The Responsibility to Protect in International Law

This book will consider a rapidly emerging guiding general principle in international relations and, arguably, in international law: the responsibility to protect. This principle is a proposed solution to a key preoccupation in both international relations and international law scholarship: how the international community is to respond to mass atrocities within sovereign states. There are three facets to this responsibility: the responsibility to prevent, the responsibility to react and the responsibility to rebuild.

This doctrine will be analysed in light of the parallel development of international customary and treaty legal obligations imposing responsibilities on sovereign states towards the international community in key international law fields, such as international human rights law, international criminal law and international environmental law. These new developments demand academic study, and this book fills this lacuna by rigorously considering all of these developments as part of a trend towards assumption of international responsibility. This must include the responsibility on the part of all states to respond to threats of genocide, crimes against humanity, ethnic cleansings and large-scale war crimes. The discussion surrounding aggravated state responsibility is also explored, with the author concluding that this emerging norm within international law is closely related to the responsibility to protect, in its imposition of an international responsibility to act in response to an international wrong.

This book will be of great interest to scholars of international law, the law of armed conflict, security studies and IR in general.

Susan Breau is Professor of International Law and Head of the School of Law at the University of Reading, UK.

Routledge Research in International Law

Available:

International Law and the Third World
Reshaping Justice
*Edited by Richard Falk,
Balakrishnan Rajagopal and
Jacqueline Stevens*

International Legal Theory
Essays and Engagements,
1966–2006
Nicholas Onuf

The Problem of Enforcement in International Law
Countermeasures, the Non-Injured State and the Idea of International Community
Elena Katselli Proukaki

International Economic Actors and Human Rights
Adam McBeth

The Law of Consular Access
A Documentary Guide
John Quigley, William J. Aceves and S. Adele Shank

State Accountability under International Law
Holding States Accountable for a Breach of Jus Cogens Norms
Lisa Yarwood

International Organizations and the Idea of Autonomy
Institutional Independence in the International Legal Order
Edited by Richard Collins and Nigel D. White

Self-Determination in the Post-9/11 Era
Elizabeth Chadwick

Participants in the International Legal System
Multiple Perspectives on Non-State Actors in International Law
Edited by Jean d'Aspremont

Sovereignty and Jurisdiction in the Airspace and Outer Space
Legal Criteria for Spatial Delimitation
Gbenga Oduntan

International Law in a
Multipolar World
Edited by Matthew Happold

The Law on the Use of Force
A Feminist Analysis
Gina Heathcote

The ICJ and the Evolution of
International Law
The Enduring Impact of the Corfu
Channel Case
*Edited by Karine Bannelier,
Théodore Christakis and Sarah
Heathcote*

UNHCR and International
Refugee Law
From Treaties to Innovation
Corinne Lewis

Asian Approaches to
International Law and the Legacy
of Colonialism
The Law of the Sea, Territorial
Disputes and International Dispute
Settlement
*Edited by Jin-Hyun Paik, Seok-Woo
Lee and Kevin Y. L. Tan*

The Right to Self-determination
Under International Law
"Selfistans," Secession, and the Rule
of the Great Powers
Milena Sterio

Reforming the UN Security
Council Membership
The Illusion of Representativeness
Sabine Hassler

Threats of Force
International Law and Strategy
Francis Grimal

The Changing Role of Nationality
in International Law
*Edited by Alessandra Annoni and
Serena Forlati*

Criminal Responsibility for the
Crime of Aggression
Patrycja Grzebyk

Regional Maintenance of
Peace and Security under
International Law
The Distorted Mirrors
Dace Winther

International Law-making
Essays in Honour of Jan Klabbers
*Edited by Rain Liivoja and
Jarna Petman*

Resolving Claims to
Self-Determination
Is There a Role for the International
Court of Justice?
Andrew Coleman

The Rise of Tamil Separatism in
Sri Lanka
From Communalism to Secession
*Gnanapala Welhengama and
Nirmala Pillay*

The United Nations and
Collective Security
Gary Wilson

Justice for Victims before the
International Criminal Court
Luke Moffett

Public-Private Partnerships
and Responsibility under
International Law
A Global Health Perspective
Lisa Clarke

Cultural Diversity in International Law
The Effectiveness of the UNESCO Convention on the Protection and Promotion of the Diversity of Cultural Expressions
Edited by Lilian Richieri Hanania

Incitement in International Law
Wibke K. Timmermann

The Cuban Embargo under International Law
El Bloqueo
Nigel D. White

Resisting United Nations Security Council Resolutions
Sufyan Droubi

The Changing Nature of Customary International Law
Methods of Interpreting the Concept of Custom in International Criminal Tribunals
Noora Arajärvi

The International Criminal Court in Search of its Purpose and Identity
Edited by Triestino Mariniello

Power and Law in International Society
International Relations as the Sociology of International Law
Mark Klamberg

The International Criminal Court and Global Social Control in Late Modernity
International Criminal Justice in Late Modernity
Nerida Chazal

International Law and Boundary Disputes in Africa
Gbenga Oduntan

Means of Transportation and Registration of Nationality
Transportation Registered by International Organizations
Vincent P. Cogliati-Bantz

Reciprocity in International Law
Its impact and function
Shahrad Nasrolahi Fard

Forthcoming titles in this series include:

Technology and the Law on the Use of Force
New Security Challenges in the Twenty-First Century
Jackson Maogoto

Seeking Justice in International Law
The Significance and Implications of the UN Declaration on the Rights of Indigenous Peoples
Mauro Barelli

Legal Accountability and Britain's Wars 2000–2014
Peter Rowe

Fragmentation vs. the Constitutionalisation of International Law
A Practical Inquiry
Edited by Andrzej Jakubowski and Karolina Wierczyńska

International Law and the Rights of those Displaced by Armed Conflict
Elena Katselli Proukaki

The Responsibility to Protect in International Law
An emerging paradigm shift

Susan Breau

LONDON AND NEW YORK

First published 2016 by Routledge

2 Park Square, Milton Park, Abingdon, Oxfordshire OX14 4RN
711 Third Avenue, New York, NY 10017

Routledge is an imprint of the Taylor & Francis Group, an informa business

First issued in paperback 2018

Copyright © 2016 Susan Breau

The right of Susan Breau to be identified as author of this work has been
asserted by her in accordance with sections 77 and 78 of the Copyright,
Designs and Patents Act 1988.

All rights reserved. No part of this book may be reprinted or reproduced or
utilised in any form or by any electronic, mechanical, or other means, now
known or hereafter invented, including photocopying and recording, or in any
information storage or retrieval system, without permission in writing from
the publishers.

Notice:
Product or corporate names may be trademarks or registered trademarks, and
are used only for identification and explanation without intent to infringe.

British Library Cataloguing in Publication Data
A catalogue record for this book is available from the British Library

Library of Congress Cataloguing in Publication Data
Publication DataNames: Breau, Susan Carolyn, 1955– author.
Title: The responsibility to protect in international law : an emerging
paradigm shift / Susan Breau. Description: New York : Routledge, 2016. |
Series: Routledge research in international law |
Includes bibliographical references and index.
Identifiers: LCCN 2015040268 | ISBN 9781138830516 (hbk) |
ISBN 9781315737287 (ebk)
Subjects: LCSH: Responsibility to protect (International law)
Classification: LCC KZ4082.B74 2016 | DDC 341.4/8–dc23
LC record available at http://lccn.loc.gov/2015040268

ISBN: 978-1-138-83051-6 (hbk)
ISBN: 978-1-138-61431-4 (pbk)

Typeset in Galliard
by Out of House Publishing

Contents

Acknowledgements	ix
Table of cases	x
Table of treaties	xiv

Introduction	1

PART I
The theoretical roots of the responsibility to protect — 9

1	From humanitarian intervention to the responsibility to protect	11
2	International society	32

PART II
The evolution of the responsibility to protect within areas of public international law — 59

3	State responsibility: obligations on states in international law	61
4	International human rights law: rights and responsibilities	92
5	International criminal law: responsibilities within the international criminal justice system	122
6	International environmental law: the responsibility to save the planet	148

viii *Contents*

PART III
The responsibility to protect in practice   **181**

7 The responsibility to prevent   183

8 The responsibility to react   207

9 The responsibility to rebuild   233

10 Responsibilities ignored? Syria and Iraq   255

   Conclusion   276

   Bibliography   281
   Index   291

Acknowledgements

I would like to thank my colleague Professor James Green, who read and commented on sections of this book. His help and encouragement was much appreciated. I would also like to thank my colleague Dr Katja Samuel for reading and commenting on the proposal for this book.

Thanks also to my research fellow Marie Aronsson-Storrier for her assistance in preparing the book for publication.

I also wish to thank my interns at the British Institute of International and Comparative Law, who provided research assistance for Part II of the book.

And finally my most sincere gratitude to the three people who inspired my passion for this topic: Sir Christopher Greenwood, Associate Professor Chaloka Beyani, United Nations Special Rapporteur on the human rights of internally dispanced persons and Professor Alan Whitehorn.

Any errors that remain are, of course, my own.

Table of cases

Judgment of the Nuremberg International Military Tribunal
    1946 (1947) 41 AJIL 172 .... 80, 123, 124, 125, 126, 127

PCIJ (ordered chronologically)

Case of the S.S. "Wimbledon (United Kingdom, France, Italy & Japan v.
    Germany), Judgment of 17 August 1923 (1923) PCIJ Serie A,
    No 1 81
Case Concerning the Chorzów Factory (Jurisdiction), Judgment of
    26 July 1927 (1927) PCIJ, Serie A, No 9 63
Case Concerning the Factory at Chorzów (Merits), Judgment of 13
    September 1928 (1928) PCIJ Serie A, No 17 79
Certain German Interests in Polish Upper Silesia (Merits),
    Judgment of 25 May 1926 (1926) PCIJ Serie A, No 7 72
The Mavrommatis Palestine Concessions, Judgment of 30 August
    1924 (1924) PCIJ Serie A, No 2 65

ICJ (ordered chronologically)

Nottebohm Case (Liechtenstein v. Guatemala) (Second Phase),
    Judgment of 6 April 1955 (1955) ICJ Rep 4 67
South West Africa Cases (Ethiopia v. South Africa; Liberia v. South
    Africa) (Second Phase), Judgment of 18 July 1966 (1966)
    ICJ Rep 6 .... 81, 96
Case Concerning the Barcelona Traction, Light and Power Company,
    Limited (Belgium v. Spain) (Second Phase), Judgment of 5 February
    1970 (1970) ICJ Rep 3 .... 80, 81, 85, 96, 116
Case Concerning United States Diplomatic and Consular
    Staff in Tehran (United States of America v. Islamic Republic
    of Iran), Judgment of 24 May 1980 (1980) ICJ Rep 3 65
Case Concerning Military and Paramilitary Activities in and
    Against Nicaragua (Nicaragua v. United States of America)
    (Merits), Judgment of 27 June 1986 (1986)
    ICJ Rep 14 .... 12, 28, 73, 74, 75, 116

Table of cases xi

Case Concerning East Timor (Portugal v. Australia) (Preliminary
Objections), Judgment of 30 June 1995 (1995) ICJ Rep 90........... 85

Legality of the Threat or Use of Nuclear Weapons, Advisory Opinion
of 8 July 1996 (1996) ICJ Rep 226... 153

*Case Concerning the Application of the Convention on the Prevention
and Punishment of the Crime of Genocide (Bosnia and
Herzegovina v. Yugoslavia)* (Preliminary Objections),
Judgment of 11 July 1996 (1996) ICJ Rep 595........................ 85, 86

*Case Concerning the Gabčikovo-Nagymaros Project
(Hungary v. Slovakia)* (Merits), Judgment of
25 September 1997 (1997) ICJ Rep 7..................................... 76, 154

*Case Concerning Legality of Use of Force (Yugoslavia v. Belgium,
Canada, France, Germany, Italy, Netherlands, Portugal
and the United Kingdom)* (Provisional Measures), Order
of 2 June 1999 (1999) 17

LaGrand Case (Germany v. United States of America) (Merits),
Judgment of 27 June 2001 (2001) ICJ Rep 466 .... 78, 79

*Case Concerning the Arrest Warrant of 11 April 2000 (Democratic
Republic of the Congo v. Belgium),* Judgment of
14 February 2002 (2002) ICJ Rep 3 .... 88, 89, 136, 137, 193

*Legal Consequences of the Construction of a Wall in the Occupied
Palestinian Territory,* Advisory Opinion of 9 July 2004
(2004) ICJ Rep 136.. 89

*Case Concerning Pulp Mills on the River Uruguay
(Argentina v. Uruguay),* Judgment of 20 April 2010 (2010)
ICJ Rep 14... 154

*Accordance with International Law of Unilateral Declaration of
Independence in Respect of Kosovo,* Advisory Opinion of
22 July 2010 (2010) ICJ Rep 403.. 243

International Arbitral Awards (ordered chronologically)

*Laura M. B. Janes et al. (United States of America) v. United Mexican
States* (1925) RIAA Vol IV, 82 66

*Teodoro García and M. A. Garza (United Mexican States) v. United
States of America* (1926) RIAA Vol IV, 119 66

*Walter H. Faulkner (United States of America) v. United Mexican
States* (1926) RIAA Vol IV, 67 66

Harry Roberts (United States of America) v. United Mexican States
(1926) RIAA Vol IV, 77 66

Gustave Caire (France) v. United Mexican States (1929)
RIAA Vol V, 540 73

Trail Smelter Case (United States of America v. Canada)
(1941) RIAA Vol III, 1905 .... 152, 153, 154, 155, 156

Rainbow Warrior (New Zealand v. France) (1990)
RIAA Vol XX, 215.. 63, 79

xii   *Table of cases*

Iron Rhine (Belgium v. Netherlands) (2005) RIAA Vol XXVII, 35......... 154

Seabed Disputes Chamber of the International Tribunal for the Law of the Sea

Advisory Opinion on Responsibilities and Obligations of States
  Sponsoring Persons and Entities with Respect to Activities in
  the Area, 1 February 2011, Case No. 17 Advisory
  Opinion (2011) 50 *ILM* 458.. 178

EctHR

Artico v. Italy (1980) 3 EHRR 1 [33].. 105
X and Y v. Netherlands (1985) 8 EHRR 235 107
Vilvarajah and others v. United Kingdom (1991) 14 EHRR 248........... 114
Chahal v. UK paragraph 80 (1996) 23 EHRR 413 .... 113, 114
Ahmed v. Austria (1996) 24 EHRR 278.. 114
Jabari v. Turkey (2000) 29 EHHR CD178 114
Conka v. Belgium (2002) 34 EHRR 54 114

ICTY

Prosecutor v. Dusko Tadic (Judgment) IT-94-1-A
  (ICTY, 15 July 1999)... 73, 74, 75
Prosecutor v. Anto Furundzija (Judgment) IT-95-17/1-T
  (ICTY, 10 December 1998) 89

ICTR

Prosecutor v. Jean-Paul Akayesu (Judgment) ICTR-96-4-T
  (ICTR, 2 September 1998) 74

IACtHR

Velásquez Rodríquez Case, Judgment of 29 July 1988
  (1988) Inter-Am. CtHR, Series C, No. 4........................ 73, 107, 133

Iran–United States Claims Tribunal

Petrolane Inc v. Islamic Republic of Iran (1991) 27 Iran-USCTR 64 73

African Commission

The Social and Economic Rights Action Center for Economic and
  Social Rights v. Nigeria , African Commission on Human
  and Peoples' Rights, Comm. No. 155/96 (2001) 106, 107

Table of cases   xiii

National courts

Israel

Attorney General v. *Adolf Eichmann,* Judgment of 11 December
1961, Criminal Case No 40/61, District Court
of Jerusalem 134, 135

United Kingdom

R v. *Bow Street Metropolitan Stipendiary Magistrate,*
Ex Parte *Pinochet Ugarte (No 3)* [1998]
UKHL 41, [1998] 3 WLR 1456 .... 131, 136, 193

United States of America

The Court Martial Of Henry Wirz (1865) General Court
Martial Orders No. 607.. 124
Ex Parte Quirin (1942) 317 US 1 127

Table of treaties (ordered chronologically)

Hague Convention (IV) Respecting the Laws and Customs of War on Land and Its Annex: Regulations Concerning the Laws and Customs of War on Land, 18 October 1907 64

Hague Convention (V) Respecting the Rights and Duties of *Neutral* Powers and Persons in Case of War on Land, 18 October 1907 (entered into force 26 January 1910) USTS 540 109

Treaty of Peace between the Allied and Associated Powers and Germany, 28 June 1919 (entered into force 10 January 1920) 225 Consol TS 188 125

United Nations and Statute of the International Court of Justice, 26 June 1945 (entered into force 24 October 1945) 1 UNTS XVI 24, 25, 33, 35, 38, 77, 94, 97, 118, 119, 130, 141, 152, 181, 202, 211, 214, 218, 227, 238

Charter of the International Military Tribunal – Annex to the Agreement for the prosecution and punishment of the major war criminals of the European Axis, 8 August 1945, 82 UNTS 279 125

Control Council Law No. 10, Punishment of Persons Guilty of War Crimes, Crimes Against Peace and Against Humanity, 20 December 1945, 3 Official Gazette Control Council for Germany 50-55 (1946) 126

Convention on the Prevention and Punishment of the Crime of Genocide, 9 December 1948 (entered into force 12 January 1951) 78 UNTS 277 .... 2, 71, 128, 269

Geneva Convention for the Amelioration of the Condition of the Wounded and Sick in Armed Forces in the Field (First Geneva Convention), 12 August 1949 (entered into force 21 October 1950) 75 UNTS 31 .... 87, 89

Geneva Convention for the Amelioration of the Condition of Wounded, Sick and Shipwrecked Members of Armed Forces at Sea (Second Geneva Convention), 12 August 1949 (entered into force 21 October 1950) 75 UNTS 85 .... 87, 89

Table of treaties xv

*Geneva Convention Relative to the Treatment of Prisoners of War
(Third Geneva Convention)*,12 August 1949 (entered
into force 21 October 1950) 75 UNTS 135 .... 87, 89
*Geneva Convention Relative to the Protection of Civilian Persons in
Time of War (Fourth Geneva Convention)*, 12 August 1949
(entered into force 21 October 1950) 75 UNTS 287 .... 87, 89
Convention Relating to the Status of Refugees, 28 July 1951
(entered into force 22 April 1954) 189 UNTS 137 ...... 108, 109, 110
Geneva Convention on the High Seas, 29 April 1958
(entered into force 30 September 1962) 450 UNTS 82 109
*Protocol Additional to the Geneva Conventions of 12 August 1949,
and relating to the Protection of Victims of International Armed
Conflicts (Protocol I)*, 8 June 1977 (entered into force
7 December 1978) 1125 UNTS 3 73
*Protocol Additional to the Geneva Conventions of 12 August 1949,
and relating to the Protection of Victims of Non-International
Armed Conflicts (Protocol II)*, 8 June 1977 (entered into force
7 December 1978) 1125 UNTS 609 138
International *Convention on the Elimination of all Forms of Racial
Discrimination*, 21 December 1965 (entered into force
4 January 1969) 660 UNTS 195 .... 94, 97
International Covenant on Civil and Political Rights,
16 December 1966 (entered into force 23 March 1976)
999 UNTS 171 .... 95, 96, 100
International Covenant on Economic, Social and Cultural Rights,
16 December 1966 (entered into force 3 January 1976)
993 UNTS 3 .... 95, 105, 116, 191
Optional Protocol to the International Covenant on Civil and Political
Rights, 16 December 1966 (entered into force 23 March 1976)
999 UNTS 171 100
*Declaration of the United Nations Conference on the Human
Environment*, 16 June 1972, 11 ILM 1416 .... 149, 150, 152, 155
*International Convention on the Suppression and Punishment
of the Crime of Apartheid*, 30 November 1973 (entered into
force 18 July 1976) 1015 UNTS 243 129
*Convention on the Elimination of All Forms of Discrimination
Against Women*, 18 December 1979 (entered into force
3 September 1981) 1249 UNTS 13 .... 95, 97
United Nations Convention on the Law of the Sea,
10 December 1982 (entered into force 16 November
1994) 1833 UNTS 3 .... 109, 154, 156
*Convention Against Torture and Other Cruel,
Inhuman or Degrading Treatment or Punishment*, 10
December 1984 (entered into force in 26 June 1987) 1465
UNTS 85 .... 95, 97, 134, 145, 193

xvi   *Table of treaties*

1987 Montreal Protocol to the Vienna Convention for the Protection
of the Ozone Layer, 16 September 1987 (entered into force
1 January 1989) 1522 UNTS 3... 148, 157, 161, 164, 165, 166, 167,
169, 175

Basel Convention on the Control of Transboundary Movement of
Hazardous waste Vienna convention on Early Notification of Nuclear
Accidents, 22 March 1989 (entered into force 5 May 1992)
1773 UNTS 126 156

Vienna Convention on Early Notification of Nuclear Accidents,
22 March 1989 (entered into force 5 May 1992) 1773
UNTS 126 156

Convention on the Rights of the Child, 20 November 1989 (entered
into force 2 September 1990) 1577 UNTS 3 .... 95, 97, 100

International Convention on the Protection of the Rights of
All Migrant Workers and Members of their Families,
18 December 1990 (entered into force 2003)
2220 UNTS 3 .... 95, 98

Bamako Convention on the Ban of Import into Africa and the Control of
Transboundary Movement and Management of Hazardous Wastes
Within Africa, January 29 1991 (entered into force 22 April
1998) 2101 UNTS 177 157

United Nations Framework *Convention on Climate Change*
9 May 1992 (entered into force 21 March 1994) 1771
UNTS 107 .... 157, 161, 164

Convention on Biological Diversity, 5 June 1992
(entered into force 29 December 1993) 1760
UNTS 79 .... 161, 171, 176, 177

Rio Declaration on Environment and Development,
14 June 1992, 31 ILM 874 150

Convention on the Prohibition of the Development, Production,
Stockpiling and Use of Chemical Weapons and on their
Destruction, 3 September 1992 (entered into force 29 April
1997) 1974 UNTS 75 272

1997 Kyoto Protocol to the Framework Convention on Climate Change,
11 December 1997 (entered into force 16 January 2005)
2303 UNTS 148 .... 161, 167, 168, 169, 170, 171

Rome Statute of the International Criminal Court (last amended
2010), 17 July 1998 (entered into force 1 July 2002)
2187 UNTS 3 .... 2, 123, 129, 140, 141, 142

Optional Protocol to the Convention on the Elimination of
Discrimination Against Women, 6 October 1999 (entered
into force 22 December 2000) 2131 UNTS 83 100

Cartagena Protocol on Biosafety to the Convention on Biological
Diversity, 29 January 2000 (entered into force on 11 September
2003) 2226 UNTS 208 176

Table of treaties xvii

UN Security Council, Statute of the International Criminal
Tribunal for the Former Yugoslavia (as amended on
17 May 2002), 25 May 1993 138
UN Security Council, Statute of the International Criminal
Tribunal for Rwanda (as amended on 13 October 2006)
8 November 1994 139
Convention on the Rights of Persons with Disabilities, 12 December 2006
(entered into force 3 May 2008) 2515 UNTS 3 .... 95, 98, 100
Optional Protocol to the Convention on the Rights of Persons with
Disabilities, 13 December 2006 (entered into force 3 May
2008) UN Doc A/61/106 100
*International Convention for the Protection of All Persons from
Enforced Disappearance* 20 December 2006 (entered into force
23 December 2010) 2716 UNTS 3 .... 95, 98
*Optional Protocol to the International Covenant on Economic, Social and
Cultural Rights,* 10 December 2008 (entered into force on 5 May
2013) UN Doc A/63/117 100
Optional Protocol to the Convention on the Rights of the Child on a
communications procedure, 19 December 2011 (entered into
force 14 April 2014) UN Doc A/66/138 100

Regional treaties

Africa

*Convention Governing the Specific Aspects of Refugee Problems in
Africa,* 10 September 1969 (entered into force 20 June
1974) 1001 UNTS 45 112
African Charter on Human and Peoples' Rights, 27 June 1981
(entered into force 21 October 1986) 1520 UNTS 217 .... 95, 112
Constitutive Act of the African Union, adopted 11 July 2000
and entered into force 26 May 2001, 2158 UNTS 3 224

Americas

American Convention on Human Rights, 22 November 1969
(entered into force 18 July 1978) 1144 UNTS 123 95

Europe

*European Convention for the Protection of Human Rights and
Fundamental Freedoms,* 4 November 1950 (entered into
force 3 September 1953) 213 UNTS 222 .... 94, 95
Charter of Fundamental Rights of the European Union [2000]
OJ C 364/01 111

Introduction

Subject of this work

> We are obliged to respect, defend and maintain the common bonds of union and fellowship that exist among all members of the human race.[1]

The responsibility to protect, at first glance, encompasses a radical and controversial new approach in international relations and international law. The basic definition of the concept embodies two interlinking elements. The first of these is that sovereignty implies responsibility in the state apparatus to ensure the protection of all persons residing within the territory of the state from genocide, crimes against humanity, ethnic cleansing and war crimes. The second element of the doctrine asserts an international responsibility upon all states to act when the population of another state is suffering serious harm from the international crimes outlined above – as a result of internal war, insurgency, repression or state failure – and the sovereign state concerned is unwilling or unable to halt or avert the suffering.[2] The novel feature of this concept is in the second element: the idea of an obligation of a state not only to protect the welfare and human rights of persons within its borders, but as a member of the international community of states, to protect humanity as a whole. However, as the above quote from the Roman Senator Cicero reveals, the notion of duties owed to all mankind has existed throughout recorded history.

Notwithstanding the long theoretical provenance of the concept, it is the putting into practice of the international element of the responsibility to protect, as a guiding principle on how the community of states reacts to massive abuses of human rights, that has demonstrated real momentum since it was first introduced in 2000.[3] This book does not seek to establish that the

---

[1] Marcus Tullius Cicero, *De Officiis*, translated by W. Miller (Cambridge, MA: Harvard University Press, 1913).

[2] International Commission on Intervention and State Sovereignty, *The Responsibility to Protect* (Ottawa, 2001), p. XI.

[3] The responsibility to protect was first introduced in a report from the Netherlands; see Advisory Council on International Affairs and Advisory Committee on Issues of Public International Law, *Humanitarian Intervention* (The Hague, 2000).

2 Introduction

responsibility to protect is an existing doctrine of customary international law. There is neither the state practice nor the *opinio juris* to assert a legal obligation to intervene in another state when threshold conditions exist for intervention (such as crimes against humanity, war crimes, ethnic cleansing or genocide).[4] Nevertheless, it can be asserted that the evolution of legal obligations constituting responsibilities of states towards other states and their populations in several fields of international law point to an evolution towards international responsibility that might at some point crystallize into international law obligations to protect peoples.[5] Furthermore, the crimes from which the responsibility to protect seeks to protect persons are all crimes established within international law. Under customary international law and treaty law, states already have obligations to prevent and punish genocide, crimes against humanity and war crimes.[6]

If this trend in practice continues, the doctrine could indeed constitute an emerging norm of public international law constituting a legal, rather than moral, obligation. It is argued here that it is presently a concept based on 'well-established principles of international law'.[7] Nevertheless, in many of the current international crises, such as Syria and Iraq, politicians, media and non-governmental organizations, in calling for a response from the international community, have used the language of the responsibility to protect as a mandatory, rather than voluntary, obligation.[8] This is astonishing considering the relatively recent history of the support by the General Assembly of the concept.[9] Given this momentum, it is the purpose of this book to engage in a systematic international law analysis of the controversial responsibility to protect concept.

The analysis in this book primarily focuses on the second element of the responsibility to protect: protection of persons not within a sovereign state's territory. Although there has been much discussion of the practice of 'humanitarian intervention' within international law and international relations,[10] there are doctrinal developments within international law that ultimately support the emergence of the practice of the responsibility to

---

[4] Statute of the International Court of Justice Article 38(1).

[5] Articles on State Responsibility, GA Res. 56/83, 28 January 2002.

[6] UN General Assembly, Convention on the Prevention and Punishment of the Crime of Genocide, 9 December 1948, 78 UNTS 277 and UN General Assembly, Rome Statute of the International Criminal Court (last amended 2010), 17 July 1998.

[7] A. Bellamy, 'A Chronic Protection Problem: The DPRK and the Responsibility to Protect' (2015) 91 *International Affairs* 225, p. 228.

[8] See, for example, Global Centre for the Responsibility to Protect, International Crisis Group, International Coalition for the Responsibility to Protect.

[9] GA Res. 60/1, 24 October 2005, paras 138 and 139.

[10] Two leading examples are: S. Chesterman, *Just War or Just Peace? Humanitarian Intervention in International Law* (Oxford: Oxford University Press, 2001); S.D. Murphy, *Humanitarian Intervention: The United Nations in an Evolving World Order* (Philadelphia: University of Pennsylvania Press, 1996).

Introduction 3

protect and may provide the foundations of international law doctrine. Most important is the work of the International Law Commission on the law of state responsibility. In tandem with the development of the responsibility to protect, the International Law Commission concluded its work on drafting Articles on State Responsibility. The General Assembly endorsed these articles in 2002.[11] With these articles was a chapter containing a new developing doctrine of international law entitled 'aggravated state responsibility', which, it will be argued in this book, embodies similar obligations to the responsibility to protect.[12] The commentary written by James Crawford to these articles acknowledges that aggravated state responsibility is also a 'developing doctrine'.[13] In fact, the developing part of both aggravated state responsibility and the responsibility to protect is the idea of a state being responsible to a higher entity, the international community. This is the emerging paradigm shift. Instead of a voluntary assumption of international obligations, both the responsibility to protect and aggravated state responsibility entail mandatory regimes of duties owed to a community of values, embodied in the international community.

The originating principles of law underpinning both the responsibility to protect and aggravated state responsibility can be gleaned from the custom and treaties in areas of international law such as the international protection of human rights, international criminal law and international environmental law. All of these areas of international law have introduced within their treaties and treaty enforcement systems notions of responsibility to the international community, and some of the doctrines are arguably peremptory norms known in international law as norms of *jus cogens*. This again is a second level of analysis; clearly international law imposes obligations within a sovereign state, but we are interested in analysing those obligations imposed upon states that are owed to the international community as a whole. All these important categories of international law contain rules resulting in obligations *erga omnes*.[14]

An important level of international law research goes beyond the development of rules of law to state practice. It is argued within this monograph that

---

[11] International Law Commission, Draft Articles on Responsibility of States for Internationally Wrongful Acts, November 2001, Supplement No. 10 (A/56/10), Chapter IV.E.1 and UN Doc. GA Res. 56/83, 12 December 2001.

[12] Ibid., Chapter III 'Serious Breaches of Obligations under Peremptory Norms of General International Law', Articles 40 and 41.

[13] J. Crawford, *State Responsibility: The General Part* (Cambridge: Cambridge University Press, 2013) and *The International Law Commission's Articles on State Responsibility: Introduction, Text and Commentaries* (Cambridge: Cambridge University Press, 2002) and the chapters on Aggravated State Responsibility.

[14] See M. Shaw, *International Law*, 7th edition (Cambridge: Cambridge University Press, 2014), p. 88 for definition of *erga omnes*, which is procedural concerning the scope of the application of the relevant rule meaning obligations of states (with respect to these rules) to the international community as a whole.

4   *Introduction*

in addition to the emergence of international law doctrine, the responsibility to protect is becoming embedded within the practice of states. There has emerged within the United Nations' architecture and practice all three elements within the proposed doctrine: the responsibility to prevent, the responsibility to react and the responsibility to rebuild.[15] This is an important component of state practice, as it is the states making up the United Nations that have adopted a fundamental change in the way the international organization responds to international crises. As Innis Claude argues with respect to the United Nations: 'the world organisation has come to be regarded, and used, as a dispenser of politically significant approval and disapproval of claims, policies and actions of states.'[16]

The transformation with the United Nations is marked. Civilian protection mandates have become the norm in the practice of peacekeeping and in peace enforcement operations, and there are many examples of missions incorporating prevention, reaction and rebuilding within the Security Council resolution mandates that establish such operations.[17] Furthermore, there is a change in the architecture of the United Nations system, particularly after the sixtieth anniversary summit in 2005, enabling a more focused response to these three levels of responsibility.

Outline of the work and methodology

Given this evolution of the responsibility to protect in the twenty-first century, it merits a full discussion in international law and not just within the narrow focus of debate within *jus ad bellum* (the lawfulness of resort to force) concerning the legality of unilateral humanitarian intervention. Although the concept emerges from a critical debate within *jus ad bellum*, it involves other areas of international law. Military intervention is evidence of a failure of the responsibility to prevent human rights catastrophes and is only to be utilized in the more extreme circumstances. Furthermore, the responsibility to protect is emerging as a doctrine to justify collective action under the auspices of the United Nations system, not as a method to justify unilateral intervention by force.[18] This book does not propose to revisit arguments of legality of unilateral humanitarian intervention, but concedes that in the most extreme circumstances, if the United Nations is unable or unwilling to act, there might be an evolving doctrine of lawful intervention on the basis of collective responsibility.[19]

---

[15] International Commission on Intervention and State Sovereignty, *The Responsibility to Protect*, p. XI Elements.

[16] I. Claude, *The Changing United Nations* (New York: Random House, 1967) p. 73.

[17] Recent examples are: UN Doc. SC Res 1975, 30 March 2011 (Ivory Coast), UN Doc. SC Res 1973, 17 March 2011 (Libya), UN Doc. SC Res 2127, 5 December 2013 (Central African Republic).

[18] Ibid.

[19] S. Breau, *Humanitarian Intervention: The United Nations and Collective Responsibility* (London: Cameron May, 2005). In this book I examined with several examples of state

Introduction 5

Therefore, this book is a systematic analysis of how the responsibility to protect concept could develop into a doctrine of public international law. This is a complex task as it involves theoretical, historical and doctrinal analysis. In order to trace the philosophical roots of the concept, it is necessary to delve into both international legal and international relations theories that engage in debate about the nature of the international system. There are many different views of the international legal system, and there is a continuing theoretical discussion about whether there is an emerging international constitution that would provide these mandatory international obligations.[20]

The first part of the book will engage in an interdisciplinary analysis of the foundational theories for international responsibility to prevent and react to massive violations of human rights in international law and international relations. This part will examine the theories of the emergence of an international legal order and the important role of protection of individuals within that order. Chapter 1 of this book will set the scene for the subsequent analysis. It will engage in a historical analysis of the development of the responsibility to protect from its first introduction in a report from the Netherlands, through the Canadian International Commission on Intervention and State Sovereignty to the various United Nations reports and resolutions supporting the concept. It is vital to understand the complexity of the concept within the literature as it foreshadows the third part of the book's discussion of the three levels of responsibility. Chapter 2 will engage in the interdisciplinary theoretical analysis of the international relations and international law discussion of the idea of an international community to which responsibility is owed. Both international relations and international legal theorists debate whether an international community is an anarchical system of states or an entity that exists independently of the nation-state. Again there has been an evolution towards a notion of international society, but there are important historical antecedents that reveal that this discussion is also a continuation of an age-old debate about international law and relations.

The second part of the book will be a doctrinal examination utilizing the procedure set out in Article 38(1)(a) and (b) of the Statute of the International Court of Justice, which outlines various ways in which the International Court could determine international law.[21] The first task will be to examine whether there are any international conventions that establish rules expressly recognized by states containing notions of international responsibility. The prime areas of international law that have extensively codified international

---

practice the debate concerning the lawfulness of unilateral and collective humanitarian intervention. I concluded that unilateral humanitarian intervention was not an exception to the prohibition on the use of force contained in Article 2(4) of the United Nations Charter.

[20] A. von Bogdandy, 'Constitutionalism in International Law: Comment on a Proposal from Germany' (2006) 47 *Harvard International Law Journal* 223.

[21] United Nations, *Statute of the International Court of Justice*, 26 June 1945, Article 38.

6 *Introduction*

responsibilities are: the law of state responsibility; international criminal law; the international protection of human rights; and international environmental law. The second task will be an exploration of the customary international law rules within these fields, which embody obligations to the international community as a whole: obligations *erga omnes*. Chapter 3 will discuss the developments in treaty law in the area of state responsibility, as at its heart this concept impacts on how states relate to the international community. The evolving notion of aggravated state responsibility, which triggers international responsibility for violations of peremptory norms of international law that occur in other states, is remarkably similar to the responsibility to protect. Human rights treaties, more than any other, specify the content of the responsibility of the state towards its populations. Chapter 4 will review these treaties, their enforcement mechanisms and the developments towards positive obligations on states in the international protection of human rights. Although the human rights system primarily imposes obligations on states, international criminal law imposes obligations on state officials. Chapter 5 will review the developments in treaty, custom and jurisprudence in international criminal law, again supporting notions of responsibility to a higher authority. Finally, the newest area of international law development is international environmental law, which, due to the transboundary nature of pollution, naturally involves obligations beyond a state's borders. Chapter 6 will review the evolution of treaties and customary law rules in international environmental law, which imposes obligations on states in environmental protection and pollution reduction.

The third part of the book will examine the emergence of state practice, which is an important part of the development of customary international law as set out in Article 38(1)(b) of the Statute of the International Court of Justice.[22] A particular focus is to examine the emerging international practice supporting the three different pillars of the doctrine: the responsibility to prevent, the responsibility to react and the responsibility to rebuild. Chapter 7 will discuss the responsibility to prevent, the least developed part of the doctrine. Chapter 8 will review the recent United Nations practice in the responsibility to react, as the key focus is on the nature of obligations within international society, rather than establishing rights to unilateral humanitarian intervention. Chapter 9 will discuss the responsibility to rebuild, the development of the Peacebuilding Commission and the growing and significant practice in post-conflict reconstruction. Finally, Chapter 10 will discuss the latest situation that has engaged the responsibility of states: the crisis in Syria and Northern Iraq. This crisis will be examined in two phases: the long-standing civil war in Syria and the emergence of the radical Islamic State. The latter, particularly, has engaged in crimes against humanity and war crimes, and it is evident that there has been a rather tepid response from the international community.

---

[22] Ibid.

Introduction 7

The conclusion to this book will discuss significant caveats with respect to the important responsibility to protect doctrine. It has the potential to be abused in international practice, and specific legal and institutional safeguards need to be developed to ensure the proper application of the principle.

Debates are emerging as to whether these obligations fall into a category of legitimacy or of moral dicta. The central argument of this book is that the responsibility to protect is an emerging legal norm within customary international law as 'the moral claims of today are often the legal rights of tomorrow'.[23] The responsibility to protect may not at this point in history constitute a binding international legal obligation. However, as Orford argues, the responsibility to protect develops 'an ambitions conceptual framework aimed at systematizing and giving formal expression to the protective authority exercised by international actors in the decolonized world since 1960'.[24]

Conclusion

The responsibility to protect is argued in this book to be an obligation essential to the functioning of an international society, which places human protection at the forefront. As Orford asserts, it is not a form of law that imposes duties on subjects, but, rather, it is a form of law that confers power of a public or official nature[25] – in this case on the international community of states that make up the United Nations. The main reason for the crisis of confidence in the United Nations, as a result of the Rwanda and Srebrenica genocides, was the pitiful response of the international community to genocide and crimes against humanity. Syria and Northern Iraq remind us that the United Nations – in spite of more robust and extensive mandates – needs to develop a systematic approach to the prevention of mass murder. This must involve a spectrum from prevention to reaction and, if necessary, to rebuilding. There is a plethora of recommendatory reports on the responsibility to protect doctrine, but these proposals will only come to fruition if they are incorporated into a system of international responsibility of individuals, states and the international community.

---

[23] H. Lauterpacht, *International Law and Human Rights* (New York: Frederick Praeger, 1950) p. 74.

[24] A. Orford, *International Authority and the Responsibility to Protect* (Cambridge: Cambridge University Press, 2011) p. 3.

[25] Ibid., p. 25, taken from H.L.A. Hart, *The Concept of Law* (Oxford: Clarendon Press, 1961) p. 28.

Part I
The theoretical roots of the responsibility to protect

1 From humanitarian intervention to the responsibility to protect

Introduction

The responsibility to protect has long philosophical roots ranging from the writings of Cicero in the ancient world, to Grotius in the Renaissance and to Kant in the Age of Enlightenment.[1] But in recent history, the concept emerges from the long-standing debate concerning humanitarian intervention. This legally disputed justification for the use of force can be seen as an integral part of just war theory, which can trace its lineage back to Plato, and was then further developed by Cicero and St Augustine.[2] The most accessible definition of the just war is provided by St Thomas Aquinas, who states:

> it is necessary that the belligerents should have a rightful intention, so that they intend the advancement of good, or the avoidance of evil. Hence Augustine says...'True religion looks upon as peaceful those wars that are waged not for motives of aggrandizement, or cruelty, but with the object of securing peace, of punishing evil-doers, and of uplifting the good'.[3]

Humanitarian intervention was incorporated into just war theory by Grotius, who asserted that any king would have the right to depose a tyrant who

---

[1] Marcus Tullius Cicero, *De Officiis*, translated by W. Miller (Cambridge, MA: Harvard University Press, 1913); Hugonis Grotii, *De Jure Belli ac Pacis, libri tres, In quibus ius naturae & Gentium: item iuris publici preciptae expilicantur* (Paris: Apud Nicalaum Buom, 1625, cum privilegio regis via Gallica (the French National Library)); I. Kant, *Perpetual Peace: A Philosophical Essay* (London: G. Allen & Unwin Limited, 1903).

[2] R. Tuck, *The Rights of War and Peace: Political Thought and the International Order from Grotius to Kant* (Oxford: Oxford University Press, 1999); H. Bull, B. Kingsbury and A. Roberts (eds), *Hugo Grotius and International Relations* (Oxford: Clarendon Press, 1990); Cicero, *De Officiis*; Augustine of Hippo, *City of God*, Book 19. See also M. Meyer and H. McCoubrey, *Reflections on the Law of Armed Conflict: The Selected Works of Colonel Draper* (The Hague: Kluwer, 1998).

[3] St Thomas Aquinas, *Summa Theologica, Part II Question 40* (Cincinnati: Benziger Bros edition, 1947).

12   Part I: Theoretical roots of responsibility to protect

abused his peoples.[4] Just war theory seems to remain a feature in the debates concerning the legitimacy of an armed conflict to this day,[5] but the controversy concerning whether it was legal to engage in humanitarian intervention reached its apex in the late twentieth century.

In addition to theorists postulating national duties to an international society – to be discussed in the next chapter – the responsibility to protect has emerged from debates within international law and international relations surrounding a series of historical events, justified on the basis of humanitarian intervention, some of which long predate the emergence of the United Nations Charter.[6] There have been many armed conflicts conducted on the basis of protecting people from religious or racial persecution.[7] The enactment of the United Nations (UN) Charter in 1945 intensified the controversy. International lawyers then focused on whether a right of unilateral humanitarian intervention was permitted as part of the UN Charter regime for the use of force, or whether it was lawful within the customary international law on the use of force, which was confirmed in the *Nicaragua* decision to sit alongside the Charter.[8] This question occupied many international law and relations scholars who specialized in the use of force, particularly during the 1990s. However, the historical event that brought the controversy to a head was the 1999 Northern Atlantic Treaty Organization (NATO) intervention in Kosovo. It is the reports following this conflict that represented a historical turning point. In this chapter the analysis will focus primarily on governmental reports emerging in the late twentieth century and early twenty-first century arguing for a fundamental reshaping of state sovereignty towards protection responsibilities. There have been other publications that examined the conflicts up to Kosovo within the lens of humanitarian intervention, but they will not be discussed here.[9] These reports followed along a continuum from the justification of the Kosovo conflict on the basis of a right to intervene in human catastrophes – humanitarian intervention – the

---

[4] Grotii, *De Jure Belli ac Pacis.*

[5] Most particularly in the 'global war on terror' as described in the rhetoric of the Bush administration.

[6] See, for example, B. Simms and J.D.B. Trim, *Humanitarian Intervention: A History* (Cambridge: Cambridge University Press, 2011).

[7] Ibid., and see I. Brownlie, *International Law and the Use of Force by States* (Oxford: Clarendon Press, 1963).

[8] *Case Concerning Military and Paramilitary Activities in and Against Nicaragua (Nicaragua v. United States of America)* (Merits), International Court of Justice Judgment 27 June 1986, [1986] ICJ Rep 14, para. 175.

[9] Danish Institute of International Affairs, *Humanitarian Intervention: Legal and Political Aspects* (Copenhagen: Danish Institute of International Affairs, 1999); United Kingdom, House of Commons, Foreign Affairs Committee, Fourth Report, available at http://www.parliament.the-stationery-office.co.uk/pa/cm199900/cmselect/cmfaff/28/2802.htm, accessed 18 November 2015; Independent International Commission on Kosovo (Chair Richard Goldstone), *The Kosovo Report: Conflict, International Response, Lessons Learned* (Oxford: Oxford University Press, 2000).

Humanitarian intervention/responsibility to protect 13

finding that humanitarian intervention was not an accepted international legal justification for intervention,[10] and the resulting reports examined here recommending a new concept – the responsibility to protect.[11] Sovereignty as responsibility had been introduced prior to the Kosovo conflict in a seminal report to the Brookings Institute by Francis Deng and others. It is acknowledged that the two governmental reports borrowed heavily from this report, which will be discussed in the context of these two post-Kosovo reports.[12]

This first chapter also adds substance to the meaning of the responsibility to protect. The International Commission on Intervention and State Sovereignty report, entitled *The Responsibility to Protect*, contains extensive discussion of three aspects of the responsibility to protect: the responsibility to prevent; the responsibility to react; and the responsibility to rebuild. The delineation of the responsibility to protect also includes discussion of the right authority for utilizing the concept, as well as a series of precautionary principles. The right authority and the precautionary principles are part and parcel of the expanded definition of the responsibility to protect and will be discussed here.

This chapter will also outline the post-2003 Iraq War reports on the use of force, culminating in the consensus General Assembly Resolution in 2005. Following from this landmark resolution, the apparatus of the United Nations began to operationalize the concept with the institutional architecture. Important to the institution were the various implementation reports of Ban Ki-moon and the establishment of the offices of the Special Adviser on the Prevention of Genocide and the Special Adviser on the Responsibility to Protect.

The organization of the chapter is as follows. The first part of the chapter will discuss only briefly the debate concerning humanitarian intervention that led to the initiation of a series of reports following the Kosovo conflict. The second part of the chapter will discuss in some detail the contents of the reports in terms of what is the actual meaning of the responsibility to protect. This part will also review the subsequent United Nations General Assembly and Security Council activity in changing the organizational structure of the UN system, although it will not embark on an analysis of any responsibility to protect collective security missions, as that discussion will wait for Part III of this book. Finally, we will review the major activity in developing in the concept that is well underway in the United Nations architecture, including several implementation reports by the Secretary-General and the appointments

---

[10] Ibid.

[11] Advisory Council on International Affairs and Advisory Committee on Issues of Public International Law, *Humanitarian Intervention* (The Hague, 2000) and International Commission on Intervention and State Sovereignty (ICISS), *The Responsibility to Protect* (Ottawa, 2001).

[12] F.M. Deng *et al.*, *Sovereignty as Responsibility: Conflict Management in Africa* (Washington DC: The Brookings Institute, 1996).

14   *Part I: Theoretical roots of responsibility to protect*

and reports of the Special Advisers on Genocide and the Responsibility to Protect.

Humanitarian intervention

Humanitarian intervention has been defined in many ways, but Vevrey introduces an adequate definition of the term in a 1992 contribution. It is:

> [t]he threat or use of force by a state or states abroad, for the sole purpose of preventing or putting a halt to a serious violation of fundamental human rights, in particular the right to life of persons, regardless of their nationality.[13]

By the early nineteenth century, states began to justify armed conflicts on the basis of a right to intervene to protect oppressed peoples. Although the prohibition on the use of force did not yet exist, these types of interventions were categorized as just wars. An early-recorded case was the intervention of France, Russia and Great Britain against the Ottoman Empire from 1827–1830 to protect Greek Christians.[14] Other cases in the nineteenth century included the French occupation of Syria in 1860–1861, the Russian interventions in Bosnia–Herzegovina and Bulgaria from 1877 to 1879, the United States invention in Cuba in 1898 and the collective intervention in Macedonia from 1903–1908.[15] The academic debate concerning these interventions focused on whether these were wars of imperialism or just wars to protect oppressed peoples. Brownlie, examining these interventions in the mid-twentieth century, conceded that the French occupation of Syria was the only exception to his general conclusion that no unequivocal practice in support of such a right existed prior to the UN Charter.[16] Armed conflict (and the inter-state use of military force more generally) was not per se unlawful during the nineteenth century, but it was important politically that there be a justification such as self-defence or protection of persons in the post-Napoleonic period.[17]

Since the adoption of the United Nations Charter in 1945 there have been legions of books, articles and chapters debating whether a unilateral intervention to protect peoples from human rights abuses, without a Chapter VII

---

[13] Wil Vevrey, 'Legality of Humanitarian Intervention after the Cold War' in E. Ferris (ed.), *The Challenge to Intervention: A New Role for the United Nations* (Uppsala: Life and Peace Institute, 1992).

[14] Francis Kofi Abiew, *The Evolution of the Doctrine and Practice of Humanitarian Intervention* (Dordrecht: Kluwer Law International 1999), p. 48.

[15] Brownlie, *International Law and the Use of Force by States*, p. 340.

[16] Ibid.

[17] For a history of the period see Part I of the recently published M. Weller (ed.), *The Oxford Handbook of the Use of Force in International Law* (Oxford: Oxford University Press, 2015).

Humanitarian intervention/responsibility to protect 15

authorization from the Security Council, was in compliance with the international law on the use of force, *jus ad bellum*.[18] Most scholars argued that humanitarian intervention was not in accordance with any exception to Article 2(4)'s prohibition on the use of force.[19] However, there were a minority of scholars, including Christopher Greenwood and Fernando Tesón, who argued that humanitarian intervention was in accordance with the purposes of the United Nations and that, as such, it constituted a customary international law exception to the prohibition supported by state practice and *opinio juris*.[20] The difficulty in their analysis of state practice is that, in most cases, states did not justify their interventions solely on humanitarian grounds. In the majority of instances that might be viewed as having been examples of humanitarian intervention, such as India in Bangladesh (1971), Tanzania in Uganda (1978) or Vietnam in Cambodia (1978), the primary justification advanced by the intervening state was self-defence. The only cases prior to the 1990s where states seemed to justify intervention on purely humanitarian grounds were France in the Central African Republic (1983), when French troops assisted in toppling Bokassa, and India in Sri Lanka in 1986, when aid was delivered by Indian forces to Tamil rebels and their families.[21] The 1990s saw an increase in cases of humanitarian intervention, such as the 'coalition of the willing' intervening in Iraq to assist Kurdish and southern Shi'a peoples following the Gulf War (1990–1991), and the Economic Community of West African States (ECOWAS) interventions in the civil wars in Liberia (1993) and Sierra Leone (1996–1998).[22] Cases of non-intervention also ignited international debate and condemnation. These were the civil wars in Rwanda and Yugoslavia, which resulted in genocide, when the United Nations dithered over intervention (with the delay resulting in the deaths of hundreds of thousands of people).[23] One situation more than any of

---

[18] Notable examples are: M. Akehurst, 'Humanitarian Intervention' in Hedley Bull (ed.), *Intervention in World Politics* (Oxford: Oxford University Press, 1984) and W.D. Vevrey, 'Humanitarian Intervention under International Law' (1985) 32 *Netherlands International Law Review* 357.

[19] Two leading examples are: S. Chesterman, *Just War or Just Peace? Humanitarian Intervention in International Law* (Oxford: Oxford University Press, 2001); S.D. Murphy, *Humanitarian Intervention: The United Nations in an Evolving World Order* (Philadelphia: University of Pennsylvania Press, 1996). I published a book with the same conclusion, S. Breau, *Humanitarian Intervention: The United Nations and Collective Responsibility* (London: Cameron May, 2005).

[20] C. Greenwood, 'International Law and the NATO Intervention in Kosovo' in (2000) 49 *International and Comparative Law Quarterly* 926; F.R. Tesón, *Humanitarian Intervention: An Inquiry into Law and Morality* (Dobbs Ferry, NY: Transnational Publishers Inc., 1988).

[21] Breau, *Humanitarian Intervention*, in which I discuss each one of these interventions in detail.

[22] Ibid.

[23] United Nations Department of Public Information, *The United Nations and Rwanda, 1993–1996* (New York: UN, 1996), and UN General Assembly, *Report of the Secretary-General Pursuant to General Assembly Resolution 53/35: The Fall of Srebrenica*, 15 November 1999, A/54/549.

16   *Part I: Theoretical roots of responsibility to protect*

the others provoked not only academic debate, but also resulted in major governmental and intergovernmental investigations.[24] This was the NATO intervention in Kosovo in 1999.

In March 1999 the states making up NATO engaged in an armed intervention in Kosovo by way of a bombing campaign, principally in Serbia. Some states argued these attacks were in compliance with international law, by a right of humanitarian intervention, to use force to prevent Slobodan Milosevic and the Serbian forces from repeating the slaughter visited upon Bosnia–Herzegovina.[25]

[24] Danish Institute of International Affairs, *Humanitarian Intervention*; United Kingdom, House of Commons, Foreign Affairs Committee, Fourth Report; Advisory Council on International Affairs and Advisory Committee on Issues of Public International Law, *Humanitarian Intervention*; ICISS, *The Responsibility to Protect*; S. Blockmans, 'Moving into Unchartered Waters: An Emerging Right of Unilateral Humanitarian Intervention?' (1999) 12 *Leiden Journal of International Law* 759; M. Brenfors and M. Petersen, 'The Legality of Humanitarian Intervention – A Defence' (2000) 69 *Nordic Journal of International Law* 449; I. Brownlie and C. J. Apperley, 'Kosovo Crisis Inquiry: Memorandum on the International Law Aspects' (2000) 49 *The International and Comparative Law Quarterly* 878; A. Cassese, 'Ex Injuria ius Oritur: Are We Moving towards Legitimation of Forcible Humanitarian Countermeasures in the World Community?' (1999) 10 *European Journal of International Law* 23; 'Editorial Comments: NATO's Kosovo Intervention' (1999) 9(3) *American Journal of International Law* 824–862 comments by Henkin, Wedgwood, Charney, Chinkin, Falk, Franck and Reisman; Christine Gray, 'The Legality of NATO's Military Action in Kosovo' in Sienho Yee and Tieya Wang (eds), *International Law in the Post-Cold War Worlds: Essays in Memory of Li Haopei* (London: Routledge, 2001); Greenwood, 'International Law and the NATO Intervention in Kosovo'; C. Greenwood, 'Humanitarian Intervention: The Case of Kosovo' (2002) 10 *Finnish Yearbook of International Law* 141; N. Krisch, 'Unilateral Enforcement of the Collective Will: Kosovo, Iraq and the Security Council' (1999) 3 *Max Planck United Nations Yearbook* 59; D. Kritsiotis, 'The Kosovo Crisis and NATO's Application of Armed Force against the Federal Republic of Yugoslavia' (2000) 49 *International and Comparative Law Quarterly* 330; V. Lowe, 'International Legal Issue Arising in the Kosovo Crisis' (2000) 49 *International and Comparative Law Quarterly* 934; C. Portela, *Humanitarian Intervention, NATO and International Law* (Berlin: BITS, 2000); A. Roberts, 'NATO's "Humanitarian War" over Kosovo' (1999) 41 *Survival* 102; N. Ronzitti, 'Lessons of International Law from NATO's Armed Intervention against the Federal Republic of Yugoslavia' (1999) 34 *The International Spectator* 45; B. Simma, 'NATO, the UN and the Use of Force: Legal Aspects' (1999) 10 *European Journal of International Law* 1; Abraham D. Sofaer, 'International Law and Kosovo' (2000) 36 *Stanford Journal of International Law* 1; S. Wheatley, 'The NATO Action against the Federal Republic of Yugoslavia: Humanitarian Intervention in the Post-Cold War Era' (2000) 50 *Northern Ireland Legal Quarterly* 47.

[25] FCO NOTE, 'FRY/Kosovo: The Way Ahead: UK View on Legal Base for Use of Force' 7 October 1998; Roberts, 'NATO's "Humanitarian War" over Kosovo', p. 571. See several other statements of UK public officials including Robin Cook, Baroness Symons and Tony Lloyd, as quoted in UKMIL, 70 BYIL 387 at pp. 571–598. UN Doc. S/PV.3988(1999) (Sir Jeremy Greenstock UK) and UN Doc. S/PV.3988(1999) (Mr Van Walsum for the Netherlands) and Department of Foreign Affairs and International Trade, 'Notes for an address by the Honourable Lloyd Axworthy, Minister of Foreign Affairs Canada', 31 March 1999, www.dfait-maeci.gc.ca, accessed 1 September 2002.

Humanitarian intervention/responsibility to protect   17

This conflict also ended up in the International Court of Justice with a claim brought by Serbia against the NATO powers for an unlawful use of force, contrary to the United Nations Charter.[26] This case never proceeded beyond the provisional measures stage, so there was not a court determination concerning the lawfulness of humanitarian intervention.

However, in the wake of the controversy surrounding the legality of this action, numerous reports were commissioned to examine intervention for human protection purposes. There were traditional reports examining humanitarian intervention. This also became a favourite subject for academic analysis in international law and several books were written in the 1990s and early 2000s on the subject.[27] It became evident from these reports and academic commentary that it was not possible to argue that humanitarian intervention was an exception to the prohibition on the use of force and customary international law in spite of a few scholars – such as Greenwood and Tesón – taking the opposite position.[28] If this ever-increasing practice of unilateral intervention continued, it could have constituted a fundamental threat to the post-war use of force legal regime. In spite of quite of few examples of humanitarian intervention that had occurred since the advent of the UN Charter, on each occasion many states had expressed serious objections, including the group of non-aligned states with respect to the intervention in Kosovo.[29] Just war theory was just that, a theory, and lawfulness depended on one of the recognized exceptions to the use of force being employed, which were self-defence or a collective security action authorized by the UN Security Council.[30] In spite of this 'logjam' in state and academic views, there were two reports that took an entirely different approach, and thus began the process of constituting a historical turning point.

The reports

The two pivotal reports were studies from the Netherlands and Canada with a stated purpose to examine humanitarian intervention; but instead of going down the usual path of examining the legality of intervention, they

---

[26] *Case Concerning Legality of Use of Force (Yugoslavia v. Belgium, Canada, France, Germany, Italy, Netherlands, Portugal and the United Kingdom)*, International Court of Justice, 1999 – Request for the Indication of Provisional Measures heard May 1999, Order of 2 June 1999 38 ILM 1167. The case did not proceed beyond this stage.

[27] See notes 20, 21 and 24 above.

[28] Ibid.

[29] The Permanent Representative of South Africa wrote to the President of the Security Council on 21 April 1991 on behalf of the Movement of non-aligned Countries, as found in UN Doc. S/1999/452.

[30] See the various editorials in (1999) 93 AJIL 824 where a number of international law scholars debate the international law issues in the Kosovo intervention.

18 *Part I: Theoretical roots of responsibility to protect*

introduced a novel concept of a 'responsibility to protect'.[31] The first report was from the Netherlands. In October 1999 the Dutch Minister of Foreign Affairs instructed the Advisory Council on International Affairs jointly with the Advisory Committee on Issues of Public International Law to produce a report on the issues raised by humanitarian intervention. The report concluded that there was no clear evidence of a customary international law emerging for humanitarian intervention without a Security Council mandate.[32] The committees, instead, concentrated on an argument for the emergence of legal obligations to protect human rights as a counterpoint to state sovereignty. The report from the joint committees stated that:

> the international duty to protect and promote the rights of individuals and groups has thus developed into a universally valid obligation that is incumbent upon all states in the international community, both individually and collectively...The CAAV and the AIV therefore consider it extremely desirable that, as part of the doctrine of state responsibility, efforts be made to further develop a justification ground for humanitarian intervention without a Security Council mandate.[33]

Although the report never uses the term 'responsibility to protect', it is clear that this obligation to protect and promote rights of individuals ('the international duty to protect') is very similar. Furthermore, this doctrine is argued to be part of the law of state responsibility. The Dutch and Canadian committees both recommended an assessment framework for intervention that has also been proposed in subsequent reports. The first step is that a state or group of states should attempt to obtain Security Council authorization for the use of force for humanitarian purposes by means of a draft resolution and, should that fail, a Uniting for Peace resolution should be introduced into the General Assembly as the secondary body for the maintenance of peace and security.[34] The assessment framework proposed for reviewing the draft resolution includes three important caveats that have also been adopted in subsequent reports:

1. States engaging in intervention should be parties to regional and universal conventions for the protection of human rights, with preference given to states in the particular region and states as part of international organizations.[35]

---

[31] Advisory Council on International Affairs and Advisory Committee on Issues of Public International Law, *Humanitarian Intervention*; ICISS, *The Responsibility to Protect*.

[32] Advisory Council on International Affairs and Advisory Committee on Issues of Public International Law, *Humanitarian Intervention*, p. 23.

[33] Ibid., p. 24.

[34] Ibid., pp. 26–27 and UN Doc. A/377 A, the General Assembly Resolution adopted on 3 November 1950, which was given the title '*Uniting for Peace*'.

[35] Ibid., p. 28.

Humanitarian intervention/responsibility to protect   19

2. The situation must be one in which fundamental human rights are being or are likely to be seriously violated on a large scale and there is an urgent need for intervention.[36]
3. The legitimate government is unwilling or unable to provide the victims with appropriate care.[37]

The actual phrase the 'responsibility to protect' was introduced in the second of the two reports, by the International Commission on Intervention and State Sovereignty (ICISS). This report was commissioned by the Government of Canada primarily to review the legality of humanitarian intervention and to answer the question posed by Kofi Annan in his speech to the General Assembly Summit for the Millennium:

> If humanitarian intervention is, indeed, an unacceptable assault on sovereignty, how should we respond to a Rwanda, to a Srebrenica – to gross and systematic violations of human rights that offend every principle of common humanity...But surely no legal principle – not even sovereignty – can ever shield crimes against humanity...Armed intervention must always remain the option of last resort, but in the face of mass murder, it is an option that cannot be relinquished.[38]

The twelve commissioners on the ICISS charged with this task represented all areas of the globe and include Cyril Ramaphosa (South Africa), Michael Ignatieff (Canada), Klaus Naumann (Germany) and Fidel Ramos (Philippines), along with Gareth Evans (Former Australian Foreign Minister) and Mohamed Sahnoun (Algeria – Special Advisor to the UN Secretary-General) as co-chairs. The unique aspect of this commission is described by one of the commissioners, Ramesh Thakur. He states the ICISS had six distinguishing features: 'balance, outreach, independence, comprehensiveness, innovativeness and political realism'.[39] The commissioners, given these features, unanimously agreed to the report. In addition to relying on their own intensive discussion, and research reports from their own research group led by Thomas Weiss, the group held a series of round-table discussions in Beijing, Cairo, Geneva, London, Maputo, New Delhi, New York, Ottawa, Paris, Santiago and Washington, where they met with academics, politicians and representatives of civil society.[40]

The ICISS report deals with the fundamental issue of state sovereignty. It was heavily influenced by a previous report, *Sovereignty as Responsibility*, authored

---

[36] Ibid.

[37] Ibid.

[38] K. Annan, Millennium Report of the Secretary-General, UN Doc. A/54/2000, Chapter 3.

[39] R. Thakur, *The United Nations and Peace and Security* (Cambridge: Cambridge University Press, 2006), p. 247.

[40] Ibid., p. 248.

20 *Part I: Theoretical roots of responsibility to protect*

by Francis Deng and others and published by the Brookings Institute.[41] It is the *Sovereignty as Responsibility* report that introduced the idea – based on the work of Lon Fuller – that responsibility for 'life sustaining standards for its citizens', rather than control over subjects, should be seen as the essence of state sovereignty.[42] The sovereign does not exist above the law; rather, he or she is judged according to the law.[43] Deng took this idea further and argued that 'these principles impose on the international community a correlative responsibility for their enforcement'.[44] It is this second level of responsibility that was adopted by the drafters of *The Responsibility to Protect*.

The final ICISS report was presented to Kofi Annan on 18 December 2001 by Paul Heinbecker, the Canadian Permanent Representative to the United Nations. In its central recommendation, the report argues that there is an emerging principle in favour of intervention for human protection purposes. The key recommendation in the report is that:

> Where a population is suffering serious harm, as a result of internal war, insurgency, repression or state failure, and the state in question is unwilling or unable to halt or avert it, the principle of non-intervention yields to the international responsibility to protect.[45]

The ICISS report outlines three specific elements of the responsibility to protect. These are:

a. The responsibility to prevent: to address both the root causes and direct causes of internal conflict and other man-made crises putting populations at risk.
b. The responsibility to react: to respond to situations of compelling human need with appropriate measures, which may include coercive measures like sanctions and international prosecution, and in extreme cases military intervention.
c. The responsibility to rebuild: to provide, particularly after a military intervention, full assistance with recovery, reconstruction and reconciliation, addressing the causes of the harm the intervention was designed to halt or avert.[46]

Even if in the last resort military intervention is contemplated, the Commission presents a detailed set of conditions prior to 'military intervention for human protection purposes' (the report does not use the term

---

[41] Deng *et al.*, *Sovereignty as Responsibility*.
[42] Ibid., p. xviii.
[43] L.L. Fuller, 'Positivism and Fidelity to Law – A Reply to Professor Hart' (1958) 71 *Harvard Law Review* 630 at p. 657.
[44] Deng *et al.*, *Sovereignty as Responsibility*, p. 6.
[45] ICISS, *The Responsibility to Protect*, p. XI.
[46] Ibid.

Humanitarian intervention/responsibility to protect 21

'humanitarian intervention'). The first set of criteria is the 'Just Cause threshold', which includes large-scale loss of life, and actual or apprehended or large-scale ethnic cleansing. The 'precautionary principles' include the idea of the right intention. This means that the primary purpose of the intervention is to halt or avert human suffering, but that did not have to be the only motive. The second principle is that the intervention has to be as a last resort after every non-military option has been explored. The third principle is that the intervention has to use proportional means and it should be the minimum necessary to secure the human protection objective. Finally, there must be a reasonable chance of success in halting or averting the suffering.[47]

The report also outlines the international law issues surrounding the use of force for human protection purposes. The 'Right Authority' conditions include, first, that there is no better or more appropriate body than the Security Council to authorize military intervention for human protection purposes. Following from that principle, the second condition is that Security Council authorization should be sought in all cases. Third, the Security Council should deal promptly with any request for authority to intervene. Fourth, the Permanent Five members should agree not to apply the veto. Fifth, if the Security Council requests a proposal or fails to act, there should be either consideration of the matter under a General Assembly 'Uniting for Peace' procedure or action by a regional or sub-regional organization under Chapter VIII of the UN Charter. Finally, concerned states may not rule out other means to meet the gravity and urgency of the situation if the Security Council fails to act, thereby affecting the 'stature and credibility of the United Nations'.[48] Clearly the drafters of the report favour United Nations action, but they, unanimously, do not rule out unilateral armed intervention.

International reaction

Initially, the reports from the Netherlands and Canada seem to have gathered dust, particularly in the wake of the terrorist attacks on the World Trade Center on 11 September 2001 and the armed conflict with the Taliban regime in Afghanistan commencing in late 2001, an intervention again without an enabling Security Council resolution but supported by a wide coalition of states as an exercise in self-defence.[49] However, there was a revival of attention in 2003 when the international community was left badly divided over the legality of the unilateral armed intervention in Iraq, which began on 19 March and was led by the United States and the United Kingdom. It was perceived that the Security Council was in major crisis and a High-Level Panel was commissioned by the Secretary-General of the United Nations to

[47] Ibid.
[48] Ibid., pp. XII–XIII.
[49] See UN Doc. S/Res/1373, 28 September 2001.

22 *Part I: Theoretical roots of responsibility to protect*

examine the threats, challenges and change facing the Security Council.[50] At the same time, another major humanitarian crisis emerged in Darfur, Sudan when, once again, the international community dithered over what action to take in the face of large-scale human suffering.

On 4 November 2003 the Secretary-General of the United Nations constituted a High-Level Panel to study global security threats. The mandate of the committee was to:

(a) Examine today's global threats and provide an analysis of future challenges to international peace and security. Whilst there may continue to exist a diversity of perception on the relative importance of the various threats facing particular Member States on an individual basis, it is important to find an appropriate balance at a global level. It is also important to understand the connections between different threats.

(b) Identify clearly the contribution that collective action can make in addressing these challenges.

(c) Recommend the changes necessary to ensure effective collective action, including but not limited to, a review of the principal organs of the United Nations.[51]

In December 2004 the Secretary-General's High-Level Panel on Threats, Challenges and Change released its report, *A More Secure World: Our Shared Responsibility*. Gareth Evans, who had co-chaired the ICISS, was also a member of the High-Level Panel. The panel seized on the notion of a responsibility to protect as part of its strategy for reforming the way the Security Council authorized the use of force under Chapter VII of the United Nations Charter:

> The Panel endorses the emerging norm that there is a collective international responsibility to protect, exercisable by the Security Council authorizing military intervention as a last resort, in the event of genocide and other large-scale killing, ethnic cleansing or serious violations of humanitarian law which sovereign Governments have proved powerless or unwilling to prevent.[52]

As with the original ICISS report, a formula of five criteria are introduced in *A More Secure World* for the use of force in situations of human catastrophe. These are:

---

[50] UN Press Release SG/A/857 04/11/2003.

[51] Ibid.

[52] *A More Secure World: Our Shared Responsibility. Report of the Secretary-General's High-Level Panel on Threats, Challenges and Change* (New York: United Nations, 2004), UN Doc. A/59/565, 2 December 2004, p. 85.

(a) *Seriousness of threat* – genocide and other large-scale killing, ethnic cleansing or serious violations of international humanitarian law, actual or imminently apprehended.
(b) *Proper purpose* – primary (not sole) purpose to halt or avert the threat in question.
(c) *Last resort* – every non-military option for meeting the threat having been explored with reasonable grounds for believing other measures will not succeed.
(d) *Proportional means* – scale, duration and intensity the minimum necessary to meet the threat.
(e) *Balance of consequences* – reasonable chance of military action being successful with the consequences not likely to be worse than consequences of inaction.

These are virtually the same criteria as those set out in *The Responsibility to Protect* and the report recommended that these guidelines be embodied in declaratory resolutions by the Security Council and the General Assembly.[53]

Secretary-General Kofi Annan also contributed significantly in the momentum towards the adoption of the responsibility to protect. In April 2004, on the tenth anniversary of the beginning of the Rwandan Genocide, the Secretary-General launched a five-point action plan to prevent genocide.[54] The first of these elements is to prevent armed conflict, as genocide almost always occurs during war. The second element is to ensure the protection of civilians in armed conflict. The third element is ending impunity for those who perpetrate genocide. The fourth element is early and clear warning of genocide. The fifth heading of the action plan is the need for *swift and decisive action* when, in spite of all efforts, the international community learns that genocide is happening or is about to happen.[55]

The Secretary-General followed the action plan to prevent genocide with his report, *In Larger Freedom*, presented to the General Assembly in September 2005. That report also endorsed the responsibility to protect. The Secretary-General developed the notion in his section, freedom to live in dignity, under the section entitled 'Rule of Law':

> 135. The International Commission on Intervention and State Sovereignty and more recently the High-Level Panel on Threats, Challenges and Change, with its 16 members from all around the world, endorsed what they described as an 'emerging norm that there is a collective responsibility to protect' (see A/59/565, para. 203). While I am well aware of the sensitivities involved in this issue, I strongly agree with this approach. **I believe that we must embrace the responsibility to**

---

[53] Ibid., p. 86.
[54] United Nations Document SG/SM/9245 of 7 April 2004.
[55] Ibid., emphasis in original.

24   *Part I: Theoretical roots of responsibility to protect*

protect, and, when necessary, we must act on it. This responsibility lies, first and foremost, with each individual State, whose primary raison d'être and duty is to protect its population. But if national authorities are unable or unwilling to protect their citizens, then the responsibility shifts to the international community to use diplomatic, humanitarian and other methods to help protect the human rights and well-being of civilian populations. When such methods appear insufficient, the Security Council may out of necessity decide to take action under the Charter of the United Nations, including enforcement action, if so required.[56]

Due to these influential reports, the responsibility to protect concept has come to the forefront of international politics and has attracted the attention of international law academics.[57] The High-Level Panel and Secretary-General's reports were discussed at the special High-Level Plenary Summit of the General Assembly on the occasion of the sixtieth anniversary of the founding of the United Nations. This summit, in spite of disagreement on general issues of United Nations reform, adopted a crucial and unanimous statement on the Responsibility to Protect, which, due to its historical importance, is set out in full here:

Responsibility to protect populations from genocide, war crimes, ethnic cleansing and crimes against humanity

138. Each individual State has the responsibility to protect its populations from genocide, war crimes, ethnic cleansing and crimes against humanity. This responsibility entails the prevention of such crimes, including their incitement, through appropriate and necessary means. We accept that responsibility and will act in accordance with it. The international community should, as appropriate, encourage and help States to exercise this responsibility and should support the United Nations to establish an early warning capability.

139. The international community, through the United Nations, also has the responsibility to use appropriate diplomatic, humanitarian and other peaceful means, in accordance with Chapter VI and VIII of the Charter, to help protect populations from genocide, war crimes, ethnic cleansing and crimes against humanity. In this context, we are prepared to take collective action, in a timely and decisive manner, through the Security Council, in accordance with the UN Charter, including Chapter VII, on a case by case basis and in cooperation with relevant regional organizations as appropriate, should peaceful means be inadequate and national

---

[56] K. Annan, *In Larger Freedom: Towards Development, Security and Human Rights for All,* UN Doc. A/59/2005, 21 March 2005, p. 35.

[57] The Conference by the American Society of International Law and the Asser Institute in The Hague focused on United Nations reform, including the responsibility to protect, and was addressed by Lord David Hannay, a member of the High-Level Panel.

authorities manifestly fail to protect their populations from genocide, war crimes, ethnic cleansing and crimes against humanity. We stress the need for the General Assembly to continue consideration of the responsibility to protect populations from genocide, war crimes, ethnic cleansing, and crimes against humanity and its implications, bearing in mind the principles of the Charter of the United Nations and international law. We also intend to commit ourselves, as necessary and appropriate, to help states build capacity to protect their populations from genocide, war crimes, ethnic cleansing and crimes against humanity and to assist those which are under stress before crises and conflicts break out.[58]

It can be argued that this resolution marks the critical historical turning point. This was a consensus resolution, as no state actively opposed it, although China and India expressed major reservations some time later.[59] It is simply astonishing that only four years after its first introduction, the Responsibility to Protect was endorsed in a declaratory United Nations resolution. In 2005, 60 years after the founding of the United Nations and almost two centuries after the first asserted instance of humanitarian intervention, the concept finally received its proper burial in this resolution. From this point on, the focus of international debate would be on the notion of international responsibility. The critical difference between the two concepts of humanitarian intervention and the responsibility to protect is evident in this resolution. Nowhere is there any discussion of a right to intervene but, rather, the resolution is a confirmation of an international responsibility to react to genocide, crimes against humanity, ethnic cleansing and war crimes.

From the viewpoint of an international lawyer, it has to be acknowledged that nowhere in the resolution of the special High-Level Plenary Summit of the General Assembly is there mandatory language. The responsibility to protect is to be exercised on a 'case by case' basis. This is not language that would result in a clear and concise legal doctrine. Yet it does declare an important principle in unequivocal terms. A state and the international community have protection responsibilities towards populations. The consensus resolution establishes these two levels of activity; state sovereignty is no longer a shield preventing interference in matters of international criminality. Thus this idea of international responsibility opens the door to further clarification by practice. Ten years later we see that this resolution on the sixtieth anniversary of the UN, in addition to activity resulting from the reports on the genocides in Rwanda and Srebrenica, resulted in substantial changes to the architecture of the United Nations system, including the abolition of the perceived ineffectual Human Rights Commission and the introduction

---

[58] UN Doc. A/Res/60/1, 24 October 2005.
[59] UN General Assembly Debate on Responsibility to Protect, July 2009.

26 *Part I: Theoretical roots of responsibility to protect*

of the Human Rights Council.[60] There were also substantial reforms within the United Nations concerning the prevention of, and reaction to, genocide, which will be the focus of the next section.

Action within the United Nations system

The first reform activity in the United Nations system in relation to the responsibility to protect surprisingly came from the Security Council. In paragraph 10 of Security Council Resolution 1366 of 30 August 2001, on the role of the Security Council in the prevention of armed conflict, the Council invited the Secretary-General to refer to the Council information and analysis from within the United Nations system on cases of serious violations of international law, including international humanitarian law and human rights law.[61]

On 7 April 2004, the tenth anniversary of the Rwandan genocide, UN Secretary-General Kofi Annan outlined a five-point action plan for preventing genocide:

1. Prevent armed conflict, which usually provides the context for genocide;
2. Protect civilians in armed conflict, including through UN peacekeepers;
3. End impunity through judicial action in national and international courts;
4. Gather information and set up an early-warning system; and
5. Take swift and decisive action, including military action.[62]

In a letter to the President of the Security Council dated 12 July 2004, Kofi Annan informed him of his decision to appoint a Special Advisor on the Prevention of Genocide.[63] Juan Méndez was the first Special Advisor and was succeeded in 2007 by Francis Deng. In the same 2004 letter, the Secretary-General listed the Special Adviser on the Prevention of Genocide's responsibilities as follows:

- Collecting existing information, in particular from within the United Nations system, on massive and serious violations of human rights and international humanitarian law of ethnic and racial origin that, if not prevented or halted, might lead to genocide;
- Acting as a mechanism of early warning to the Secretary-General, and through him to the Security Council, by bringing to their attention situations that could potentially result in genocide;

---

[60] Report of the Independent Inquiry into the Actions of the United Nations during the 1994 Genocide in Rwanda, UN Doc. S/1999/1257, 16 December 1999, and UN Doc. A/54/549, 15 November 1999, Report of the Secretary-General on the Fall of Srebrenica.

[61] UN Doc. S/Res/1366, 30 August 2001.

[62] UN Doc. Press Release SG/SM/9197, 7 April 2004.

[63] UN Doc. S/2004/567, 12 July 2004.

Humanitarian intervention/responsibility to protect 27

- Making recommendations to the Security Council, through the Secretary-General, on actions to prevent or halt genocide; and
- Liaising with the United Nations system on activities for the prevention of genocide and work to enhance the United Nations' capacity to analyze and manage information regarding genocide or related crimes.[64]

After the adoption of the consensus General Assembly Resolution on the responsibility to protect in 2005, the apparatus of the United Nations began to operationalize the concept, and it was to be part and parcel of the existing prevention of genocide apparatus. The Secretary-General of the United Nations wrote a letter to the President of the Security Council recommending that a Special Adviser on the Responsibility to Protect be appointed:

> To enable the Special Representative (on genocide) to have greater operational impact and in recognizing the link between large scale atrocities and threats to peace and security, his office needs to be strengthened. As part of this effort, and based on the agreement contained in paragraphs 138 and 139 of the 2005 World Summit Outcome Document, I intend to designate a Special Adviser on the Responsibility to Protect at the level of Assistant Secretary-General, on a part-time basis. Recognizing the fledgling nature of agreement on the responsibility to protect, the Special Adviser's primary roles will be conceptual development and consensus-building.[65]

The first Special Adviser on the Responsibility to Protect was Edward Luck, who was appointed in 2008 and replaced in 2012 by Jennifer Welsh.[66] In January of 2009 the Secretary-General released a report entitled *Implementing the Responsibility to Protect*, which was largely prepared by Mr Luck.[67] This was a very important document, as Welsh has stated that it made clear that renegotiation of the responsibility to protect was not on offer.[68]

The strategy for implementation is based on a three-pillar approach. Pillar one is the primary protection responsibilities of states. Pillar two is international assistance and capacity-building and pillar three is timely and decisive response. The strategy focused on the first aspect of the responsibility to protect – the responsibility to prevent – and if that prevention fails, the notion of 'early and flexible response tailored to the specific circumstances of each case'. Thus the design of the system of protection was a first level of individual state

---

[64] Ibid.

[65] UN Doc. S/2007/721, 7 December 2007.

[66] For biographies of advisers and descriptions of roles, see www.un.org/en/preventgenocide/ adviser/adviser.shtml, accessed 4 July 2015.

[67] *Implementing the Responsibility to Protect.* Report of the Secretary-General. UN Doc. A/ 63/677, 12 January 2009.

[68] J. Welsh, 'Implementing the Responsibility to Protect', Policy Brief No. 1 2009, Oxford Institute for Ethics, Law and Armed Conflict.

28 *Part I: Theoretical roots of responsibility to protect*

responsibility, a second level of capacity-building and a third level, if both previous levels fail, of reaction by the United Nations. It is from this date that it was clear that implementing the responsibility to protect became one of the activities of the United Nations peace and security apparatus.

Two days after Secretary-General Ban Ki-moon presented his implementation report, members of the General Assembly of the United Nations debated the responsibility to protect over three days. The plenary debate took place on 23, 24 and 28 July 2009.[69] A total of 94 member states and 2 observer missions took the floor and 86 others chose to be represented by some of those speaking. Only 12 of the 192 United Nations member states were not part of the debate. Over 50 statements in the debate explicitly endorsed the three-pillar strategy as the route for implementing the responsibility to protect. And at least two thirds of all the statements had positive words for the report of the Secretary-General.

By contrast, only four countries called the responsibility to protect into question and clearly did not support the concept or its implementation, and these were: Cuba, Nicaragua, Sudan and Venezuela. Other states expressed concern about its implementation, preferring to focus on pillars one and two, and some remained hostile, or at least fearful, about pillar three. But only a handful of states explicitly objected to pillar three (including Iran, North Korea, Pakistan and Sri Lanka), considerably fewer than the 27 members that specifically acknowledged the need to consider coercive measures as a last resort.[70] Later, within its regular annual session, the General Assembly passed resolution 63/308, in which the Assembly confirmed its intention 'to continue its consideration of the responsibility to protect' as called for in the 2005 World Summit Outcome.[71]

Due to the consistent work of the Special Advisor on the Responsibility to Protect, the Secretary-General releases implementation reports annually. The first report from the Secretary-General was in July 2010, entitled, *Early Warning, Assessment and the Responsibility to Protect.*[72]

In 2011 the Secretary-General authored a second report entitled, *The Role of Regional and Sub-regional Arrangements In Implementing the Responsibility to Protect.*[73] The next report, in July 2012, was entitled, *Responsibility to Protect: Timely and Decisive Response.*[74] In July 2013 came the report, *Responsibility to Protect: State Responsibility and Prevention.*[75]

---

[69] International Coalition of the Responsibility to Protect, 'Report on the General Assembly Plenary Debate on the Responsibility to Protect', 15 September 2009, available at www.responsibilitytoprotect.org/ICRtoP%20Report-General_Assembly_Debate_on_ the_Responsibility_to_Protect%20FINAL%209_22_09.pdf, accessed 1 July 2015.
[70] Ibid.
[71] UN Doc. G/Res/63/308, 7 October 2009.
[72] UN Doc. A/64/864, 9 August 2010.
[73] UN Doc. A/65/877-S2011/393, 12 July 2011.
[74] UN Doc. A/66/874-S/2012/578, 25 July 2012.
[75] UN Doc. A/67/929-S/2013/399, 9 July 2013.

Humanitarian intervention/responsibility to protect 29

The sixth report of the Secretary-General was released 11 July 2014 entitled, *Fulfilling our Collective Responsibility: International Assistance and the Responsibility to Protect.*[76]

It is to be noted that the emphasis of the work of the Special Advisor who drafts these reports is primarily on prevention and the initial level of protection responsibility within the state. Only the report in 2012 emphasized the second level of international responsibility. This report deals with the pillar three collective responsibility, but argues that pillar three should be less and less utilized if a state is enabled to fulfil its responsibility to eliminate the international crimes that mandate an international response.[77] The Secretary-General discusses levels of reaction from diplomacy, referral to the International Criminal Court, sanctions and, if all else fails, use of force pursuant to Chapter VII.[78] It is not surprising that he does not contemplate unilateral forcible action by states. The significance of this report is that the Secretary-General is recommending to the members of the United Nations that there will be occasions for a non-peacekeeping type of action that requires a military response and that the United Nations system has to adopt comprehensive strategies to deal with the types of situations that require the responsibility to protect.

It is a bit surprising, given the activity of the Special Advisors, that the newly constituted Human Rights Council and the office of the UN High Commissioner for Human Rights were slow to address the responsibility to protect. In June 2012 there was a 'side event' on the responsibility to protect addressed by Navi Pillay, the then High Commissioner.[79] This was in response to a request from Australia, Hungary, Thailand, Nigeria and Uruguay that the Human Rights Council discuss its role regarding the responsibility to protect. On 12 June 2012 the Human Rights Council passed a resolution on Syria, reminding Syria of its responsibility to protect its population.[80]

The actual activity of the United Nations towards the promotion of the responsibility to protect has to be viewed within its peace and security activity, which will be the subject of the final part of this book. However, it is clear from the above discussion that the architecture of the United Nations bureaucracy has undergone a substantial change with the introduction of the Special Advisors on Genocide and the Responsibility to Protect, who ensure annual reporting on the implementation of the concept.

The NGO community, in contrast, has enthusiastically embraced the concept, as there is a Global Centre for the Responsibility to Protect, an International Coalition for the Responsibility to Protect and an Asia Pacific

---

[76] UN Doc. A/68/947-S/2014/449, 11 July 2014.
[77] UN Doc. A/66/874-S/2012/578, 25 July 2012, para. 18.
[78] Ibid., paras 27–32.
[79] See www.una.org.uk/sites/default/files/Navi%20Pillay%20Message%20to%20Human%20
Rights%20Council%20R2P%20event%2019-06-12.pdf, accessed 6 July 2015.
[80] UN Doc. A/HRC/RES/S-19/1, 4 June 2012.

30   *Part I: Theoretical roots of responsibility to protect*

Centre for the Responsibility to Protect.[81] All prepare numerous policy papers that are forwarded to the United Nations and governments, which detail protection responsibilities. The latter group, located at the University of Queensland and partly sponsored by the Australian Government, also hosts a Global Responsibility to Protect Journal for the academic community.[82]

Another community that has been slow to react to this new concept is the international law scholarly community. Only very recently have there been studies emerging on the international law aspects of the concept.[83] In the same way that the community had been opposed to an argument of unilateral humanitarian intervention evolving into customary international law, so too is there opposition to any kind of international legal status for the responsibility to protect.[84]

Conclusion

It is difficult to minimize the seismic shift in the international debate when situations of massive abuses of human rights occur. No longer do states focus on rights of intervention: the language is now of duty and responsibility. Even though the sceptic can point to many examples of the international community failing in its international responsibility, no one seriously argues that the responsibility does not exist. It is evident that a historical turning point took place from 2001 to 2005, when the General Assembly adopted its consensus resolution. It is clear that this resolution did not set out rules of international law as the language is not mandatory. But the lack of clarity regarding the responsibility to protect resulted in activity by the United Nations, particularly in the implementation reports, to clarify the content of the concept. This process continues to this day and has resulted in the beginning of a blueprint for action, which we shall discuss in the final part of this book. The final chapter will review a current example of a failure of intervention (the situation in Syria and Iraq), but the third part of this book will continue the discussion of a fundamental change in the way the United Nations peace and security apparatus conducts its business.

---

[81] See www.globalr2p.org/, accessed 5 July 2015; www.responsibilitytoprotect.org/, accessed 5 July 2015; www.r2pasiapacific.org/, accessed 5 July 2015.

[82] Ibid., and see www.brill.com/cn/global-responsibility-protect, accessed 5 July 2015.

[83] A. Orford, *International Authority and the Responsibility to Protect* (Cambridge: Cambridge University Press, 2011); G. Zyberi (ed.), *An Institutional Approach to the Responsibility to Protect* (Cambridge: Cambridge University Press, 2013). See also the upcoming book by R. Barnes and V.P. Tzevelekos (eds), *Beyond the Responsibility to Protect: Generating Change in International Law*, to be published by Routledge.

[84] See, for example, C. Focarelli, 'The Responsibility to Protect and Humanitarian Intervention: Too Many Ambiguities for a Working Doctrine' (2008) 13 *Journal of Conflict and Security Law* 191; A. Kapur, 'Humanity as the A and Ω of Sovereignty: Four Replies to Anne Peters' (2009) 20 *European Journal of International Law* 560; G. Molier, 'Humanitarian Intervention and the Responsibility to Protect after 9/11' (2006) 53 *Netherlands International Law Review* 37.

Humanitarian intervention/responsibility to protect 31

However, prior to undertaking a close examination of the practice of the international community, it is necessary to set the context in which the responsibility to protect emerged. In the next chapter it will be useful to review the debate within international law and international relations about the entity known in the consensus resolution as the international community. After this, the second part of the book will review how responsibility as a concept has become embedded within several areas of international law, particularly within the law of state responsibility. It can be argued that not only did historical events lead us to the adoption of international responsibility, but that for many years the developments within key areas of international law had also been leading us in that direction.

2 International society

The responsibility to protect may have emerged in the context of a long-standing political dispute over how to respond to massive abuses of human rights, but the theoretical debate underpinning the concept has also existed for centuries. There are several strands of relevant theoretical discussion that it would be possible for one to examine in relation to the responsibility to protect, but this book will concentrate on the most important facet within the doctrine, the debate concerning the nature of the international system.[1] There have been many publications concerning issues of *jus ad bellum*, particularly focusing on the long-standing just war theory. But as this book argues throughout, the responsibility to protect engages the theorist on an entirely different level: it is not focused on the justification of the use of force or armed conflict. The only aspect of *jus ad bellum* the discussion of the doctrine in this book touches upon is the collective security, Chapter VII aspect. This will be discussed in Part III. The theoretical focus for the responsibility to protect is on the second aspect of the doctrine, the state's responsibility to the international community. The question posed by Annan following Kosovo on sovereignty versus responsibility has to be predicated on a query – responsibility to whom or to what? The fascinating theoretical question is what exactly *is* the 'international community'. This question, again, has involved scholarly debate for centuries.

Therefore, the genesis of the responsibility to protect emerges from literature concerning the nature of the international political and legal system, as can be seen from Deng's original report.[2] There is a large body of international law and international relations theoretical scholarship supporting various visions of an international system with rights and responsibilities on the part of sovereign states towards other states and, arguably, towards citizens from other states. It follows a continuum of propositions from a

---

[1] These debates include the role of the individual in the international system, the nature of responsibility and a discussion of collective security. These issues are discussed as part of the chapters on state responsibility, human rights and the responsibility to react.

[2] F.M. Deng *et al.*, *Sovereignty as Responsibility: Conflict Management in Africa* (Washington DC: The Brookings Institute, 1996).

loose society of states to a cosmopolitan/Kantian vision of an integrated constitutional system. Dupuy states that a constitution can have two meanings: first, the material or substantial sense of the term, which is 'a set of legal principles of paramount importance for every one of the subjects belonging to the social community ruled by it', and second, in the organic and institutional sense, which points to 'the designation of public organs, the separation of powers and the different institutions which are endowed each with its own competencies'.[3] It is the first sense of a constitution that occupies the theoretical debate: does the international system have a community ruled by a set of legal principles of paramount importance? Many theorists in both international law and international relations argue that there is, indeed, an international community or international society governed by a set of legal principles.[4]

The first part of this chapter will review the vibrant debate within international legal theory about the international community. The second part of this chapter will discuss some of the international relations theories arguing for the existence of international society. International relations scholarship is relevant as the two main schools discussed within international relations – the 'English School' and cosmopolitanism – view international law as providing the guiding rules and principles of an international society.

The international community in international legal theory

Whether there is indeed an international society or system has long occupied international legal theory.[5] Grotius – the so-called 'father of international law' – defined international society as:

> The *universal society* of the human race being an institution of nature herself, that is to say, a necessary consequence of the nature of man, – all men, in whatever stations they are placed, *are bound to cultivate it, and to discharge its duties.*[6]

---

[3] P.-M. Dupuy, 'The Constitutional Dimension of the Charter of the United Nations Revisited' (1997) 1 *Max Plank Yearbook of International Law* 1, p. 3.

[4] See, for example: J. Crawford, *State Responsibility: The General Part* (Cambridge: Cambridge University Press, 2013), p. 362; J. Habermas, *The Divided West* (Cambridge: Polity Press, 2006), p. 115; A.-M. Slaughter and W. Burke-White, 'An International Constitutional Moment' (2003) 43 *Harvard International Law Journal* 1.

[5] For an excellent synopsis of the history of international legal theory, see R. Tuck, *The Rights of War and Peace: Political Thought and the International Order from Grotius to Kant* (Oxford: Oxford University Press, 1999).

[6] Hugonis Grotii, *De Jure Belli ac Pacis, libri tres, In quibus ius naturae & Gentium: item iuris publici preciptae expilicantur* (Paris: Apud Nicalaum Buom, 1625, cum privilegio regis via Gallica (the French National Library)), Book I, Chapter I, III, original emphasis.

34   *Part I: Theoretical roots of responsibility to protect*

The philosopher Kant argued in 1793 that there needed to be an international institution with power over sovereign states to ensure a law of world citizenship:[7]

> Since the narrower or wider community of the peoples of the earth has developed so far that a violation of rights in one place is felt throughout the world, the idea of a law of world citizenship is no high-flown or exaggerated notion. It is a supplement to the unwritten code of the civil and international law, indispensable for the maintenance of the public human rights and hence also of perpetual peace.[8]

In the twenty-first century this argument has been taken up by Jürgen Habermas, who argues that the world dominated by nation-states 'is indeed in transition towards the postnational constellation of a global society'.[9] Slaughter and Burke-White have argued that this constitutional moment is based on the emergence of a basic norm of civilian inviolability.[10]

The German School

It has long been accepted by many legal scholars that there is at least some version of an international legal system.[11] Von Bogdandy supports this vision of a 'global legal community that frames and directs political power in light of common values and common good'.[12] The decision to characterize the international system as 'global legal community' was earlier embodied in the work of Hermann Mosler and Christian Tomuschat, who imparted their vision of the international legal system in their seminal Hague Academy lectures.[13] Tomuschat's work resonates as a prudent vision of the current international system as his view is primarily reliant on the positivist method of studying the practice of sovereign states, which he argues supports an international legal community with additional important elements of participation from individuals and civil society.[14] This view is again supported by Jürgen Habermas,

---

[7] Ibid.

[8] I. Kant, *Perpetual Peace: A Philosophical Essay* (London: G. Allen & Unwin Limited, 1903), Third Definitive Article.

[9] Habermas, *The Divided West*, p. 115.

[10] Slaughter and Burke-White, 'An International Constitutional Moment'.

[11] R. Higgins, *Problems and Process* (Oxford: Oxford University Press, 1994), Chapters 1–3, where she discusses the international legal system.

[12] A. von Bogdandy, 'Constitutionalism in International Law: Comment on a Proposal from Germany' (2006) 47 *Harvard International Law Journal* 223, p. 223.

[13] H. Mosler, 'The International Society as a Legal Community' (1974) 140 *Recueil Des Cours* 1; C. Tomuschat, 'Obligations Arising for States without or against their Will' (1993) 241 *Recueil Des Cours* 195; C. Tomuschat, 'International Law: Ensuring the Survival of Mankind on the Eve of a New Century' (1999) 288 *Recueil Des Cours* 1.

[14] Ibid.

who argues that the international condemnation of the conflict in Iraq supports an idea of an emerging international constitutional order.[15]

Notwithstanding these compelling views, there are deep divisions among international legal theorists between such groupings as legal positivists, critical legal theorists and liberal internationalists.[16] Brierly argued that when we speak of the 'law of nations', we are assuming that a 'society of nations exists'.[17] There are several terms used almost interchangeably within international law and international relations; examples are: international society, the international community, the international legal community, the international system and the international legal order. Whatever the term employed, the major theoretical controversy is whether the international community is anything other than a grouping of nations. With the evolution of the United Nations system, the end of the cold war and the phenomenon of globalization, this theoretical debate became more complex, with certain scholars arguing that an international constitutional system had emerged, with the Charter of the United Nations as its constitutional document.[18]

Writing in the period just after the enactment of the Charter, Hersch Lauterpacht discussed the notion of international society in his definition of international law, which he saw as 'predominantly the body of rules which are voluntarily accepted or imposed by the existence of international society and which govern the conduct of states and are subject to enforcement by external sanctions'.[19] However, contrast this definition with one described as the traditional definition of international law: 'the minimal law necessary to enable state-societies to act as closed systems internally and to act as territory-owners in relation to each other.'[20]

More recently, von Bogdandy proposed that there is a German version of the international system that combines the positivist vision of the emergence of international law with liberal ideas of an international society into the view of an international legal community.[21] This vision of a legal community is attractive when one discusses the responsibility to protect as an emerging legal

---

[15] Habermas, *The Divided West*, p. 115.

[16] D.M. Johnston, 'World Constitutionalism in the Theory of International Law' in R. St John Macdonald and D.M. Johnston, *Towards World Constitutionalism: Issues in the Legal Ordering of the World Community* (Leiden: Martinus Nijhoff, 2005), pp. 3–29. Johnston identifies 12 idealistic models of international law.

[17] J.L. Brierly, *The Law of Nations*, 6th edition (Oxford: Oxford University Press, 1963), pp. 41–42.

[18] Leading this analysis is Bardo Fassbender; see 'The United Nations Charter as Constitution of the International Community' (1998) 36 *Columbia Journal of Transnational Law* 529 and *UN Security Council Reform and the Right of Veto* (The Hague: Kluwer Law, 1998).

[19] H. Lauterpacht, *International Law and Human Rights* (New York: Frederick Praeger, 1950), p. 93.

[20] P. Allott, *Eunomia* (Oxford: Oxford University Press, 1990), p. 324.

[21] For a good summary of the German position, in particular the views of Tomuschat, see Bogdandy, 'Constitutionalism in International Law'.

36 *Part I: Theoretical roots of responsibility to protect*

norm. In an influential Hague Academy Lecture entitled, 'The International Society as a Legal Community', given by Hermann Mosler in 1974, we see an early definition of the international legal community:

> the fact that a certain number of independent societies organized on a territorial basis exist side by side, and the psychological element in the form of a general conviction that all these units are partners mutually bound by reciprocal, generally applicable, rules granting rights, imposing obligations and distributing competences.[22]

There are within this definition two parallel origins of the legal order: sovereign states and the awareness of legal rules that constrain their sovereignty.[23] Although at first glance this may seem to be a traditionalist version of international law, Mosler discusses the expansion of international law and the obligations of the several great powers living in a certain balance to protect the position of the other members, which is the equivalent of internal constitutional law.[24] The state is the only institution capable of guaranteeing law, order and welfare within society.[25] Mosler argues that the rules of conduct between states are based on rational argument.[26] The legal order in which the only sanction is self-help by its members is always in danger of being turned upside down by the strongest member.[27] The international legal community is not working towards the disappearance or transformation of the state, but towards acceptance of the centrality of the nation-state.[28]

Mosler does not neglect the United Nations, as he argues that the organizational element is the second significant feature of modern international society, after the increase in the number of states. Membership in international organizations has introduced an element of permanent obligations that restricts freedom of action of states. Sovereignty is diminished through the activities of these organizations.[29] Writing at the height of the cold war, Mosler argues that the third element of the international system was the balance of power between the two superpowers, the United States and the Union of Soviet Socialist Republics. This is a deeply realistic vision of the international legal community, influenced by the fact that it was written during the cold war struggle. At that time, Mosler argued that it was perhaps too ambitious to include the individual in the structure of the international society.[30]

[22] Mosler, 'The International Society as a Legal Community' (1974), p. 18.
[23] Ibid., p. 19.
[24] Ibid., p. 27.
[25] Ibid., p. 28.
[26] H. Mosler, *The International Society as a Legal Community* (Alphen aan den Rijn, the Netherlands: Sijthoff & Noordhoff, 1980), p. 3.
[27] Ibid., p. 15.
[28] Ibid., p. 15.
[29] Mosler, 'The International Society as a Legal Community' (1974), pp. 27–29.
[30] Ibid., p. 30.

International society   37

Notwithstanding the cold war era of power politics, Mosler introduced the question of an international constitution that was then taken up by subsequent scholars. He argued that the statutes of the present organizations of states, such as the United Nations Charter, represented a considerable element of constitutional life in international society. The basic principle that made international society into an international legal community was the agreement of the members to develop the rules and principles by which they are to be bound, which is a law-creating process.[31] Mosler argues that these rules and principles constitute the public order of the international community, which is a wider concept than *jus cogens*.[32] Writing in 1974, Mosler acknowledged that these principles of the public order of the international community had not yet been developed.[33]

It was Christian Tomuschat who built upon the work of Mosler in his provocative and compelling view of the international legal community. In his two series of Hague Academy lectures he carefully and systematically traces developments in international law towards an international legal community governed by international law. In the wake of the end of the cold war, he built on Mosler's work towards rules and principles that govern the international legal community. In his lectures entitled 'Obligations Arising for States without or against their Will',[34] given to the Hague Academy in 1993, Tomuschat argues that, '[g]iven the developments triggered by the UN Charter, today a community model of international society would seem to come closer to reality than any time before in history'.[35] He goes on to assert:

> States live, as from their birth, within a legal framework of a limited number of basic rules which determines their basic rights and obligations with or without their will, leaving them, however, sufficient room for self-responsible action within the openings of that legal edifice. One may call this framework, from which every State receives its legal entitlement to be respected as a sovereign entity, the constitution of international society or, preferably, the constitution of the international community, community being a term suitable to indicate a closer union than between members of a society.[36]

This statement would seem to encapsulate the development of a constitutional framework for the international community that includes the basic rules that are the norms of *jus cogens* and obligations *erga omnes*, but that also permit sovereign action.

[31] Ibid., pp. 31–32.
[32] Ibid., p. 35.
[33] Ibid., p. 44.
[34] Tomuschat, 'Obligations Arising for States'.
[35] Ibid., p. 211.
[36] Ibid., p. 211.

38   *Part I: Theoretical roots of responsibility to protect*

In support of his thesis, Tomuschat argues that there a number of instruments that set out the rules of the international legal order or what he calls, 'the juridical architecture of the international system'. They include: Article 2(1) of the Charter, which sets out the principle of the sovereign equality of states; Article 38(1) of the Statute of the International Court of Justice, which contains a list of the different categories of rules of international law including customary law and treaty law; and Article 26 of the Vienna Convention on the Law of Treaties, which declares that every treaty in force is binding on the parties to it and must be performed in good faith.[37] Tomuschat gives the example of an unwritten constitution, that of the United Kingdom, as the 'prime example of a constitution whose relevant components cannot be found in a single document', but where one can identify 'certain rules and statutes as forming part and parcel of the substantive constitution'.[38] He argues that the Charter of the United Nations aims to some extent to become that common law for all states, particularly in its mechanisms for the maintenance of international peace and security – somewhat mirroring the British constitutional model. He concludes that:

> the international community can indeed be conceived of as a legal entity, governed by a constitution, a term which, as pointed out, serves to denote the basic functions of governance within that entity. The international community and its constitution were created by States. Over centuries up to the present time, buttressed in particular by the UN Charter, the idea of a legal framework determining certain common values as the guiding principles States are bound to observe and respect has gained ground and has been progressively strengthened. Today, international legal discourse is profoundly marked by the concept of international community, and precisely in documents established by State representatives.[39]

Tomuschat therefore introduces the concept of an international constitution, but one that relies on the establishment of its rules by sovereign states. In 1999 his Hague Academy course was entitled, 'International Law: Ensuring the Survival of Mankind on the Eve of a New Century'. He reveals that his approach to public international law is grounded in positivism as the international legal order is based on foundations that were brought into being by a collective effort primarily of states that encapsulates a common understanding, but that today, 'is independent of the consent of any individual state'. He says that positivism 'respects the consensus-based structure of international law'. However, Tomuschat's positivism is tempered by an acknowledgement almost mirroring Kant, that the international legal order does not only contain principles and rules, but also basic values that 'permeate its entire

[37] Ibid., pp. 211–212.
[38] Ibid., p. 217.
[39] Ibid.

International society 39

texture, capable of indicating the right direction when new answers have to be sought for new problems'.[40]

In his positivist analysis of the history of the development of international law, and specifically the international community, he concludes that there is indeed such a community where states, 'which by no means lose their capacity as the basic units of the international system', 'have established a considerable number of mechanisms and institutions for the discharge of certain tasks which they are no longer able to deal with acting in isolation'. This international society for Tomuschat is at the mid-point between the traditional model of sovereign states and a world government.[41]

Bardo Fassbender takes probably the most radical view in the German School, when he argues that the United Nations Charter is a constitution of the international community.[42] He engages with three views on the international system: the school founded by the Viennese jurist Alfred Verdross (and later Bruno Simma), the New Haven School and the authors (primarily Mosler and Tomuschat) focusing on the idea of an international community. Fassbender takes issue with Tomuschat's hesitancy to argue that the United Nations Charter is the constitution of the international community. He states that, 'the international community, as it exists today, provides a sufficient social basis for a constitutional charter, a charter which, as an element of a broader process of integration, will further strengthen the community it governs'.[43]

His argument is that the United Nations is the primary institutional representative of the international community and that the drafting of the United Nations Charter was the true constitutional moment in international law.[44] Fassbender concludes that the Charter is an authoritative statement of both the fundamental rights and responsibilities of the international community and the values of that community, and it established defined community institutions.[45] To Fassbender, the structure of the international legal community is centred on the United Nations, not on a consensual coalition of sovereign states. Fassbender, however, seems out of step with his German contemporaries. His view of the United Nations Charter seems utopian and, although it may be an authoritative statement, it is based on sovereign equality of states and does not, as do most constitutions, impose a statement of values on those states.

A more realistic view, supportive of the Tomuschat vision, is argued by Bruno Simma in his Hague Academy lecture, 'From Bilateralism to Community Interest in International Law'.[46] This work continued on from

---

[40] Tomuschat, 'International Law', p. 38.
[41] Ibid., pp. 89–90.
[42] Fassbender, 'The United Nations Charter' and *UN Security Council Reform*.
[43] Fassbender, 'The United Nations Charter', p. 566.
[44] Ibid., pp. 567 and 573.
[45] Ibid., p. 617.
[46] B. Simma, 'From Bilateralism to Community Interest in International Law (1994) **250** *Recueil Des Cours* 217.

40 *Part I: Theoretical roots of responsibility to protect*

his previous work with the Austrian jurist Verdross.[47] He argued for an international community without the inclusion of the word 'legal'. Simma defines community interest as a 'consensus according to which respect for certain fundamental values is not to be left to the free disposition of States individually or *inter se* but is recognized and sanctioned by international law as a matter of concern to all States'.[48] Simma gives examples of the substance of community interests including international peace and security, solidarity between developed and developing countries, protection of the environment, the common heritage concept and the international concern with human rights.[49] He takes issue, however, with calling the international community an international legal community, as then it would be viewed exclusively as a community under international law. To argue that an international society/community could be held together by legal norms alone seems to Simma to overestimate the capacity of law (or at least of international law). He disagrees with Tomuschat that the normative reality of the international community can be deduced from the universal acceptance of legal documents. Simma argues that there is also a certain moral and political unity necessary in addition to international law. He states that what will be decisive is not the use of the term 'international community' as such, but rather 'concrete institutions, principles and rules through which commitment to the interests common to humankind can be activated'.[50] The tension is between the need to make international law express and support universally held moral beliefs and the need to make it reflect the political context.[51] It can be argued that Simma supports Tomuschat's vision of an international community but with the addition of the importance of institutional structures as well as values.

In 2005 a massive publication, edited by two Canadian international lawyers, Ronald St John Macdonald and Douglas Johnston, brought together theorists of an international constitution.[52] Their book also has contributions from Tomuschat and Fassbender, but they added a Canadian perspective to the debate. Johnston introduces the subject by acknowledging how controversial is the debate over the idea of an international constitution. After examining various models of international law, he argues that one way modern international law can be envisioned idealistically, in ethical and institutional terms as 'a collective effort to achieve universal order through the development of constitutional structure and procedure among nations'.[53] Modern international law, to Johnston, reflects three features of

---

[47] A. Verdross and B. Simma, *Universelles Völkerrecht: Theorie und Praxis*, 3rd edition (Berlin: Duncker & Humblot, 1984). For discussion of this book, see Fassbender, 'The United Nations Charter', pp. 542–544.

[48] Simma, 'From Bilateralism to Community Interest', p. 233.

[49] Ibid., pp. 236–243.

[50] Ibid., p. 248.

[51] Ibid., p. 249.

[52] R. St John MacDonald and D. Johnston, *Towards World Constitutionalism: Issues in the Legal Ordering of the World Community* (Leiden: Martinus Nijhoff, 2005).

[53] Johnston, 'World Constitutionalism', p. 19.

constitutionalism: the paramount legal status of the UN Charter; the difficulty of achieving legal amendment of the Charter; and an ethical core of the system by virtue of a 'bill of rights' nucleus of civil rights principles and instruments.[54] However, he argues this is not enough and that constitutionalism in the international system is a 'work-in-progress'. The trends towards constitutionalism, he asserts, are within the fields of human rights, international trade law, international criminal law and the phenomenon of globalization.[55] To advance the project of constitutionalism, Johnston argues that there must be an 'open-ended coalition of state and non-state institutions, so that the voices of civil society can be heard within the chambers of the power-holders'.[56] This echoes a cosmopolitan vision of society advanced by international relations theorists.

The New Haven School

The German School of international legal scholarship is focused on the structure of the system as a society of states. On the other hand the New Haven School focuses on the normative process within the international system as its social process model emphasizes a universal order of human dignity. The function of government may be exercised not only by the government itself, but also by local populations, private pressure organizations, business enterprises, churches and others. The state is an independent community organized for making and enforcing policy.[57] *Law and Minimum World Public Order* was written in 1961 by Yale Law School scholars Myers McDougal and Florentino Feliciano.[58] There are three major tenets of the theory. First, that there is a world community that embraces the whole arena of world and space. Second, there is a world community process through which decisions are taken and enforced by severe deprivations or high indulgences that are inclusive in their reach and effect. Third, there is a process of authoritative and controlling decision that is global in its reach. There are two general conclusions on international law. First, the perception of law as rules is rejected, as in the international arena law is a continuing process of authoritative decisions. Second, international law is about policy and decisions are policy-oriented.[59]

---

[54] Ibid., p. 18.

[55] Ibid., p. 19.

[56] Ibid., p. 27.

[57] M.S. McDougal and Associates, *Studies in World Public Order* (New Haven: Yale University Press, 1960), pp. 62–63.

[58] M.S. McDougal and F.P. Feliciano, *Law and Minimum World Public Order: The Legal Regulation of International Coercion* (New Haven: Yale University Press, 1961).

[59] I. Brownlie, *Principles of Public International Law*, 7th edition (Oxford: Oxford University Press, 2008) (written before his untimely death – an 8th edition was published in 2012), pp. 8–11 for an excellent discussion of this doctrine.

42 *Part I: Theoretical roots of responsibility to protect*

The New Haven School theory is based on a universal order of human dignity. Human dignity is referred to 'as a social process in which values are widely and not narrowly shared, and in which private choice, rather than coercion, in emphasized as the predominant modality of power'.[60] In the global process described above, the nation-state would stand out as a major participant, but 'one would note the rising power of many functional groups of the individual as the ultimate actor in all groups'.[61] McDougal and Reisman argued that the sovereignty of the nation-state was limited by the 'global constitutive process'. They stated that:

> Officials of nation-states, drawing on the vast resources of these composite entities, continue to be important decision-makers, but they are joined by the officials of international organizations, both governmental and intergovernmental, as well as a variety of non-territorial entities, which participate in all decision functions.[62]

Therefore, the minimum world public order perspective does allow for the state being a major participant in the world social process of effective power, but it is not the only actor, and the power of individuals and other actors is rising to challenge the predominance of the state. Again, this is a cosmopolitan vision of international society. There has to be a balance struck between the inclusive, shared competence of the entire community of states and the exclusive, non-shared competence of individual states.[63] However, there is a strong natural law/idealist Kantian component, as even within the exclusive competence area policies are made by the 'maintenance of democratic access to participation within such competence, thus ensuring that peoples in fact primarily affected by decisions have a voice in determining such effects'.[64]

In terms of the normative content in this theory, there are core values that hold international society together that can be found in treaties, the decisions of international tribunals, resolutions of international organizations, the writings of authorities and the statements and actions of states.[65] There are four core values in the international system: the maintenance of minimum public order (meaning the avoidance of behaviour that would risk war); self-determination; minimum human rights; and the raising of living

---

[60] McDougal and Associates, *Studies in World Public Order*, p. 16.

[61] M.S. McDougal and W. Michael Reisman, 'International Law in Policy-Oriented Perspective' in R. St John MacDonald and D.M. Johnston, *Towards World Constitutionalism: Issues in the Legal Ordering of the World Community* (Leiden: Martinus Nijhoff, 2005), p. 105.

[62] Ibid., p. 107.

[63] M. McDougal, 'The Impact of International Law upon National Law: A Policy Oriented Perspective' in M. McDougal and Associates, *Studies in World Public Order* (New Haven: Yale University Press, 1960), p. 158.

[64] Ibid., pp. 158–159.

[65] S.D. Krasner, *Sovereignty: Organised Hypocrisy* (Princeton: Princeton University Press, 1999), p. 46.

International society 43

standards throughout the world.[66] Although, at its heart, this is a system analysis approach, there are aspects of natural law theories in the notion of a universal order of human dignity. It is a compelling theory about the legal process.

Liberalism

Another theory that examines the international system, and also places the individual at the centre, is international liberalism. The contrast between the two theories is that the New Haven School is process-oriented and does not advocate one political model, whereas liberal theories advocate one model – democracy – as the ideal for the preservation of human dignity. Liberal internationalism also argues for the existence of an international society, but one that is founded on key principles of liberalism. The liberal theory based on Kant's *Perpetual Peace* saw a great deal of interest amongst international law scholars in the late twentieth century. Three prominent advocates are Fernando Tesón, Anne-Marie Slaughter and John Rawls.

Fernando Téson relies on Kant not for his cosmopolitan vision, but for his view of an international society. The just international society, then, is the one 'formed by an alliance of separate free nations, united by their moral commitment to individual freedom, by their allegiance to the international rule of law, and by the mutual advantages derived from peaceful intercourse'.[67] Téson argues that, for Kant, international society was neither a global community of individuals nor simply a society of states. Kant was neither cosmopolitan nor realist. States have a role in preserving different cultural traditions within the bounds of human rights and democracy.[68] The Kantian vision that Tesón supports is an international arrangement of an alliance of democracies, not a superstate. The requirement to join the community of civilized nations under international law is the observance of human rights. There cannot be a federation of tyrannical states.[69]

John Rawls' *Law of the Peoples* was a recent formulation of his liberal theories in the context of international law. This study invoked a 'Law of Peoples' promoted as a particular liberal political conception of right and justice. This theory is applied to the principles and norms of international law and practice. The term 'Society of Peoples' is introduced to mean all those people who follow the ideals and principles of the Law of Peoples in their mutual relations. The peoples would all have their own internal governments, but these must be either constitutional liberal democracies or

---

[66] T. Farer, 'Problems of an International Law of Intervention' (1962) 3 *Stanford Journal of International Studies* 20, p. 22.

[67] F. Tesón, 'Kantian International Liberalism' in David R. Mapel and Terry Nardin (eds), *International Society* (Princeton: Princeton University Press, 1998), pp. 103–104.

[68] Ibid., pp. 105–106.

[69] F. Tesón, *A Philosophy of International Law* (Boulder, CO: Westview, 1998), p. 7.

44   *Part I: Theoretical roots of responsibility to protect*

non-liberal but decent governments (these must have basic institutions that meet conditions of political rights and justice). The conception of justice to Rawls, as developed in *A Theory of Justice*, is premised on the idea of a social contract based on rights and justice, a realistic utopia.[70] In this world peace and justice would be achieved between liberal and decent peoples both at home and abroad.[71]

Rawls allows for political systems that are not democratic, but his baseline is on minimum standards of civilization. He argues that:

> I believe that the idea of a realistic utopia is essential. Two main ideas motivate the Law of Peoples. One is that the great evils of human history – unjust war and oppression, religious persecution and the denial of liberty of conscience, starvation and poverty, not to mention genocide and mass murder – follow from political injustice, with its own cruelties and callousness...The other main idea...is that, once the gravest forms of political injustice are eliminated by following just (or at least decent) social policies and establishing just (or at least decent) basic institutions, these great evils will eventually disappear.[72]

As with Tesón, Rawls referred back to Kant and *Perpetual Peace*. Rawls relied on the Kantian notion of *foedus pacificum*. This meant the idea that, at the second level, constitutionally democratic regimes were to make agreements with other liberal peoples. This would be an undertaking *between peoples* to maintain the Law of Peoples.[73] In spite of Rawls' title of the *Law of the Peoples*, at its heart his is a regime theory based on democratic regimes; it is statist in that peoples will elect those democratic governments, but they will not be direct participants in the international system.

Liberal legal theory is very similar to the natural law theories, but the difference is that the focus is on a political model rather than any notion of inherent rights. It has to be noted that there is a profound bias towards liberal democracies within this theory and the Rawlsian vision of a decent regime. It can be asserted that regimes that respect the International Covenants on Human Rights can be classified as decent regimes even if they are not democratic.

Finally, Anne-Marie Slaughter has written extensively on the relationship between international relations and international law theory. In 1995, in an article entitled 'International Law in a World of Liberal States', she asserted that:

> The most distinctive aspect of Liberal international relations theory is that it permits, indeed mandates, a distinction among different types of States based on their domestic political structure and ideology. In

[70] J. Rawls, *The Law of Peoples* (Cambridge, MA: Harvard University Press, 1999), pp. 3–5.
[71] Ibid., p. 6.
[72] Ibid., pp. 6–7.
[73] Ibid., p. 10.

particular, a growing body of evidence highlights the distinctive quality of relations among liberal democracies, evidence collected in an effort to explain the documented empirical phenomenon that liberal democracies very rarely go to war with one another. The resulting behavioural distinctions between liberal democracies and other kinds of States, or more generally between liberal and non-liberal States, cannot be accommodated within the framework of classical international law.[74]

The Slaughter model postulates international law between liberal states. The world of liberal states would be a world of disaggregated states. The state would be composed of multiple centres of political authority – legislative, administrative, executive and judicial. These institutions would be co-representative and regulative of the people. The proliferation of transnational economic and social transactions would create links between these institutions and individuals and groups. This would generate contacts between political institutions of multiple states. These interactions would be based on an awareness of a common or complementary function transcending national identity and a recognition of an obligation to defend and promote the interests of individuals and groups in transnational society.[75] Once again, the vision is of a society of states.

Slaughter argues that contemporary human rights law was founded on the recognition that domestic political conditions have consequences for international security. She argues that the existing catalogue of fundamental human rights expands to include a right of 'democratic governance', a right that Thomas Franck proposes based in part on empirical evidence of peace among liberal states. In that respect international law will take the first step toward an explicit distinction among states based on domestic regime-type.[76]

There are serious concerns about liberal internationalism, shared by this author, as the theory views international society as a contrast between 'legitimate states' that belong to the society and 'illegitimate states' that do not. As Simpson states:

> Liberal anti-pluralism is related to the reformist or revolutionist projects...in the sense that some anti-pluralist thought is dedicated to a radical reformation of the international order through the imposition of substantive political preferences on all states within the international system.[77]

---

[74] A.M. Slaughter, 'International Law in a World of Liberal States' (1995) 6 *European Journal of International Law* 503, pp. 504–505.

[75] A.M. Slaughter, *A New World Order* (Princeton: Princeton University Press, 2005); A.M. Slaughter, 'A Global Community of Courts' (2003) 44 *Harvard International Law Journal* 191; A.M. Slaughter, 'Global-Government Networks, Global Information Agencies and Disaggregated Democracy' (2002–2003) 24 *Michigan Journal of International Law* 1041.

[76] Slaughter, 'International Law in a World of Liberal States', p. 538.

[77] G. Simpson, *Great Powers and Outlaw States* (Cambridge: Cambridge University Press, 2004), p. 15.

46 *Part I: Theoretical roots of responsibility to protect*

It can be argued that, at this time, core minimum values based on natural law do not include rights to democratic governance. External responsibility to the international community by sovereign states is currently based primarily on membership in the United Nations and the doctrines of public international law. This re-characterization from sovereignty as control to sovereignty as responsibility is arguably accepted by all states by virtue of their signature of the UN Charter, creating both internal and external duties. This is responsibility to the international community through the UN.[78]

Conclusions on a legal theory of the international community

As acknowledged by most of these authors in their publications, the notion of an international legal community is confronted by one major challenge post-9/11, and that is the idea of American Hegemony. Douglas Johnston labels the phenomenon as 'US exceptionalism' with two strands: the traditional idea of America as the exemplar nation, or America as the missionary nation. He states that, subsequent to 9/11: '[i]t is a difficult time in world history to convince most Americans that their foreign policy should be further constrained by global constitutional norms and procedures that are likely to be applied against them by unfriendly foreigners'.[79]

Tomuschat also addresses the issue of multilateralism in the age of US Hegemony. He commences by challenging the definition of hegemony and proposing the idea, based on a quotation from Harry Truman, that hegemony is nothing else than responsible leadership.[80] In spite of this definition, Tomuschat gives example after example of the United States' violations of international law with the major examples being the war in Iraq and Guantánamo Bay. He argues throughout his discussion of these examples that the United States does not reject multilateralism as a matter of principle, and that it has active participation not only in the United Nations but also in a vast array of other multilateral agencies, providing proof of its preparedness to cooperate with other nations.[81] Furthermore, he states in his conclusion that 'open challenge to the existing legal order entails considerable costs in a globalized world'.[82]

However, the most compelling theorist in addition to Tomuschat for the purposes of this analysis is the political philosopher Jürgen Habermas. He supports Tomuschat's vision of the international legal community and discusses the issue of an international constitution within that community. What is so influential is that he writes after the crisis to the international system that was

---

[78] Ibid., p. 14.
[79] Johnston, 'World Constitutionalism', p. 24.
[80] C. Tomuschat, 'Multilateralism in the Age of US Hegemony' in R. St John Macdonald and D.M. Johnston (eds), *Towards World Constitutionalism: Issues in the Legal Ordering of the World Community* (Leiden: Martinus Nijhoff, 2005), p. 34.
[81] Ibid., p. 71.
[82] Ibid., p. 74.

the division over the legality of the invasion of Iraq and the rise of United States Hegemony. His thesis of a constitution is based on examining the dispute between Kantian idealists and the Carl Schmitt realists over the limits to the 'juridification of international relations'.[83] The clash concerns whether justice is possible in international relations, particularly in light of the US Government ignoring international law (first in its 2002 National Security Strategy, second in its establishment of Guantanamo Bay and the policy of rendition, and third in its 2003 invasion of Iraq).[84] In spite of the imperial strategy of the United States, Habermas explores the idea of the constitutionalization of international law. He first argues that classical international law accords only equal status to sovereign states with no supranational authority existing to sanction or punish violations of international law. This means that war is the price to be paid for sovereign equality.[85] He contrasts this with Kant's cosmopolitan vision.

For Habermas, Kant conceives of a legal peace between nations as a pre-condition for his republican perspective. The idea of a peaceful community of nations is a principle of right, not merely a command of morality, and it is the right of the major participants in the system – not the states, but the world citizenry. The cosmopolitan constitution guarantees a union of all peoples under public laws.[86] However, Habermas takes issue with Kant's idea of a world republic as a 'rash move' and argues that the constitutionalization of international law does not need to lead to a structure such as a republic.[87] Habermas takes a step back and argues that even classical international law is already a kind of constitution in the sense that it creates 'a legal community among parties with formally equal rights'.[88] The democratic federal state as a world republic is the wrong model as it does not relate to an inclusive world organization such as the United Nations, the World Trade Organization (WTO) or the European Union, as they have only specific, 'carefully circum-scribed functions'.[89] However, they can be construed as political organiza-tions for a 'decentered world society as a multilevel system' that lacks the characteristics of a state. Habermas' vision is of a 'suitably reformed world organization' performing the vital functions of securing peace and promot-ing human rights.[90] Thus, Habermas also includes the process within the structure of the system. He addresses the important issue of democracy and the criticism that world organization is anti-democratic as it does not have a legislature that is representative of citizens. He argues that international organizations such as the WTO do take into account protection of human rights, but acknowledges that the constitutionalization of international law

---

[83] Habermas, *The Divided West*, p. 116.
[84] Ibid. Guantánamo Bay, renditions of suspects and allegations of torture of terrorist suspects could also be argued to be serious violations of international law.
[85] Ibid., p. 119.
[86] Ibid., pp. 121–122.
[87] Ibid., p. 123.
[88] Ibid., p. 133.
[89] Ibid., p. 134.
[90] Ibid., p. 136.

48 *Part I: Theoretical roots of responsibility to protect*

'retains a derivative status because it depends on "advances" of legitimation from democratic constitutional states'.[91]

In his history of the development of international law, Habermas examines the United Nations Charter and highlights three innovations that point to it being a constitutional document:

- the explicit connection of the purpose of securing peace with a politics of human rights;
- the linkage of the prohibition on the use of violence with a realistic threat of prosecution and sanctions; and
- the inclusive character of the world organization and the universal validity it claims for the law it enacts.

In Habermas' opinion, the Charter provides a framework in which member states are not exclusively the subjects of international law, but one in which they act together with their citizens as the constitutional pillars of a 'politically constituted world society'.[92] Habermas acknowledges the weakness of the United Nations and supports the chorus of reformers (specifically with respect to issues of massive violations of human rights), and argues that the Security Council has to operate independently of national interests and must bind itself 'to actionable rules that lay down, in general terms, when the UN is authorized *and obligated* to take up a case'.[93]

A compelling model for the international legal community based on a society of states with agreed values may be the structural model of federalism. The noted Canadian scholar of federalism, Ronald Watts, argued, 'we appear to be in the midst of a paradigm shift which is taking us from a world of sovereign nation-states to a world of diminished state sovereignty and increased interstate linkages of a constitutionally federal character.'[94] The reasons Watts gives for this trend seem to accord with the other scholars arguing for an international constitutional order; these are developments in transportation, social communications, technology and industrial organization, and the goals shared by Western and non-Western societies for progress, a rising standard of living and social justice. Watts indicates that there is worldwide interdependence in an era where both mass destruction and mass construction are possible.[95] He defines federations as:

> compound polities, combining strong constituent units and a strong general government, each possessing powers delegated to it by the people through a constitution, and each empowered to deal directly with the

[91] Ibid., pp. 140–141.
[92] Ibid., pp. 160–161.
[93] Ibid., p. 173, original emphasis.
[94] R.L. Watts, *Comparing Federal Systems*, 2nd edition (Montreal and Kingston: McGill-Queen's University Press, 1999), p. 4.
[95] Ibid., p. 4.

citizens in the exercise of its legislative, administrative and taxing powers, and each directly elected by the citizens.[96]

The key factor missing from the model in the case of the international legal community governed by the United Nations is the element of the people, as they do not directly elect the members of the General Assembly or the Security Council. A second weakness is obviously the element of 'strong' central government. However, the element of international legal obligations as developed in the international legal community does imply the aspect of governance, as we shall see in Chapter 3 on state responsibility.

All of these international law theories have one element in common: the notion that sovereign states have responsibility – to a lesser or greater extent – to common values and, perhaps, even to an international constitution.[97] This debate is mirrored in international relations theory, particularly those theories that support the idea of an international system based on the rules of international law.

International society in international relations theory

International relations also has various groupings of theorists, all with radically differing visions of the structure of the system. These include members of the English School, cosmopolitanists and functionalist/regime theorists. It is the English School that resembles most closely the Tomuschat vision of the international legal community, as it relies upon a vision of a society of states.

These theorists, as with the international law theorists, do not agree on the nature of the international political system. The main function of international relations theorists is to engage in debates on the nature of the relation between various actors in the international system and on the nature of the international system itself. There are many schools of international relations theory and this book does not purport to propose the ideal theory to explain international relations. However, there are schools in international relations theory that are similar to the international legal theories discussed above. First, the English School postulates a society in which states are shaped by and shape the system.[98] The key notion in this theory is that of an international society. Buzan defines international society as 'the institutionalization of shared interest and identity among states, and puts the creation and

---

[96] Ibid., p. 8.
[97] See also J.P. Trachtman, *The Future of International Law: Global Government* (Cambridge: Cambridge University Press, 2013), who uses a modified theory of functionalism to argue for global government based on rules of international law.
[98] B. Buzan, *From International to World Society? English School Theory and the Social Structure of Globalization* (Cambridge: Cambridge University Press, 2004), p. 8, original emphasis.

50   *Part I: Theoretical roots of responsibility to protect*

maintenance of shared norms, rules and institutions at the centre of IR theory. I call this *interstate society*.'[99]

The English School

Martin Wight, described as the 'intellectual forefather' of the English School with its vision of an international society, divided the history of international relations theory into three traditions. The first was the realist or Machiavellian tradition with adherents such as Carr and Morgenthau. The second was the Revolutionists or Kantians, embodied by advocates for the French or Russian Revolution. The third tradition was the Grotian or rationalist tradition derived from natural law thinkers and including Locke, Burke, Roosevelt and Churchill. This third tradition postulated a relation between states characterized not only by conflict but also cooperation. It is from this third tradition that Wight's theory of International Society emerged.[100] Therefore, the emergence of the English School had its genesis in Grotius.

Grotius, in his work *Jure Belli ac Pacis*, argued for the law of nations based on the law of nature. Although he placed sovereign states as the primary actor in international law, he also gave rights and duties in international law to individuals. He also argued that states did not have to live in conflict, but that they could be bound by common customs as set out in the law of nations.[101] Hedley Bull, another leading member of the English School, noted that '[t]he Grotian prescription for international conduct is that all states, in their dealings with one another, are bound by the rules and institutions of the society they form'.[102] Therefore, to this school of international relations, international law is the key component in relations between states.

In his book *The Anarchical Society*, Bull devoted a chapter to international law and international order. He argued:

> The international law to which, in some measure, all states in the global international system give their formal assent still serves to carry out its traditional functions of identifying the idea of a society of states as the operational principles of world politics, starting with the basic rules of coexistence and facilitating compliance with those and other rules.[103]

This theory of international society – as with international law – places the state as the central participant in the society.

---

[99] Ibid.

[100] R. Fawn and J. Larkins, 'International Society after the Cold War: Theoretical Interpretations and Practical Implications' in R. Fawn and J. Larkins (eds), *International Society after the Cold War* (Basingstoke and London: MacMillan Press, 1996), pp. 2–3.

[101] Ibid., p. 4.

[102] H. Bull, *The Anarchical Society* (Basingstoke: Palgrave, 1977), p. 25.

[103] Ibid., pp. 154–155.

International society 51

One area that caused divisions in this school of international relations was intervention and human rights. Wheeler argued that there was a tension between those like Hedley Bull and Wight who adhered to a pluralist position that argued that states were the principal bearers of rights, and those like Grotius and Vincent who argued for a 'solidarist' position that asserted the duty of collective humanitarian intervention in cases of extreme suffering.[104] Vincent, who had changed his position from his earlier work on 'non-intervention', asserted that there was an increasingly cosmopolitan sentiment that would encourage citizens of states to force their states to act on behalf of individuals mistreated by other states.[105]

It is evident that if an international society is based on international law and its customary norms, then it is possible that a norm for non-intervention can evolve into an accepted customary norm for intervention in extreme human rights catastrophes. But the question remains as to whether an international society can accommodate a responsibility to protect. Within the English School there is just such a debate about the emergence of a world community or a global civil society. These notions challenge the pluralist vision of Bull and Wight. Shaw has argued that at the core of the development of global civil society is the concept of 'global responsibility'.[106]

However, in his conclusion to his seminal work (and in other works), Bull conceded that a study of order in world politics needed to be complemented by a study of justice.[107] He also argued that the element of international society shares the stage with world politics with its elements of war and conflict and the element of human community. A 'world order' was a wider concept than 'international order' or 'order among states', and was 'also more fundamental and primordial than it, and morally prior to it'. Therefore, the system of states would have to be continually reassessed.[108] Bull, then, leaves open the door to a possibility of the centrality of human security as a value within international society, but writing in 1966 he argued this solidarist concept of international society was premature.[109]

Nicholas Wheeler examined humanitarian intervention within an English School framework. *Saving Strangers* is a leading international relations book

---

[104] N. Wheeler, 'Pluralist or Solidarist Conceptions of International Society: Bull and Vincent on Humanitarian Intervention' (1992) 21 *Millennium; Journal of International Studies* 464.

[105] R.J. Vincent, *Human Rights and International Relations* (Cambridge: Cambridge University Press, 1986), in contract to his earlier work *Nonintervention and International Order* (Princeton: Princeton University Press, 1974).

[106] M. Shaw, 'Global Society and Global Responsibility' in R. Fawn and J. Larkins (eds), *International Society after the Cold War* (Basingstoke and London: MacMillan Press, 1996) p. 57.

[107] H. Bull, 'The Grotian Conception of International Society' in H. Butterfield and M. Wight (eds), *Diplomatic Investigations* (London: Allen & Unwin, 1966), pp. 51–74.

[108] Bull, *The Anarchical Society*, pp. 307–308.

[109] Bull, 'The Grotian Concept of International Society', p. 63.

52   *Part I: Theoretical roots of responsibility to protect*

that examines humanitarian intervention.[110] The focus of Wheeler's examination is the extent to which humanitarian intervention had become a legitimate practice in international society. Although he accepts that states form a society of states constrained by rules of sovereignty, non-intervention and the non-use of force, the notion of international legitimacy creates norms that 'constrain even the most powerful states in the international system'.[111] Wheeler identifies a division within the English School between pluralists who focus on states sharing different conceptions of justice and solidarist voices who focus on strengthening the legitimacy of international society 'by deepening its commitment to justice'.[112] Solidarists acknowledge that individuals have rights and duties in international law, but acknowledge that these rights can only be enforced by states.[113] This society of states is one 'in which states accept not only the moral responsibility to protect the security of their own citizens', but also the wider one of 'guardianship of human rights everywhere'.[114] The solidarist claim is that 'states that massively violate human rights should forfeit their rights to be treated as legitimate sovereigns, thereby morally entitling other states to use force to stop the oppression'.[115] This solidarist theory is extremely close to the modern argument of a responsibility to protect. In the remainder of his book, Wheeler sought to demonstrate the emergence of the solidarist position in the 1990s. In his conclusion he argued:

> The problem with the realist view is that it does not sufficiently distinguish between power that is based on relations of domination and power that is legitimate because it is based on shared norms. A good example of this is the shaming power of humanitarian norms, which is a form of power not derived from the political and economic hegemony of Western states; rather, it stems from the fact that even repressive governments recognize the need to legitimate their actions as being in conformity of global human rights standards.[116]

Systems theory

A related theory to the English School is the pluralist model of 'complex interdependence' describing an order in which non-state actors, both economic

---

[110] N. Wheeler, *Saving Strangers* (Oxford: Oxford University Press, 2000). See also the excellent collection of essays in J.L. Holzgrefe and R.O. Keohane, *Humanitarian Intervention: Ethical, Legal, and Political Dilemmas* (Cambridge: Cambridge University Press, 2003). For an early solidarist discussion of these concepts see Vincent's *Human Rights and International Relations.*

[111] Wheeler, *Saving Strangers*, pp. 6–7.

[112] Ibid., p. 11.

[113] Ibid., p. 11.

[114] Ibid., p. 12.

[115] Ibid., pp. 12–13.

[116] Ibid., pp. 290–291.

International society 53

and social, as well as states engage in the exercise of power, regime-building and agenda-setting.[117] This is the school of modern international relations theory in which many North American political theorists view states as constituting a system.[118] Bull distinguished a system from a society, stating:

> A *system of states* (or international system) is formed when two or more states have sufficient contact between them, and have sufficient impact on one another's decisions, to cause them to behave – at least in some measure – as parts of a whole...A *society of states* (or international society) exists when a group of states, conscious of certain common interests and common values, form a society in the sense that they conceive themselves to be bound by a common set of rules in their relations with one another, and share in the working of common institutions.[119]

This is one of the major divisions between the realist schools of international relations and the English School. 'System', according to Jackson, is a term that 'invites the positivist billiard ball image of international relations as a "clash of forces". The focus is not on the rules, stratagems or what might be going on in the mind of statesmen but on the nature or structure of the system.'[120]

Regime theory

A closely related school in international relations theory, very similar to the New Haven School in international legal theory, is regime theory, which examines the processes within the international system. As Noortmann states: 'Regime theory seeks to explain international relations in systemic, institutional and cooperative relationships as an alternative concept to both power politics and normative approaches.'[121] The leading proponent of regime theory is the international relations theorist Robert Keohane.[122] Once again, as with the New Haven School, there is an emphasis on process,

---

[117] R.O. Keohane and J.S. Nye, *Power and Interdependence* (Boston, MA: Little, Brown & Co., 1977).

[118] See K. Waltz, *Theory of International Politics* (Reading, MA: Addison-Wesley Publishing Company, 1979) for a discussion of neo-realism.

[119] Bull, *The Anarchical Society*, pp. 9–10 and 13, emphasis in original.

[120] R. Jackson, 'The Political Theory of International Society' in K. Booth and S. Smith (eds), *International Relations Theory Today* (Cambridge: Polity Press, 1995), pp. 111–112.

[121] M. Noortmann, *Enforcing International Law* (Aldershot: Ashgate, 2005), p. 129.

[122] See particularly, R.O. Keohane, *After Hegemony: Cooperation and Discord in the World Political Economy* (Princeton: Princeton University Press, 1984); R.O. Keohane, 'International Institutions: Two Approaches' in R.J. Beck, A.C. Arend and R. Vander Lugt (eds), *International Rules: Approaches from International Law and International Relations* (Oxford: Oxford University Press, 1996); R.O. Keohane, 'The Demand for International Regimes' in S.D. Krasner (ed.), *International Regimes* (London: Cornell University Press, 1983).

54 *Part I: Theoretical roots of responsibility to protect*

but the systems analysis is a complex method of viewing international relations as regimes are artificial constructs in which states operate by a system of agreed principles and norms.[123] S.D. Krasner, another leading proponent of regime theory, defines regimes as a set of 'implicit or explicit principles, norms, rules and decision-making procedures around which actors' expectations converge in a given area of international relations'.[124] As Noortmann points out, this could well include international legal principles in the rules and decision-making procedures part of the definition.[125] This theory is a very interesting and innovative way to examine the international political and legal system and can contribute to the debate on the responsibility to protect by viewing the political and systemic process of norm creation as an emerging doctrine.

Cosmopolitanism

The final relevant international relations theory is cosmopolitanism, which can be traced back to the work of Kant. Cosmopolitanism is a departure from the English School and regime theory as it views international society not as a society of states or a regime, but as a political community. This theory is very similar to liberal internationalism as both have their roots in Kantian philosophy. The term cosmopolitanism has been defined as a political system in which citizens have political representation in international affairs independently of their own governments.[126] The argument is that the modern state 'is increasingly embedded in webs of regional and global interconnectedness'. Sovereignty is challenged as political authority is moved to regional and global power systems.[127] Interdependence means that a state cannot deliver basic services to its citizens without international cooperation in every area of state function. This includes trade, world economy and culture. The cosmopolitan sees significant institutionalization of world politics including the United Nations, regional organizations and a vast array of 'formal suprastate bodies' including the WTO.[128]

Cosmopolitanism is associated with the movement towards cosmopolitan democracy. According to the model, a more democratic form of inter-state organization can evolve despite diversity of domestic regimes.[129]

---

[123] Keohane, 'The Demand for International Regimes', p. 158.

[124] S.D. Krasner, 'Structural Causes and Regime Consequences: Regimes as Intervening Variables' in S.D. Krasner, *International Regimes* (London: Cornell University Press, 1983), p. 1.

[125] Noortmann, *Enforcing International Law*, pp. 135–138.

[126] D. Archibugi and D. Held, 'Introduction' in D. Archibugi and D. Held (eds), *Cosmopolitan Democracy* (Cambridge: Polity Press, 1995), p. 13.

[127] D. Held and A. McGrew, *Globalization/Anti-Globalization* (Cambridge: Polity Press 2003), p. 23.

[128] Ibid. p. 59.

[129] Ibid.

International society 55

The argument is that effective political power cannot be limited to national governments and it is shared between national, regional and international levels.[130] State sovereignty has not disappeared but has been transformed into a system of multiple and combined power centres with overlapping authority.[131] Held and McGrew argue that adherents to this process are not globalists but tranformationalists, as globalization is 'reconstituting or "re-engineering" the power, functions and authority of national governments'.[132] Complex global systems mean that functions of governance – from financial to ecological – are bound by new forms of organizations that transcend national boundaries.[133] Barry argued that institutional cosmopolitanism postulates some 'ideal of world political organization in which states and state-like units have significantly diminished authority in comparison with the status quo and supranational institutions have more'.[134]

The overlap in governance is labelled by Held and McGrew as 'cosmopolitan social democracy', as this idea nurtures some of the most important values in social democracy – the rule of law, political equality, democratic politics, social justice, social solidarity and economic effectiveness – while applying them to the new global politics. The goal is to promote impartial administration of law at the international level, greater transparency, accountability and democracy in global governance, commitment to social justice in pursuit of a more equitable distribution of the world's resources, regulation of the global economy through public management of global financial and trade flows, the provision of global public goods and the engagement of leading stakeholders in global governance.[135]

Part of the agenda of cosmopolitan democracy is reform of the United Nations. Archhibugi argued that there should be three main reforms: first, a project for creating an Assembly of the Peoples of the United Nations, which would directly represent citizens; second, strengthening the world judicial powers including reforming the International Court of Justice; and third, modifying the world executive powers, principally the Security Council and the veto power.[136] Held argues that the cosmopolitan model of democracy has required elements. The first is a transitional measure to ensure that the UN system actually lives up to its Charter. This would involve pursuing measures to implement key elements of the rights conventions, enforcing

---

[130] Ibid., p. 123.
[131] Ibid., and see D. Held, 'Law of States, Law of Peoples: Three Models of Sovereignty' (2002) 8 *Legal Theory* 1.
[132] Held and McGrew, *Globalization/Anti-Globalization*, p. 126.
[133] Ibid., p. 127.
[134] B. Barry, 'International Society from a Cosmopolitan Perspective' in D. Mapel and T. Nardin (eds), *International Society* (Princeton: Princeton University Press, 1998), p. 144.
[135] Held and McGrew, *Globalization/Anti-Globalization*, p. 131.
[136] D. Archibugi and D. Held (eds), *Cosmopolitan Democracy* (Cambridge: Polity Press, 1995), p. 13.

56 *Part I: Theoretical roots of responsibility to protect*

the prohibition on the discretionary right to use force, and activating the collective security system envisaged by the Charter.[137] In addition to this step would be the creation of regional parliaments or enhancement of those that already exist, such as the European Parliament, as 'legitimate independent sources of law'.[138] In addition there could be general referenda of groups cutting across nations on issues such as energy policy. Finally, there could be the formation of an 'authoritative assembly of all democratic states and agencies' – a reformed General Assembly of the United Nations.

David Held has argued that there is an emerging framework of 'cosmopolitan law' that 'circumscribes and delimits' the power of individual states. Components of that law are international laws governing war and concerning crimes against humanity, environmental issues and human rights.[139] Additionally, he argues that there should be a new international human rights court.[140] This means that states cannot treat their citizens as they see fit. Cosmopolitan legal theory postulates the international rule of law, liberal democracy and human rights as universal standards of civilization.[141] Although a state might retain the ultimate legal claim to supremacy over its own territory, this has to be juxtaposed with the expanding jurisdiction of international institutions and the obligations of international law.[142] This theory could also be closely linked to the vision of Fassbender and an international constitution.

Conclusions on international relations theory

The cosmopolitan vision – as with Fassbender's constitutionalism – still seems premature in the current context. However, there is no doubt that there is an exponential growth in transnational courts, tribunals and government structures. The new international economic order, as illustrated by limitations on trade in the GATT process, and integrated economic systems such as NAFTA and the European Community, point to an evolution towards an international community where the state is only a component in the process.[143] This vision, however, is some time off. The reforms suggested by Held and Archibugi in 1995 are unlikely to take place as even more moderate proposals for a limitation on the veto and expanded membership of the UN Security Council failed in 2005.

---

[137] Held and McGrew, *Globalization/Anti-Globalization*, p. 106.

[138] D. Held, 'Democracy and the International Order' in D. Mapel and T. Nardin (eds), *International Society* (Princeton: Princeton University Press, 1998), p. 108.

[139] Held and McGrew, *Globalization/Anti-Globalization*, p. 20.

[140] Held, 'Democracy and the International Order', p. 107.

[141] Held and McGrew, *Globalization/Anti-Globalization*, p. 62.

[142] Ibid., p. 126.

[143] But see E. Kwakwa, 'Regulating the International Economy: What Role for the State' in M. Byers (ed.), *The Role of Law in International Politics* (Oxford: Oxford University Press, 2000), in which he argues that the role of the state is indispensable to regulating the international economy.

Conclusion

It is evident from this review of the theoretical unpinning of the responsibility to protect that there are two very compelling theories, one from the international law tradition and one from international relations. Both are linked. The German School of international law and the English School of international relations encompass a vision of an international society of states bound by the rules of international law. Although Fassbender, the New Haven School and the Cosmopolitan School would argue for a community bound by a fully developed international constitution, thus far this seems a utopian vision. As Thakur argues:

> Gradually over the course of the last century the idea of an international community bound together by shared values, benefits and responsibilities, and common rules and procedures, took hold of people's imaginations. The UN is the institutional expression of that development.[144]

This does not mean that the United Nations is a world government; rather it is the repository of the values of this international society. The superior norm for this preferred theory of an international society is the notion of responsibility to follow the rules of international law, and responsibility on each state to each of the other states within that society.

Tomuschat and Habermas both argue the emergence of collective responsibility of states. One area they did not canvas that might have strengthened the argument of an international community of states bound by rules of international law is the burgeoning area of the law of state responsibility. State responsibility provides the content to the rules that bind the international community of states, which include obligations to protect individuals within those states. The next part of this book examines the rules that represent the responsibilities of states to the international community.

---

[144] R. Thakur, *The United Nations and Peace and Security* (Cambridge: Cambridge University Press, 2006), p. 11.

Part II

The evolution of the responsibility to protect within areas of public international law

3 State responsibility
Obligations on states in international law

Introduction

The international law of state responsibility is closely linked to the two major elements of the definition of the responsibility to protect. The focus of legal obligation in this first element of the responsibility to protect is on the primary responsibility of states towards its own citizens. In addition to domestic legislation, the content of this responsibility stems from states' international treaty and customary international law obligations, which set out rules requiring domestic implementation. In the second element of the responsibility to protect the focus is on states as the major legal actors in the international community and the responsibilities that the state owes to persons living in other nations. Both of these elements of state obligations are also included in the traditional customary international law of state responsibility and in the Articles on State Responsibility drafted by the International Law Commission and recommended to the international community by the General Assembly in 2002.[1] Unlike the other elements of international law examined in this book, the secondary rules of the law of state responsibility is based on customary international law developed over centuries. These articles are not a treaty but rather contain both long-standing customary international law rules and proposed rules that might eventually evolve into customary international law.

It is argued in this book that the development in international relations of the principle of the responsibility to protect is supported by the parallel development in the international law of state responsibility. It is the thesis of this book that the development of the responsibility to protect and the introduction of the notion of aggravated state responsibility have to be examined in tandem as there is so much resonance between the two concepts. Therefore, this chapter traces the codification of the secondary rules of state responsibility.[2] Although the Articles on State Responsibility only deal with secondary

---

[1] International Law Commission (ILC), Draft Articles on Responsibility of States for Internationally Wrongful Acts, November 2001, Supplement No. 10 (A/56/10), Chapter IV.E.1, as recommended to states in UN Doc. GA Res. 56/83? (cf. fn 11, p. 3), 28 January 2002.

[2] Ibid.

62 Part II: Evolution in public international law

rules of state responsibility, the commentaries concerning these rules and the context of some of them tended to stray into consideration of primary rules of state conduct. This is particularly the case for 'aggravated state responsibility', describing consequences for violations of peremptory norms of public international law. However, in order to examine the content of the primary obligations on a sovereign state in international law, it is necessary to view the development of the law of state responsibility prior to adoption of the articles. There are two titans of international law who have written extensively on this topic, the late Professor Ian Brownlie and Professor James Crawford (now Judge of the International Court of Justice (ICJ)). Brownlie's work is an excellent source for the traditional law of state responsibility prior to the adoption of the Articles on State Responsibility.[3] Crawford was primarily responsible for the bringing to a final resolution of the development of the Articles on State Responsibility, and his latest book on state responsibility and his commentary on the articles are essential sources for understanding the current law.[4]

This chapter is divided into three parts. The first part describes the development of the traditional notions of the responsibility of states, which have been developed over the last 160 years, particularly in a series of rulings by Arbitration Commissions.[5] The second part reviews in detail the articles of 'ordinary state responsibility' with the Articles on State Responsibility and the relevance these articles might have to the responsibility to protect. The third part of the chapter discusses the radical new approach in the concept of 'aggravated state responsibility'. This part will discuss the legal precedents that led the International Law Commission to include such a section in place of articles attributing criminal responsibility to states. The final part of the chapter will analyse this notion of 'aggravated state responsibility' with reference to the reports and resolutions recommending the responsibility to protect to the international community.

It is acknowledged here that there is nothing within the traditional law of state responsibility or the aggravated responsibility articles that provide a legal basis for a unilateral military response to egregious violations of international law by a state. However, these articles provide an international law basis for a state's responsibility to the international community for violations of *jus cogens* rules.

---

[3] I. Brownlie, *System of the Law of Nations: State Responsibility (Part 1)* (Oxford: Clarendon Press, 1983).

[4] J. Crawford, *State Responsibility: The General Part* (Cambridge: Cambridge University Press, 2013) and *The International Law Commission's Articles on State Responsibility: Introduction, Text and Commentaries* (Cambridge: Cambridge University Press, 2002).

[5] Crawford, *State Responsibility: The General Part*, p. 4, in which he states that state responsibility was not systematically dealt with until the second half of the nineteenth century by August Wilhelm Heffter in his *Le Droit International Public de l'Europe* (1857), and although he engages in a fascinating discussion of original international law theorists such as Gentili and Grotius, this will not be discussed here.

Traditional rules of state responsibility

State responsibility is a core concept of customary international law.[6] States have duties with regard to the fulfilment of obligations of treaties or of customary international law in matters such as international commerce, international finance and international administration.[7] The state is also responsible for tortuous liability for treatment of aliens outside of the accepted international standards.[8] As Crawford asserts, in international law there is no distinction between the types or degrees of liability such as crime, contract, tort or delict.[9] As stated in the *Rainbow Warrior* arbitration: 'the violation of a State of any obligation, of whatever origin gives rise to State responsibility'.[10]

State responsibility is closely linked to the procedure of making claims in international law and the remedies for breaches of obligations.[11] In the Judgment in the *Chorzów Factory* case, the Permanent Court of International Justice discussed the element of reparation in state responsibility:

> It is a principle of international law that the breach of an engagement involves an obligation to make reparation in an adequate form. Reparation therefore is the indispensable complement of a failure to apply a convention and there is no necessity for this to be stated in the convention itself.[12]

The *Chorzów Factory* case sets out that if a state violated an international obligation under a treaty or a rule of customary international law, it owed legal duty to compensate the victim state for such a violation.[13]

The content of the international law of state responsibility developed from a series of arbitration commissions in the nineteenth century that involved cases concerning claims brought by one state for the lack of protection for their citizens or property located in another state. Traditional state responsibility focused on bilateral relations between states and not on the community of states. It was divided into two branches. The first consisted of primary rules of international law – those customary and treaty rules that governed the conduct of states. The second branch set out the rules establishing the conditions on when breach of the primary rules might have occurred and the legal consequences of such breaches.[14] The formula for a claim of state responsibility

---

[6] I. Brownlie, *The Rule of Law in International Affairs: International Law at the Fiftieth Anniversary of the United Nations* (The Hague: Kluwer Law, 1998), p. 79.

[7] H. Lauterpacht, *International Law and Human Rights* (New York: Frederick Praeger, 1950), pp. 40–41.

[8] Crawford, *State Responsibility: The General Part*, p. 23.

[9] Ibid., p. 51.

[10] *Rainbow Warrior (New Zealand* v. *France* (1990) RIAA Vol. XX, 215), p. 551.

[11] Brownlie, *The Rule of Law in International Affairs*, p. 79.

[12] *Chorzów Factory* (Jurisdiction) case (1927), PCIJ, Series A, No. 9, p. 21.

[13] Ibid., p. 241.

[14] Ibid., p. 243.

64 *Part II: Evolution in public international law*

involved three aspects: a call for preventive measures, a claim for the punishment of those responsible and a demand for payment of compensation.[15]

Although there was agreement in the international community that there were primary rules of conduct that might engage responsibility between states, there has never been agreement as to the content of those rules.[16] Brownlie, in his influential study, delineated causes of action alleging the responsibility of states that had been invoked in practice. Although he examined several heads of relief in pleadings, he found only a few that directly related to state responsibility. His final list was:

(a) State responsibility arising from a breach of a treaty obligation
(b) State responsibility arising otherwise from a breach of duty set by general international law (customary international law)
(c) Claims of sovereignty or title
(d) Action for a declaration of the validity of a State measure in general international law
(e) Violation of the sovereignty of a State by specified acts
(f) Infringement of the freedom of the high seas or outer space
(g) The unreasonable exercise of a power causing loss or damage (abuse of rights)
(h) Usurpation of jurisdiction
(i) Breach of an international standard concerning the treatment of aliens (denial of justice)
(j) Breach of human rights standards, in particular the forms of unlawful discrimination
(k) Unlawful confiscation or expropriation of property
(l) Unlawful seizure of vessels.[17]

Cassese also examined the content of internationally wrongful acts and agreed that they evolved out of the practice of states and a wealth of cases brought before international arbitral tribunals.[18] He argued that very few treaty rules existed, but a prominent one was Article 3 of the Fourth Hague Convention of 1907, on the Laws and Customs of War on Land:

> A belligerent party, which violated the provisions of the said Regulations, shall if the case demands, be liable to pay compensation. It shall be responsible for all acts committed by persons forming part of its armed forces.[19]

[15] Brownlie, *System of the Law of Nations: State Responsibility (Part 1)*, p. 26.
[16] Crawford, *State Responsibility: The General Part*, pp. 216–217.
[17] Ibid., p. 85.
[18] A. Cassese, *International Law*, 2nd edition (Oxford: Oxford University Press, 2005).
[19] Ibid., p. 242, and Hague Convention (IV) Respecting the Laws and Customs of War on Land and Its Annex: Regulations Concerning the Laws and Customs of War on Land, 18 October 1907.

State responsibility in international law 65

This was one of the few provisions that specified the primary laws that could be breached. Generally there is a vague statement of responsibility for breach of an international rule. Cassese concludes that the rules on state responsibility were rudimentary as they did not (1) specify some general elements of international delinquency or, (2) the legal consequences of international wrongs.[20]

Greig further clarifies the law of state responsibility by dividing the claims of state responsibility into two categories: direct international wrongs or indirect international wrongs.[21] Examples of direct international wrongs would be invasion of a state's territory, the sinking or seizing of a ship flying its flag, the shooting down of a plane, the arrest of an ambassador and the breach of treaty obligations owed to a state. There are three categories of indirect international wrongs. The first is when the injury suffered by the claimant state is indirect. An example would be the seizure of property of a national of state B by the officials of state A. The second type of indirect wrong is when the responsibility of the respondent state would only arise indirectly. An example of another type of indirect international wrong is if the injury to state B is direct but it concerns the acts of individuals of state A where lack of due care of state A can be shown. An example could be if a crowd of demonstrators protesting against the policies of state B get out of control and seize the embassy of state B in state A. A third category is when both the injury and responsibility are indirect. An example would be the injury of a national of state B by a private individual in state A, and the police are so inefficient that the incident is not investigated properly so as to give rise to what is known as a 'denial of justice'.[22]

This theory of indirect responsibility was supported by the Permanent Court of International Justice in the *Mavrommatis* case. The court ruled that:

> in taking up the case of one of its nationals, by resorting to diplomatic action or international judicial proceedings on his behalf, a State is in reality asserting its own rights, the right to ensure in the person of its nationals respect for the rules of international law.[23]

A critical point on the content of these rules was that customary rules on the legal consequences of wrongful acts were normally lumped together with the substantive rules governing state behaviour – chiefly the customary rules concerning the treatment of foreigners. These customary rules had crystallized as a result of a series of arbitral decisions on the treatment by developing nations (particularly in Latin America) of nationals of developed states (especially

[20] Ibid., p. 242.
[21] D.W. Greig, *International Law* (London: Butterworths, 1976), chapter on state responsibility.
[22] Ibid., p. 522, and see *US Diplomatic and Consular Staff in Tehran* case (1980) ICJ Reports 3.
[23] *Mavrommatis* case (1924) PCI Report, Series A, No. 2, p. 12.

66   Part II: Evolution in public international law

the United States). Therefore, state responsibility is often wrongly associated with the obligation to respect the rights of foreign nationals and their property.[24] As can be seen in the Brownlie list, which seems the most comprehensive, the primary obligations on sovereign states were far more extensive.

For the purpose of this review in relation to the responsibility to protect, it should be noted that several of the categories of primary rules of state responsibility concern breaches of human rights both in terms of violations of treaty obligations and rules of customary international law. A number of cases that were known under the traditional head of protection of aliens concerned serious abuses of human rights. There were several arbitration cases in the nineteenth century concerning unlawful killing or wounding of aliens, unlawful expulsion and standards of detention. In the *García and Garza* case before the General Claims Commission, between Mexico and the United States of America, the commissioners argued that there was an international standard of appraising human life, which was breached by reckless use of firearms.[25] In the *Faulkner* case in the same commission, the commissioners decided that Mexico had breached international standards in holding a detainee in filthy, unsanitary conditions.[26] This was echoed in the *Roberts* claim, where the Commissioners stated that the test was 'whether aliens are treated in accordance with the ordinary standards of civilization'. Arguing that the conditions in jail were the best that Mexico could provide was not sufficient.[27] Another aspect of the responsibility of states towards aliens was the necessity to investigate allegations of unlawful killing. In the *Janes* claim Mexico was ordered to pay $12,000 to the United States Government for failure to apprehend and punish those responsible, stating that the Mexican Government had not 'measured up to its duty of diligently prosecuting and properly punishing the offender'.[28]

These cases fall into another important head of responsibility – the denial of justice. Article 9 of the Harvard Draft of the Responsibility of States described a denial of justice as a 'denial, unwarranted delay or obstruction of access to courts, gross deficiency in the administration of judicial or remedial process, failure to provide those guarantees which are generally considered indispensable to the proper administration of justice, or a manifestly unjust judgment'.[29] Greig argued that the international law standard was based upon two propositions:

1. If the standards of the local administration of justice are higher than those of the minimum standards required by international law, the alien would be entitled to the benefits of the higher standards either on the

---

[24] Cassese, *International Law*, p. 243.
[25] *García and Garza* claim, RIAA IV, pp. 120–121.
[26] *Faulkner* claim, RIAA IV, pp. 70–71.
[27] *Roberts* claim, RIAA IV, p. 80.
[28] *Janes* claim, RIAA IV, p. 87.
[29] *Harvard Draft on the Responsibility of States* (1929) 23 AJIL Supp., p. 173.

State responsibility in international law   67

ground that he should not be the subject of discrimination, or because international law will insist on the observance of those standards irrespective of discrimination.

2. It is, however, no defence to show that an alien has been treated no worse than nationals of the respondent State if the standard of treatment is lower than the minimum standards required by international law.[30]

Greig and Brownlie argued in the 1970s and 1980s that non-discrimination had yet to receive general acceptance as a rule of customary international law. In the context of state responsibility it is accepted that:

> it would fall short of the standards of non-discrimination required by customary international law for a State to grant to nationals procedural advantages in the administration of justice not accorded to aliens, irrespective of whether the advantage exceeded the minimum standards of international law.[31]

It may well be argued that the prohibition against discrimination might have subsequently become a doctrine of customary international law.[32]

Another claim for violation of rights of aliens that resonates with the topic at hand is state responsibility for mass expulsion of aliens. As Brownlie discussed, there is a prima facie power of expulsion and therefore the claimant state would have to prove conditions of illegality such as arbitrary conduct and discrimination. The leading case referred to in this area was the *Nottebohm* case, where Liechtenstein alleged that Mr Nottebohm had been expelled by Guatemala unlawfully.[33] Goodwin-Gill argued that the power to expel aliens had to be exercised in good faith and not for some ulterior motive such as genocide, confiscation of property or the surrender of some individual to persecution.[34]

Finally, there was the issue of confiscation, expropriation and destruction of the property of aliens. Although a state has a right to expropriate property of aliens upon payment of appropriate compensation, unlawful confiscation or destruction are internationally wrongful acts.[35]

The case law of the arbitration commissions had identified groupings of rules of state responsibility and these cases had also developed consequences,

---

[30] Greig, *International Law*, p. 554.

[31] Ibid., pp. 554–555.

[32] See, for example, G. Verdirame, *The UN and Human Rights: Who Guards the Guardians?* (Cambridge: Cambridge University Press, 2011), p. 190.

[33] *Nottebohm Case (Liechtenstein v. Guatemala)* (Second Phase), Judgment of 6 April 1955 [1955] ICJ Rep 4.

[34] G. Goodwin-Gill, 'The Limits of the Power of Expulsion in Public International Law' (1976) 47 *British Yearbook of International Law* 56, p. 96, and see his discussion of claims for unlawful expulsion at pp. 131–133.

[35] Crawford, *State Responsibility: The General Part*, p. 516.

68 *Part II: Evolution in public international law*

mainly financial, of the breach of these primary rules. However, the law of secondary rules of state responsibility did not emerge in a coherent fashion until the work of the International Law Commission (ILC). However, the many cases of the arbitration commission focused on the kinds of violations that are now set out in the many international and regional human rights treaties. It was evident even before the drafting of these treaties subsequent to the Second World War that a state did not have the right to take the life of, confiscate the property of or injure an alien within their jurisdiction. Human rights conventions then set out that these same minimum standards applied to citizens of these states as well. This development will be discussed in the next chapter, but it is clear that by the time the Articles on State Responsibility were completed, violations of the treaties and customs of international law also included violations of the treaties that constituted the international bill of human rights.

Articles on the Responsibility of States for Internationally Wrongful Acts

On 28 January 2002 the General Assembly passed Resolution 56/83 with an annex attached containing the Articles on the Responsibility of States for Internationally Wrongful Acts (ARSIWA). The operative paragraph of the resolution states that the General Assembly:

> 3. *Takes note* of the articles on responsibility of States for internationally wrongful acts, presented by the International Law Commission, the text of which is annexed to the present resolution, and commends them to the attention of Governments without prejudice to the question of their future adoption or other appropriate action.[36]

These articles do not constitute a multilateral convention, but the resolution recommends them to states. Nevertheless, the resolution is very significant as these articles in some parts are reflective of customary international law, and other articles could evolve into customary law, even if no further codification by treaty takes place. In 2007 a document accompanying the various state views on the articles stated that no less than 129 cases before international or domestic courts and tribunals had cited with approval the ARSIWA or the Draft Articles.[37]

This resolution was a result of over 40 years work by the ILC (the first report on state responsibility went to the International Law Commission in 1956) and finalized the Draft Articles, which had their first reading in

---

[36] ILC, Draft Articles on Responsibility of States for Internationally Wrongful Acts, emphasis in original.

[37] Crawford, *State Responsibility: The General Part*, p. 41.

State responsibility in international law 69

1996.[38] This was not the first effort to codify rules of state responsibility. The League of Nations from 1924 to 1930 attempted to codify customary international law and one of the topics was 'Responsibility of States for Damages done in their Territory to the Person or Property of Foreigners'. This effort was unsuccessful due to the disagreement on what would be an accepted minimum standard of treatment.[39]

The law of state responsibility was therefore greatly expanded after the Second World War by the work of the ILC, which had been established in 1948 by the UN General Assembly to codify rules of international law. This was part of the initial work programme established by the ILC, and the work commenced in 1956 with the appointment of the first Special Rapporteur, F.V. Garcia Amador of Cuba. Due to the efforts of a number of Special Rapporteurs, with the last and most successful being James Crawford, the secondary rules of the law of state responsibility were codified in a series of provisions that outlined the consequences of violating international obligations and various procedural items, such as who might be responsible for breaches and defences that could be raised to a claim of wrongfulness. These articles clarify who might act on behalf of a state, what circumstances might preclude wrongfulness and what actions a wronged state might take.[40] Secondary rules of state responsibility were defined as: 'the general conditions under international law for the State to be considered responsible for wrongful actions or omissions, and the legal consequences which flow therefrom.'[41]

Cassese argues that the new law has important features. First, the law of state responsibility has been unfastened from the set of substantive rules on the treatment of foreigners. In the new format the distinction is made between the primary rules of international law, which are the customs and treaty rules laying down substantive obligations for states, with examples such as state immunities, treatment of foreigners, diplomatic and consular immunities, and respect for territorial sovereignty, and the secondary rules. These secondary rules establish the conditions under which a breach of a primary rule could be held to have occurred and what the legal consequences are of such a breach. The articles then codified the secondary rules as the law of state responsibility.[42]

The second important feature of the development in this area, as identified by Cassese, is that the current rules on state responsibility have been clarified and given precision. The third feature is that agreement has been achieved on the need to distinguish between two forms or categories of state

---

[38] J. Crawford, 'The Earl A. Snyder Lecture in International Law: Responsibility to the International Community as a Whole' (2001) 8 *Indiana Journal of Global Legal Studies* 303, p. 304.

[39] Cassese, *International Law*, p. 183.

[40] See Crawford, *The International Law Commission's Articles on State Responsibility*, Introduction at pp. 1–60 for a history of the Articles on State Responsibility.

[41] Ibid., p. 74.

[42] Cassese, *International Law*, p. 244.

70   Part II: Evolution in public international law

responsibility: ordinary breaches and a class of aggravated responsibility for violations of some fundamental general rules that enshrine essential values. The fourth feature is that it is no longer permitted for a state to immediately take forcible action. Instead, there are a series of successive steps including requests of reparation, negotiations, conciliation, arbitration and other peaceful means. Only if these measures do not work can there be peaceful countermeasures.[43]

The finalized articles are divided into four parts. The first part, in five chapters, sets out: the general principles, attribution of conduct to a state, breach of an international obligation, responsibility of a state in connection with the act of another state and circumstances precluding wrongfulness. Cassese points out that in this first part of the articles the basic preconditions of state responsibility are defined with subjective and objective elements. The subjective elements are imputability to a state of conduct of an individual, and in some instances the fault of the state official in performing the act. The objective elements are the inconsistency of a particular conduct with international obligations, the existence of material or moral damage and the absence of circumstances precluding wrongfulness.

Article I specifies that: 'Every internationally wrongful act of a State entails the international responsibility of that State.'[44] In his commentary to the article, Crawford discusses three separate views of this statement. The first is that the consequences of an internationally wrongful act should be seen exclusively in the bilateral relations between states. Another view, associated with Kelsen, is that the legal order is a coercive order, that general international law empowers the injured state to react to a wrong and the obligation to make reparations is treated as subsidiary by the way in which the responsible states could avoid the application of coercion. The third and prevailing view, according to Crawford, is that the consequences of an internationally wrongful act cannot be limited either to reparation or sanction, and that in international law a wrongful act may give rise to various types of legal relations, depending on the circumstances.[45] The critical factor of this new system of legal relations is that some wrongful acts can engage the responsibility of the state concerned towards several or many States and even towards the international community as a whole.[46] Even in this early stage of the articles there is an acknowledgement of international responsibility.

Article 2 sets out the constituent elements of such an act:

> There is an internationally wrongful act of a State when conduct consisting of an action or omission:

[43] Ibid., p. 245.
[44] ILC, Draft Articles on Responsibility of States for Internationally Wrongful Acts, Article 1.
[45] Crawford, *The International Law Commission's Articles on State Responsibility*, pp. 78–79.
[46] Ibid., p. 79.

State responsibility in international law 71

(a) is attributable to the State under international law; and
(b) constitutes a breach of an international obligation of the State.[47]

Crawford, in his commentary to this section, seeks to avoid the distinction between objective and subjective responsibility. Interestingly, he uses the Genocide Convention to support his argument. Article II of the Genocide Convention states that:

> In the present Convention, genocide means any of the following acts committed with intent to destroy, in whole or in part, a national, ethnical, racial or religious group, as such.[48]

In this case Crawford argues that the breach has to have intention or knowledge on the part of relevant state organs or agents, and in that sense it may be a subjective test. Therefore, whether the responsibility is objective or subjective depends on the circumstances of the obligation.[49] The terminology of breach of an international obligation covers treaty and non-treaty obligation and corresponds to the language of Article 36(2)(c) of the Statute of the International Court of Justice.[50] Along with the difficulty of describing the content of the rules, there are other conceptual problems with the law of state responsibility. The first major problem is that it is not clear whether state responsibility can arise only if the state officials act wilfully and maliciously or negligently, or if instead the fact that an international rule is broken was sufficient. This is the critical question of fault and whether there needs to be an element of intentional or negligent conduct on the part of the person concerned, or whether, like some criminal offences, there is a strict liability test.[51] In his analysis, Brownlie argues the concept of objective responsibility:

> Technically, objective responsibility rests on the doctrine of the voluntary act: provided that agency and causal connection are established, there is a breach of duty by result alone.[52]

His assertion is that in the conditions of international life, the public law concept of *ultra vires* acts is more realistic than seeking a subjective *culpa*.[53]

---

[47] ILC, Draft Articles on Responsibility of States for Internationally Wrongful Acts, Article 2.
[48] UN General Assembly, Convention on the Prevention and Punishment of the Crime of Genocide, 9 December 1948, United Nations Treaty Series, vol. 78, p. 277.
[49] Crawford, *The International Law Commission's Articles on State Responsibility*, pp. 81–82.
[50] Ibid., p. 83.
[51] M. Shaw, *International Law*, 5th edition (Cambridge: Cambridge University Press, 2003), p. 698.
[52] Brownlie, *System of the Law of Nations: State Responsibility (Part 1)*, p. 38.
[53] Ibid.

72   Part II: Evolution in public international law

Shaw argues that the majority of cases and academic opinion tend towards the strict liability, objective theory of responsibility.[54] Nevertheless, Brownlie argues that the principle of *faute* or *culpa* could still play an important role in certain contexts. Where the loss complained of results from the acts of individuals not employed by states, the responsibility of the state would be of a failure to control. In this type of case questions of knowledge would be important in establishing an omission, or more properly, responsibility for failure to act. In the *Corfu Channel* case, the effect of the judgment was that Albania had been under a duty to take reasonable care to discover the activities of alleged trespassers.[55]

Brownlie also argues that where the *ultra vires* action of an official is accompanied by malice, proof of intention to harm or *dolus* might not affect the liability issue, but might have the effect of causing an award of penal damages.[56] This is related to the doctrine of abuse of rights, which was accepted by several systems, including Article 1912 of the Mexican Civil Code. In the case concerning *Certain German Interests in Polish Upper Silesia* the Permanent Court of International Justice held that the right to dispose of state property in the territory remained with Germany, but alienation of that property would constitute of breach of its obligations and a misuse of that right.[57] Brownlie does not accept that there needed to be a separate principle of abuse of rights, but that responsibilities for excess of authority would exist independently of an abuse of rights.[58]

Chapter II of the articles concerns attribution of conduct to a state. Of interest to the study of a responsibility to protect is Article 7, dealing with the question of unauthorized or *ultra vires* acts of state organs or entities. Article 7 states:

> The conduct of an organ of a State or of a person or entity empowered to exercise elements of the governmental authority shall be considered an act of the State under international law if the organ, person or entity acts in that capacity, even if it exceeds its authority or contravenes instructions.[59]

Crawford points out that a state cannot take refuge behind the notion that these acts ought not to have occurred or ought to have taken a different form. This is so even when the organs of the state have disavowed the conduct of

---

[54] Shaw, *International Law*, p. 698.
[55] Brownlie, *System of the Law of Nations: State Responsibility (Part 1)*, pp. 46–47 and *Corfu Channel Case (United Kingdom v. Albania)* (Merits) [1949] ICJ Rep 4.
[56] Brownlie, *System of the Law of Nations: State Responsibility (Part 1)*, p. 46.
[57] *Certain German Interests in Polish Upper Silesia* (1926) PCIJ Series A, No. 7, p. 30.
[58] Brownlie, *System of the Law of Nations: State Responsibility (Part 1)*, p. 52.
[59] ILC, Draft Articles on Responsibility of States for Internationally Wrongful Acts, Article 7.

State responsibility in international law 73

the organ or entity that has committed unlawful acts. Otherwise a state could rely on its internal law to escape liability. The British Government has stated that 'all Governments should always be held responsible for all acts committed by their agents by virtue of their official capacity'.[60] This rule is also supported in the 1977 Geneva Protocol I, which provides that a 'party to a conflict...shall be responsible for all acts by persons forming part of its armed forces.[61]

A further issue to be determined in establishing the responsibility of a state is set out in the Iran–United States Claims Tribunal, and that is whether the act has been 'carried out by persons cloaked with governmental authority'.[62] One way of making this determination, according to Crawford, is to see if the conduct is systematic or recurrent, such that the state ought to have known about it and taken steps to prevent it. These acts do not include private acts by persons who happen to be government officials.[63]

The next Article, Article 8, sets out the provisions dealing specifically with imputability of conduct to a state, as discussed extensively in the *Nicaragua* case decided in the ICJ and the *Tadić* cases decided by the International Criminal Tribunal for Yugoslavia (ICTY). It is clear that responsibility only arises if the acts of the individuals involved are imputable to a state. There is a distinction between an act committed by, or with authorization of, the government of a state and unauthorized acts of the agents of the state, or acts of nationals and aliens living in the territory of the state.[64] Particularly as regards massive abuses of human rights, the individuals involved may not have the formal status and rank of a state official, but there is evidence that they act on behalf of the state.

This distinction is important and the law of state responsibility has to deal with this aspect. However, the Judgments in the *Nicaragua* case in the ICJ and in the *Tadić* case in the ICTY took different approaches to this issue. In the *Nicaragua* case three factors were used to identify whether individuals were under the 'effective control of a State'. These were whether they were state officials or (1) they were paid or financed by a state, (2) their action had been coordinated and supervised by that state and (3) the state had issued specific instructions concerning each of their unlawful actions.[65] The *Tadić* case

---

[60] Crawford, *The International Law Commission's Articles on State Responsibility*, p. 106.

[61] 1977 Geneva Protocol I Additional to the Geneva Conventions of 12 August 1949, Article 91. See also the *Caire* case, RIAA V 516 (1929), p. 531, and *Velásquez Rodríguez*, Inter-Am. CtHR, Series C, No. 4 (1989), at para. 170; 95 ILR 259, p. 296.

[62] *Petrolane Inc. v. Islamic Republic of Iran* (1991) 27 Iran–UCTR 64 at p. 92.

[63] Crawford, *The International Law Commission's Articles on State Responsibility*, p. 108.

[64] Brownlie, *System of the Law of Nations: State Responsibility (Part 1)*, p. 36. Brownlie is very critical of the distinction between original and vicarious state responsibility. He argues that it implies a fiction as the use of the term 'vicarious responsibility' is erroneous.

[65] Cassese, *International Law*, p. 249.

74 Part II: Evolution in public international law

employed a much wider ambit for attribution to a state. There were three aspects. The first is whether single individuals or groups lacking military organization acted under specific instructions or subsequent public approval of the state. The second, in the case of armed groups or militarily organized groups (paramilitaries), is whether they were under the overall control of a state without receiving specific instructions for each act. In the third aspect the test is whether individuals actually behave as state officials within the structure of a state.[66] The issue for the International Law Commission was whether the ICJ or ICTY view constituted customary international law. They decided as follows:

Article 8

Conduct directed or controlled by a State

The conduct of a person or group of persons shall be considered an act of a State under international law if the person or group of persons is in fact acting on the instructions of, or under the direction or control of, that State in carrying out the conduct.

Article 9

Conduct carried out in the absence or default of the official authorities

The conduct of a person or group of persons shall be considered an act of a State under international law if the person or group of persons is in fact exercising elements of the governmental authority in the absence or default of the official authorities and in circumstances such as to call for the exercise of those elements of authority.

Article 10

Conduct of an insurrectional or other movement

1. The conduct of an insurrectional movement which becomes the new government of a State shall be considered an act of that State under international law.
2. The conduct of a movement, insurrectional or other, which succeeds in establishing a new State in part of the territory of a pre-existing State or in a territory under its administration shall be considered an act of the new State under international law.
3. This article is without prejudice to the attribution to a State of any conduct, however related to that of the movement concerned, which is to be considered an act of that State by virtue of articles 4 to 9.[67]

These articles therefore reveal a preference for how the issue had been treated in the *Nicaragua* case.[68] In such instances it is necessary to

---

[66] Ibid., p. 249.

[67] ILC, Draft Articles on Responsibility of States for Internationally Wrongful Acts, Articles 8–10.

[68] *Military and Paramilitary Activities in and against Nicaragua* (Merits), [1986] ICJ Rep 14; Case IT-94-I-A, *Prosecutor v. Tadić* (1999) 38 ILM 1518; ICTR-96-4-T, *Prosecutor v. Akayesu.*

State responsibility in international law   75

establish a real link between the persons or group performing the internationally wrongful act and the state apparatus. This could be accomplished by means of recruiting private individuals such as paramilitary groups or directing civilian activity. However, this provision is disappointing as the latter fact is difficult to establish. In the *Nicaragua* case the Court held that the United States was responsible for planning, direction and support for the Contras.[69] In the case of insurgencies, the general principle set out in Article 10 is that if the insurgency becomes the new government, they are responsible for the past acts.[70] These articles again do not resolve the difference of opinion over the actual mechanism of state control, which is so important in situations such as the actions of the Janjeweed in Darfur, Sudan and the militia forces in Syria. The test in the *Tadić* case would be preferable. Cassese predicts that under this formulation it will be very difficult to prove that the state is responsible for acts performed by individuals, as it will be necessary to prove that every single action contrary to international law had been the subject of specific instructions by the state.[71]

Chapter III is entitled 'Breach of an international obligation'. Article 12 states:

Existence of a breach of an international obligation

There is a breach of an international obligation by a State when an act of that State is not in conformity with what is required of it by that obligation, regardless of its origin or character.[72]

This general statement encompasses all those areas outlined by Brownlie in his list of possible breaches, and supports the views expressed by Crawford that there is no room in international law for a distinction between the breach of a responsibility under a treaty or for a breach of another rule of international law, generally customary international law.

Within Chapter IV are those provisions outlining the responsibility of a state in connection with those acts of another state. These provisions were not in the earlier Draft Articles, as Brownlie had discussed that the practice of states in this area was non-existent. He had argued in his study that he could see that there could be joint responsibility for international wrongs.[73] These articles provide for aiding and assistance, direction or control and coercion, and, as a result, develop the law of state responsibility in this area.

---

[69] *Military and Paramilitary Activities in and against Nicaragua* (Merits), p. 51, para. 86; Crawford, *The International Law Commission's Articles on State Responsibility*, p. 111.

[70] Crawford, *The International Law Commission's Articles on State Responsibility*, p. 117.

[71] Cassese, *International Law*, p. 250.

[72] ILC, Draft Articles on Responsibility of States for Internationally Wrongful Acts, Article 12.

[73] Brownlie, *System of the Law of Nations: State Responsibility (Part 1)*, p. 189.

76 *Part II: Evolution in public international law*

Chapter V of Part I outlines the six circumstances precluding wrongfulness, which had pre-existed in customary international law. Crawford describes these articles as a shield against an otherwise well-founded claim.[74] In these defences arising out of treaty obligation, the law of treaties and the law of state responsibility have to be applied. As outlined in the *Gabčikovo-Nagymaros Project* case, the ICJ held that even if the defence of a state of necessity was found to exist, it was not a ground for the termination of the treaty. It would only be invoked to exonerate the state from failure to implement a treaty and the treaty could be resumed once the conditions justifying the defence no longer existed.[75]

There is one critical aspect of these defences that relates directly to issues involving the responsibility to protect, and this concerns the non-applicability of these defences when they conflict with a peremptory norm. The primary obligation is the peremptory norm of customary international law. As the provision states:

> Article 26
>
> Compliance with peremptory norms
> Nothing in this chapter precludes the wrongfulness of any act of a State, which is not in conformity with an obligation arising under a peremptory norm of general international law.[76]

Cassese describes an example of how this provision might work in practice. A state may not take countermeasures amounting to genocide in reaction to the genocidal action of another state.[77] This is the same type of situation as set out in Article 53 of the Vienna Convention of the Law of Treaties, which was described by Fitzmaurice as follows: 'a treaty obligation the observance of which is incompatible with a new rule or prohibition of international law in the nature of *jus cogens* will justify the non-observance of any treaty obligation involving such incompatibility.'[78]

There was one interesting situation in relation to circumstances precluding wrongfulness that involve norms of *jus cogens*. In the deliberations of the ILC, the question arose as to whether any military intervention – and, specifically, humanitarian intervention – could be seen as a necessity rather than an internationally wrongful act. The defence that could be used in these cases of dire emergency is necessity, which is defined in Article 25:

> *Necessity*
>
> 1. Necessity may not be invoked by a State as a ground for precluding the wrongfulness of an act not in conformity with an international obligation of that State unless the act:

---

[74] Crawford, *The International Law Commission's Articles on State Responsibility*, p. 160.
[75] *Gabčikovo-Nagymaros Project* case [1997] ICJ Rep 63.
[76] ILC, Draft Articles on Responsibility of States for Internationally Wrongful Acts, Article 26.
[77] Cassese, *International Law*, p. 257.
[78] G. Fitzmaurice, 'Fourth Report on the Law of Treaties', quoted in Crawford, *The International Law Commission's Articles on State Responsibility*, p. 187.

> (a) is the only way for the State to safeguard an essential interest against a grave and imminent peril; and
>
> (b) does not seriously impair an essential interest of the State or States towards which the obligation exists, or of the international community as a whole.[79]

The key concept of relevance is that of a state safeguarding an essential interest against grave and imminent peril, and whether that could include other obligations to the international community, including protecting populations of other states in grave and imminent peril.

James Crawford and his committee contemplated the possibility of this defence being used in cases of humanitarian intervention. In the International Law Commission report on the Draft Articles in 1999, there was a lengthy commentary on the relationship of necessity to humanitarian intervention and the relationship of the use of force to peremptory norms of *jus cogens*. Because of its importance it is set out here in full. In the previous draft Article 26 had been Article 33:

> 286. One of the issues discussed at some length in the commentary is the relationship between the plea of necessity as a circumstance precluding wrongfulness and the doctrine of humanitarian intervention as a ground for the use of force on the territory of another State. There are two difficulties here. First of all, of course, is the continuing controversy over whether and to what extent measures of forcible humanitarian intervention, not sanctioned pursuant to Chapters VII or VIII of the Charter of the United Nations, may be lawful under modern international law. This is not a question on which the Commission can take a position in formulating the secondary rules of responsibility, nor does the commentary purport to do so. But there is a second difficulty, in that article 33 expressly excludes from the scope of the plea of necessity violations of peremptory norms of international law, among which the rules relating to the use of force referred to in Articles 2(4) and 51 of the Charter certainly rank. Thus it could be argued that article 33, while purporting not to take a position on the exception of humanitarian intervention, in fact does so, since such an exception cannot stand with the exclusion of obligations under peremptory norms. The commentary appears to suggest that this difficulty can be avoided by differentiating between the peremptory status of some aspects of the rules relating to the use of force (e.g., the prohibition of aggression) and the non-peremptory status of other aspects (e.g., the injunction against a use of force even when carried out for limited humanitarian purposes). By implication, therefore, necessity can excuse the wrongfulness of genuine humanitarian action, even if it

---

[79] ILC, Draft Articles on Responsibility of States for Internationally Wrongful Acts, Article 25.

78   Part II: Evolution in public international law

involves the use of force, since such action does not, at any rate, violate a peremptory norm.

287. This construction raises complex questions about the 'differentiated' character of peremptory norms which go well beyond the scope of the draft articles. For present purposes it seems enough to say that either modern State practice and *opinio juris* license humanitarian action abroad in certain limited circumstances, or they do not. If they do, then such action would appear to be lawful in those circumstances, and cannot be considered as violating the peremptory norm reflected in Article 2(4) of the Charter. If they do not, there is no reason to treat them differently than any other aspect of the rules relating to the use of force. In either case, it seems than the question of humanitarian intervention abroad is not one which is regulated, primarily or at all, by article 33. For these reasons, it is suggested that the exception in article 33 for obligations of a peremptory character should be maintained.[80]

This commentary is directly related to individual states using force unilaterally in a humanitarian action. In his later commentary Crawford emphasized that necessity could not excuse a breach of a peremptory norm.[81] This clearly would not be applicable to a United Nations sanctioned intervention. This commentary does seem to preclude any military action, such as one based on an argument of a responsibility to protect, being conducted on a unilateral basis. This commentary was yet another indication that humanitarian intervention was not compatible with *jus ad bellum* and, as a result, another paradigm had to be found to combat the scourge of genocide.

Part Two of the articles are entitled: Content of the International Responsibility of a State. This part is divided into three chapters. The first chapter contains general principles and the second concerns reparation for injury. Article 30 of the articles specifies that a state that is responsible for an internationally wrongful act is under an obligation to cease that act and offer assurances of non-repetition.[82] In the ICJ in the *LaGrand* case, Germany sought assurances that the failure of consular notification would not be repeated and the Court held that 'the commitment expressed by the United States to ensure implementation of the specific measures adopted in performance of its obligations...must

---

[80] Second Report on State Responsibility by Mr James Crawford, Special Rapporteur, International Law Commission, Fifty-First Session, 1999, A/CN.4/498/Add.2.

[81] Crawford, *The International Law Commission's Articles on State Responsibility*, p. 188.

[82] ILC, Draft Articles on Responsibility of States for Internationally Wrongful Acts, Article 30.

be regarded as meeting Germany's request for a general assurance of non-repetition'.[83]

In Chapter II of the articles, on reparations, Article 34 states that full reparation for injury takes the form of restitution, compensation and satisfaction, either singly or in combination. The primary principle set out in Article 35 is that a state responsible for an internationally wrongful act is under an obligation to re-establish the situation that existed before the wrongful act was committed unless this is impossible. This article reflects the ruling in the *Chorzów Factory* case.[84] The other methods of compensation are also specifically set out, including satisfaction, which represents an expression of regret, a formal apology or another appropriate modality.[85] This modality is to remedy moral and legal damage.[86]

One area that is not dealt with by the articles is the issue of discrimination. In the 1961 articles there was a statement that 'aliens enjoy the same rights and the same legal guarantees as nationals, but these rights and guarantees shall in no case be less that the human rights and fundamental freedoms recognised and defined in contemporary international instruments.'[87] An explanation is that these rules stray into the primary rules of state responsibility as to treatment of aliens. At the present time the corpus of human rights obligations codify the minimum standard of treatment.[88] It cannot be seriously argued that there are variable standards for situations that involve the right to life and freedom from torture.

The discussion of these rules is important, as it is clear that situations that give rise to claims of responsibility to protect are the same types of violations of treaty and customary obligations that give rise to situations that might engage the principle of the responsibility to protect. It is critical to understand imputability and defences, as they apply equally to the situations triggering international activity. However, there is another critical element in the discussion and that is the fact that those breaches that engage international responsibility are systematic and widespread. In that regard, they trigger a different level of state responsibility.

Aggravated state responsibility

It is important to trace the development of those articles designed to deal with the most egregious violations of the primary rules of state

---

[83] *LaGrand Case (Germany v. United States of America)* (Merits) 27 June 2001 (2001) ICJ. Reports 466.

[84] *Factory at Chorzów* (Merits) (1928) PCIJ Series A, No. 17, p. 48.

[85] ILC, Draft Articles on Responsibility of States for Internationally Wrongful Acts, Articles 34–37.

[86] *Rainbow Warrior Arbitration*, RIAA XX, 217, pp. 272–273.

[87] Revised draft on International Responsibility of the State for Injuries caused in its Territory to the Person or Property of Aliens, Art. 1, 1961, *Yearbook International Law Commission*, Volume II, p. 46.

[88] See discussion of standards in Chapter V of the Articles.

80   Part II: Evolution in public international law

responsibility. In Crawford's monograph this topic is introduced under the title 'responsibility for breaches of communitarian norms'.[89] This title supports the argument advanced in Chapter 2 that there are paramount values in international society. Prior to Crawford's term as Special Rapporteur, one of the main roadblocks to completion of the work on state responsibility was draft Article 19, which had introduced the notion of criminal responsibility. It was one of the most contested areas in the various reports on state responsibility as the controversy had been over whether or not a state could commit a criminal act. Criminal responsibility was first included in the 1976 Draft Articles.[90] Article 19(2) stated:

> An internationally wrongful act which results from the breach by a State of an international obligation so essential for the protection of the fundamental interests of the international community as a whole constitutes an international crime.[91]

The justification for inclusion of such a provision was based on the passage in the *Barcelona Traction* case introducing the concept of obligations *erga omnes*.[92] The case invoked the responsibility for states to the international community as a whole where obligations *erga omnes* were involved. Prohibition against aggression and human rights norms were given as examples of these obligations. However, this case did not mention criminal liability or the responsibility of other states to intervene.[93] Roslyn Higgins in her discussion of Article 19 does not agree that the *erga omnes* concept requires the formulation of a category of international crimes. She states:

> It requires sliding from the concept of *erga omnes* to the category of *jus cogens*, and then making the further assumption that the breach of either is necessarily an international crime.[94]

This provision was deleted from the Draft Articles, as it did not attract general acceptance from states, including the United States and the United Kingdom.[95] There was certainly no agreement as to what action might be taken against a state that committed an international crime, as the Nuremberg and Tokyo Military Tribunals had tried individuals rather than states. It was

---

[89] Crawford, *State Responsibility: The General Part*, p. 362.

[90] M. Spinedi, 'International Crimes of State: The Legislative History' in J.H.H. Weiler, A. Cassese and M. Spinedi (eds), *International Crimes of State: A Critical Analysis of the ILC's Draft Article 19 on State Responsibility* (Berlin/New York: De Gruyter, 1989) for a drafting history of this article.

[91] ILC 1996 Report, GAOR, 51st Session, Supp. 10, p. 125.

[92] *Barcelona Traction, Light and Power Company Limited* (Second Phase) [1970] ICJ Rep 3.

[93] Shaw, *International Law*, p. 545.

[94] R. Higgins, *Problems and Process* (Oxford: Oxford University Press, 1994), p. 167.

[95] GAO 31st Sess. 1976, A/C/SR 18, para. 35.

State responsibility in international law 81

evident that there had not been the development of penal consequences for states.[96]

Brownlie also argues against criminal responsibility. Since 1920 there had been a considerable number of writers and resolutions of non-governmental bodies calling for criminal responsibility of states and individuals. He acknowledges that in a domestic legal system there could be imposition of criminal penalties on corporate bodies. Brownlie asserts that the international system is unsuitable for the imposition of criminal responsibility on states and it is doubtful that governments are prepared to accept the notion. He states that:

> State responsibility as a matter of law is, and in principle should be, limited to the obligation to make reparation, to compensate. Unfortunately the precise legal incidents of an 'international crime' in respect of States are a matter of uncertainty.[97]

The compromise position was introduced during Crawford's term as Special Rapporteur, as the notion of 'aggravated state responsibility'. This was the idea of obligations of a state towards the international community as a whole. Crawford described communitarian norms as obligations *erga omnes*, which he defined as:

> multilateral rights and obligations, established in the interest of and owed to the international community as a whole, entailing a recognised legal interest of each of its members to invoke compliance.[98]

The key feature is the 'sense of binding force for all states'.[99] But on the issue of enforcement, Crawford relies on the Sir Percy Spender opinion in the Second Phase of the *South West Africa* cases and points out that enforcement can only take place 'through a collective form of invocation within the framework of an international organization'.[100]

He argued that these communitarian norms predated the *Barcelona Traction* case. The first case was the *Wimbledon* case, decided in 1923 by the Permanent Court, which involved a claim brought by the United Kingdom, France, Italy and Japan against Germany concerning freedom of navigation of the Kiel Canal. The Court held that freedom of navigation, which had been identified by Hugo Grotius, resulted in the Kiel Canal being available for the use of the whole world.[101] Another case relevant to the responsibility

---

[96] See Crawford, *The International Law Commission's Articles on State Responsibility*, pp. 243–245 for an explanation as to why the criminal provision was deleted.
[97] Brownlie, *System of the Law of Nations: State Responsibility (Part 1)*, pp. 32–33.
[98] Crawford, *State Responsibility: The General Part*, p. 362.
[99] Ibid.
[100] Ibid., p. 365, and *South West Africa Cases (Ethiopia v. South Africa; Liberia v. South Africa)*, Second Phase [1966] ICJ Rep 6, p. 35.
[101] *SS Wimbledon* case (1923) PCIJ Series A, No. 1, 33.

82   Part II: Evolution in public international law

to protect is the *Aland Island* report by the International Commission of Jurists in 1920. This case concerned the treaty provisions on the obligation to demilitarize the islands: 'until these provisions are duly replaced by others, every State interested has the right to insist on compliance with them.'[102] Long before the United Nations Charter these cases established that there were norms that involved the interest of all states.

Crawford correctly argues that there is no complete agreement on the enumeration of these norms and that the law is this area is still developing, but the principle that in certain cases any state had standing to protest against breaches of certain fundamental norms, and if necessary to institute proceedings to vindicate its interest as a member of the international community, has long been accepted.[103]

However, the concept of aggravated state responsibility is also contested even though state actions are no longer labelled as international crimes. States such as India, Sierra Leone, France, Japan, the United Kingdom and the United States object to gradations of seriousness and argue that this does not reflect general customary international law. Nevertheless, other states such as the Nordic countries, Austria, the Netherlands and Slovenia support the compromise in Chapter III.[104] Chapter III of the articles, entitled 'Serious breaches of obligations under peremptory norms of general international law', introduces the concept of a second tier of obligations identified as 'aggravated state responsibility'.[105]

The compromise is as follows:

Article 40

1.   This chapter applies to the international responsibility which is entailed by a serious breach by a State of an obligation arising under a peremptory norm of general international law.
2.   A breach of such an obligation is serious if it involves a gross or systematic failure by the responsible State to fulfil its obligation.[106]

Article 41

1.   States shall cooperate to bring to an end through lawful means any serious breach within the meaning of article 40.

---

[102] Report of the International Commission of Jurists on the Aland Islands Question (1920) LNOJ Spec. Supp. No. 3, 17.
[103] Crawford, *State Responsibility: The General Part*, p. 365.
[104] J. Crawford, *Fourth Report on State Responsibility*, UN Doc. A/CN.4/517, 12 April 2001.
[105] See Cassese, *International Law*, pp. 200–204 on 'aggravated' state responsibility.
[106] ILC, Draft Articles on Responsibility of States for Internationally Wrongful Acts, Article 40.

State responsibility in international law 83

2. No State shall recognize as lawful a situation created by a serious breach within the meaning of article 40, nor render aid or assistance in maintaining the situation.
3. This article is without prejudice to the other consequences referred to in this part and to such further consequences that a breach to which this chapter applies may entail under international law.[107]

It should be evident that these two articles do not open the door for an argument for a responsibility to protect. The first reason is that these articles only relate to secondary rules of state responsibility and do not set out primary rules for responsibilities of states. The second reason is that even the drafters of the articles acknowledged that aggravated state responsibility was not yet a developed doctrine in customary international law. In his commentaries, Crawford recognizes that paragraph 1 may not be part of general international law, but could constitute a progressive development of the law.[108] There may be future development of 'a more elaborate regime of consequences entailed by such breaches'.[109] The movement in international law had been from 'sovereignty to obligation' and from 'immunity to accountability'.[110] It seems that both the reports on humanitarian intervention and the Articles on State Responsibility called for another approach to serious human rights breaches. An important similarity is the developmental aspect of the argument. The Articles on Aggravated State Responsibility and the responsibility to protect are both proposed avenues for legal responses to serious breaches of international law.

However, there are stark similarities in the approach of the committees considering the responsibility to protect and that of the ILC committee. It was obvious that the Articles on State Responsibility as passed by the General Assembly do not contain specific provisions outlining a responsibility to protect or a duty by other states to intervene when this responsibility is ignored. However, the articles on serious breaches of obligations, specifically Article 41, do prescribe positive duties of cooperation and response to violations of peremptory norms of international law. The original reports from the Dutch and Canadian governments argue just that international responsibility. They also examine the most serious and sustained violations of peremptory norms of international law. These reports are attempting to push forward a development of a customary doctrine, not in favour of a right of humanitarian intervention, but in favour of a duty to intervene. Although neither the reports nor the Draft Articles reflect the current situation of the international

---

[107] Ibid., Article 41.
[108] Crawford, *The International Law Commission's Articles on State Responsibility*, p. 249.
[109] Ibid., p. 253.
[110] Crawford, *State Responsibility: The General Part*, pp. 307 and 309.

84   *Part II: Evolution in public international law*

law of state responsibility, the reports introducing the responsibility to protect do introduce what is perhaps the logical conclusion of the notion of aggravated state responsibility – that the international community has an obligation to intervene in some fashion to stop serious abuses of human rights that violate norms of *jus cogens*.

However, this is not a new idea: Heffter, for instance, had previously discussed obligations 'owed to the international community as a whole'.[111] Amongst these obligations were: not to attempt world domination, the inviolability of diplomats and obligations to suppress piracy and the slave trade.[112] This concept is astonishing in its similarity to the responsibility to protect. Cassese asserts that aggravated state responsibility arises when a state violates a rule laying down a 'community obligation' that is either a customary obligation *erga omnes* protecting such fundamental values as peace, human rights or self-determination of peoples, or an obligation *erga omnes contractantes* laid down in a multilateral treaty safeguarding those fundamental values. This section on aggravated state responsibility tends to stray into the primary rules of state responsibility in that it defines the content of international obligations.

To begin with, Article 40 defines serious breaches as those involving gross or systematic failure by the responsible state to fulfil its obligation arising under a peremptory norm of general international law. The community obligation is owed to all other members of the international community and, therefore, there is a community right belonging to any other state. As a result, this community right can be exercised by any other state, whether or not it is damaged by the breach. However, this right is exercised on behalf of the international community, not on the part of the claimant state.[113] Article 40(2) specifies that the breach must be gross or systematic, serious or large scale, and examples given are aggression, genocide or grave atrocities against one's own nationals or all persons belonging to an ethnic group.[114] As with the language employed in the various reports recommending a responsibility to protect, it is clear that all members of the international legal community become victims of the breach of their community rights or, dare we say, constitutional values.

Cassese argues that this new form of responsibility has come into being as a result of a number of factors. First of all, the UN Charter provisions on the ban of force and the methods of response to acts of aggression brought about the idea that there existed rules envisaging reactions to international delinquencies different and more serious than the usual response. A second feature is the practice concerning reaction to gross and large-scale violations

---

[111] A. Heffter, *Le Droit International Public de l'Europe* (Berlin: H.W. Muller, 1857), pp. 203–204.

[112] Cassese, *International Law*, pp. 207–208.

[113] Ibid., pp. 200–201. Cassese also included obligations to states bound by multilateral treaties, but that does not seem to be included in Chapter III.

[114] Ibid., p. 201.

State responsibility in international law 85

of human rights that involves a collective dimension. Finally Cassese argues the emergence in the world community of values such as peace, human rights and self-determination, which are deemed of universal significance and not subject to derogation. This has led many states to believe that gross infringements of such values must require a stronger reaction than those normally taken in response to violation of bilateral legal relations. The reaction should be public and reactive.[115]

Examples of collective action by states are of course the actions of the Security Council in situations of a breach of the UN Charter, which is a multilateral treaty. Examples given are the economic measures against Southern Rhodesia, South Africa, the Federal Republic of Yugoslavia, Libya, Liberia and Haiti.[116] The two other categories mentioned by Cassese are the international treaty regimes, particularly in human rights and international humanitarian law, and in the cases under international criminal law. These will be examined in subsequent chapters as regimes of responsibility, the focus of the analysis in this book.

Indeed, many of the situations that have resulted in putative cases of humanitarian intervention have fallen into this category with massive and systematic breaches of right to life or freedom from torture. Chapter III is an important advance towards clarifying how obligations to the international community trigger the secondary rules of state responsibility. At the core of Article 40 is the notion of obligations *erga omnes* as set out in the *Barcelona Traction* case, the *Namibia* opinion, the *Case Concerning East Timor* and the *Application of the Convention on the Prevention and Punishment of the Crime of Genocide (Bosnia and Herzegovina* v. *Yugoslavia)* case. The types of serious breaches as set out in those cases were genocide, aggression, apartheid and forcible denial of self-determination. These breaches 'shock the conscience of mankind'; they should therefore attract serious consequences and thus merit a separate chapter in the Draft Articles.[117] As Crawford states, the *Barcelona Traction* case was the first to make a distinction between 'the position of an injured State in the context of diplomatic protection with the position of all States in respect of the breach of an obligation towards the diplomatic community as a whole'.[118] In the *East Timor* case the Court held that 'Portugal's assertion that the right of peoples to self-determination, as it evolved from the Charter and from United Nations practice, has an *erga omnes* character is irreproachable'.[119] In a critical statement the Court in the *Application of the Convention on the Prevention and Punishment of the Crime of Genocide*

---

[115] Ibid., p. 263.
[116] Ibid., pp. 263–264.
[117] Crawford, *The International Law Commission's Articles on State Responsibility*, pp. 18–19.
[118] Ibid., p. 242.
[119] *East Timor (Portugal* v. *Australia)* (Preliminary Objections) (1995) ICJ Reports 90, p. 102, para. 29.

86 Part II: Evolution in public international law

case states that 'the rights and obligations enshrined by the [Genocide] Convention are rights and obligations *erga omnes*'.[120]

Articles 53 and 64 of the Vienna Convention on the Law of Treaties are cited by the drafters of these articles, as the Convention recognizes the existence of substantive norms of a fundamental character from which no derogation is permitted.[121] In this same way this chapter of the articles recognizes that there could be 'egregious breaches of obligations owed to the community as a whole, breaches which warrant some response by the community and its members'.[122]

It is the consequences of serious breach of obligations under peremptory norms that are a dramatic departure from ordinary state responsibility. The first important factor is that *all* other states can take action. All other states are entitled to: (a) invoke the aggravated responsibility by bringing their claim to the notice of the state, (b) demand cessation of the wrong, (c) claim reparation on behalf of the victims, (d) bring the matter to competent international bodies such as the UN or regional organization, (e) if that international organization takes no action, then states can take *peaceful* countermeasures on an individual basis, and finally (f) to resort to collective self-defence in the case of aggression subject to their consent.[123]

States are placed under a positive obligation by the term 'shall' to cooperate in order to bring an end to serious breaches of obligations owed under a peremptory norm of international law. Article 41 regrettably does not specify the form this cooperation should take; it could be organized under the auspices of the United Nations, but it also could be 'non-institutionalized cooperation'.[124] Article 41(2) obliges other states not to recognize as lawful a situation created by a serious breach, nor to render aid or assistance to that state.

These articles must be read in conjunction with two other articles of ARSIWA: Articles 42 and 48 in Part III. Article 48 is entitled 'Invocation of responsibility by a State other than an injured State':

1. Any State other than an injured State is entitled to invoke the responsibility of another State in accordance with paragraph 2 if:

    a. The obligation breached is owed to a group of States including that State, and is established for the protection of a collective interest of the group; or
    b. The obligation breached is owed to the international community as a whole.

---

[120] *Application of the Convention on the Prevention and Punishment of the Crime of Genocide (Bosnia and Herzegovina v. Yugoslavia)* (Preliminary Objections) (1996) ICJ Reports 595, p. 616, para. 31.

[121] Crawford, *The International Law Commission's Articles on State Responsibility*, p. 243.

[122] Ibid., p. 20.

[123] Ibid., pp. 203–204.

[124] Ibid., p. 249.

2. Any State entitled to invoke responsibility under paragraph 1 may claim from the responsible State:
   a. Cessation of the internationally wrongful act, and assurances and guarantees of non-repetition in accordance with article 30; and
   b. Performance of the obligation of reparation in accordance with the preceding articles, in the interest of the injured State or of the beneficiaries of the obligation breached.
3. The requirements for the invocation of responsibility by an injured State under articles 43, 44 and 45 apply to an invocation of responsibility by a State entitled to do so under paragraph 1.[125]

Article 42 is entitled 'Invocation of responsibility by an injured State', and states:

A State is entitled as an injured State to invoke the responsibility of another State if the obligation breached is owed to:

a. That State individually; or
b. A group of States including that State, or the international community as a whole, and the breach of the obligation:
   i. Specially affects that State; or
   ii. Is of such a character as radically to change the position of all the other States to which the obligation is owed with respect to the further performance of the obligation.[126]

Both of these articles on the implementation of the international responsibility of a state contemplate obligations owed to the international community as a whole. Crawford traces this notion to the work of Fitzmaurice as a Special Rapporteur to the International Law Commission on the Law of Treaties. He introduced the notion of 'integral obligations' in treaties, defined as 'self-existent, absolute and inherent for each party'.[127] Among the examples given were obligations under the Genocide Convention, human rights conventions and the 1949 Geneva Conventions.[128] There is another relevant article that supports this view:

Article 54

Measures taken by States other than an injured State

This chapter does not prejudice the right of any State, entitled under article 48, paragraph 1, to invoke the responsibility of another State, to take lawful measures against that State to ensure cessation of the breach

---

[125] ILC, Draft Articles on Responsibility of States for Internationally Wrongful Acts, Article 48.
[126] Ibid., Article 42.
[127] Fitzmaurice, Second Report, ILC Ybk, 1957/II, 28.
[128] Ibid., p. 54, and Fitzmaurice, Third Report, ILC Ybk 1958/II, 44.

88 *Part II: Evolution in public international law*

and reparation in the interest of the injured State or of the beneficiaries of the obligation breached.[129]

As Pronto asserts, this provision allows a third state to involve the responsibility of the wrong-doing state if the wrongful actions of that state violate an obligation owed to the third state or the international community as a whole.[130] This provision further supports Articles 40, 41 and 48.

However, commentaries on Articles 40 and 41 dismiss their use in humanitarian intervention. In his discussion of state practice and aggravated state responsibility, Cassese specifically refers to the Kosovo intervention by NATO as a clear breach of the UN Charter and of the *jus cogens* principle banning the use of force. He does not accept that intervention could be a community response to serious breaches of obligations.[131] Crawford, the Special Rapporteur of the committee on state responsibility, has a definite objection to states taking military action to assist victims and stated:

> Presently we have the spectre of certain States galloping to the aid of victims who are clear that they do not want such aid. As the Court said in the Nicaragua case, if a State purports to act in collective self-defense of another, it must act with the consent of the State which is said to be the victim of the attack. The same principle should apply to State responsibility, especially so far as reparation is concerned.[132]

Neither of these responses to the use of aggravated state responsibility answers the question as to what exactly states are to do within 'lawful means' when their international responsibility is engaged.

In a decision on universal jurisdiction, the *Case Concerning the Arrest Warrant of 11 April 2000 (Democratic Republic of the Congo v. Belgium)*, in the separate opinion of Judges Higgins, Kooijmans and Buergenthal, there is a discussion of the evolution of international law. In paragraph 51 the opinion states:

> The series of multilateral treaties with their special jurisdictional provisions reflect a determination by the international community that those engaged in war crimes, hijacking, hostage taking, torture should not go unpunished...And those States and academic writers who claim the right to act unilaterally to assert a universal criminal jurisdiction over persons

---

[129] ILC, Draft Articles on Responsibility of States for Internationally Wrongful Acts, Article 54.

[130] A.N. Pronto, 'The International Law Commission' in G. Zyberi (ed.), *An Institutional Approach to the Responsibility to Protect* (Cambridge: Cambridge University Press, 2013).

[131] J. Crawford, *The International Law Commission's Articles on State Responsibility,: Introduction, Text and Commentaries*, p. 205.

[132] Crawford, *State Responsibility: The General Part*, p. 321.

State responsibility in international law   89

committing such acts, invoke the concept of acting as 'agents for the international community'.[133]

Although the case itself concerns universal jurisdiction, this concept of responsibility to the community as a whole is a mirror image of a claim of universal jurisdiction. In fact the whole design of ad hoc International Criminal Tribunals and the International Criminal Court reflect this trend of responsibility towards the international community for crimes that are part and parcel of those items that constitute serious breaches of international obligations. In the *Furundzija* Trial Chamber decision in the ICTY there is a reference to aggravated responsibility. The Judgment states:

> Under current international humanitarian law, in addition to individual criminal liability, State responsibility may enure as a result of a State official engaging in torture or failing to prevent torture or to punish torturers. If carried out as an extensive practice of State officials, torture amounts to a serious breach on a widespread scale of an international obligation of essential importance for safeguarding the human being, thus constituting a grave wrongful act generating State responsibility.[134]

The reports of the ICISS and the Dutch committee specify a number of these rules such as the prohibition against genocide, the rules set out in the Geneva Conventions and the obligations set out in various human rights treaties. Agreement on these rules could only be established by examining the practice of states and decisions of the various international courts and tribunals, and save for the Brownlie study in the 1970s this has not yet been accomplished. Controversy still exists over whether any of them constitute peremptory norms.

The most important decision with respect to ARSIWA is the ICJ's 2004 *Wall* Advisory Opinion. First, it was held that the obligations *erga omnes* violated by Israel in building its barrier were the obligation to respect the right of the Palestinian people to self-determination and other obligations under international humanitarian law.[135] The Court held that all states were under an obligation not to render aid or assistance in maintaining the situation created by the construction of the wall. All other states were to see to it 'that any impediment, resulting from the construction of the wall, to the exercise by the Palestinian people of its right to self-determination is brought to an end'.

---

[133] *Case Concerning the Arrest Warrant of 11 April 2000 (Democratic Republic of the Congo v. Belgium)* [2002] ICJ Rep 1, Joint Separate Opinion of Judges Higgins, Kooijmans and Buergenthal, para. 51.

[134] *Prosecutor* v. *Anto Furundzija* (Trial Judgment), IT-95-17/1-T, International Criminal Tribunal for the former Yugoslavia (ICTY), 10 December 1998, para. 142.

[135] *Advisory Opinion Concerning Legal Consequences of the Construction of a Wall in the Occupied Palestinian Territory* [2004] ICJ Rep 136, pp. 199–200.

90   Part II: Evolution in public international law

States were also obligated to ensure compliance with international humanitarian law. The Court recommended that the United Nations, particularly the General Assembly and the Security Council, consider what further action should be taken to end 'the illegal situation'. Crawford argues that this case not only endorsed the ILC provisions on communitarian norms but went a step further in the development of the consequences of violations of *erga omnes* obligations.[136]

Crawford comments at length on the obligation set out in Article 41(1) that states must engage in lawful collective action to bring to an end any situation created through the breach. Crawford indicates that the article does not specify how any collective action would be coordinated, but acknowledges that the obvious force to do so would be the United Nations, and particularly the Security Council acting under Chapter VII.[137] He briefly addresses humanitarian intervention, stating:

> Another difficulty lies in assessing what is considered 'lawful' within international law, particularly where questions relating to the use of force and humanitarian intervention are concerned: what some states consider lawful, others may not, leading to a situation in which, pending an authoritative determination of legality which seldom emerges with immediacy, either the parties to the adventure are in breach of international law, or their detractors are acting contrary to the precepts of Article 41(1).[138]

It is a shame that Crawford did not take the next logical step and assert that the responsibility to protect could emerge as a lawful response to these violations. In spite of the trend towards responsibility in the Draft Articles and these two reports, it would be completely premature to argue that state responsibility to comply with international obligations had evolved towards a duty to act when citizens of another state were at risk from massive human rights violations that their own state was unwilling or unable to prevent. None of the human rights, international criminal law or humanitarian law treaties force sovereign states to act in these circumstances. There is a responsibility on a state within its own boundaries to respect and abide by international law, but that same state is not compelled to act outside its territory unless mandated by the United Nations Charter. Even the practice of the Security Council in its resolutions is to call on states to volunteer armed forces to the Security Council, rather than compelling states to intervene. One might argue that in circumstances of genocide, such as those seen in Rwanda and Srebrenica, there should be a duty of this kind, but it is clear that neither international conventions nor customary international law imposes such a duty.[139]

[136] Crawford, *State Responsibility: The General Part*, p. 371.
[137] Ibid., p. 386.
[138] Ibid., p. 387.
[139] Pronto, 'The International Law Commission', p. 195.

Conclusion

Cassese, in his conclusion to his examination of aggravated responsibility, argues that although ordinary responsibility is firmly embedded in the world community, 'aggravated responsibility' plays a minor role. Cassese acknowledges that there is evidence of a consistent but 'thin' practice pointing to the legal regime of 'aggravated responsibility'.[140] He acknowledges that international practice clearly showed that states consider that (1) the protection of some fundamental values laid down in legal obligations requires that the legal reaction to possible breaches of such obligations should be different from that envisaged by an 'ordinary' wrongful act; (2) such reaction should first of all be decided or agreed upon within the framework of international bodies; and (3) in some circumstances states might act alone to enforce community values. However, the practice described in the commentary to the articles did not seem to be as limited as Cassese suggests, and covered a number of critical international law decisions.

A key aspect to international responsibility is the notion of responsibility for violations to the rights of individuals and, particularly, the violation of obligations *erga omnes*. The international legal community through the development of the Articles on State Responsibility has now developed secondary rules compelling accountability for states for violations of the rights of individuals. In addition, these rules establish state responsibility for the actions of individuals, the actions of whom, and for which they may be individually criminally responsible, *also* trigger responsibility for states to act to put an end to the violations of international law. The next chapters with respect to human rights, criminal law, environmental law – and Part III on state and United Nations practice in the three aspects of the responsibility to protect – reveal that this practice may not be as 'thin' as it seems at first glance.

[140] Cassese, *International Law*, p. 277.

4 International human rights law
Rights and responsibilities

Introduction

More than any other legal regime, the international protection of human rights impinges on the traditional positivist notion of the absolute sovereignty of the state and supports the idea of an emerging international constitutional system, or at the very least supports the idea of an international community of states bound by fundamental norms.[1] Although the criminal justice system in a state may help to protect peoples from abuses such as genocide, war crimes, ethnic cleansing and crimes against humanity, at the core of the protection of a population is a robust system of human rights protection. It is when human rights are violated on a large scale that international crimes occur, a phenomenon that the responsibility to protect seeks to address. As argued in the previous chapter, massive violations of human rights of norms of *jus cogens* also involve obligations on states *erga omnes*, which trigger consideration of aggravated state responsibility.

The evolution of human rights instruments and practices in human rights courts, committees and commissions have imposed limits on the power of states over their own populations. The international protection of human rights encompasses obligations on the part of states and their officials to protect citizens and resident aliens, including asylum seekers, from abuses to their fundamental human rights. However, this is primarily a statist notion of legal protection and the first level of the responsibility to protect. The question under consideration for this book is whether these obligations on states within human rights practice and jurisprudence extend to the protection of all individual members of the international community rather than just citizens within a nation-state, which is the fundamental core of both the responsibility to protect and aggravated state responsibility.

There are three separate facets to this chronological and progressive analysis of the relationship between human rights and the responsibility to protect. The reason a historical framework is necessary is that it could not be argued that in 1945, even in the wake of the Holocaust, the international community

[1] B. Simma, 'From Bilateralism to Community Interest in International Law' (1994) 250 *Recueil Des Cours* 217, pp. 236–243.

International human rights law 93

accepted the responsibility to protect all of humanity. Although these may be artificial divisions, there are perhaps three phases to this evolution. The first part of this chapter traces the development of what has been called the International Bill of Rights, a series of human rights treaties complete with enforcement mechanisms. This is also extended to the regional instruments of human rights protection and promotion, which contain the first court-based enforcement systems. This is not meant to be a repetition of well-known history but a discussion of how, even in these instruments, there are notions of universality both in agreement and in application. The first tier of obligation is clearly domestic, but each treaty contains within its preamble notions of international responsibility.

The second part of this chapter considers the momentum towards extending human rights protection towards positive obligations that mandate the creation of environments that promote human rights, not only from a government to its population, but also horizontally from person to person within society. Positive obligations have developed from the practices of treaty enforcement systems. The specialized area of refugee and asylum law, more than any other area of human rights, triggers positive obligations of protection on receiving states and the international community towards those fleeing persecution. Furthermore, part of the doctrine of international protection of asylum seekers is predicated on notions of a state being unable or unwilling to protect its people even from abuses not perpetrated by the state itself.

The third and final part of this chapter considers the evolution of notions of international responsibility in the evolution of customary human rights law, including the controversial notions of *jus cogens* and obligations *erga omnes*. This final part extends the parameters of human rights protection beyond national boundaries to the global community at large. This results in the development of the notion of international responsibility within the corpus of the treaty obligations and practice of human rights. Thus this international responsibility can lead to both aggravated state responsibility and the responsibility to protect.

The emergence of the treaty regime of human rights protection – the International Bill of Rights

One way in which protection of human rights is argued to extend beyond territorial boundaries is in its theoretical framework. Human rights law has been associated with natural law theory. The natural law vision is of a common humanity bound by inherent legal principles that acknowledges human vulnerability and dignity and espouses general rules of non-violence.[2] Inherent rights are viewed within the framework of the standard of civilization. States as part of civilization share common preoccupations with life, liberty, dignity, security and other fundamental rights. Within this vision, states must exist for

---

[2] R. Jackson, *Quasi-states: Sovereignty, International Relations and the Third World* (Cambridge: Cambridge University Press, 1990), p. 141.

94   *Part II: Evolution in public international law*

the good of the people, and not the reverse. Natural law rights are immune from political intervention. Even if this common law of mankind cannot be enforced without the acquiescence of states, human rights provide a legal standard for bringing them into international accountability.[3] As discussed in Chapter 2, the scholar most associated with this vision is Kant, and its modern-day adherents in international law would be the school of international liberalism.[4]

Lauterpacht argued that human rights must be supported by the 'twin sanction of the law of nature and the law of nations'.[5] However, to address those who did not share his natural law perspective, he embarked on a positivist analysis that will be employed in this chapter. In the context of the law of nations, he investigated the evolution in positive law of the 'International Bill of Rights of Man'.[6] He argued that prior to the Charter of the United Nations, the idea of the existence of international human rights was controversial. There had been occasional recognition of fundamental human rights in treaties, the most outstanding examples being the several minority protection treaties concluded after the First World War.[7] The Charter of the United Nations was a legal document containing the language of international law. In affirming repeatedly the 'fundamental human rights' of the individual, it referred to legal rights recognized both by international law and domestic law. Although rights may be only imperfectly enforceable, the correlation of rights and remedies was not as close in international law as in domestic law. Lauterpacht asserted that members of the United Nations had a legal duty to respect fundamental human rights and if they did not do so, they committed a breach of the Charter. Even if there was no international tribunal endowed with compulsory jurisdiction over human rights, violations that did not deprive them of their legal character. As the Charter formed part of the municipal law of its members, then it would be enforceable as such.[8]

In the 70 years since the advent of the Charter, and the 65 years since Lauterpacht's treatise on human rights, a myriad of human rights multilateral conventions have been adopted both at an international and regional level, the first being the European Convention for the Protection of Human Rights and Fundamental Freedoms adopted in Rome in 1950.[9] These treaties have included mechanisms for enforcement of international

---

[3] Ibid., pp. 142–145.

[4] I. Kant, *Perpetual Peace: A Philosophical Essay* (London: G. Allen & Unwin Limited, 1903) and see F. Tesón, 'Kantian International Liberalism' in D.R. Mapel and T. Nardin (eds), *International Society* (Princeton: Princeton University Press, 1998).

[5] H. Lauterpacht, *International Law and Human Rights* (New York: Frederick Praeger, 1950), p. 94.

[6] Ibid., p. 3.

[7] Ibid., p. 32.

[8] Ibid., pp. 34–35.

[9] The 10 key international instruments are: International Convention on the Elimination of All Forms of Racial Discrimination, 21 December 1965; International Covenant on Civil and

International human rights law   95

human rights responsibility. There are also thousands of national and international human rights organizations constituting what has been labelled as international civil society.[10] Many of these NGOs have special consultative status recognized by the Economic and Social Rights Council.[11] This focus on human rights has also been supported by the mass media, so that Kant's prediction that 'a violation of rights in one place is felt throughout the world' is borne out.[12]

In 1945 the UN Charter mandated the General Assembly to initiate studies and make recommendations for the purpose of assisting in the realization of human rights and fundamental freedoms for all without distinction as to race, sex, language or religion. This led to the establishment of a Human Rights Commission and the development of instruments to protect human rights.[13] In spite of cold war paralysis in the area of peace and security, the development of a series of instruments specifying obligations to promote and protect human rights that attracted almost universal agreement was truly impressive.

The General Assembly adoption of the Universal Declaration of Human Rights in 1948 (UDHR) was the first step in the codification of human rights.[14] It was not a binding treaty but a statement of aspirations. The provisions contained 'general principles of law and elementary considerations of humanity'.[15] The vision of the drafters of the UDHR was of national political systems that guaranteed fundamental human rights, including the right to life, freedom from torture, rights to fair trial, freedom of movement,

---

Political Rights, 16 December 1966; International Covenant on Economic, Social and Cultural Rights, 16 December 1966; Convention on the Elimination of All Forms of Discrimination against Women, 18 December 1979; Convention against Torture and other Cruel, Inhuman or Degrading Treatment or Punishment, 10 December 1984; Convention on the Rights of the Child, 20 November 1989; International Convention on the Protection of the Rights of All Migrant Workers and Members of their Families, 18 December 1990; Convention on the Rights of Persons with Disabilities, 12 December 2006; International Convention for the Protection of All Persons from Enforced Disappearance, 20 December 2006. Regional conventions are: Council of Europe, European Convention for the Protection of Human Rights and Fundamental Freedoms, as amended by Protocols Nos 11 and 14, 4 November 1950; Organization of American States (OAS), American Convention on Human Rights, 'Pact of San Jose', Costa Rica, 22 November 1969; Organization of African Unity (OAU), African Charter on Human and Peoples' Rights ('Banjul Charter'), 27 June 1981, CAB/LEG/67/3 rev. 5, 21 ILM 58 (1982).

10 A. Colás, *International Civil Society* (Cambridge: Polity Books, 2002).
11 For the current list see https://esango.un.org/civilsociety/documents/E-2014-INF-5.pdf, accessed 25 September 2015.
12 Kant, *Perpetual Peace*.
13 United Nations, Charter of the United Nations, 24 October 1945, 1 UNTS XVI, Article 13.
14 UN General Assembly, Universal Declaration of Human Rights, 10 December 1948, UN Doc. GA/RES/217 A (III) (UDHR).
15 I. Brownlie, *Principles of Public International Law*, 5th edition (Oxford: Oxford University Press, 1998).

96 *Part II: Evolution in public international law*

assembly, association and expression and freedom from poverty.[16] Many of the rights outlined in the Universal Declaration became part of customary international law, and some evolved into norms of *jus cogens* such as the right to life, fair trial and freedom from torture.[17]

As with the Charter, notions of development (freedom from want) and human rights (freedom from fear) went hand in hand. In the preamble the Declaration stated:

> Whereas the peoples of the United Nations have in the Charter reaffirmed their faith in fundamental human rights, in the dignity and worth of the human person and in the equal rights of men and women and have determined to promote social progress and better standards of life in larger freedom.[18]

The rights within this declaration included a group that are characterized as economic, social and cultural rights. Amongst these were:

> Article 22
>
> Everyone, as a member of society, has the right to social security and is entitled to realization, through national effort and international co-operation and in accordance with the organization and resources of each State, of the economic, social and cultural rights indispensable for his dignity and the free development of his personality.[19]

This provision introduced the notion of 'international co-operation'. Even in 1948, human rights were to be secured not just nationally but internationally as well. Other unique features of the UDHR were notions of inherence and universality – all humanity, by virtue of their being human, were entitled to share in these fundamental civil, political, economic, social and cultural rights.[20]

In spite of the bipolar divisions between the Western and Soviet blocs resulting from the cold war, the Economic and Social Council's Human Rights Commission developed a whole series of both generalized and specialized human rights conventions. The two major general instruments are the International Covenant on Civil and Political Rights (ICCPR) and the International Covenant on Economic and Social and Cultural Rights

---

[16] UDHR, Articles 3, 5, 13, 18, 19, 20.

[17] Ibid., Articles 3, 10 and 5, and confirmation of *jus cogens* in *South West Africa Cases* (Second Phase) [1966] ICJ Rep 6, para. 291 and *Case Concerning the Barcelona Traction, Light and Power Company Limited (Belgium v. Spain)* [1970] ICJ Rep 3, para. 34.

[18] UDHR, Preamble.

[19] Ibid., Article 22.

[20] Ibid., Preamble.

International human rights law 97

(ICESCR), which were opened for signature in 1966 and in effect from 1976.[21] These two conventions added specificity and detail to the rights enunciated in the UDHR. Within the preamble to both conventions was the statement of universality:

> *Considering* the obligation of States under the Charter of the United Nations to promote universal respect for, and observance of, human rights and freedoms.[22]

There followed in the next decades a whole series of specialized conventions on the rights of women, children, migrant workers, disabled peoples and those facing racial discrimination. The International Convention on the Elimination of All Forms of Racial Discrimination (CERD) was signed in 1965 and entered into force in 1969. Within the preamble to this convention was yet another statement of universal application:

> *Resolved* to adopt all necessary measures for speedily eliminating racial discrimination in all its forms and manifestations, and to prevent and combat racist doctrines and practices in order to promote understanding between races and to build an international community free from all forms of racial segregation and racial discrimination.[23]

In 1979 the Convention on the Elimination of All Forms of Discrimination against Women (CEDAW) was adopted and came into force in 1981. There was a sweeping statement of the importance of equality of women to the international community:

> *Convinced* that the full and complete development of a country, the welfare of the world and the cause of peace require the maximum participation of women on equal terms with men in all fields.[24]

The Convention against Torture and Other Cruel, Inhuman or Degrading Treatment or Punishment (CAT) was adopted in 1984 and came into force in 1987. The preamble contained a similar paragraph to those in the ICCPR and ICESCR. The General Assembly adopted the Convention on the Rights of the Child (CRC) on 20 November 1989 and it came into force on 2 September 1990. This convention had an even clearer statement of international obligation: *Recognizing* the importance of international cooperation for improving the living conditions of children in every country, in particular the developing countries.[25]

---

[21] ICESCR and ICCPR 1966, Preamble, original emphasis.

[22] Ibid., original emphasis.

[23] Convention on the Elimination of All Forms of Racial Discrimination, 1966, Preamble, original emphasis.

[24] CEDAW, 1979, Preamble, original emphasis.

[25] CRC, 1989, Preamble.

98   *Part II: Evolution in public international law*

The International Convention on the Protection of the Rights of All Migrant Workers and Members of their Families (ICRMW) was adopted by General Assembly Resolution on 18 December 1990 and came into force on 1 July 2003.[26] This convention returned to the general language of universality:

> *Convinced therefore* of the need to bring about the international protection of the rights of all migrant workers and members of their families, reaffirming and establishing basic norms in a comprehensive convention which could be applied universally.[27]

The Convention of the Rights of Persons with Disabilities was adopted on 13 December 2006 and quickly came into force on 3 May 2008. Again, the preamble contains the language of universal obligation:

> Recognizing the importance of international cooperation for improving the living conditions of persons with disabilities in every country, particularly in developing countries.[28]

The International Convention for the Protection of All Persons from Enforced Disappearance, adopted the same year, came into force on 23 December 2010. This treaty contains an interesting statement on enforced disappearance concerning the international impact of the crime. It states:

> *Aware* of the extreme seriousness of enforced disappearance, which constitutes a crime and, in certain circumstances defined in international law, a crime against humanity.[29]

These treaties form the corpus of what has been called the International Bill of Rights and have been signed, ratified or acceded to by the majority of states – and the CRC has almost universal acceptance. Although there are many provisions with respect to the rights to be protected on a national basis, they are all premised on notions of universality, which is that persons within the globe are entitled to these rights no matter where they reside, and that international cooperation in promoting economic development

---

[26] The ICCPR has two Optional Protocols, one adopted in 1966 for a complaints mechanism and one in 1989 on the death penalty. The CEDAW has one Optional Protocol on a complaints mechanism, adopted in 1999. The CRC has two optional protocols, adopted in 2000 – one on child soldiers and the other on child pornography and prostitution. The CAT has one optional protocol, adopted in 2002, on torture in detention.

[27] ICRMW, 1990, Preamble, original emphasis.

[28] Convention on the Rights of Persons with Disabilities, 13 December 2006.

[29] International Convention for the Protection of All Persons from Enforced Disappearance, 20 December 2006.

International human rights law 99

might secure these rights.[30] These treaties reinforce the existence of the international community. With respect to international cooperation, these treaties mandate responsibility on states to aid and assist other nations in fulfilling their human rights responsibilities. This is directly relevant to the first branch of the responsibility to protect – the responsibility to prevent. Providing international assistance, particularly in economic, social and cultural rights, might help prevent abuses that occur in the absence of the realization of these rights.

Included within this proliferation of human rights treaties are mechanisms of enforcement of human rights obligations. Each treaty establishes its own system of monitoring of compliance, but there are similarities within each monitoring committee. Generally, the international system relies on voluntary compliance with supervision by a series of treaty bodies. These treaty-monitoring committees of each of the international conventions are composed of influential and experienced human rights experts. Part of their working sessions is devoted to formulating general comments for guidance on the meaning and scope of the rights set out in their respective conventions. These general comments have been cited in the jurisprudence of human rights courts and committees, and in the review of states reports that are mandated under human rights conventions.[31]

General comments are predicated on universality. The comments are based on the universal meaning and application of these standards. The Human Rights Committee (HRC) has the most comprehensive set of general comments. Of particular interest are General Comment 29 on derogations and General Comment 31 on the nature of the general legal obligation imposed on states parties. General Comment 29 limits the power of states to depart from their treaty obligations even in states of emergency:

> 2. Measures derogating from the provisions of the Covenant must be of an exceptional and temporary nature. Before a State moves to invoke article 4, two fundamental conditions must be met: the situation must amount to a public emergency which threatens the life of the nation, and the State party must have officially proclaimed a state of emergency. The latter requirement is essential for the maintenance of the principles of legality and rule of law at times when they are most needed. When proclaiming a state of emergency with consequences that could entail derogation from any provision of the Covenant, States must act within their constitutional and other provisions of law that govern such proclamation and the exercise of emergency powers; it is the task of the Committee to monitor the laws in question with respect to whether they enable

---

[30] One criticism of the International Bill of Rights is that it is a Western notion that does not take into account cultural sensitivities, but this is a discussion for another publication.

[31] P. Alston and R. Goodman, *International Human Rights* (Oxford: Oxford University Press, 2012). See Part D for discussion of international and regional enforcement of human rights.

100 *Part II: Evolution in public international law*

and secure compliance with article 4. In order that the Committee can perform its task, States parties to the Covenant should include in their reports submitted under article 40 sufficient and precise information about their law and practice in the field of emergency powers.[32]

This mandatory language is common to most of the general comments, which set out wide powers of review of compliance by the Human Rights Committee. General Comment 31 is specific regarding domestic legal requirements:

> 7. Article 2 requires that States Parties adopt legislative, judicial, administrative, educative and other appropriate measures to fulfill their legal obligations. The Committee believes that is important to raise levels of awareness about the Covenant not only among public officials and State agents but also among the population at large.[33]

In the international system personal petitions are allowed under the Protocols to the International Covenant on Civil and Political Rights, the Convention on the Elimination of Discrimination against Women, the Convention on the Rights of the Child and the Convention on the Rights of Persons with Disabilities.[34] The Optional Protocol to the International Covenant on Economic, Social and Cultural Rights entered into force on 5 May 2013, and this finally brought personal petition rights to this convention.[35]

Personal petitions allow citizens of many countries to complain about violations of their human rights in their own country. Although these committees cannot make legal orders against these nations, they can publish influential recommendations. These recommendations, known as views, often lead to alteration of offending policies by the state complained about. The final paragraph contained in the views released by the HRC in a case concerning the Republic of Korea stated:

> 10. Bearing in mind that, by becoming a party to the Optional Protocol, the State party has recognized the competence of the Committee to determine whether there has been a violation of the Covenant or not

---

[32] General Comment to the ICCPR 29, UN Document CCPR/C/21/Rev.1/Add.11, 31 August 2001.

[33] General Comment to the ICCPR 31, UN Document CCPR/C/74/CRP. 4/Rev.6, 21 April 2004.

[34] Optional Protocol to the International Covenant on Civil and Political Rights, December 1966; Optional Protocol to the Convention on the Elimination of Discrimination against Women, December 1999; Optional Protocol on the Rights of Persons with Disabilities, December 2006; Optional Protocol to the Convention on the Rights of the Child on a communications procedure, December 2011.

[35] Optional Protocol to the International Covenant on Economic, Social and Cultural Rights, December 2008.

International human rights law 101

and that, pursuant to article 2 of the Covenant, that State party has undertaken an obligation to ensure to all individuals within its territory or subject to its jurisdiction the rights recognized in the Covenant and to provide an effective and enforceable remedy in case a violation has been established, the Committee wishes to receive from the State party, within 90 days, information about the measures taken to give effect to the Committee's Views. The State party is also requested to publish the Committee's Views.[36]

All of the treaty-monitoring bodies that allow individual petitions issue similar statements and will monitor the response of states to the views issued by the committees.

The foundational principle of this system of human rights conventions is the notion of international monitoring of states' compliance with their obligations under the treaty provisions. In order to comply with treaty obligations under all of the international human rights treaties, states parties are required to produce narrative reports on the domestic enforcement of their international obligations. The monitoring committee of international human rights experts then reviews these reports, often in consultation with various civil society organizations, and then questions members of the delegations of the member states. It issues concluding observations on the record of compliance. Each set of concluding observations ends with a statement that the state party should provide relevant information on the implementation of the committee's recommendation within one year.

Concluding observations of the reports submitted by states parties contain startling mandatory language. For example, in the Concluding Observations of Columbia's compliance under the ICCPR, the HRC expressed concern about the significant number of arbitrary detentions, abductions, forced disappearances, cases of torture, extrajudicial executions and murders, and stated:

> The State party should take immediate and effective steps to investigate these incidents, punish and dismiss those found responsible and compensate the victims, so as to ensure compliance with the guarantees set forth in articles 2, 3, 6, 7, and 9 of the Covenant.[37]

In addition to the extensive treaty-monitoring mechanisms, the Human Rights Commission employs special procedures for serious and systemic violations of human rights. The first is the system of appointment by the Human Rights Commission of Special Rapporteurs on various issues in human

---

[36] Views of the Human Rights Committee in Jeong-Eun Lee and the Republic of Korea UN Document CCPR/C/84/D/1119/2002, 12 August 2005.

[37] Concluding Observations of the Human Rights Committee: Columbia 26/05/2005, UN Document CCPR/CO/80/COL, 26 May 2004.

102 *Part II: Evolution in public international law*

rights or specific countries. Special Rapporteurs provide regular reports on their issues, often to the Security Council in addition to the Human Rights Commission. In addition, there can be working groups on thematic issues in human rights, for example the Working Group on Arbitrary Detention. Although the mandates may vary slightly, they are usually to examine, monitor, advise and publicly report on human rights situations in various countries or on a major phenomenon of human rights violations worldwide. These thematic mandates certainly impose common duties on all nations to prevent such abuses as extrajudicial, summary or arbitrary executions, disappearances and arbitrary detention.[38]

The terms of reference for these missions impose strenuous disclosure obligations on states. Although the states in principle provide invitations to Special Rapporteurs, there are mandated rules with respect to these study visits. These include:

(a) Freedom of movement in the whole country, including facilitation of transport, in particular to restricted areas;
(b) Freedom of inquiry, in particular as regards:

  (i) Access to all prisons, detention centers and places of interrogation;
  (ii) Contacts with central authorities of all branches of government;
  (iii) Contacts with representatives of non-governmental organizations, other private institutions and the media;
  (iv) Confidential and unsupervised contact with witnesses and other private persons, including persons deprived of their liberty, considered necessary to fulfil the mandate of the special rapporteur; and
  (v) Full access to all documentary material relevant to the mandate;

(c) Assurance by the Government that no persons, official or private individuals who have been in contact with the special rapporteur/representative in relation to the mandate will for this reason suffer threats, harassment or punishment or be subjected to judicial proceedings;
(d) Appropriate security arrangements without, however, restricting the freedom of movement and inquiry referred to above;
(e) Extension of the same guarantees and facilities mentioned above to the appropriate United Nations staff who will assist the special rapporteur/ representative before, during and after the visit.[39]

Nations comply with these guidelines as revealed in the report of the Working Group on Arbitrary Detentions, which welcomed the cooperation of Iran

---

[38] Conclusions and Recommendations of Thematic Special Rapporteurs and Working Groups, UN Document E/CN.4/2004/3/.

[39] Terms of Reference for Fact-finding Missions by Special Rapporteurs/Representatives of the Commission on Human Rights, available at http://www.ohchr.org/Documents/ HRBodies/CHR/TermsOfReference.doc, accessed 17 November 2015.

International human rights law   103

and Argentina in providing transparency and no major hindrance to the investigations.[40]

To be sure, the regional systems are far more sophisticated and are similar to domestic courts in their methods and procedures. The European Court of Human Rights (ECtHR), the Inter-American Court of Human Rights and the embryonic African Court of Human Rights are mandated to issue legally binding orders including provision for compensation and costs. Consideration of the procedures and jurisprudence of these courts has to be left to others, but these courts support notions of international accountability for domestic human rights enforcement to the extent of having to pay compensation to victims as ordered by an international court. This provides individuals with direct access to these international tribunals and a supranational system of justice for the effective guarantee of domestic obligations.[41] This is only available in a small part of the world, but it is a model that attracts human rights advocates around the world.

Notwithstanding the myriad of enforcement mechanisms, there is no question that the international system is weak and subject to political favouritism with 'no-go areas' of enforcement. This problem has been discussed extensively to the extent that the Human Rights Commission was replaced by the Human Rights Council in 2006.[42] These reforms have not, as yet, changed the Human Rights Committee procedures and there is no effort towards establishment of a universal Human Rights Court.

The jurisprudence of these courts and the views, comments and responses to state reports of the international commissions has been influential and has developed the content and scope of human rights protection. These cases are cited in national courts and inform domestic legislation. As with the general comments, these cases have defined the meaning and scope of human rights obligations. But it is argued here that all of these developments have defined and expanded the concept of responsibility of a state to the international community. Human rights are binding legal obligations set out within treaties and customary international law that can be enforced within the law of state responsibility. This is particularly the case in our next discussion of positive obligations.

Positive obligations and international responsibility[43]

General positive obligations under human rights conventions

It is evident that human rights protection requires different levels and sets of obligations. Positive rights are the entitlement of the person that the state

---

[40] Conclusions and Recommendations of Thematic Special Rapporteurs and Working Groups, UN Document E/CN.4/2004/3/.

[41] R. Higgins, *Problems and Process* (Oxford: Oxford University Press, 1994), p. 95.

[42] UN Doc. A/RES/60/251, 15 March 2006.

[43] See A.R. Mowbray, *The Development of Positive Obligations under the European Convention on Human Rights by the European Court of Human Rights* (Oxford: Hart Publishing, 2004) for

104 Part II: Evolution in public international law

acts in particular ways to benefit the individual, such as providing education or health care. These positive obligations impose duties on states to provide the necessary institutions to ensure the respect of human rights.[44] Closely linked with this notion is the idea of horizontal obligations. Horizontal obligations imply that states parties to human rights conventions ensure that rights are protected as between private individuals, as opposed to vertical obligations that protect the individual from abuse by state power. A concrete example would be an obligation to ensure the provision of crisis housing for persons who are victims of domestic violence, in order that they may escape further violence.

Higgins argued 'a right is just as much a right if its implementation requires positive steps rather than negative abstinence' and that positive duties were increasingly becoming 'part and parcel of the normative requirements of civil and political rights'.[45] This view is borne out by an examination of the treaty provisions and the general comments. Article II of the ICCPR sets out obligations of states:

> Each State Party to the present Covenant undertakes to respect and to ensure to all individuals within its territory and subject to its jurisdiction the rights recognised in the present Covenant, without distinction of any kind, such as race, colour, sex, language, religion, political or other opinion, national or social origin, property, birth or other status.

The article provides for positive horizontal obligations, as the expression 'to ensure' implies that states not only respect rights of individuals but engage in prevention to ensure that rights are not violated by the state or other citizens.

Steiner and Alston discussed the importance of positive duties with respect to international human rights conventions:

> To understand the significance and implications of the rights stated in the ICCPR, CEDAW and other human rights treaties, it is helpful to examine the related duties/obligations of states – even though human rights conventions rarely talk of duties. Attention to such duties both clarifies the significance of the related rights and thus helps to work out ideas, and points to strategies and change. The effort, then, is to decompose a right into its related state duties, and thereby gain a clearer notion of the content or proposed content of the right itself.[46]

---

an excellent survey of the jurisprudence in the ECtHR, and more recently D. Xenos, *The Positive Obligations of the State under the European Convention of Human Rights* (Routledge Research in Human Rights Law) (Abingdon: Routledge, 2013).

44 H.J. Steiner and P. Alston, *International Human Rights in Context*, 2nd edition (Oxford: Oxford University Press, 2000), p. 363.

45 Higgins, *Problems and Process*, p. 100.

46 Steiner and Alston, *International Human Rights in Context*, pp. 180–181.

International human rights law   105

The Human Rights Committee in General Comment 31 discussed both positive obligations and the horizontal effect of human rights obligations:

> The article 2, paragraph 1, obligations are binding on States [Parties] and do not, as such, have direct horizontal effect as a matter of international law. The Covenant cannot be viewed as a substitute for domestic criminal or civil law. However the positive obligations on States Parties to ensure Covenant rights will only be fully discharged if individuals are protected by the State, not just against violation of Covenant rights by its agents, but also against acts committed by private persons or entities that would impair the enjoyment of Covenant rights in so far as they are amenable to application between private persons or entities. There may be circumstances in which a failure to ensure Covenant rights as required by article 2 would give rise to violations by States Parties of those rights, as a result of States Parties' permitting or failing to take appropriate measures or to exercise due diligence to prevent, punish, investigate or redress the harm caused by such acts by private persons or entities.[47]

The practice of regional courts supports the view that the minimum duty required from a state is to ensure that their governments act to ensure an environment where a citizen is protected from public or private violations of their fundamental rights.[48] This is significant as it imposes a layer of obligation on the international community, not just to punish violations of rights but also to ensure a legal and political system designed to ensure these rights exist. This particularly engages with the prevention element of the responsibility to protect, since prevention requires addressing the systemic causes of human rights abuses. These human rights abuses do not necessarily result from governmental action but can also result from a failure to protect citizens from their fellow citizens.

There are also a series of positive obligations set out under the International Covenant on Economic, Social and Cultural Rights and its jurisprudence. These obligations, as with all other human rights conventions, are based on three principles: to respect, to protect and to fulfil. While the principle to respect is the classical non-interference in rights approach, the principle to fulfil implies responsibilities of states to take measures to ensure that individuals are not deprived of their basic rights, including the right to food.[49] In General Comment 3 these have also been termed obligations of conduct and obligations of result.[50]

---

[47] United Nations Document CCPR/C/21/Rev.1/Add.13, General Comment no. 31 (80) adopted 29 March 2004.

[48] *Artico* v. *Italy* (1980) 3 EHRR 1 [33].

[49] A. Eide, 'Economic, Social and Cultural Rights as Human Rights' in A. Eide, C. Krause and A. Rosas (eds), *Economic, Social and Cultural Rights: A Textbook* (Dordrecht: M. Nijhoff, 1995), pp. 21–40.

[50] General Comment 3, 'The nature of States parties obligations', CESCR, 14 December 1990.

106   *Part II: Evolution in public international law*

General Comment 12 on the right to food discusses the positive obligations on the state:

> The right to adequate food, like any other human right, imposes three types or levels of obligations on States parties: the obligations to respect, to protect and to fulfil. In turn, the obligation to fulfil incorporates both an obligation to facilitate and an obligation to provide...The obligation to fulfil (facilitate) means that the State must pro-actively engage in activities intended to strengthen people's access to and utilization of resources and means to ensure their livelihood, including food security.[51]

General Comment 14 also emphasizes positive obligations, arguing that health is a fundamental human right indispensable for the exercise of other human rights.[52] The linkage is also made to other human rights:

> 3. The right to health is closely related to and dependent upon the realization of other human rights, as contained in the International Bill of Rights, including the rights to food, housing, work, education, human dignity, life, non-discrimination, equality, the prohibition against torture, privacy, access to information, and the freedoms of association, assembly and movement. These and other rights and freedoms address integral components of the right to health.[53]

The positive obligations are inherent in the definition of the right. As the Committee on Economic, Social and Cultural Rights stated in their general comment:

> The right to health contains both freedoms and entitlements...By contrast, the entitlements include the right to a system of health protection, which provides equality of opportunity for people to enjoy the highest attainable level of health.[54]

As the Committee on Economic, Social and Cultural Rights only recently provided for individual petition, there is no jurisprudence available. The African Commission, on the other hand, has considered economic, social and cultural rights as they are incorporated into the African Charter on Human and People's Rights. The case decided by this body was *The Social and Economic Rights Action Center for Economic and Social Rights v. Nigeria*. This case dealt with the involvement of the military government of Nigeria in oil production through the state oil company in a consortium

---

[51] General Comment 12, UN Doc. E/C.12/1999/5, 12 May 1999.
[52] General Comment 14, UN Doc. E/C.12/2000/4, 11 August 2004.
[53] Ibid., para. 3.
[54] Ibid., para. 8.

with Shell Petroleum Development. The oil production was alleged to have caused environmental degradation and health problems resulting from the contamination of the environment among the Ogoni peoples. Nigeria was found to be in violation of Articles 2, 4, 14, 16, 18(1), 21 and 24 of the African Charter. Two critical paragraphs of the Judgment supported notions of positive obligations:

> 44. Internationally accepted ideas of the various obligations engendered by human rights indicate that all rights – both civil and political rights and social and economic – generate at least four levels of duties for a State that undertakes to adhere to a rights regime, namely the duty to respect, protect, promote, and fulfil these rights. These obligations universally apply to all rights and entail a combination of negative and positive duties.

> 47. The last layer of obligation requires the State to fulfil the rights and freedoms it freely undertook under the various human rights regimes. It is more of a positive expectation on the part of the State to move its machinery towards the actual realisation of the rights. This is also very much intertwined with the duty to promote mentioned in the preceding paragraph. It could consist in the direct provision of basic needs such as food or resources that can be used for food (direct food aid or social security).[55]

The case also supported the notion of horizontal obligations under economic, social and cultural rights:

> 57. Governments have a duty to protect their citizens, not only through appropriate legislation and effective enforcement but also by protecting them from damaging acts that may be perpetrated by private parties (*See Union des Jeunes Avocats /Chad* [Communication 74/92]). This duty calls for positive action on part of governments in fulfilling their obligation under human rights instruments. The practice before other tribunals also enhances this requirement as is evidenced in the case *Velásquez Rodríguez* v. *Honduras*. In this landmark judgment, the Inter-American Court of Human Rights held that when a State allows private persons or groups to act freely and with impunity to the detriment of the rights recognised, it would be in clear violation of its obligations to protect the human rights of its citizens. Similarly, this obligation of the State is further emphasised in the practice of the European Court of Human Rights, in *X and Y* v. *Netherlands*. In that case, the Court pronounced that there was an obligation on authorities to take steps to make sure that

---

[55] *The Social and Economic Rights Action Center for Economic and Social Rights* v. *Nigeria*, African Commission on Human and Peoples' Rights, Comm. No. 155/96 (2001).

108 *Part II: Evolution in public international law*

> the enjoyment of the rights is not interfered with by any other private person.[56]

The judgment referred to positive and horizontal obligations in the right to shelter. The government's obligation would extend to preventing the violation of any individual's right to housing by any other individual or non-state actor such as landlords, property developers and landowners. This included access to legal remedies and precluding further deprivations, and also extended to the right to food, where it was held that not only should the government not destroy or contaminate food sources, but it should also not allow private persons to destroy or contaminate food sources.[57]

Domestic courts have also begun to consider economic, social and cultural rights. The Supreme Court of India and the South African Constitutional Courts have considered positive obligations on the state to provide economic, social and cultural rights, specifically the rights to housing and medical care.[58]

Positive obligations in refugee and asylum law

Asylum and refugee law is the clearest example of the relationship between positive obligations and international responsibility. This law concerns the duty of states to provide asylum in their own territories to victims of distress who arrive at their frontiers seeking entry. It is a crucial right of physical safety for individuals to leave states where their lives are in danger and to be permitted entry to the first country they reach where they have no fear of persecution.[59] Even though the 1951 Refugee Convention is not clear on a right or duty of granting entrance for persons in need, it has been argued that this is a positive legal obligation, especially noting the Article 33 non-refoulement provision.[60]

Asylum law has its roots in two areas: the obligation to provide for persons who have been shipwrecked and the obligation of neutral countries to offer 'offices of humanity' to belligerents. Neff outlined that in the eighteenth and nineteenth centuries it was common practice in the law of the sea for treaties of friendship to provide for persons shipwrecked in the territories of the contracting states.[61] This principle has evolved in modern international law

---

[56] Ibid.

[57] Ibid.

[58] For an up-to-date list, see the database located at www.escr-net.org/caselaw, accessed 5 August 2015.

[59] G. Robertson, *Crimes against Humanity. The Struggle for Global Justice* (London: Penguin, 2002), p. 105.

[60] Convention Relating to the Status of Refugees, 1951, Article 33, Prohibition of expulsion or return ('refoulement').

[61] S. Neff, 'Rescue across State Boundaries: International Legal Aspects of Rescue' in M. Menlove and A. McCall Smith (eds), *The Duty to Rescue: The Jurisprudence of Aid* (Aldershot: Dartmouth Publishing Company, 1993), pp. 176–177.

International human rights law 109

to encompass the rescuing of persons in distress on the high seas. The 1958 Geneva Convention on the High Seas requires in Article 12 each state party to impose on the masters of all ships under their flag a duty to render assistance to persons in distress on the high seas.[62]

Another field of asylum concerns the duties of neutral countries during wartime. From the seventeenth to the nineteenth centuries the customary law doctrine of neutral countries affording 'offices of humanity' to belligerents was replaced by the rather more precise rules of the law of neutrality.[63] Neutral states had the right but not the duty to afford asylum to victims of war. However, at the end of the nineteenth century these conditions became increasingly detailed and strict. Three different categories of war-related asylum seekers were recognized: able-bodied armed forces, prisoners of war and wounded and sick persons. Different rules were crafted concerning the treatment of each of these on neutral territory. Neutral states that admitted belligerent troops into their territory were required to supply the internees during the internment period with food, clothing and 'relief required by humanity'. This duty of interment had been inscribed into treaty law in the Hague Convention V respecting the Rights and Duties of Neutral Powers and Persons in Case of War on Land of 1907.[64] Article 13 of the Hague Convention on Neutrality on Land stated that, concerning the second category of persons, prisoners of war admitted to a neutral country by belligerent troops were to be set free by the host state government.[65] None of these provisions provided for a duty to rescue the victims of war.

The law after 1945 regarding peacetime asylum for civilian victims of persecution is similar to that governing wartime asylum, in that the basic foundation is the sovereign right of states to decide whether to admit persons. Neff stresses that the question of responsibility concerns the treatment of these people during their stay, rather than on admission per se.[66]

In the historical context, it is critical to see the provisions of the UDHR and the 1951 Convention Relating to the Status of Refugees[67] in light of the guilt on the part of many states that turned away or refused to accept Jewish refugees from Nazism.[68] The UDHR has two provisions on asylum. Article 13(2) of the UDHR provides that 'Everyone has the right to leave

---

[62] Geneva Convention on the High Seas, 29 April 1958, 450 UNTS 82, Article 12. See also the UN Convention on the Law of the Sea, 10 December 1982, UN Doc. A/CONF.61/122 and Corr.1–11 (1982), Article 98.

[63] Neff, 'Rescue across State Boundaries', p. 177.

[64] *Hague Convention* (V) Respecting the Rights and Duties of *Neutral* Powers and Persons in Case of War on Land, USTS 540, 2 AJIL Supp. 117, Articles 11 and 12.

[65] Ibid., Article 13.

[66] Neff, 'Rescue across State Boundaries', p. 179.

[67] UN General Assembly, Convention Relating to the Status of Refugees, vol. 189, p. 137.

[68] An excellent book on Canada's record is I. Abella and H. Troper, *None Is Too Many: Canada and the Jews of Europe 1933–1948* (Toronto: L&O Dennys, 1986).

110 *Part II: Evolution in public international law*

any country, including his own, and to return to his country'. Article 14(1) states that 'every person has the right to seek and enjoy in other countries asylum from persecution'. Even though this has been drafted as a right, there is a corresponding duty on the receiving state to ensure this freedom from persecution.

The 1951 Convention relating to the Status of Refugees is even more explicit. It first defines a refugee as a person 'owing to well-founded fear of being persecuted for reasons of race, religion, nationality, membership of a particular social group or political opinion' who is 'outside the country of his nationality...or who, not having a nationality and being outside the country of his former habitual residence' and 'owing to such fear, is unwilling to avail himself of the protection of that country'.[69] There are a number of articles imposing obligations on states. Two of the critical ones are:

Article 32 Expulsion

1. The Contracting States shall not expel a refugee lawfully in their territory save on grounds of national security or public order.
2. The expulsion of such a refugee shall be only in pursuance of a decision reached in accordance with due process of law. Except where compelling reasons of national security otherwise require, the refugee shall be allowed to submit evidence to clear himself, and to appeal to and be represented for the purpose before competent authority or a person or persons specially designated by the competent authority.
3. The Contracting States shall allow such a refugee a reasonable period within which to seek legal admission into another country. The Contracting States reserve the right to apply during that period such internal measures as they may deem necessary.

Article 33 Prohibition of expulsion or return ('refoulement')

1. No Contracting State shall expel or return ('refouler') a refugee in any manner whatsoever to the frontiers of territories where his life or freedom would be threatened on account of his race, religion, nationality, membership of a particular social group or political opinion.
2. The benefit of the present provision may not, however, be claimed by a refugee whom there are reasonable grounds for regarding as a danger to the security of the country in which he is, or who, having been convicted by a final judgement of a particularly serious crime, constitutes a danger to the community of that country.[70]

[69] UN General Assembly, Convention Relating to the Status of Refugees, Article 1.
[70] Ibid., Articles 32 and 33.

International human rights law 111

In the European Union, the Charter of Fundamental Rights (2000) Articles 18 and 19 are the relevant provisions, which incorporate these *non-refoulement* provisions.

Article 18

Right to asylum

The right to asylum shall be guaranteed with due respect for the rules of the Geneva Convention of 28 July 1951 and the Protocol of 31 January 1967 relating to the status of refugees and in accordance with the Treaty establishing the European Community.

Article 19

Protection in the event of removal, expulsion or extradition

1. Collective expulsions are prohibited.
2. No one may be removed, expelled or extradited to a State where there is a serious risk that he or she would be subjected to the death penalty, torture or other inhuman or degrading treatment or punishment.[71]

Critics argue that non-refoulement is not a right to be admitted to the host country in the first place.[72] It is a curious position that states have a duty to treat refugees humanely, for example not to expel them, *if* the refugees happen to be in a state's territory, but that they have no explicit duty to rescue them by allowing them to enter in the first place has to be seen in a more nuanced way. Logically the de facto rejection at a border of a person would be to 'compel' the person to return to the place where he or she was threatened with persecution. Goodwin-Gill states that even if in 1951 the principle of non-refoulement did not encompass non-rejection at the frontier, state practice and the analysis of international organizations of the past 45 years have established a broader understanding of non-refoulement.[73] 'As a matter of fact, anyone presenting themselves at a frontier post, port, or airport will already be within State territory and jurisdiction.'[74] If the refugee qualifies in the strict legal sense of the term (well-founded fear), non-refoulement applies at the moment of presenting themselves or being within the jurisdiction of the state, and therefore the duty of admission under refugee law applies. Yet one has to admit that state practice to date has not recognized directly correlative duties obliging states to adjust visa and immigration policies accordingly. The Syrian, Afghan and Iraq refugee crisis is just such an example of the variation in admission procedures in Europe.

[71] EU, Charter of Fundamental Rights, 2000.
[72] Neff, 'Rescue across State Boundaries', p. 180; A. Grahl-Madsen, *The Status of Refugees in International Law*, Vol. 2 (Leiden: A.W. Sijthoff, 1972), pp. 94–99.
[73] G.S. Goodwin-Gill, *The Refugee in International Law* (Oxford: Clarendon Press, 1996), pp. 121ff.
[74] Ibid.

112   *Part II: Evolution in public international law*

The broad non-refoulement understanding was reflected in the Convention on Refugees of the Organization of African Unity (OAU).[75] Article II(3) states:

> [n]o person shall be subject…to measures such as *rejection at the frontier* [emphasis added], return or expulsion, which would compel him to return or remain in a territory where his life, physical integrity or liberty would be threatened.[76]

The African Charter on Human and Peoples' Rights, adopted in 1981, provides explicitly in its Article 12(3):

> Every *individual* shall have the right, when persecuted, to seek and obtain asylum in other countries in accordance with laws of those countries and international conventions.[77]

At the international level an attempt to draft a legally binding convention on territorial asylum in the 1970s failed, however.[78] The 1967 Declaration on Territorial Asylum by the UN General Assembly,[79] which states that persons fleeing from persecution have a right of admission into states to whose frontiers they flee, is left as a 'not legally binding' recommendation.

Unfortunately, states continually try to shirk their international responsibility. Europe has been known as 'Fortress Europe' and the United States has been known to turn back Haitian boat people.[80] In 2001 Australia refused landing rights to a Norwegian merchant vessel, the *Tampa*, which had rescued several hundred refugees as part of its maritime legal duty as their boat had sunk.[81] However, the international reaction to that and their subsequent detention practices reveal that there was an understanding that Australia bore a humanitarian duty to land them and to consider their asylum claims.[82]

The United Nations High Commissioner for Refugees (UNHCR) Report on International Protection to the General Assembly, however, reaffirmed the duty of states in paragraph 11:

---

[75] Convention on Refugee Problems in Africa, 10 September 1969, 1001 UNTS 45.

[76] Emphasis added.

[77] Original emphasis.

[78] On this initiative, see P. Weis, 'The Draft United Nations Convention on Territorial Asylum' (1979) 50 *British Yearbook of International Law* 151.

[79] General Assembly Resolution 2312, UN Doc. A/6716 (1967), 81.

[80] Amnesty International, 'The Human Cost of Fortress Europe' (London: Amnesty International, 2014) and CNN International, 'Boat People Fleeing Haitian Crisis', 26 February 2004, available at http://edition.cnn.com/2004/WORLD/americas/02/25/haiti.revolt/, accessed 1 August 2015.

[81] Amnesty International, 'How Tampa became a turning point', 14 June 2007, available at www.amnesty.org.au/refugees/comments/how_tampa_became_a_turning_point/, accessed 1 August 2015.

[82] See, for example, UN Doc. A/HRC/28/68/Add.1, report of UN Special Rapporteur on Torture, 6 March 2015.

International human rights law 113

The 1951 Convention is undermined where people seeking international protection are unable to gain access to territory. Interception on land and at sea, security checks and other measures have made legal access to a territory where asylum can be claimed increasingly difficult...UNHCR continued to train border guards, police, and provincial, immigration and airport officials the world over to enhance awareness of their responsibilities, particularly as regards non-refoulement.[83]

The Council of Europe has issued a similar statement:

Nowhere are the acceleration of procedures and the absence of guarantees more absolute than in the case of individuals returned immediately upon arrival, without even being given the opportunity to apply for asylum at all. This practice is particularly prevalent in the larger airports of Europe, in which, through spurious legal fictions, foreigners are often considered not to have entered the territory of the state. There can, however, be no justification at all for this alarming violation of the principle of non-refoulement.[84]

If states are not complying with these obligations of protecting people, they are 'reminded' by international bodies such as the UN Human Rights Committee (HRC). In its Country Report on Uzbekistan, the HRC states:

The State party should ensure that individuals who claim that they will be subjected to torture, inhuman or degrading treatment, or the death penalty in the receiving state, have the opportunity to seek protection in Uzbekistan or at least assured of non-refoulement (arts. 6 and 7 of the Covenant).[85]

Jurisprudence in the ECtHR also supports notions of positive obligations even though the European Convention on Human Rights (ECHR) does not have an explicit provision on refugees. The Court has held for a non-refoulement if this would amount to a breach of Articles 2 or 3. In such circumstances Articles 2 and 3 establish an obligation not to expel the person in question to that country, thereby engaging the responsibility of the state in question. In the case of *Chahal* v. *UK*, Mr Chahal had been granted leave to remain by the Home Secretary, but following suspected terrorist activities,

---

[83] Executive Committee of the High Commissioner's Programme, Note on the International Protection to the General Assembly, 56th session, 3–7 October 2005, A/AC.96/1008 (4 July 2005).

[84] Council of Europe, Commissioner for Human Rights, 4th Annual Report January to December 2003 to the Committee of Ministers and Parliamentary Assembly, CommDH (2004)10, Strasbourg, 15 December 2004.

[85] Concluding observations of the Human Rights Committee: Uzbekistan, UN Document, CCPR/CO/71/UZB, 26 April 2004, para. 13.

114 *Part II: Evolution in public international law*

his deportation to India was ordered on national security grounds. He was detained for six years pending deportation. The European Court held that Article 3 would be relevant:

> whenever substantial grounds have been shown for believing that an individual would face a real risk of being subjected to treatment contrary to Article 3 if removed to another State the responsibility of the Contracting State to safeguard him or her against such treatment is engaged in the event of expulsion.[86]

Ahmed v. *Austria* found that deportation of a Somali convicted of a serious criminal offence was a violation of Article 3 if the applicant was at risk of being subjected to inhuman and degrading treatment by non-state agents upon expulsion;[87] *Jabari* v. *Turkey* found a violation of Article 3 in the case where deportation would return a woman who had committed adultery to Iraq.[88] Finally, in the case of *Conka* v. *Belgium* the Court held that the detention and return of rejected Roma asylum seekers to Slovakia constituted a violation of Article 5, as well as the prohibition against 'collective expulsion' under Protocol 4.[89]

Statements concerning the non-refoulement provisions of asylum conventions and the jurisprudence of the ECtHR reveal positive obligations to protect citizens of other nations from well-founded fear of persecution. These expansions of positive obligations towards persecuted humanity contained in refugee law are a short leap away from the notion of responsibility to humanity in general. It is also important to note that refugees who claim asylum flee the very situations the responsibility to protect has been designed to respond to. However, if the summers of 2014 and 2015 are any indication, European states are less and less likely to respond favourably to refugee crises. It is estimated that thousands have perished trying to reach Europe by boat.[90]

The evolution of international responsibility in international human rights law

Save for refugee and asylum law, and general statements concerning universality in the international treaties, the vision of human rights discussed thus

---

[86] European Court of Human Rights, *Chahal* v. *UK paragraph 80* (see also *Vilvarajah and others* v. *UK*, 30 October 1991, para. 103).
[87] European Court of Human Rights, *Ahmed* v. *Austria*, Judgment of 17 December 1996.
[88] European Court of Human Rights, *Jabari* v. *Turkey*, Judgment of 11 July 2000.
[89] European Court of Human Rights, *Conka* v. *Belgium*, Judgment of 5 February 2002.
[90] H. Alexander, 'Record Numbers of Migrants Die Trying to Cross into Europe', *The Telegraph*, 30 September 2014, available at www.telegraph.co.uk/news/worldnews/europe/11131118/Record-numbers-of-migrants-die-trying-to-cross-into-Europe.html, accessed 5 August 2015.

far seems mainly focused on the sovereign state and its obligations towards its own citizens or those who seek protection within its borders. However, human rights in the international community is a broader notion than domestic civil liberties. This idea was first expressed in the United Nations Charter and followed in the UDHR. The preamble to the UDHR sets out the key principles of universality and asserts the premise that persons are central to an international rule of law:

> *Whereas* the peoples of the United Nations have in their Charter reaffirmed their faith in the fundamental human rights, in the dignity and worth of the human person and in the equal rights of men and women and have determined to promote social progress and better standards of life in larger freedom.
>
> *Whereas* Member States have pledged themselves to achieve, in cooperation with the United Nations, the promotion of universal respect for the observance of human rights and fundamental freedoms.[91]

This 'universal respect', which is repeated in the general statements discussed above, is reminiscent of natural law philosophy discussed earlier. There are two sides to this obligation, as set out in the UDHR preamble: the obligations of states toward the international community in the observance of human rights and fundamental freedoms, and the obligation of the international community as embodied in the United Nations to promote universal respect for human rights.

Responsibility/obligations of states towards the international community

As we have seen in the discussion of state responsibility, signature of a multilateral convention signifies obligations owed to all the other states parties to that convention.[92] However, human rights are not just a series of treaty obligations. First of all, many of the concepts making up human rights conventions exist in national constitutions and have been acknowledged by most states as legally binding obligations. In the light of state practice, it has been argued that certain human rights have entered into customary international law, and indeed might constitute *jus cogens* and obligations *erga omnes*, violations of which trigger aggravated state responsibility. These would include the prohibition against torture, genocide and slavery and the principle of non-discrimination.[93] The UDHR has influenced many constitutions of

---

[91] Original emphasis.

[92] International Law Commission, Draft Articles on Responsibility of States for Internationally Wrongful Acts, November 2001, Supplement No. 10 (A/56/10), Chapter IV.E.1, as recommended to states in UN Doc. GA Res. 56/83, 12 December 2001, Article 1.

[93] Third US Restatement of Foreign Relations Law, St Paul, 1987, vol. II, p. 161.

116   *Part II: Evolution in public international law*

emerging post-colonial states and was itself influenced by constitutions such as the American Declaration of Independence and the French Declaration on the Rights of Man. As a result it is evident that at least parts of the contents of the UDHR constitute part of customary international law. This is due to the fact that some General Assembly resolutions that purport to contain declarations of rules of international law can emerge as part of the corpus of customary international law.[94]

As the *Nicaragua* case affirmed, customary law and treaty law exist in tandem. Therefore, the content of many of the multilateral conventions also constitute provisions in customary international law.[95] This is particularly the case of the international covenants and the Convention on the Right of the Child, conventions that have attracted almost universal ratification. Sadly, as of yet, there is no study of customary human rights law, which could be conducted in a similar fashion to the International Committee of the Red Cross study of customary humanitarian law.[96]

As discussed above, international human rights law incorporated duties of states to the international community. Some of the human rights originally reflected in the UDHR, such as the right to life, freedom from torture, right to a fair trial and non-discrimination, have also evolved into peremptory norms.[97] As Meron argues, the *Barcelona Traction* case has confirmed that a hierarchy of human rights norms exists.[98] As we have seen in our discussion of the development of international law, these customary norms of *jus cogens* relate closely to obligations *erga omnes*. The codification of the Articles on State Responsibility in the novel idea of aggravated state responsibility specify obligations of states to the international community as a whole, which have resulting, but as not yet specified enforcement obligations.[99] It seems clear, however, that only the most egregious violations of human rights trigger an international response. It is suggested here that this response be part and parcel of the responsibility to protect.

Responsibility of the international community

Within the corpus of human rights conventions, it is the International Covenant on Economic, Social and Cultural Rights that has the clearest

---

[94] For a comprehensive discussion of this subject, see B. Sloan, 'General Assembly Resolutions Revisited (Forty Years Later)' (1987) *British Yearbook of International Law* 37.

[95] *Case Concerning Military and Paramilitary Activities in and against Nicaragua (Nicaragua v. United States of America)* (Merits), International Court of Justice Judgment 27 June 1986, [1986] ICJ Rep 14, para. 175.

[96] J.-M. Henckaerts and L. Doswald Beck, *Customary International Humanitarian Law, Volume I: Rules* (Cambridge: Cambridge University Press, 2005).

[97] T. Meron, 'On a Hierarchy of International Human Rights' (1986) 80 *American Journal of International Law* 1.

[98] Ibid., p. 1, and *Barcelona Traction, Light and Power Company Limited (Belgium v. Spain)* (Second Phase) [1970] ICJ Rep 6.

[99] ILC, Draft Articles on Responsibility of States for Internationally Wrongful Acts, Chapter on Aggravated State Responsibility.

International human rights law 117

statements on responsibilities of the international community. The international community has an obligation to provide aid should positive obligations on states to provide food, housing and health care not be adhered to.[100] The second level emerging from notions of positive obligations and minimum core obligations is to establish the emergence of international responsibility if compliance domestically drops beneath the floor described above. Mbazira argues that the international community has a duty to ensure realization of these rights, and his argument is based on the evidence of aid and development activity in support of economic, social and cultural rights in various African states by the international community, including international organizations and civil society.[101] However, there is also support for international obligation not just in the actions of the international community in delivering aid and development, but also in the provisions and general comments to the ICESCR.

This thesis of international responsibility is first supported by the general statement contained in Article 2(1) ICESCR, which states:

> 1. Each State Party to the present Covenant undertakes to take steps, individually and *through international assistance and co-operation*, especially economic and technical, to the maximum of its available resources, with a view to achieving progressively the full realization of the rights recognized in the present Covenant by all appropriate means, including particularly the adoption of legislative measures.[102]

In General Comment 3 drafted by the Committee on Economic, Social and Cultural Rights (CESCR) the duties under the ICESCR have also been termed obligations of conduct and obligations of result.[103] This positive obligation to fulfil all of the provisions of the Covenant is not only on the sovereign state but also on all states making up the international community. The general comment to this article emphasizes that international cooperation for development and the realization of economic, social and cultural rights is an obligation placed on all states. In the absence of an active programme of international assistance and cooperation on the part of all of those states that are in a position to undertake such a programme, the full realization of economic, social and cultural rights will 'remain an unfulfilled aspiration in

---

[100] ICESCR, Article 2(1).

[101] C. Mbazira, 'A Path to Realizing Economic, Social and Cultural Rights in Africa? A Critique of the New Partnership for Africa's Development' (2004) 4 *African Human Rights Law Journal* 34, p. 39. See also D. Rieff, 'Charity on the Rampage: The Business of Foreign Aid' (1997) 76 *Foreign Affairs* 132, in which he illustrates the pressure on states to provide aid in emergency situations such as Bosnia, Rwanda and eastern Zaire, but see also his analysis that there are 'scoundrels' in the aid world.

[102] ICESCR, Article 2(1), emphasis added.

[103] General Comment 3, 'The nature of States parties obligations', CESCR, 14 December 1990.

118 *Part II: Evolution in public international law*

many countries'.[104] It thus seems evident that the framework of economic, social and cultural rights includes within the positive obligations the duty of all states in the international community that are in a position to do so to provide humanitarian assistance, not just within the framework of a humanitarian emergency but also within the framework of providing aid to realize these critical human rights.

This interpretation of the Covenant by the CESCR is supported in academic opinion. Dennis and Stewart argue that the CESCR has consistently documented that the realization of these rights contain a dimension of international obligation including the general comments as discussed above, but they caution that the degree of this international obligation is not specified in the Covenant.[105]

Another pertinent article in the Covenant mandating humanitarian aid is Article 11, which states in part:

> 1. The States Parties to the present Covenant recognize the right of everyone to an adequate standard of living for himself and his family, including adequate food, clothing and housing, and to the continuous improvement of living conditions. The States Parties will take appropriate steps to ensure the realization of this right, recognizing to this effect the essential importance of international co-operation based on free consent.

Even within this most basic provision for the necessities of life – food, clothing and housing – the importance of international cooperation is set out and is further amplified in the general comment to this article.[106]

This approach is further developed in the analysis of the right to physical and mental health. Article 12 states:

---

[104] Ibid., para. 14.

[105] M.J. Dennis and D.P. Stewart, 'Justiciability of Economic, Social and Cultural Rights: Should There Be an International Complaints Mechanism to Adjudicate the Rights to Food, Water, Housing and Health? (2004) 98 *American Journal of International Law* 462 at 498–500.

[106] General Comment 12 on the right to food discusses the international obligations set out in Article 36. It states: 'In the spirit of article 56 of the Charter of the United Nations, the specific provisions contained in articles 11, 2(1), and 23 of the Covenant and the Rome Declaration of the World Food Summit, States parties should recognize the essential role of international cooperation and comply with their commitment to take joint and separate action to achieve the full realization of the right to adequate food. In implementing this commitment, States parties should take steps to respect the enjoyment of the right to food in other countries, to protect that right, to facilitate access to food and to provide the necessary aid when required. States parties should, in international agreements whenever relevant, ensure that the right to adequate food is given due attention and consider the development of further international legal instruments to that end.' General Comment 12, E/C.12/1999/5, 12 May 1999.

Int*ernational human rights law*   119

1. The States Parties to the present Covenant recognize the right of everyone to the enjoyment of the highest attainable standard of physical and mental health.

International obligation to secure this highest attainable standard is set out in the very developed General Comment 14 adopted by the CESCR in 2004. It includes a framework for international cooperation in providing adequate health care, including economic and technical international assistance and cooperation, which will be accomplished by joint and separate action.[107] The general comment argues that there is inequality in the health status of people, particularly between developed and developing countries, as well as within countries, which is politically, socially and economically unacceptable and is, therefore, of common concern to all countries.[108] There is a critical statement in this general comment of direct relevance to the issues addressed in this chapter:

> 40. States parties have a joint and individual responsibility, in accordance with the Charter of the United Nations and relevant resolutions of the United Nations General Assembly and of the World Health Assembly, to cooperate in providing disaster relief and humanitarian assistance in times of emergency, including assistance to refugees and internally displaced persons.[109]

It has to be noted that general comments are only interpretive instruments with respect to the Covenant, but these comments are highly influential and agreed upon by human rights experts in the area representing the international community of states.

In support of their thesis of international obligation, Dennis and Stewart analyse the analysis of state reports by the CESCR. Although the ICESCR does not require any specific amount of international cooperation or

---

[107] General Comment 14, 'The right to the highest attainable standard of health', CESCR, 11 August 2004.

[108] Ibid., para. 38, and see also para. 39, which states: 'To comply with their international obligations in relation to article 12, States parties have to respect the enjoyment of the right to health in other countries, and to prevent third parties from violating the right in other countries, if they are able to influence these third parties by way of legal or political means, in accordance with the Charter of the United Nations and applicable international law. Depending on the availability of resources, States should facilitate access to essential health facilities, goods and services in other countries, wherever possible and provide the necessary aid when required...States parties which are members of international financial institutions, notably the International Monetary Fund, the World Bank, and regional development banks, should pay greater attention to the protection of the right to health in influencing the lending policies, credit agreements and international measures of these institutions.'

[109] Ibid., para. 40, which goes on to state:

120 *Part II: Evolution in public international law*

assistance, consideration by the CESCR has involved the controversial issue of whether a given state has provided a sufficient level of financial assistance. In its concluding observations to states reports the Committee now urges developed countries to ensure that their official development assistance meets the UN target of 0.7 per cent of GNP.[110]

Another highly influential international declaration is the Millennium Declaration, adopted in 2000 on consensus by all states. Within this declaration, adopting Millennium Development Goals is a pivotal statement on international responsibility:

- **Shared responsibility**
  Responsibility for managing worldwide economic and social development, as well as threats to international peace and security, must be shared among the nations of the world and should be exercised multilaterally. As the most universal and most representative organization in the world, the United Nations must play the central role.[111]

Therefore, it can be established within human rights discourse that international assistance is an important feature in the realization of economic, social and cultural rights as part of a development agenda, particularly in positive

> Each State should contribute to this task to the maximum of its capacities. Priority in the provision of international medical aid, distribution and management of resources, such as safe and potable water, food and medical supplies, and financial aid should be given to the most vulnerable or marginalized groups of the population. Moreover, given that some diseases are easily transmissible beyond the frontiers of a State, the international community has a collective responsibility to address this problem. The economically developed States parties have a special responsibility and interest to assist the poorer developing States in this regard.

[110] Dennis and Stewart, 'Justiciability of Economic, Social and Cultural Rights', pp. 500–501. See also Concluding Observations of the ESCR Committee Ireland, para. 38 UN Doc. E./C./12.1/Add.77 (2002); Concluding Observations of the ESCR Committee Germany, para. 33, UN Doc. E/C.12/1/Add.68 (2001).

[111] United Nations Millennium Declaration, General Assembly Resolution 55/2, adopted 18 September 2000. The Declaration also contains a specific provision for international responsibility in humanitarian aid. It states:

> VI. Protecting the vulnerable

> 26. We will spare no effort to ensure that children and all civilian populations that suffer disproportionately the consequences of natural disasters, genocide, armed conflicts and other humanitarian emergencies are given every assistance and protection so that they can resume normal life as soon as possible.
> We resolve therefore:

> - To expand and strengthen the protection of civilians in complex emergencies, in conformity with international humanitarian law.
> - To strengthen international cooperation, including burden sharing in, and the coordination of humanitarian assistance to, countries hosting refugees and to help all refugees and displaced persons to return voluntarily to their homes, in safety and dignity and to be smoothly reintegrated into their societies.

obligations to fulfil these key rights. It can be concluded, at least with respect to economic, social and cultural rights, that states making up the international community have obligations towards assisting other states in providing economic development.

Conclusion

In the past 70 years the evolution of the content and practice of international human rights law has moved inexorably towards notions of positive duties and obligations towards humanity in general. This is primarily reflected in the well-developed jurisprudence of the European Court of Human Rights and in the general comments and concluding observations of the Human Rights Committee. It is in asylum and refugee law that the linkage is made between national protection and international obligation. Furthermore, the treaty provisions and general comments in economic, social and cultural rights reveal notions of responsibility of the international community to contribute to development.

It is apparent that the scope of treaty obligations, practice and custom impose significant limitations on the conduct of state officials. Yet the revolution in human rights goes even further than imposition of obligations on governmental officials for their own conduct, requiring a positive atmosphere for the protection and promotion of human rights beyond the citizen-to-state relationship.

Nevertheless, ideas of responsibilities to the international community are still controversial in international human rights law, although there is a developing corpus of law supporting this concept. At this point, the notions of *jus cogens* and obligations *erga omnes* only encompass a few of the specified human rights. In human rights catastrophes violations of the rights to life and freedom from torture are the two major components, and they are arguably norms of *jus cogens* that trigger obligations *erga omnes*. Therefore, in situations of large loss of human life and barbarity towards persons, international responsibility is engaged. This is further supported by the next area of international law to be reviewed, international criminal law, which criminalizes violations of these peremptory norms and brings individuals to account under the international judicial system.

5 International criminal law
Responsibilities within the international criminal justice system

Introduction

As we have seen in the discussion of human rights in the last chapter, sovereign states have the primary responsibility for the protection of their citizens and those who live within their borders. In a domestic legal system, the criminal justice system is another one of the primary mechanisms of protection, not only to prosecute crimes that take place between members of the public but also to hold accountable public officials who might be criminally charged for exceeding their legal authority by engaging in practices that threaten the health or safety of the citizenry. In our model of the international legal community, criminal law is also internationalized with a rudimentary justice system holding both public servants and private individuals accountable for international crimes. International crimes are defined as acts that the international community recognizes not only as a violation of domestic criminal law but also as being so serious that they are matters for international concern. All international crimes are also widespread or systemic human rights or international humanitarian law violations.[1] Cassese defines international criminal law as 'a body of international rules designed both to proscribe international crimes and to impose upon States the obligation to prosecute and punish at least some of those crimes.'[2] The community of states has an interest in prosecuting these crimes as they threaten the international legal order, and if they are left unpunished, the resulting culture of impunity may lead to anarchy. Moreover, these crimes imply that individuals in positions of power have responsibility to the international community to ensure international crimes do not take place. This is evident in the number of indictments issued, thus far, in the International Criminal Court (ICC).[3]

---

[1] C. de Than and E. Shorts, *International Criminal Law and Human Rights* (London: Sweet & Maxwell, 2003), p. 13.

[2] A. Cassese, 'International Criminal Law' in M. Evans (ed.), *International Law* (Oxford: Oxford University Press, 2003), p. 721.

[3] For the latest list see www.icc-cpi.int/en_menus/icc/situations%20and%20cases/Pages/situations%20and%20cases.aspx, accessed 25 September 2015.

International criminal law 123

International criminal law as an important branch of international law provides another unique development in international law – which is that individuals participate in the system not only as perpetrators but also as victims. Victims can participate in the international criminal justice system and seek compensation. This is particularly the case in the developments in the ICC, which has formalized victim compensation.[4] The individual becomes subject to the rules of conduct, but is also treated as an object for protection, entitled to receive some type of legal remedy.

Although the provisions of international criminal law may directly impact on the individuals who represent the state, there are specific state responsibilities within the corpus of international criminal law, not only to prosecute and punish in domestic law, but also in many cases to surrender suspects to and cooperate with investigations of other national courts or international tribunals. These obligations are not only reflected in the various resolutions and treaties establishing international criminal tribunals, but also in the content of the offences in international criminal law and the jurisprudence being established in the various tribunals.[5]

The development of international criminal law prior to, and immediately following, the Second World War is the first point of analysis for this chapter. This brief historical survey reveals that obligations of individuals to the international community date from the Middle Ages. However, the Nuremberg process after the Second World War crystallized the content of international criminal responsibility and the idea that perpetrators of international crimes cannot hide behind notions of state sovereignty. The crimes, in themselves, signify the idea of international responsibility, both in terms of aggravated state responsibility in international law and the responsibility to protect.

The second aspect in the development of international criminal law as part of the corpus of responsibility is the steady growth in treaties, particularly in international humanitarian law, that called for international criminal prosecution of individuals if the sovereign state was unable or unwilling to act. The 1990s led to a dramatic increase of activity in international criminal justice, culminating in the establishment of the International Criminal Court and a renewed debate on universal jurisdiction. This analysis will examine both responsibilities of states and rights of victims within the system.

The final part of this review of international criminal law is to formulate how it directly relates to the responsibility to protect and aggravated state responsibility. In terms of the responsibility to protect, international criminal justice becomes involved in the three elements of responsibility: the responsibility to prevent, the responsibility to react and the responsibility to rebuild. At each stage the perpetrators of massive violations of human rights can come into contact with the system of international criminal justice. As far as

---

[4] UN General Assembly, Rome Statute of the International Criminal Court (last amended 2010), 17 July 1998, Article 75, Reparations for the Victim.
[5] Ibid., Part IX, International Cooperation and Judicial Assistance.

124   *Part II: Evolution in public international law*

aggravated state responsibility is concerned, no other state can ignore a situation where international crimes are taking place, and it is argued here that there is an international responsibility to respond.

The Nuremberg legacy

The evolution of international criminal justice is often dated back to the Nuremberg Tribunal, but actually international criminal justice has a much longer pedigree. In 1474 Sir Peter von Hagenback was tried and executed in Breisach, Austria for atrocities committed against civilians from that town. He was tried before 28 judges from the confederate entities of the Holy Roman Empire, which convicted him of murder, rape, perjury and other crimes against the 'laws of God and man'. This is the first recorded trial of an international character.[6]

Captain Henry Wirz, the Confederate Commandant of the infamous Andersonville Prison, was tried by the Union army and executed for war crimes on 10 November 1865. On 23 August 1865 a Military Commission of the War Department, on the orders of the president, filed two charges against Wirz: the first alleging that he had conspired with Jefferson Davis, John H. Winder and various other high-ranking Confederate officials to 'impair the health and destroy the lives' of Union prisoners of war. The second charge had 13 specifications, alleging that Wirz had murdered 13 Union prisoners of war at Andersonville by shooting, stomping, subjecting such prisoners to the mauling of bloodhounds and various other mistreatment.[7] The finding of the Commission referred to international standards:

> And the said Henry Wirz, still pursuing his wicked and cruel purpose, wholly disregarding the usages of civilized warfare, did, at the time and place aforesaid, maliciously and willfully subject the prisoners aforesaid to cruel, unusual, and infamous punishment.[8]

One could argue that this proceeding was a domestic criminal proceeding as the war had ended and the states were once again unified. However, the trial was for events that occurred when arguably two sovereign states were at war – the Union and Confederacy. The notion of civilized warfare discussed in the Commission's finding signified that there were international standards in the conduct of armed conflict that Captain Wirz had violated.

[6] K. Kittichaisaree, *International Criminal Law* (Oxford: Oxford University Press, 2001), p. 14.

[7] The Official Records of the War of Rebellion, Henry Wirz Court Martial, Charges and Specifications, www.civilwarhome.com/chargesandspecifications.htm, accessed on 25 September 2005.

[8] Henry Wirz Court Martial, Finding of the Court, www.civilwarhome.com/findingofcourt.htm, accessed on 25 September 2005.

International criminal law 125

In 1919, after the First World War, a Commission on the Responsibility of the Authors of the War and on Enforcement of Penalties listed 32 categories of violations of the laws and customs of war committed by the governments and armed forces of Germany, Italy, Austria and their allies. It recommended the establishment of an international tribunal that would try individuals for 'order[ing], or, with knowledge thereof and with power to intervene, abstain[ing] from preventing or taking measures to prevent, putting an end to or repressing, violations of the laws or customs of war'.[9] The particular focus was on the German Emperor Kaiser Wilhelm II. Article 227 of the Treaty of Versailles of 1919 mandated that a special tribunal be established to try Wilhelm II for 'a supreme offence against international morality and the sanctity of treaties'. The tribunal was to consist of judges from the United States, Great Britain, France, Italy and Japan.[10] However, it later emerged that the United States was not prepared to support the idea of war crimes being punished by an international tribunal and the Netherlands refused to extradite the Kaiser.[11] The court was established but failed due to a lack of cooperation on the part of countries where the accused persons had been found to surrender them to the court. In the end only 13 German soldiers were brought to trial in Germany and 6 were acquitted. Once again the argument had been that these were offences against international morality, implying an offence against a larger entity than a sovereign state.

In 1921 the Advisory Committee of Jurists appointed by the Council of the League of Nations recommended that the League establish a High Court of International Justice alongside the Permanent Court of International Justice to try international crimes. This proposal did not meet with success due to two objections. The first was that there was a view that individuals were not the subjects of international law, and the other that while war crimes were established, the same could not be said of international crimes in times of peace.[12] Nevertheless, the mere fact that this was attempted by the League of Nations revealed consensus that there were international crimes in times of war.

It was not until the end of the Second World War that international criminal tribunals were finally established to try international crimes resulting from armed conflict. These first courts were the International Military Tribunal at Nuremberg[13] and the Tribunal for the Far East in Tokyo. It cannot be

---

[9] Commission on the Responsibility of the Authors of the War and on Enforcement of Penalties, Report Presented to the Preliminary Peace Conference, 19 March 1919, reprinted in (1920) 14 *American Journal of International Law* 95.

[10] Treaty of Peace between the Allied and associated Powers and Germany (Treaty of Versailles), 28 June 1919 (entered into force 10 January 1920) 225 Consol TS 188, Article 227.

[11] Kittichaisaree, *International Criminal Law*, p. 15.

[12] Ibid., p. 16.

[13] Charter of the International Military Tribunal – Annex to the Agreement for the prosecution and punishment of the major war criminals of the European Axis, 8 August 1945, 82 UNTS 279.

126   *Part II: Evolution in public international law*

seriously argued that these tribunals were true international courts as they were courts of military occupation set up by the four victorious powers, Great Britain, France, the Soviet Union and the United States of America. The jurisdiction of the tribunal at Nuremberg was established by the London Charter on 8 August 1945. Article 6 of the Charter specified that the tribunal was established to try and punish the major war criminals of the European Axis countries for crimes against peace (which were defined as the planning, preparation, initiation or waging of a war of aggression, or a war in violation of international treaties), war crimes (defined as violations of the laws or customs of war) and a new offence, crimes against humanity (defined as murder, extermination, enslavement, deportation and other inhumane acts committed against any civilian population, or persecutions on political, racial or religious grounds). Article 7 specified that the official position of the defendants, whether as heads of state or responsible officials in government departments, would not be considered as freeing them from responsibility. Finally, Article 8 set out that the fact that a defendant acted pursuant to orders of his government did not free him from responsibility, but may be used as mitigation in punishment. These provisions were subsequently repeated in Control Council Law No. 10, entitled 'Punishment of Persons Guilty of War Crimes, Crimes Against Peace and Against Humanity', and which led to many prosecutions of German war criminals.[14]

This was the first recognition by the international community of the existence of crimes against humanity. The Tribunal limited its jurisdiction in this case to crimes taking place during the war, although the specification in the London Charter had been broader to extend to crimes against humanity that took place before and during the war. The significant aspect of this notion of crimes against humanity was that they were crimes regardless of whether they were committed in accordance with the national law of the accused persons. The crimes were punishable by a law superior to that of the law of the state.[15]

It was the jurisprudence, more than the composition of the Tribunal, that set the standard for international criminal justice, both in terms of content of crimes and methods of establishing culpability. Under Control Council Law no. 10 there were several other trials other than the major trial at Nuremberg. However, it was the Judgment at Nuremberg that discussed the relationship between individual and state criminal responsibility. The Judgment included these critical paragraphs on the responsibility of the individual to the international community:

> It was submitted that international law is concerned with the action of sovereign States, and provides no punishment for individuals; and further, that where the act in question is an act of state, those who carry it

[14] Official Gazette Control Council for Germany 50–55 (1946), 20 December 1945.
[15] H. Lauterpacht, *International Law and Human Rights* (New York: Frederick Praeger, 1950), pp. 35–36.

International criminal law 127

out are not personally responsible, but are protected by the doctrine of the sovereignty of the State. In the opinion of the Tribunal, both these submissions must be rejected. That international law imposes duties and liabilities upon individuals as well as upon States has long been recognised. In the recent case of Ex Parte Quirin (1942 317 US 1), before the Supreme Court of the United States persons were charged during the war with landing in the United States for purposes of spying and sabotage. The late Justice Stone, speaking for the Court, said:

From the very beginning of its history this Court has applied the law of war as including that part of the law of nations which prescribes for the conduct of war the status, rights and duties of enemy nations as well as enemy individuals.

He went on to give a list of cases tried by the Courts, where individual offenders were charged with offences against the laws of nations, and particularly, the laws of war. Many other authorities could be quoted, but enough has been said to show that individuals can be punished for violations of international law. Crimes against international law are committed by men, not by abstract entities, and only by punishing individuals who commit such crimes can the provisions of international law be enforced.

...the very essence of the Charter is that individuals have international duties which transcend the national obligations of obedience imposed by the individual State. He who violates the laws of war cannot obtain immunity while acting in pursuance of the authority of the State if the State in authorising action moves outside its competence under international law.[16]

These paragraphs gives the view of the members of the Tribunal that states cannot move outside their legal authority under international law and that the individuals who lead these states will not be above international law. The mandate of the Nuremberg Tribunal was subsequently endorsed by the fledgling United Nations. On 11 December 1946 the United National General Assembly adopted Resolution 95(1), which endorsed the principles of international law recognized in the Charter of the Nuremberg Tribunal. On 12 December 1950, upon the recommendation of the International Law Commission, the General Assembly adopted the detail of crimes against peace, war crimes and crimes against humanity that had been set out in the London Charter.[17]

In the years following the Second World War there were a series of treaties developed by the United Nations and the International Committee of

---

[16] *Judgment of the Nuremberg International Military Tribunal 1946* (1947) 41 AJIL 172 (also followed in this respect by the International Military Tribunal for the Far East).

[17] UN Doc. GA/RES/95(1), 11 December 1946.

128 *Part II: Evolution in public international law*

the Red Cross on international criminal and international humanitarian law, and there was an aborted attempt to create an international criminal code. The Convention on the Prevention and Punishment of the Crime of Genocide of 1948 established that genocide, whether committed in peace or war, was a crime under international law, that the states parties to the treaty undertook to prevent the crime and that the persons responsible would be punished whether they were public officials or private individuals.[18] Lauterpacht in 1950 argued that the state should also be criminally responsible for the breach of the convention due to the 'magnitude of the interests involved'.[19]

A problem with the Convention was that, on its face, in Article 6 it stated that 'persons charged with genocide shall be tried in the territory on which the genocide was committed or by an international tribunal'.[20] This meant no prosecutions for this crime for many years as there was no international tribunal and states did not try their leaders for genocide. This only changed in international practice with the establishment of ad hoc criminal tribunals and the concept of universal jurisdiction, both to be discussed below.

The four Geneva Conventions of 1949 were drawn up to codify the international rules relating to the treatment of prisoners of war and civilians in occupied territory. Each of the conventions contained specific definition of 'grave breaches', which were war crimes under international law for which there was individual criminal liability and for which states had a corresponding duty to prosecute. The states parties of these conventions had the obligation to search for, prosecute and punish perpetrators of grave breaches unless they were handed over to another state party for trial.[21] The Commentary to the Conventions confirmed that the obligations to prosecute was 'absolute' and therefore, according to Scharf, amnesties or impunity from prosecution were not to be granted.[22] These provisions on grave breaches traditionally were held only to apply to international armed conflict. Once again, the provision for prosecution was weak as it compelled states either to prosecute or hand over the perpetrators to other states, which did not occur. *Aut dedere aut punire* – the Latin expression for this duty was an empty phrase, again until the establishment of ad hoc criminal tribunals that provided the enforcement mechanism. Even domestically war crimes trials were very rare and many Second World War criminals escaped punishment in the wake of the commencement of the cold war.

---

[18] Convention on the Prevention and Punishment of the Crime of Genocide, 1948, 78 UNTS 277, Articles 1 and 4.

[19] Lauterpacht, *International Law and Human Rights*, p. 45.

[20] Convention on the Prevention and Punishment of the Crime of Genocide, 1948, Article 6.

[21] M. Scharf, 'The Letter of the Law: The Scope of the International Legal Obligations to Prosecute Human Rights Crimes' (1996) 59 *Law & Contemporary Problems* 41, p. 44.

[22] Ibid.

International criminal law 129

However, Article 1 of the four 1949 Geneva Conventions contained the obligation for states parties to react by any appropriate means to any violation of an international humanitarian obligation, even though the underlying act was not attributable to the state concerned. As this duty was confirmed in Articles 1 and 89 of the Additional Protocol I of 1977 and was given universal ratification of all four Geneva Conventions, there is support for the view that the duty to respond to violations of international humanitarian law has become part of customary international law.[23]

In the 1950s the International Law Commission worked on the Draft Code of Offences against the Peace and Security of Mankind. This Code was to codify the concept of individual criminal responsibility developed by the International Military Tribunals. Article 1 stated that 'Offences against the peace and security of mankind, as defined in this Code, are crimes under international law, for which the responsible individuals shall be punished'. Article 2 set out the criminal acts against the peace and security of mankind, including aggression, terrorism, raising of armed bands against another state and:

(10) Acts by the authorities of a State or by private individuals committed with intent to destroy, in whole or in part, a national, ethnic, racial or religious group as such, including:
  (i) Killing members of the group;
  (ii) Causing serious bodily or mental harm to members of the group;
  (iii) Deliberately inflicting on the group conditions of life calculated to bring about its physical destruction in whole or in part;
  (iv) Imposing measures intended to prevent births within the group;
  (v) Forcibly transferring children of the group to another group.

This part of the article repeated the key provisions of the Genocide Convention and extended, as had the Convention, individual responsibility from members of the state apparatus to private individuals. The next part of the article included acts in violation of the laws and customs of war, and the next two articles repeated the Nuremberg formula that acting under orders or as a member of a government did not absolve an individual from responsibility.[24] Regrettably, the International Law Commission abandoned its work on this international criminal code in 1954 due to lack of agreement on an acceptable definition of the crime of 'aggression'.[25]

In 1973 the International Convention on the Suppression and Punishment of the Crime of Apartheid was adopted and it subsequently entered into force in 1976.[26] Article 1 declared:

---

[23] O. Triffterer *et al.*, *Commentary on the Rome Statute of the International Criminal Court*, 2nd edition (Oxford: Hart, 2008), pp. 1060–1061.

[24] International Law Commission, Draft Code of Offences Against the Peace and Security of Mankind 1954.

[25] Kittichaisaree, *International Criminal Law*, p. 8.

[26] International Convention on the Suppression and Punishment of the Crime of Apartheid, 30 November 1973 (entered into force 18 July 1976) 1015 UNTS 243.

130 *Part II: Evolution in public international law*

1. The States Parties to the present Convention declare that apartheid is a crime against humanity and that inhuman acts resulting from the policies and practices of apartheid and similar policies and practices of racial segregation and discrimination, as defined in article II of the Convention, are crimes violating the principles of international law, in particular the purposes and principles of the Charter of the United Nations, and constituting a serious threat to international peace and security.

In Articles IV and V of the Convention a system of universal jurisdiction was established for the crime of apartheid:

Article IV
The States Parties to the present Convention undertake:

(a) To adopt any legislative or other measures necessary to suppress as well as to prevent any encouragement of the crime of apartheid and similar segregationist policies or their manifestations and to punish persons guilty of that crime;
(b) To adopt legislative, judicial and administrative measures to prosecute, bring to trial and punish in accordance with their jurisdiction persons responsible for, or accused of, the acts defined in article II of the present Convention, whether or not such persons reside in the territory of the State in which the acts are committed or are nationals of that State or of some other State or are stateless persons.

Article V
Persons charged with the acts enumerated in article II of the present Convention may be tried by a competent tribunal of any State Party to the Convention which may acquire jurisdiction over the person of the accused or by an international penal tribunal having jurisdiction with respect to those States Parties which shall have accepted its jurisdiction.

As apartheid regimes no longer exist, this treaty is no longer active, but it is an example of individual criminal responsibility for a state policy and at the same time a treaty establishing universal jurisdiction alongside the possibility of an international tribunal.

The next important multilateral treaty was the 1984 Torture Convention. This convention contained extensive obligations for states parties. It included in Article 2 the obligation to take 'effective legislative, administrative, judicial or other measures to prevent acts of torture in any territory under its jurisdiction'. In Article 4 a state party had to ensure that 'all acts of torture are offences under its criminal law'. The jurisdiction provisions are very complex and do not establish a true universal jurisdiction over offenders, but some type of quasi-universal jurisdiction. In Article 5 the Treaty sets out that, besides the usual territorial jurisdiction:

International criminal law 131

2.Each State Party shall likewise take such measures as may be necessary to establish its jurisdiction over such offences in cases where the alleged offender is present in any territory under its jurisdiction and it does not extradite him pursuant to article 8 to any of the States mentioned in Paragraph 1 of this article.

In Article 8 there is a specific extradition requirement:

1. The offences referred to in article 4 shall be deemed to be included as extraditable offences in any extradition treaty existing between States Parties. States Parties undertake to include such offences as extraditable offences in every extradition treaty to be concluded between them.
2. If a State Party which makes extradition conditional on the existence of a treaty receives a request for extradition from another State Party with which it has no extradition treaty, it may consider this Convention as the legal basis for extradition in respect of such offenses. Extradition shall be subject to the other conditions provided by the law of the requested State.

This treaty did not recommend an international tribunal, and in fact a human rights mechanism was established by the introduction of state reporting and individual petitions to the Committee Against Torture. However, it is clearly an international criminal treaty as it established that any state party had to treat this kind of activity as criminal. It does not state, however, that this is a crime against all mankind. This was not discussed until the famous *Pinochet* decision, as General Pinochet's crimes in Chile did not fall within the restrictive definition of the Genocide Convention.[27]

Cassese has argued two difficulties with the criminal justice treaty system. The first is that states have found means of evading their international obligations. States are not prepared to exercise jurisdiction unless express national legislation to this effect is lacking. Cassese gives the example of Egypt, which has ratified many international treaties on international crimes while failing to enact the necessary domestic legislation with regard to genocide and the 1949 Geneva Conventions. A second method is to enter reservations upon ratification. For example, Morocco stated that only Moroccan courts can deal with genocide in Morocco. A third method is for some states to pass implementing legislation that restricts or narrows the scope of grounds of jurisdiction laid down in the treaties. An example is in the United States legislation implementing the 1949 Geneva Conventions, which engages the active and passive personality principles of jurisdiction rather than universality in contradiction to the treaty.[28]

---

[27] *R v. Bow Street Metropolitan Stipendiary Magistrate, Ex Parte Pinochet Ugarte (No. 3)* [1998] UKHL 41; *3* WLR 1456 (HL 1998).

[28] A. Cassese, *International Law*, 2nd edition (Oxford: Oxford University Press, 2005), p. 305.

132   *Part II: Evolution in public international law*

Cassese has argued that the second difficulty is the lack of a customary international rule empowering or mandating states to exercise jurisdiction over war crimes, crimes against humanity, genocide, aggression, torture or terrorism, in spite of enabling legislation or specific treaty obligations. He argues that there are also no international rules that oblige states to act upon a specific ground of jurisdiction, as the choice of grounds is left to each state.[29] Cassese is no doubt correct, as we can see that each treaty discussed above seems to fall down on its basis of jurisdiction. Nevertheless, this corpus of treaty obligations has meant that in times of human rights crises involving international crimes, the international community is placed under pressure to act.

Unlike the international criminal conventions, human rights conventions are silent concerning any possible criminal consequences of massive violations of the rights enumerated within them. However, these conventions do contain provisions to 'ensure' the rights provided within.[30] A duty to prosecute violators of human rights conventions can be supported by the work of the Human Rights Committee in their consideration of state reports, general comments and communications. The first example is a communication alleging acts of torture in Zaire. The Human Rights Committee in their view stated that Zaire was 'under a duty to…conduct an inquiry into the circumstances of [the victim's] torture, to punish those found guilty of torture and to take steps to ensure that similar violations do not occur in the future'.[31] In consideration of extra-legal executions in Surinam, the Committee urged the government of Surinam 'to take effective steps…to investigate the killings…[and] to bring to justice any persons found to be responsible'.[32] In a case involving disappearances in Uruguay, the Committee found that the Government of Uruguay should take effective steps to bring to justice any persons found responsible.[33]

The Human Rights Committee has also supported this position in their general comments on the right to life and torture. In General Comment 6 on the right to life in 1982 the provision stated:

> 3. The protection against arbitrary deprivation of life which is explicitly required by the third sentence of article 6(1) is of paramount importance. The Committee considers that States parties should take measures not only to prevent and punish deprivation of life by criminal acts, but also to prevent arbitrary killing by their own security forces. The deprivation

---

[29] Ibid., p. 301.

[30] Ibid., p. 48.

[31] *Muteba* v. *Zaire*, Comm. No. 124/1982, 39 UN GAOR Supp. (No. 40) Annex XIII, UN Doc. A/39/40 (1984).

[32] *Boaboeram* v. *Surinam*, Comm. Nos 146/1983 and 148–154/1983, 40 UN GAOR Supp. (No. 40) Annex X, 13.2, UN Doc. A/40/40 (1985).

[33] See *Quinteros* v. *Uruguay*, Comm. No. 107/1981, 38 UN GAOR Supp. (No. 40) Annex XXII, UN Doc. A/38/40 (1983).

International criminal law   133

of life by the authorities of the State is a matter of the utmost gravity. Therefore, the law must strictly control and limit the circumstances in which a person may be deprived of his life by such authorities.[34]

In 1992 the Committee adopted General Comment 20 on Article 7 of the Covenant and stated:

> 8. The Committee notes that it is not sufficient for the implementation of article 7 to prohibit such treatment or punishment or to make it a crime. States parties should inform the Committee of the legislative, administrative, judicial and other measures they take to prevent and punish acts of torture and cruel, inhuman and degrading treatment in any territory under their jurisdiction.[35]

An authoritative decision on this issue is the *Velásquez Rodríguez* case, which read into the American Convention of Human Rights a duty to prosecute. The Court held:

> This obligation implies the duty of the States Parties to organize the governmental apparatus and, in general, all the structures through which public power is exercised, so that they are capable of juridically ensuring the free and full enjoyment of human rights. As a consequence of this obligation, the States must prevent, investigate and punish any violation of the rights recognized by the Convention and, moreover, if possible attempt to restore the right violated and provide compensation as warranted for damages resulting from the violation.[36]

International criminal justice enforcement

It was not until the end of the cold war that serious efforts were made to enforce international criminal justice, with the ultimate culmination of this effort being the establishment of the International Criminal Court. However, a first area of initiative took place in the domestic sphere with the growth of case law debating issues of universal jurisdiction for international crimes. The second development subsequent to the end of the cold war was the involvement of the Security Council in international criminal justice, including the establishment of ad hoc tribunals. The final development was the successful movement towards and establishment of the International Criminal Court.

---

[34] UN Doc. HR1/GEB/1/Rev.5, p. 115.
[35] UN Human Rights Committee (HRC), *CCPR General Comment No. 20: Article 7 (Prohibition of Torture, or Other Cruel, Inhuman or Degrading Treatment or Punishment)*, 10 March 1999.
[36] *Velásquez Rodríguez*, Inter-Am. Ct.H.R., Series C, No. 4 (1989), para. 164.

134   *Part II: Evolution in public international law*

Universal jurisdiction

In a 1990 statement concerning amnesty laws in Argentina, the Committee Against Torture stated: 'even before the entry into force of the Convention Against Torture, there existed a general rule of international law which should oblige all states to take effective measures to prevent torture and to punish acts of torture.'[37] Cassese argued that:

> Human rights have by now become a *bonum commune humanitatis* (a common asset of whole humankind), a core of values of great significance for the whole of humankind. It is only logical and consistent to grant the courts of all States the power and also the duty to prosecute, bring to trial, and punish persons allegedly responsible for intolerable breaches of those values. By so doing, national courts would eventually act as 'organs of the world community'. That is to say, they would operate not on behalf of their own authorities but in the name and on behalf of the whole international community.[38]

This statement represented a clear endorsement of the principle of universal jurisdiction.

Universal jurisdiction is based on the understanding that certain crimes are so harmful to international interests that all states have an obligation to bring proceedings against the perpetrator wherever the crime was committed, or whatever the nationality of the victim or the perpetrator. This is the framework of unlimited universal jurisdiction. In practice, normally the perpetrator or the victim has some connection with the prosecuting state, and this is known as limited universal jurisdiction.

In spite of Cassese's statement and the treaty obligations outlined above, very few states in practice subscribe to even limited universal jurisdiction. There are two issues: the first is whether certain crimes, by their nature, do actually give rise to a right in all states to try the perpetrators, and the second is whether these crimes give rise to only a right or a duty to prosecute the perpetrators. Regrettably, states are still grappling with the first issue and have not yet begun to consider the right v. duty issue.

One of the most famous cases often relied upon to support universal jurisdiction is the *Eichmann* case. The Jerusalem District Court found it had jurisdiction since the charges were not crimes under Israeli law alone:

> These crimes, which struck at the whole of mankind and shocked the conscience of nations, are grave offences against the law of nations itself. Therefore, so far from international law negating or limiting the jurisdiction of countries with respect to such crimes, international law is, in the

---

[37] *O.R., M.M. and M.S. v. Argentina* (1990) UN Doc. A/45/44, p. 111.
[38] Cassese, *International Law*, p. 457.

absence of an international criminal court, in need of the judicial and legislative organs of every country to give effect to its criminal interdictions and to bring criminals to court.[39]

There have been very few cases that rely on universal jurisdiction. The Princeton Principles on Universal Jurisdiction aim to clarify an increasingly important area of international criminal law – one that played a prominent role in the legal proceedings against former Chilean leader Augusto Pinochet in London and in the recent convictions of two Rwandan nuns in Belgium. The principles are being distributed to government officials, judges and legislators around the world as a resource for those seeking to extend international justice.

Mary Robinson in her foreword to the Princeton Principles stated:

> The principle of universal jurisdiction is based on the notion that certain crimes are so harmful to international interests that states are entitled – and even obliged – to bring proceedings against the perpetrator, regardless of the location of the crime or the nationality of the perpetrator or victim.[40]

The crimes covered by these principles include piracy, slavery, war crimes, crimes against peace, crimes against humanity, genocide and torture.

The 14 principles are intended to legitimize the controversial idea that ordinary national courts should be able to hear charges against anyone found within their jurisdiction who is alleged to have committed a serious crime under international law. The principles also intend to regulate the exercise of universal jurisdiction in order to eliminate the chances of improper uses of this jurisdiction. The principles mainly use a 'permissive' language (e.g. 'national courts may prosecute') and do not talk about an international 'obligation' to prosecute. Three of the key principles are:

> **Principle 5** – With respect to serious crimes under international law as specified in Principle 2(1), the official position of any accused person, whether as head of state or government or as a responsible government official, shall not relieve such person of criminal responsibility nor mitigate punishment.
>
> **Principle 7** –
>
> 1. Amnesties are generally inconsistent with the obligation of states to provide accountability for serious crimes under international law as specified in Principle 2(1).

---

[39] *Attorney General* v. *Adolf Eichmann*, District Court of Jerusalem, Israel, Judgment of 11 December 1961.

[40] Princeton Project on Universal Jurisdiction, *Princeton Principles of Universal Jurisdiction*, 2001, at http://lapa.princeton.edu/hosteddocs/unive_jur.pdf, accessed 17 November 2015.

136   *Part II: Evolution in public international law*

Principle 12 – Inclusion of Universal Jurisdiction in Future Treaties

In all future treaties, and in protocols to existing treaties, concerned with serious crimes under international law as specified in Principle 2(1), states shall include provisions for universal jurisdiction.[41]

This last principle is most significant as it makes it an obligation for states to prosecute international crimes no matter where they occur. The fact that they are agreeing to be bound by an obligation under which they have to prosecute international crimes wherever and by whomever perpetrated indicates that the international community takes seriously the responsibility to protect, and believes that prosecution of international crimes is a step towards such protection.

In neither the first nor third *Pinochet* decisions did the Lords rely on universal jurisdiction, except for Lord Millet. He stated:

> In my opinion, crimes prohibited by international law attract universal jurisdiction under customary international law if two criteria are satisfied. First, they must be contrary to a peremptory norm of international law so as to infringe a jus cogens. Secondly, they must be so serious and on such a scale that they can justly be regarded as an attack on the international legal order. Isolated offences, even if committed by public officials, would not satisfy these criteria.[42]

Several of the Judges in the International Court of Justice considered the issue of universal jurisdiction in the *Arrest Warrant* case. In the Judgment the Court stated (para. 41) that it could not rule on the issue of universal jurisdiction in the decision on the merits of the case as Congo had withdrawn its initial claim concerning Belgium's lack of jurisdiction. But the issue of universal jurisdiction was discussed in the separate opinions. Judge Guillaume, in his separate opinion, was very sceptical about universal jurisdiction, stating:

> 12. In other words, international law knows only one true case of universal jurisdiction: piracy. Further, a number of international conventions provide for the establishment of subsidiary universal jurisdiction for purposes of the trial of certain offenders arrested on national territory and not extradited to a foreign country.
>
> 16. States primarily exercise their criminal jurisdiction on their own territory. In classic international law, they normally have jurisdiction in respect of an offence committed abroad only if the offender, or at least the victim, is of their nationality, or if the crime threatens their internal or

---

[41] Ibid.
[42] *R v. Bow Street Metropolitan Stipendiary Magistrate, Ex Parte Pinochet Ugarte (No. 3).*

International criminal law 137

external security. Additionally, they may exercise jurisdiction in cases of piracy and in the situations of subsidiary universal jurisdiction provided for by various conventions if the offender is present on their territory. But apart from these cases, international law does not accept universal jurisdiction; still less does it accept universal jurisdiction *in absentia*.[43]

This view was not accepted by Judges Higgins, Kooijmans and Buergenthal, who issued a separate opinion where the concept of universal jurisdiction was discussed at length:

> 52. We may agree with the authors of the Oppenheim, 9th Edition, at page 998, that:
>
> 'While no general rule of positive international law can as yet be asserted which gives to states the right to punish foreign nationals for crimes against humanity in the same way as they are, for instance, entitled to punish acts of piracy, there are clear indications pointing to the gradual evolution of a significant principle of international law to that effect.'
>
> 73. An observance in the field of international criminal law: As we said in paragraph 49, a gradual movement towards bases of jurisdiction other than territoriality can be discerned. This slow but steady shifting to a more extensive application of extraterritorial jurisdiction by States reflects the emergence of values which enjoy an ever-increasing recognition in international society.[44]

Although these are separate opinions, they may be destined to become definitive statements on universal jurisdiction. It is a shame that the majority decision did not deal with this issue, but the separate opinions clearly point the way to systems of universal jurisdiction. However, due to the controversial nature of universal jurisdiction, the Security Council has acted to advance the cause of enforcement of international criminal law within international tribunals.

The Security Council

Two developments involved the Security Council in international criminal justice: the first was terrorist crimes, specifically the Lockerbie bombing, and the second was the massive abuses of human rights during the civil wars in the 1990s. The Security Council has acted on several occasions through Chapter VII to create binding obligations on states to bring individuals responsible for international crimes to justice. In Security Council Resolution 748 the Council required Libya to surrender to the United States

---

[43] *Case Concerning the Arrest Warrant of 11 April 2000 (Democratic Republic of the Congo v. Belgium)*, 14 February 2002 [2002] ICJ Rep 3.

[44] Ibid., Separate Opinion of Higgins, Kooijmans and Buergenthal.

138 *Part II: Evolution in public international law*

or the United Kingdom for prosecution the two Libyan officials charged with bombing Pan Am Flight 103. The Council also passed a resolution calling for the arrest of Mohamed Farrah Aidid, the Somali warlord who was allegedly responsible for the murder of 24 UN peacekeepers.[45]

The second development was the proliferation of human rights catastrophes in the 1990s. Two key Security Council resolutions established the International Criminal Tribunal for the Former Yugoslavia (ICTY) and the International Criminal Tribunal for Rwanda (ICTR). The ICTY Statute was adopted by the Security Council in Resolution 728 on 25 May 1983. The court was to be based in The Hague. It consisted of Trial Chambers and an Appeals Chamber, and it was empowered to try persons for serious violations of international humanitarian law, genocide and crimes against humanity that had taken place in the territory of the former Yugoslavia since 1991. In this court crimes against humanity had to be committed during the armed conflict.

The ICTR Statute was accepted on 8 November 1994 by Security Council Resolution 955. The Trial Chambers were based in Arusha, Tanzania and the court had jurisdiction over genocide, crimes against humanity and violations of Article 3 common to the Geneva Conventions of 12 August 1949 and Additional Protocol II of 1977. The ICTR was concerned with a civil war and therefore crimes against humanity did not have to have a connection with an armed conflict.

A unique feature of both courts is that they had concurrent and primary jurisdiction with national courts. The purpose of these two courts was not to try all the perpetrators but those who had been the primary figures in the crimes.

The Statutes also called on all states that were members of the United Nations to cooperate fully with the Tribunals, particularly in the apprehension of the persons to be tried.

Article 29 of the ICTY Statute sets out the obligations of states:

Cooperation and judicial assistance

1. States shall cooperate with the International Tribunal in the investigation and prosecution of persons accused of committing serious violations of international humanitarian law.
2. States shall comply without undue delay with any request for assistance or an order issued by the Trial Chamber, including, but not limited to:
   (a) the identification and location of persons;
   (b) the taking of testimony and the production of evidence;
   (c) the service of documents;
   (d) the arrest or detention of persons;
   (e) the surrender or the transfer of the accused to the International Tribunal.[46]

---

[45] Scharf, 'The Letter of the Law', p. 41.
[46] UN Security Council, Statute of the International Criminal Tribunal for the Former Yugoslavia (as amended on 17 May 2002), 25 May 1993.

International criminal law 139

These obligations were mandatory (shall) and comprehensive, and constituted a direct interference with a traditional sovereign activity of bringing criminals to justice. This provision was repeated in the Statute of the ICTR:

Article 28: Cooperation and Judicial Assistance

1. States shall cooperate with the International Tribunal for Rwanda in the investigation and prosecution of persons accused of committing serious violations of international humanitarian law.
2. States shall comply without undue delay with any request for assistance or an order issued by a Trial Chamber, including but not limited to:
   (a) The identification and location of persons;
   (b) The taking of testimony and the production of evidence;
   (c) The service of documents;
   (d) The arrest or detention of persons;
   (e) The surrender or the transfer of the accused to the International Tribunal for Rwanda.[47]

As with the cases of refusal to comply with treaty obligations, it is difficult to secure compliance with these obligations as this involves interaction with the traditional law of extradition.[48] However, generally it has been the case that states have ultimately surrendered the perpetrators for trial.

These courts were the first international courts since the Second World War and they provided impetus to the movement to establish the International Criminal Court. This development of institutions of criminal justice was another important evolution in the sense of individual responsibility to the international community. There have also been additional hybrid courts to try international crimes established in Sierra Leone, Cambodia, Lebanon and the Extraordinary African Chambers in Senegal, all with a large element of international participation.

---

[47] UN Security Council, Statute of the International Criminal Tribunal for Rwanda (as last amended on 13 October 2006), 8 November 1994.

[48] See, for example, Kenneth S. Gallant, 'Securing the Presence of Defendants before the International Tribunal for the Former Yugoslavia: Breaking with Extradition' in Roger S. Clark and Madeleine Sann (eds), *The Prosecution of International Crimes* (New Brunswick, NJ: Transaction Publishers, 1996), p. 355; H. Fox, 'The Objections to Transfer of Criminal Jurisdiction to the UN Tribunal' (1997) 46 *International and Comparative Legal Quarterly* 434; K.J. Harris and R. Kushen, 'Surrender of Fugitives to the War Crimes Tribunals for Yugoslavia and Rwanda: Squaring International Legal Obligations with the U.S. Constitution' (1997) 7 *Criminal Law Forum* 561; S. O'Shea, 'Interaction between International Criminal Tribunals and National Legal Systems' (1996) 28 *New York University Journal of International Law & Policy* 367; E.J. Wallach, 'Extradition to the Rwandan War Crimes Tribunal: Is Another Treaty Required?' (1998) 3 *UCLA Journal of International Law & Foreign Affairs* 59; C. Warbrick and D. McGoldrick, 'Co-operation with the International Criminal Tribunal for Yugoslavia' (1996) 45 *International and Comparative Law Quarterly* 947.

140   *Part II: Evolution in public international law*

The International Criminal Court

The International Criminal Court is an institution based on treaty and does not contain the same mandatory status as the courts created by the Security Council. However, states parties are under a general obligation to cooperate. Cooperation may be loosely divided into two categories: cooperation in relation to the surrender of persons and other forms of cooperation in relation to investigations or prosecutions. The general duty of cooperation is set out in Part 9 of the Rome Statute. This statute contains extensive provisions on the duties of states. The key provisions are:

> Article 86: General obligation to cooperate
> States Parties shall, in accordance with the provisions of this Statute, cooperate fully with the Court in its investigation and prosecution of crimes within the jurisdiction of the Court.

Article 87 contained the provision dealing with lack of cooperation:

> 7. Where a State Party fails to comply with a request to cooperate by the Court contrary to the provisions of this Statute, thereby preventing the Court from exercising its functions and powers under this Statute, the Court may make a finding to that effect and refer the matter to the Assembly of States Parties or, where the Security Council referred the matter to the Court, to the Security Council.[49]

The wording of these provisions is very similar to the wording of Article 29 of the Statute of the ICTY and Article 28 of the Statute of the ICTR.[50] However, in contrast to these Statutes the binding force of cooperation is by treaty, not a Security Council resolution binding on all states by Article 103.[51] According to the Cassese commentary:

> That States Parties are under an obligation to 'cooperate fully with the Court' implies that they are duty-bound to act promptly and with all due diligence, in accordance with the general principle of good faith governing performance of international obligations. It was, therefore, not necessary to spell out explicitly, as the Draft Statute did, that States have to comply without undue delay.[52]

Article 87 is a significant provision, as other sections of this article provide that non-states parties and intergovernmental organizations can be asked to assist

---

[49]   Rome Statute of the International Criminal Court, Articles 86 and 87.
[50]   Triffterer *et al.*, *Commentary on the Rome Statute*, p. 1051.
[51]   A. Cassese, P. Gaeta and J.R.W.D. Jones (eds), *The Rome Statute of the International Criminal Court: A Commentary* (Oxford: Oxford University Press, 2002), pp. 1611–1613.
[52]   Ibid., p. 1613.

International criminal law   141

in the prosecutions. However, the most relevant feature for the purposes of examining international responsibility is the consequence of non-compliance. It is possible for the Security Council, acting under Chapter VII of the Charter, to obligate all member states to cooperate with the Court in a given case, which would be binding under Article 103 of the Charter and not just the Rome Statute.[53] Cassese also argued that under customary international law, all states, including non-states parties, would be obliged to cooperate at least with respect to some of the crimes within the jurisdiction of the and particularly the war crimes set out in the Geneva Conventions (as discussed above).[54]

Schabas is sceptical about the power under the Statute to deal with recalcitrant states:

> What can be done when State parties, who are bound by the Statute to cooperate with the Court, refuse perfectly legal requests for assistance? Art. 87(7) states that the Court may make a finding of non-compliance and then refer the matter to the Assembly of States Parties.
>
> Where the Security Council has referred the matter to the Court, the Court may refer the matter to the Security Council, although this would hardly seem necessary as the Security Council could certainly take action in any case, pursuant to its powers under the Charter of the United Nations.
>
> As for the Assembly of States Parties, its powers, in the case of non-compliance, would appear to be limited to 'naming and shaming'.[55]

In contrast to this view, Cassese argues that there would be powers under the general rules of state responsibility. He argues that the Assembly of States Parties 'would be entitled to ask for the immediate cessation of the international wrongful act and arguably also consider the appropriateness of collective countermeasures, such as economic sanctions, against the non-cooperating State'.[56]

There is also a provision mandating that this cooperation be enacted in domestic law:

> Article 88 – Availability of procedures under national law
> States Parties shall ensure that there are procedures available under their national law for all of the forms of cooperation which are specified under this Part.[57]

Although the provisions on cooperation seem to have little teeth, there are significant reasons both in the law of state responsibility and in customary

---

[53] Triffterer et al., *Commentary on the Rome Statute*, p. 1061.
[54] Cassese, Gaeta and Jones, *The Rome Statute*, p. 1609.
[55] W. Schabas, *Introduction to the International Criminal Court*, 2nd edition (Cambridge: Cambridge University Press, 2004), p. 130.
[56] Cassese, Gaeta and Jones, *The Rome Statute*, p. 1635.
[57] Rome Statute of the International Criminal Court, Article 88.

142 *Part II: Evolution in public international law*

international law why, at least, the states parties will have significant obligations to the international community. Of course the history of cooperation with international tribunals is mixed. Just recently, the South African Government refused to surrender to the ICC President al-Bashir of Sudan, who was wanted on various charges.[58]

Another unique aspect of the International Criminal Court is the role of the victim; although both the ICTY and ICTR had provisions for protection of witnesses, they did not address in any way the special needs of the victims.[59] However, the ICC provides a special Victims and Witnesses Unit that provides counselling and assistance, but also:

> Where the personal interests of the victims are affected, the Court shall permit their views and concerns to be presented and considered at stages of the proceedings determined to be appropriate by the Court and in a manner which is not prejudicial to or inconsistent with the rights of the accused and a fair and impartial trial. Such views and concerns may be presented by the legal representatives of the victims where the Court considers it appropriate, in accordance with the Rules of Procedure and Evidence.[60]

Furthermore, there is a special scheme established for reparation:

Article 75
Reparations to victims

1. The Court shall establish principles relating to reparations to, or in respect of, victims, including restitution, compensation and rehabilitation. On this basis, in its decision the Court may, either upon request or on its own motion in exceptional circumstances, determine the scope and extent of any damage, loss and injury to, or in respect of, victims and will state the principles on which it is acting.
2. The Court may make an order directly against a convicted person specifying appropriate reparations to, or in respect of, victims, including restitution, compensation and rehabilitation.
    Where appropriate, the Court may order that the award for reparations be made through the Trust Fund provided for in Article 79.
3. Before making an order under this article, the Court may invite and shall take account of representations from or on behalf of the convicted person, victims, other interested persons or interested States.

---

[58] G. York, 'South Africa welcomes ICC fugitive to African Union summit', *The Globe and Mail*, 14 June 2015.

[59] ICTY Statute, Article 22, and ICTR Statute, Article 21.

[60] Rome Statute of the International Criminal Court, Article 68.

International criminal law 143

4. In exercising its power under this article, the Court may, after a person is convicted of a crime within the jurisdiction of the Court, determine whether, in order to give effect to an order which it may make under this article, it is necessary to seek measures under article 93, paragraph 1.

5. A State Party shall give effect to a decision under this article as if the provisions of article 109 were applicable to this article.

6. Nothing in this article shall be interpreted as prejudicing the rights of victims under national or international law.[61]

Under Article 79 of the Statute a trust fund is established by the Assembly of States Parties to provide funds for this compensation.[62] These provisions concerning victims are more extensive than in many domestic jurisdictions and provide a pivotal role to be played by the victim, not only during the proceedings but also in a compensation claim. This means that people are not only accountable to the international legal system but they can also hold to account the international criminal justice system, at least for their personal losses.

International criminal law as international responsibility

The responsibility to protect

The ICISS report *The Responsibility to Protect* assigned a role for international criminal law at all three stages in the spectrum: the responsibility to prevent, the responsibility to react and the responsibility to rebuild. In terms of prevention the ICISS argued:

> 3.23 Root cause prevention may also mean strengthening *legal* protections and institutions. This might involve supporting efforts to strengthen the rule of law; protecting the integrity and independence of the judiciary; promoting honesty and accountability in law enforcement; enhancing protections for vulnerable groups, especially minorities; and providing support to local institutions and organizations working to advance human rights.
>
> 3.29 The threat to seek or apply international legal sanctions has in recent years become a major new weapon in the international preventive armoury. In the first place, the establishment of specialist tribunals to deal with war crimes committed in specific conflicts – for the former Yugoslavia, Rwanda and most recently Sierra Leone – will concentrate the minds of potential perpetrators of crimes against humanity on the risks they run of international retribution.[63]

---

[61] Ibid., Article 75.
[62] Ibid., Article 79.
[63] Original emphasis.

144   *Part II: Evolution in public international law*

Therefore, the report argues in the first level of responsibility that having a system of both domestic and international criminal justice dealing with these types of crimes might just prevent escalation of human rights abuses to the level where a forcible reaction is needed. Although the report primarily focuses on the responsibility of states, this part dealing with international criminal law acknowledges that it is individuals who are responsible for repressive state policies and that they should know that they will be held accountable for these crimes.

International criminal law has also played a role in the legal justification for intervention. In the section on reaction, the ICISS indicated amongst other instruments the Statute of the ICC as possible support for the principle of military intervention for human protection purposes:

> 2.26 The notion that there is an emerging guiding principle in favour of military intervention for human protection purposes is also supported by a wide variety of legal sources – including sources that exist independently of any duties, responsibilities or authority that may be derived from Chapter VII of the UN Charter. These legal foundations include fundamental natural law principles; the human rights provisions of the UN Charter; the Universal Declaration of Human Rights together with the Genocide Convention; the Geneva Conventions and Additional Protocols on international humanitarian law; the statute of the International Criminal Court; and a number of other international human rights and human protection agreements and covenants. Some of the ramifications and consequences of these developments will be addressed again in Chapter 6 of this report as part of the examination of the question of authority.

By implication this paragraph argues that evidence that states are not complying with these treaty provisions could signify that the international community might have to react. The provisions outlining international crimes and the duty to cooperate with the International Criminal Court would be fundamental aspects of international obligations, violations of which trigger responsibility to protect. Therefore, if these treaties were not respected, that might be part of a justification for a responsibility to react. Inclusion of the Statute of the International Criminal Court can be explained by the treaty's definition of the international crimes of genocide, crimes against humanity and war crimes as these crimes are often the very reason for the argument for an international reaction in the first place.

Although contained within the section on reaction, there are sections of the report that endorse a system of criminal justice that deals with the perpetrators of crimes after the events and should be part and parcel of a responsibility to rebuild:

> 3.30 Secondly, the establishment of the International Criminal Court – when 60 states have ratified the 1998 Statute – will mean there is new

International criminal law 145

jurisdiction over a wide range of established crimes against humanity and war crimes, some of which are described in greater detail in the Statute than in existing instruments, such as the categories of sexual violence constituting crimes against humanity, and some of which are new, such as the prohibition on the enlistment of child soldiers. The establishment of the International Criminal Court is also to be welcomed as a measure to avoid the accusations of double standards, or 'victor's justice', which are periodically aimed at the specialist tribunals just referred to.

3.31 Apart from these international courts, present or planned, the Geneva Conventions and Additional Protocols (as well as the Convention Against Torture) establish universal jurisdiction over crimes listed in them. This means that any state party can bring to trial any person accused of such crimes. Universal jurisdiction is in any case held to exist under customary international law for genocide and crimes against humanity, and a number of countries have enacted legislation to give their courts jurisdiction in such cases. While these provisions have in the past usually been more honoured in the breach than in the observance, the prosecution and conviction in 2001 in a Belgian court of Rwandan nuns charged with complicity in the Rwandan genocide are an indication that the universal jurisdiction of these instruments is starting to be taken very seriously. Another important legal development occurred with the British House of Lords decision in 1998–99 in the General Pinochet extradition case, which went a long way to void the sovereign immunity of government leaders for crimes against humanity committed while they were in office.

This part of the report supports both universal jurisdiction to try offenders after the event and the International Criminal Court as part of this system of responsibility. The international legal community has to contain both international courts and domestic courts empowered to deal with individual offenders. This is not duplication as the International Criminal Court has been established to deal with only the most serious offenders. This is certainly controversial as states such as South Africa have chosen to employ a Truth and Reconciliation Commission rather than a system of criminal trials.

Aggravated state responsibility

As discussed in the chapter on state responsibility, the whole notion of aggravated state responsibility was developed in response to the negative reaction to a provision assigning criminal responsibility to a state.[64] Notwithstanding

---

[64] See M. Spinedi, 'International Crimes of State: The Legislative History' in J.H.H. Weiler, A. Cassese and M. Spinedi (eds), *International Crimes of State: A Critical Analysis of the ILC's Draft Article 19 on State Responsibility* (Berlin/New York: De Gruyter, 1989) for a drafting history of this article.

146 *Part II: Evolution in public international law*

the deletion of Article 19 and its substitution by Chapter III, the whole basis of aggravated state responsibility seems to be triggered in the event that international crimes occur. Surely an argument can be made that it is the very detail of international criminal law activities provided in *The Responsibility to Protect* report in its prevention, reaction and rebuilding phases that provides the answer as to how states might react to violations of international criminal law triggering aggravated state responsibility. International crimes involve norms of *jus cogens* such as the right to life and trigger the procedural obligation *erga omnes* as set out in Article 48 of ARSIWA, as discussed in Chapter 3.

Conclusion

Criminal law is above all a legal regime of individual responsibility to the community. However, international criminal law is replete with duties of states to cooperate with the emerging international criminal justice system. The International Criminal Court Statute is by far the most sophisticated and comprehensive set of obligations imposed on states parties to the treaty.

It can be seen from the history of international criminal law that crimes of aggression, genocide, crimes against humanity and war crimes are intimately connected with the formulation of public policy measures that violate international criminal law standards. International criminal law holds the leaders of the government, military or other major state actors responsible for paying the penalty for crimes that are initiated by governmental functions. Therefore, international criminal law, unlike domestic criminal law, is closely interrelated with doctrines of the responsibility of states. The debate concerning criminalizing the state itself has been resolved by the Articles on State Responsibility, but there is no question of the close link between aggravated state responsibility and genocide, crimes against humanity and war crimes.

The following extract from the address of the Canadian Prime Minister Paul Martin at the United Nations in September 2004 reflects the argument regarding the relationship of state obligations to people and international criminal law:

> International law is moving in the right direction. Existing instruments such as the Convention on Genocide and human rights treaties do acknowledge states' obligations to their people. The establishment of the International Criminal Court and criminal tribunals are further steps forward. Thus customary international law is evolving to provide a solid basis in the building of a normative framework for collective humanitarian intervention. To speed it along, member-states should now adopt a General Assembly Resolution recognising the evolution of sovereignty to encompass the international responsibility to people.[65]

---

[65] Available at http://pm.gc.ca/eng/news.asp?id=266, accessed 1 August 2005.

International criminal law goes one step further; it not only recognizes within sovereignty international responsibility to one's own people but also to the international community in general. Perpetrators have to answer for violating the international rule of law and have to be held accountable. Victims of these crimes also have another level of protection that they can seek, that of an international legal system. At this point this only extends to states parties of the International Criminal Court and those matters referred by the Security Council. Although the leaders of Sudan have not led their state into becoming a party to the International Criminal Court, the Security Council has voted (with the United States abstaining in spite of its opposition to the ICC) to bring these leaders to account for their actions.

Perhaps the most sophisticated and developed system of international responsibility is not within the areas that would lead to the responsibility to protect. In fact, it is in the rules that have developed in international environmental law, incorporating duties to the international community, which we review in the next chapter.

6 International environmental law

The responsibility to save the planet

With the spectre of climate change causing natural disasters across the globe, environmental issues have become globalized. Held and McGrew argue that 50 years of resource-intensive, high-pollution growth in areas such as Russia, Eastern Europe and the ex-Soviet states, the rapid industrialization of many parts of the South and the massive rise in global population led to 'the globalization of environmental degradation'.[1] Global warming is an issue of universal concern; for example, it is argued that the long-term fate of many Pacific islands rests on actions of tens of millions of private motorists around the globe.[2] It is clear that there is a necessity for a coordinated international effort to stem the tide of global warming – if indeed it is not too late 13 years after the Held–McGrew warning.

One of the main reasons international environmental law is of interest to the responsibility to protect and the international law of state responsibility is the fact that most environmental agreements contain obligations by states to the international community at large. For example, the Montreal Protocol on Substances that Deplete the Ozone Level of 1987 provided that sulphur dioxide emissions were to be reduced by 30 per cent against a certain baseline.[3] This treaty, as with other environmental treaties, required the establishment and enforcement of a domestic regime designed to obtain the necessary reduction in emission that required scientific and technical judgments, bureaucratic capacity and fiscal resources.[4] Another feature of the Montreal Protocol was that it was the first treaty under which the parties agreed to provide significant financial assistance to defray the incremental costs of compliance for developing countries.[5] The instruments resulting from the 1992 United Nations Conference on Environment and Development (UNCED)

---

[1] D. Held and A. McGrew, *Globalization/Anti/Globalization* (Cambridge: Polity Press, 2003), p. 128.

[2] Ibid. p. 129.

[3] *Montreal Protocol on Substances that Deplete the Ozone Layer*, 1522 UNTS 3; (1987) 26 ILM 1550.

[4] See P.-M. Dupuy and J.E. Vinuales, *International Environmental Law* (Cambridge: Cambridge University Press, 2015), pp. 135–141 for discussion of the treaty regime.

[5] Ibid.

International environmental law   149

contained similar provisions and in these treaties the obligations of the developing countries were conditioned on the provision of financial resources by developed countries.[6]

There are too many detailed and complex environmental treaties to canvass in this book; therefore, in this chapter we will review the key principles emerging from the key environmental conferences and treaties with purported customary status. The key principles of environmental law are remarkably similar to the principles in the responsibility to protect with a particular emphasis on prevention (in this case of environmental harm). These principles emerged from the 1972 Stockholm and 1992 Rio conferences and have been incorporated into many treaties. These principles constrain state sovereignty in a similar fashion to human rights and international criminal law provisions. In the second part of the chapter we will review just a few of the key treaties that emerged from the 1992 Rio Declaration, which was a fundamental turning point in international environmental law, and the further incorporation of the principles discussed in Part I. In the third part of the chapter we will consider the emerging debate concerning the responsibility to protect populations from the effects of natural disasters. This chapter will demonstrate that, in the same fashion that the notion of obligations *erga omnes* in human rights emerged, so too did ideas of the responsibility to preserve our planet for future generations crystallize, thus resulting in international legal responsibilities to the international community as a whole.

Environmental law principles

There is a large volume of environmental treaties that emerged from two declarations in the 1970s and 1990s, the Stockholm Declaration and the Rio Declaration. Despite the considerable volume of international agreements that have been concluded in recent years, many commentators contend that there has been little evidence to support assertions of an improvement in the health of the environment.[7] However, principles emerging from these two declarations have arguably become part of customary international law and thus are binding on all states.

The two conferences

The Stockholm Declaration

The 1972 UN Conference on the Human Environment in Stockholm resulted in three major products: the non-binding Stockholm Declaration

---

[6] Ibid., p. 15.

[7] P. Sands and J. Peel, *Principles of International Environmental Law*, 3rd edition (Cambridge: Cambridge University Press, 2012), pp. 14–15, and L.J. Susskind, 'A New World Order in Environmental Policy Making? A Review of the State and Social Power in Global Environmental Politics' (1995) 25 *Environmental Law* 239, p. 242.

150　*Part II: Evolution in public international law*

on the Human Environment,[8] an Action Plan and the establishment of the United Nations Environment Programme (UNEP).[9] According to Sohn, 'Stockholm enlarged and facilitated means towards international action previously limited by inadequate perception of environmental issues and by restrictive concepts of national sovereignty.'[10] The Stockholm Declaration stated the need to 'safeguard and improve the environment'.[11] As a result, this declaration contains 26 principles. The first principle affirms that it is a fundamental human right to 'adequate conditions of life, in an environment of a quality that permits a life of dignity and well-being'.[12] Principle 24 sets out that the protection and improvement of the environment should be handled 'in a cooperative spirit by all countries' through multilateral or bilateral arrangements.[13]

The Rio Declaration

Twenty years later, the Rio Declaration[14] enunciated 27 principles that develop upon those expressed in the Stockholm Declaration. The Rio Conference on Environment and Development is thought to have instigated a 'paradigm shift' in international environmental law in articulating a legal basis for the concept of sustainable development.[15] At the core of the Rio Declaration are Principles 3 and 4, which draw an express link between economic development and environmental protection.[16] Principle 4 provides that 'in order to achieve sustainable development, environmental protection shall constitute an integral part of the development process and shall not be considered in isolation from it'.[17] Principle 2 is a mirror image of Stockholm Principle 21 and will be included in the discussion below of customary law.

---

[8] See Report of UN Conference on the Human Environment, Stockholm 5–16 June 1972, UN Doc. A/CONF.48/14/Rev. 1. For a general discussion of the declaration, see Sands and Peel, *Principles of International Environmental Law*, pp. 30–33.

[9] See Report of UN Conference on the Human Environment, Stockholm 5–16 June 1972, UN Doc. A/CONF.48/14/Rev. 1

[10] L.B. Sohn, 'The Stockholm Declaration of the Human Environment' (1973) 14 *Harvard International Law Journal* 423, p. 424.

[11] Report of UN Conference on the Human Environment, Stockholm 5–16 June 1972, UN Doc. A/CONF.48/14/Rev. 1, para. 4.

[12] Ibid., Principle 1.

[13] Ibid., Principle 24.

[14] Rio Declaration on Environment and Development, UN Doc. A/CONF.151/26 (vol. I)/ (1992) 31 ILM 874.

[15] Peter Sand, 'International Environmental Law after Rio' (1993) 4 *European Journal of International Law* 377, p. 378.

[16] Rio Declaration, and see Principle 3, which provides that '[t]he right to development must be fulfilled so as to equitably meet developmental and environmental needs of present and future generations'.

[17] Ibid., Principle 4.

International environmental law   151

The legacy of the Rio Declaration's impact on international environmental law can be adduced from the fact that the principles set forth in the Rio Declaration are reflected in many subsequent treaties and arguably form part of customary international law. The Rio Declaration has had wide-ranging effects on national legal frameworks and policies, many of which incorporate some or all of the principles contained in the Declaration, including the right of all people to an appropriate environment.[18] Significantly, the Rio Declaration expands the domestic reach of international environmental law[19] in urging states to enact environmental legislation;[20] to facilitate access for individuals to information, decision-making processes and judicial and administrative proceedings at national level;[21] to adopt and 'widely' apply the precautionary approach in environmental legislation;[22] and to undertake environmental impact assessment as a 'national instrument'.[23]

Agenda 21

Another influential and prominent non-binding instrument to have been produced from the 1992 Rio Conference is Agenda 21,[24] a programme of action covering 40 different sectors and topics for introducing sustainable development into national policies, legislation, measures, plans and programmes, including areas such as conservation of biodiversity, combating desertification and managing ecosystems.[25] To fulfil the requirements of Agenda 21, most countries have prepared national environmental strategies or action plans and set up institutions for environmental management. The instrument's most significant impact has arisen through its development of the concept of sustainable development, widening the parameters of environmental policy-making in linking it to broader issues of socio-economic development.[26]

Customary provisions

Principle 21 – prevent no harm

These two conferences were so significant that environmental lawyers propose a series of customary law provisions arising from them. The first of

---

[18] UNEP, *Handbook for Global Environmental Outlook*, Chapter Three: Policy Responses GEO-2000, available at www.unep.org/geo/geo2000/english/text/0134.htm, accessed 17 November 2015.

[19] P. Birnie and A. Boyle, *International Law and the Environment*, 2nd edition (Oxford: Oxford University Press, 2002), p. 97.

[20] Rio Declaration, Principle 11.

[21] Ibid., Principle 10.

[22] Ibid., Principle 15.

[23] Ibid., Principle 17.

[24] UN GAOR, 46th Sess., Agenda Item 21, UN Doc. A/Conf.151/26 (1992).

[25] Ibid.

[26] Ibid., Chapter 1, para. 12 states the need to integrate economic and development concerns for the 'fulfilment of basic needs, improved living standards for all, better protected and managed ecosystems and a safer, more prosperous future'.

152 *Part II: Evolution in public international law*

these – and central to international environmental law's development – are two fundamental objectives: that states have sovereignty over their natural resources and that a state must not cause damage to the environment.[27] Principle 21 of the Stockholm Declaration, which is considered to be the cornerstone of international environmental law,[28] enshrines the two edifices and states:

> States have, in accordance with the Charter of the United Nations and the principles of International law, the sovereign right to exploit their own resources pursuant to their own environmental policies, and the responsibility to ensure that activities within their jurisdiction or control do not cause damage to the environment of other states or of areas beyond the limits of national jurisdiction.[29]

Intrinsic to the Principle 21 formulation is a reaffirmation of the central normative principle of state sovereignty, which permits states to conduct activities within their territories as they choose, even where these activities have detrimental consequences for their own environment.[30] Principle 2 of the Rio Declaration mirrors this language and affirms that every state is free – within the limits of international law – to determine its own environmental and developmental policies and to manage and utilize its natural resources as it wishes.[31]

This is qualified by the second component of the Principle 21/Principle 2 formulation, however, which provides that states have a responsibility not to cause damage to the environment of other states or to areas beyond their national jurisdiction.[32] What this means in practice is that the right of a state over its natural resources is not unlimited and is subject to constraints of an environmental nature. This is very similar to the two-tiered nature of the responsibility to protect, incorporating national and international responsibility.

Principle 21 and the later formulation of this principle, enunciated in Principle 2 of the Rio Declaration, are recognized to represent customary law.[33] It is now widely recognized that states are required to take adequate measures to regulate and control sources of global environmental pollution or transboundary harm that emanate from within their territory.[34] The origin of this rule can be found in the *Trail Smelter* case, where the arbitral tribunal

---

[27] Sands and Peel, *Principles of International Environmental Law*, pp. 190–191.

[28] Ibid., p. 191.

[29] Report of UN Conference on the Human Environment, Stockholm 5–16 June 1972, UN Doc. A/CONF.48/14/Rev. 1, Principle 21.

[30] Sands and Peel, *Principles of International Environmental Law*, p. 191.

[31] Ibid.

[32] Ibid.

[33] Ibid., p. 191.

[34] Ibid., p. 195.

International environmental law 153

concluded that 'no state has the right to use or permit the use of its territory in such a manner as to cause injury by fumes in or to the territory of another or the properties or persons therein'.[35]

In 1996 the International Court of Justice (ICJ) was called upon to provide an advisory opinion on the *Legality of the Threat or Use of Nuclear Weapons*. The Court emphasizes the significance of this and states:

> [T]he Court also recognizes that the environment is not an abstraction but represents the living space, the quality of life and the very health of human beings, including generations unborn. The existence of the general obligation of States to ensure that activities within their jurisdiction and control respect the environment of other States or of areas beyond national control is now part of the corpus of international law relating to the environment.[36]

This ruling confirms the customary status of Principle 21.

Whereas the older *Trail Smelter* case simply focused on trans-frontier pollution and the harm suffered by states, recent international environmental agreements have endorsed the view that states are required to protect global common areas and those areas beyond the limits of national jurisdiction such as the high seas, deep sea bed and outer space.[37] This development is significant as it reflects a new understanding of the obligation not to cause environmental harm outside the bilateral state-to-state framework, but one that also 'benefits the international community as a whole'.[38]

Birnie and Boyle contend that formulations of Principle 21 within treaty language cannot be construed as an absolute prohibition on environmental damage, nor do they confer upon states absolute freedom to exploit their natural resources without constraint.[39] The appropriate balance to be struck between the competing principles of sovereignty and environmental protection will normally be negotiated in the context of the particular treaty.[40] Treaties concerned with land-based pollution, for instance, may offer states more room for manoeuvre than those dealing with pollution from ships or nuclear accidents.[41]

---

[35] *Trail Smelter Arbitration (United States v. Canada)*, Arbitral Trib., 3 UN Rep. Int'l Arb. Awards 1905 (1941).

[36] *Legality of the Threat or Use of Nuclear Weapons*, Advisory Opinion [1996] ICJ Rep 226 at para. 29.

[37] Birnie and Boyle, *International Law and the Environment*, p. 111, and *Trail Smelter Arbitration (United States v. Canada)*, Arbitral Trib., 3 UN Rep. Int'l Arb. Awards 1905 (1941).

[38] Ibid.

[39] Ibid., p. 110.

[40] Ibid.

[41] Ibid.

154 *Part II: Evolution in public international law*

The duty to prevent, reduce and control environmental harm[42]

Where the *Trail Smelter* judgment assessed the 'no harm' principle from the perspective of state responsibility and the obligation to provide reparation for environmental damage, Principle 21, as applied in later conventions, has tended to promote preventative measures to protect the environment.[43] As a result, Birnie and Boyle argue that the rule in Principle 21 extends beyond a mere duty to provide reparation where environmental harm occurs to one of 'prevention and control'.[44] This interpretation was confirmed in the *Iron Rhine* arbitration.[45] Therefore, a state would be expected to introduce the appropriate legislative, administrative and regulatory controls applicable to public and private conduct capable of providing effective protection for the benefit of other states as well as the global environment.[46]

This duty of prevention has been affirmed by international tribunals and supported in a wide range of multilateral environmental agreements and soft law instruments.[47] In the *Case Concerning the Gabčikovo-Nagymaros Project*, the ICJ noted: 'in the field of environmental protection, vigilance and prevention are required on account of the often irreversible character of damage to the environment and of the limitations inherent in the very mechanisms of reparation of this type of damage.'[48]

The preventive approach requires each party to exercise 'due diligence', that is to act reasonably and in good faith and to regulate public and private activities subject to its jurisdiction or control that are potentially harmful to any part of the environment.[49] Thus the principle does not impose an absolute duty to prevent all harm, making the state a guarantor, but rather an obligation on each state to minimize the harmful consequences of permissible activities through regulation.[50]

Sands suggests that the principle of preventative action can be distinguished from the application of Principle 21 as having a freestanding objective of minimizing environmental damage, detached from the component of sovereignty that defines the application of Principle 21.[51] The principle of prevention is nonetheless closely aligned with Principle 21 and is more broadly

[42] Sands and Peel, *Principles of International Environmental Law*, pp. 200–203.
[43] Ibid., p. 200.
[44] Birnie and Boyle, *International Law and the Environment*, p. 111. See, for example, Article 194(2) of the United Nations Convention on the Law of the Sea.
[45] Iron Rhine *Arbitration (Belgium v. Netherlands)*, Award, ICGJ 373 (PCA 2005), 24 May 2005, Permanent Court of Arbitration.
[46] Ibid., p. 112.
[47] Sands and Peel, *Principles of International Environmental Law*, pp. 58–60, and see *Pulp Mills on the River Uruguay (Argentina v. Uruguay)*, Judgment [2010] ICJ Rep 14.
[48] *Gabčikovo-Nagymaros Project (Hungary v. Slovakia)*, Judgment, Merits [1997] ICJ Rep 88, p. 94.
[49] Birnie and Boyle, *International Law and the Environment*, p. 112.
[50] Ibid.
[51] Sands and Peel, *Principles of International Environmental Law*, p. 201.

International environmental law   155

linked with rules on mitigation and precaution, as well more general prescription of information exchange and cooperation, and therefore informs the development of international environmental law in various methodological and conceptual guises.[52]

A duty to cooperate in mitigating environmental risks and emergencies, through notification, consultation, negotiation and in appropriate cases, environmental impact assessment[53]

Another principle that has arguably entered the realm of customary law is the principle of information and consultation.[54] This principle may be described as a subset of the general principle of 'good neighbourliness' enunciated in Article 74 of the UN Charter.[55] The principle manifests itself as an obligation imposed on states to cooperate in the protection of the environment and in the mitigation of environmental risks.[56] According to Handl, the principle of permanent sovereignty includes, at the minimum, at duty of cooperation for the good of the international community.[57]

Formulations of the principle can be detected in various international agreements. The evolution of the principle requiring states to cooperate for the protection of the environment was alluded to in the *Trail Smelter* case and was restated in Principle 24 of the 1972 Stockholm Declaration. Principle 24 of the Stockholm Declaration calls for international cooperation 'to effectively control, prevent, reduce, and eliminate adverse environmental effects resulting from activities conducted in all spheres, in such a way that due account is taken of the sovereignty and interest of all states'.[58] Furthermore, Principle 7 of the Rio Declaration 1992 pronounces that 'states shall co-operate in a spirit of global partnership to conserve, protect and restore the health and integrity of the Earth's ecosystem'.[59]

Although the principle of cooperation, as Cassese asserts, is framed loosely, it does fortify new understandings of the environment as a common amenity to be preserved and protected by states, even where a state has not suffered harm to its own environment.[60] However, the principle merely imposes on states a procedural requirement rather than a substantive

---

[52] T. Iwama, 'Emerging Principles and Rules for the Prevention and Mitigation of Environmental Harm' in E. Weiss (ed.), *Environmental Change and International Law* (New York: United Nations University Press, 1992).

[53] Sands and Peel, *Principles of International Environmental Law*, pp. 203–205.

[54] Ibid., p. 203.

[55] Ibid.

[56] Ibid.

[57] G. Handl, 'Environmental Security and Global Change: The Challenge to International Law' (1991) 1 *Yearbook of International Environmental Law* 3, p. 32.

[58] Rio Declaration.

[59] Ibid.

[60] A. Cassese, *International Law*, 2nd edition (Oxford: Oxford University Press, 2005), p. 489.

156   *Part II: Evolution in public international law*

obligation. In this respect, states are simply obliged to negotiate in good faith and are not limited in their actions in any way should negotiations be unsuccessful.[61]

A subcategory of the principle is that which obliges each state to immediately notify other states of where that other state is at risk of being affected by an accident that has occurred on the first state's territory or in an area under its jurisdiction.[62] The Vienna Convention on Early Notification of Nuclear Accidents[63] greatly contributed to the crystallization of the principle, which was later restated in Principle 18 of the 1992 Rio Declaration.[64] Article 198 of the United Nations Convention on the Law of the Sea 1982 provides that when a state becomes aware of threats of imminent damage to the marine environment, 'it shall immediately notify other states it deems likely to be affected by such damage, as well as competent authorities'.[65]

The precautionary principle[66]

The primary distinction between precaution and prevention is the standard of proof required before preventive action is to be taken to avert environmental harm. In international law the traditional obligation to prevent transboundary harm is triggered after 'convincing evidence' exists that such harm will occur.[67] There is, as such, a focus on foreseeability or likelihood of harm based on knowledge or ability to know.

In contrast, the precautionary approach calls for action even when there is scientific uncertainty about the precise degree of risk or the magnitude of potentially significant or irreversible environmental harm.[68] Principle 15 of the Rio Declaration elaborates a version of this formula. It states:

---

[61] Birnie and Boyle, *International Law and the Environment*, p. 128.

[62] Cassese, *International Law*, pp. 489–490.

[63] Vienna Convention on Early Notification of Nuclear Accidents, 22 March 1989 (entered into force 5 May 1992) 1773 UNTS 126.

[64] Rio Declaration.

[65] Other examples include Article 13 of the Basel Convention on the Control of Transboundary Movement of Hazardous waste, which similarly requires that in an event of an accident during the transboundary movement that is likely to present risks to human health and the environment in other states, those states are to be informed immediately.

[66] Sands and Peel, *Principles of International Environmental Law*, pp. 217–228.

[67] The *Trail Smelter* Tribunal reached a similar conclusion when it stated that, 'under the principles of international law, as well as of the law of the United States, no State has the right to use or permit the use of its territory in such a manner as to cause injury by fumes in or to the territory of another or the properties or persons therein, when the case is of serious consequence and the injury is established by clear and convincing evidence'. *Trail Smelter Arbitration (United States v. Canada)*, Arbitral Trib., 3 UN Rep. Int'l Arb. Awards 1905 (1941), p. 1965.

[68] Birnie and Boyle, *International Law and the Environment*, p. 117.

> In order to protect the environment, the precautionary approach shall be widely applied by States according to their capabilities. Where there are threats of serious or irreversible damage, lack of full scientific certainty shall not be used as a reason for postponing cost-effective measures to prevent environmental degradation.[69]

Therefore, resort to a precautionary approach to environmental protection is based on the assumption that scientific knowledge about the effects of human activities on the health of the environment is still emerging. The situation is compounded by the fact that new activities or substances may be found to be harmful only after irreversible or catastrophic damage has occurred. By focusing on the risk of harm, the precautionary approach seeks to prevent harm that may be serious or irremediable.[70]

The precautionary approach is not merely relevant to transboundary environmental risk, but it is also to be 'widely applied'[71] to global environmental issues such as biological diversity and climate change, as well as domestically in furtherance of the objective of sustainable development.[72] International instruments widely refer to and reiterate the precautionary principle. Various regulatory techniques are encompassed by it: for example, environmental quality standards, regulation or prohibition of hazardous substances, use of the best available technology, integrated environmental regulation and comprehensive environmental impact assessments.[73]

The growing acceptance of the precautionary principle is reflected in its incorporation into numerous multilateral environmental agreements. This principle gave impetus to the negotiations and subsequent adoption of the Montreal Protocol and the United Nations Framework Convention on Climate Change (which will be discussed below).[74] These agreements imposed obligations on states parties despite an absence of firm evidence establishing a causal link between the release of CFCs and the depletion of the ozone layer, the effect of greenhouses gases and climate change.[75]

---

[69] Rio Declaration, Principle 15.
[70] Birnie and Boyle, *International Law and the Environment*, p. 115.
[71] Rio Declaration, Principle 15.
[72] Birnie and Boyle, *International Law and the Environment*, p. 117.
[73] Sands and Peel, *Principles of International Environmental Law*, pp. 218–219.
[74] Montreal Protocol, Preamble, p. 1551; United Nations Conference on Environment and Development, Framework Convention on Climate Change, 1992, 31 ILM 849 (hereinafter UNFCCC); Bamako Convention on the Ban of Import into Africa and the Control of Transboundary Movement and Management of Hazardous Wastes within Africa, 29 January 1991, 30 ILM 775. Article 4(3) UNFCCC calls for the adoption of a preventative, precautionary approach to pollution problems that prohibits the release of substances without waiting for scientific proof to be demonstrated. A strong version of the precautionary principle can be found in the Cartagena Protocol on Biosafety 2000 in Articles 10(8) and 11(8), available at https://bch.cbd.int/protocol/, accessed 17 November 2015.
[75] Ibid.

158   *Part II: Evolution in public international law*

There have been many cases addressing the status of the precautionary principle in international law. A review of these cases at the international, regional and domestic level has led Sands and Peel to conclude:

> There is certainly sufficient evidence of state practice to support the conclusion that the principle, as elaborated in Principle 15 of the Rio Declaration and various international conventions, has now received sufficiently broad support to allow a strong argument to be made that it reflects a principle of customary law.[76]

Sustainable development[77]

Another paramount principle at the crux of modern international environmental law is 'sustainability', which underpins the principle of sustainable development. The most noteworthy aspect of sustainable development is that 'for the first time it makes a state's management of its own domestic environment a matter of international concern in a systematic way'.[78] This dimension of the concept is most apparent in the Convention on Biodiversity, which will be discussed in greater detail below.

The term 'sustainable development' first appeared in the Brundtland Report of the World Commission on Environment and Development, which defined 'sustainable development' as 'development that meets the needs of the present without compromising the ability of future generations to meet their own needs'.[79] Subsequently, the Rio Conference on Environment and Development called for the further development of international law in the field of sustainable development. The Rio Declaration enjoins states to 'decrease the disparities in standards of living and better meet the needs of the majority of the people of the world',[80] and urges states to take cognisance of 'the special situation and needs of developing countries'.[81]

The concept of sustainable development is composed of four elements, which Sands and Peel have described as follows:

1. The need to preserve natural resources for the benefit of future resources (the principle of inter-generational equity);
2. The aim of exploiting natural resources in a manner that is 'sustainable', or 'prudent', 'rational' or 'wise' or 'appropriate' (the principle of sustainable use);

---

[76] Sands and Peel, *Principles of International Environmental Law*, p. 228.
[77] Ibid., pp. 206–217.
[78] Birnie and Boyle, *International Law and the Environment*, p. 85.
[79] Report of the World Commission on Environment and Development, General Assembly Resolution 42/187, 11 December 1987, p. 43.
[80] Rio Declaration, Principle 5.
[81] Ibid., Principle 6.

International environmental law   159

3. The 'equitable use of natural resources', which implies that use by one
   state must take account of the needs of other states (the principle of
   equitable use, or intra-generational equity);
4. The need to ensure that environmental considerations are integrated
   into economic and other development plans, programmes and projects,
   and that development needs are taken into account in applying environmental objectives (the principle of integration).[82]

These four elements are often combined, leading Sands to conclude that the
legal status of each component is not well developed.[83] Although elements
of state practice appear to recognize sustainable use as a guiding principle,
aspects of its application continue to be normatively vague.[84] Nevertheless,
Sands and Peel conclude that '[t]here can be little doubt that the concept of
"sustainable development" has entered the corpus of international customary law, requiring different streams of international law to be treated in an
integrated manner'.[85]

What is vital to the study of the responsibility to protect is that these customary international rules resulting from the Stockholm and Rio Principles
have emerged since 1992, a relatively brief period in time.[86] Furthermore, it
is the aspects of prevention that are so important. Environmental disasters,
in the same fashion as international crimes, must be prevented before they
cause irreparable harm.

Important 'soft law' principles

Despite the ongoing problems associated with implementation, monitoring and enforcement and growing treaty congestion, it is possible to detect
cross-references between treaties and a degree of convergence in many of
the common principles embodied in conventions.[87] The new stream of international 'soft law' sets out principles that, although not legally binding,
represent the policy intentions of many states and thereby enjoin them to
formulate rules and legally enforceable standards in domestic legislation that
move towards the fulfilment of the objectives enshrined in the declarations
and resolutions.[88]

---

[82] Sands and Peel, *Principles of International Environmental Law*, p. 207.

[83] Ibid.

[84] Birnie and Boyle, *International Law and the Environment*, pp. 95–96.

[85] Sands and Peel, *Principles of International Environmental Law*, p. 208.

[86] When this chapter was first drafted in 2005, the precautionary principle and sustainable development were placed under soft law principles and thus have emerged as customary law in the
past 10 years.

[87] P.-M. Dupuy 'Soft Law and the International Law of the Environment' (1991) 12 *Michigan
Journal of International Law* 420, p. 424.

[88] Birnie and Boyle, *International Law and the Environment*, p. 27.

160   *Part II: Evolution in public international law*

Polluter-pays principle[89]

The essence of the polluter-pays principle is that the costs of pollution be borne by the party responsible for causing the pollution. This principle has not received the kind of broad support that the preventative action and precautionary principles have in recent times.[90] Principle 16 of the Rio Declaration, for instance, supports the 'internalization of environmental costs', taking into account the polluter-pays principle, but only 'with due regard to the public interest and without distorting international trade and investment'. An example of an international instrument that refers expressly to the polluter-pays principle is the 1972 Organisation for Economic Co-operation and Development (OECD) Council recommendation on Guiding Principles Concerning the International Economic Aspects of Environmental Policies, which endorses the polluter-pays principle to allocate costs of pollution prevention and control measures, so as to encourage rational use of environmental resources.[91]

Common but differentiated responsibility[92]

Although remnants from the era of the 'New International Environmental Order' have all but disappeared, the principle of common but differentiated responsibilities is the modern manifestation of differential treatment for developing countries.[93] The principle of common but differentiated responsibility finds it roots in the application of equity in general international law.[94] At the heart of this principle is that while all states may have common concerns, normative responsibilities between states can be differentiated on the basis of factors such as the economic development and special needs of a state as its historic contributions to an environmental problem.[95]

The normative principle of common but differentiated responsibility surfaced in the 1992 UNCED and the Rio Declaration in two distinct but related formulations: 'The special situation and needs of developing countries, particularly the least developed and those most environmentally vulnerable, shall be given special priority.'[96] Developing this theme, Principle 7 asserts:

> States have common but differentiated responsibilities. The developed countries acknowledge the responsibility that they bear in the international pursuit to sustainable development in view of the pressures their

---

[89] Sands and Peel, *Principles of International Environmental Law*, pp. 228–233.
[90] Ibid., p. 229.
[91] OECD Council Recommendations C(72)128 (1972), 14 ILM 236 (1975).
[92] Sands and Peel, *Principles of International Environmental Law*, pp. 233–236.
[93] P. Cullet, 'Differential Treatment in International Law: Towards a New Paradigm of Inter-state Relations' 10 *European Journal of International Law* 542, p. 576.
[94] Sands and Peel, *Principles of International Environmental Law*, p. 233.
[95] Ibid.
[96] Rio Declaration, Principle 6.

International environmental law 161

societies place on the global environment and of the technologies and financial resources they command.[97]

Several multilateral environmental agreements (MEAs) provide for differentiated obligations, although the term 'common but differentiated responsibilities' is not explicitly referred to in them.[98] The most unequivocal materialization in a multilateral environmental agreement of 'common but differentiated responsibilities', in those words, is the United Nations Framework Convention on Climate Change (UNFCCC). Article 3(1) provides that '[t]he Parties should protect the climate system...on the basis of equity and in accordance with their common but differentiated responsibilities and respective capabilities'. This provision formed the basis for the differentiated scheme of commitments adopted under the Kyoto Protocol and for the provision of financial assistance and technology transfer to developing countries.[99]

Therefore, the concept of common but differentiated responsibility can be seen as an attempt to achieve an equitable balance between developed and developing states in two respects: first, in setting less onerous standards for developing states relative to developed states, and second, through the provision of 'solidarity assistance' by means of financial and technical assistance with the aim of enabling developing states to meet those standards and treaty obligations.[100]

The 'globalization' of international environmental law and the 'common concern of mankind'

In addition to the adoption of future customary rules, the 1992 United Nations Conference on Environment and Development (Rio Earth Summit) signified a pivotal moment in international environmental law's evolution. With all but six member states of the UN represented, the conference was a landmark in the history of environmental law, confirming the global character of environmental protection and its integration with development. Two new conventions were opened for signature: the UN Framework Convention on Climate Change (UNFCCC), which is sectoral in that it deals with climate and the atmosphere but is widespread in its effects, and the Convention on Biological Diversity (CBD), which seeks to bring together agriculture, forestry, fishery, land use and nature conservation in new ways.[101]

---

[97] Ibid., Principle 7.

[98] Among these are the 1991 protocol to the 1979 Convention on Long-Range Transboundary Air Pollution (LRTAP), and even more pointedly the 1987 Montreal Protocol to the Vienna Convention for the Protection of the Ozone Layer discussed below.

[99] Conference of the Parties to the Framework Convention on Climate Change: Kyoto Protocol (10 December 1997), 37 ILM 22.

[100] Birnie and Boyle, *International Law and the Environment*, pp. 101–103.

[101] *UNFCCC*; Convention on Biological Diversity (CBD) (1992) 1760 *UNTS* 79.

162   *Part II: Evolution in public international law*

The Rio Declaration portends the creation of a 'new equitable global partnership through the creation of new levels of co-operation among states, key sectors of societies and people'.[102] Principle 12 of the Declaration promotes 'environmental measures addressing transboundary or global environmental problems' and states that these 'should as far as possible be based on international consensus'. Importantly, the Rio treaties create institutional arrangements for the transference of financial and technical assistance to developing countries to enable them to achieve goals that are recognized as global objectives. States are encouraged to 'engage in a continuous and constructive dialogue' in pursuit of a 'climate of genuine co-operation' in order to achieve a more 'efficient and equitable world economy'.[103]

With these normative developments, international environmental law entered into a new era based on the assumption of global responsibilities. What has transpired in the post-Rio international order is that international environmental law is no longer simply a system based on bilateralism with a narrow focus on transnational harm; its reach now extends to environmental issues of a truly global nature.[104] The increased move towards multilateral cooperation had already been evidenced in the adoption of the Basel Convention, where it was recognized that combating problems associated with the 'exportation' of hazardous wastes, with particular respect to developing countries, would necessarily involve a global effort.

Birnie and Boyle describe the transition:

> [F]or the first time, the Rio instruments set out a framework of global environmental responsibilities, as distinct from those responsibilities which are merely regional or transboundary in character, such as air or river pollution, or which relate to common spaces, such as part XII of the 1982 UNCLOS.[105]

Where the 1972 Stockholm Declaration had only distinguished between responsibility for areas within and beyond national jurisdiction, the concept of 'common concern of mankind' was employed in the Rio agreements to designate those issues that entailed global responsibilities.[106] Therefore, the Rio treaties expressly denominate climate change and biodiversity as the 'common concern of mankind' and devise global regulatory regimes that attempt to deal with these issues.[107] This is the last and perhaps most

---

[102] Rio Declaration, Preamble.

[103] Agenda 2, Introduction, para. 2.1.

[104] F.O. Vicunna, 'State Responsibility, Liability and Remedial Measures under International Law: New Criteria for Environmental Protection' and A. Kiss 'The Implications of Global Change' in E. Weiss (ed.), *Environmental Change and International Law* (New York: United Nations University Press, 1992).

[105] Birnie and Boyle, *International Law and the Environment*, p. 97.

[106] Ibid.

[107] Ibid.

International environmental law 163

important environmental principle that relates both to the notion of aggravated state responsibility and the responsibility to protect, the idea of an international issue (in this case climate change) representing the common concern of mankind.

According to Birnie and Boyle, notions of global responsibility can be distinguished from transboundary environmental law in the following ways: global responsibilities that are labelled the 'common concern' of the international community may have an *erga omnes* character, comparable to human rights norms, which are owed to the international community as a whole and not just to states who have suffered direct harm. Another incongruity is that although these global responsibilities are held in common by all states, obligations conferred upon developing and developed parties are differentiated in various ways and incorporate elements of 'equitable balancing', which is not the case in the law relating to transboundary harm. Finally, it is in the exercise of these global responsibilities that the application of the precautionary approach can be most clearly evinced.[108]

The concept of 'common concern of mankind' is a modern invention with no prior usage in the context of international environmental law. Consequently, its definition and scope has not yet been fully ascertained.[109] It is clear, however, that the term is not to be read as synonymous with other environmental concepts such as 'common property' or 'common heritage of mankind' (which it will be recalled is a concept that is employed in the context of the global commons) and has a separate meaning of its own as well as different legal implications.[110]

Though the legal status and scope of the concept of 'common concern' remains uncertain, its inception can be attributed to an improved awareness of the fact that where global environmental degradation is concerned, no state, no matter how powerful, is immune to its effects.[111] A greater appreciation of global environmental threats has engaged a corresponding recognition that the continuing degradation of the environment threatens the existence of the common survival of the community of states and mankind itself.[112]

Germane to this appraisal is the adoption of instruments pertaining to the protection of the stratospheric atmosphere and the global climate, both of which epitomize this notion of community interest and mutual dependence. Global issues such as the protection of the ozone layer and climate change that cannot be addressed at the national level are symptomatic of what might

[108] Ibid., p. 99.
[109] Ibid.
[110] Ibid., p. 98.
[111] A.S. Timoshenko, 'Ecological Security: Responses to Global Challenges' in E. Weiss (ed.), *Environmental Change and International Law* (New York: United Nations University Press, 1992).
[112] Iwama, 'Emerging Principles and Rules'.

164   *Part II: Evolution in public international law*

be described as the globalization of international law.[113] Although the Vienna Convention and the Montreal Protocol do not explicitly refer to the phenomenon of ozone layer decimation as the common concern of mankind, it is 'in substance' treated as such in the treaties.[114]

The notion of 'common concern' combines both spatial and temporal elements, inviting consideration of the biosphere in its entirety because of the interdependence of all its elements within states and the global commons, and the need to preserve the ecosystem for the benefit of future generations. Thus there is implicit acceptance of the artificiality of spatial boundaries in the context of climate change and a recognition that the phenomena of global warming and climate change are to be treated differently from problems of transboundary air pollution, which are regional or bilateral in character.[115]

While the global atmosphere cannot be characterized as common property, and is therefore outside the domain of sovereignty of individual states, it is acknowledged that global warming and climate change are issues that affect the international community as a whole. Birnie and Boyle state: '[I]t is immaterial whether the global atmosphere comprises air space under the sovereignty of a subjacent state or not: it is a "common resource" of vital interest to mankind.'[116] This proposition was reinforced in UN General Assembly Resolution 45/53 that declared global climate change to be 'the common concern of mankind'. The United Nations Framework Convention on Climate Change constructs a global regulatory regime based on international cooperation designed to mitigate the ill effects of global climate change.

United Nations Framework Convention on Climate Change

The UN Framework Convention on Climate Change (UNFCCC)[117] was adopted in 1992. Notably, the UNFCCC was the first agreement to be negotiated by virtually all members of the international community.[118] The preamble of the Framework Convention describes the global stratosphere as the 'common concern of mankind'.[119]

The objective of the Convention is stated in Article 2, which calls for the stabilization (rather than the reversal) of greenhouse gases in the atmosphere 'at a level that would prevent dangerous anthropogenic interference with the climate system'.[120] The Convention does not specify what that the stabilization level might be, although it does assert that: '[Parties] should take

---

[113] J.L. Dunoff, 'From Green to Global: Towards the Transformation of International Environmental Law' (1995) 19 *Harvard Environmental Law Review* 241, p. 273.

[114] Birnie and Boyle, *International Law and the Environment*, p. 97.

[115] Ibid., p. 98.

[116] Ibid.

[117] *UNFCCC (1992)* 1771 *UNTS* 107, in force 21 March 1994.

[118] Sands and Peel, *Principles of International Environmental Law*, p. 276.

[119] *UNFCCC*, Preamble.

[120] Ibid., Article 2.

International environmental law **165**

precautionary measures to anticipate, prevent or minimize the causes of climate change and mitigate its adverse effects.'[121]

Parties are to draw upon the 'guiding principles' enunciated in Article 3 of the Convention when undertaking efforts to meet their obligations under the Convention. These principles are based on those expressed in the Rio Declaration and Agenda 21 and include the concept of 'intergenerational equity', the 'precautionary principle', 'common but differentiated responsibility' and the right of all parties to 'sustainable development'. In this respect Article 3 of the UNFCCC is novel in that it sketches out the contours of the subsequent instruments that are to flesh out these principles while still providing considerable manoeuvrability in how they are to be interpreted.[122]

Article 4 is based on the principle of common but differentiated responsibilities.[123] Consequently, although the obligations set forth in Article 4(1) are 'subject to specific national and regional development priorities, objectives and circumstances', they are common to all parties to the Convention. The more specific commitments inscribed in Article 4(2) apply only to developed countries and economies in transition, referred to collectively as Annex I parties.

The Convention also contains a number of provisions designed to assist developing countries in meeting their commitment through the provision of funding as well as through technology transfer.[124] Article 4(1) elaborates a number of obligations that are to be achieved by the contracting parties. Parties undertake responsibilities to inter alia:

- develop, update and publish national inventories of anthropogenic emission by sources and removal of sinks;[125]
- formulate, implement and update national and regional programmes containing measures to mitigate climate change by addressing anthropogenic emissions by sources and removals by sinks of all greenhouse gases not controlled by the Montreal Protocol;
- cooperate in preparing for adaptation to the impacts of climate change and to take climate change considerations into account to the extent feasible in their relevant social, economic and environmental policies.[126]

Although these general obligations encourage states parties to give greater consideration to the issue of climate change when formulating national

---

[121] Ibid., Article 3(3).

[122] Birnie and Boyle, *International Law and the Environment*, p. 525.

[123] *UNFCCC*, Article 3(3).

[124] Ibid., Article 4(3)–4(10).

[125] Ibid., Article 1(8) defines this as 'as any process, activity or mechanism which removes a greenhouse gas, an aerosol or a precursor of a greenhouse gas from the atmosphere of all greenhouse gases not covered by the Montréal Protocol'.

[126] Ibid., Article 4(1).

166 *Part II: Evolution in public international law*

policies, they fall short of prescribing specific international standards of conduct upon states with respect to climate change policies.[127]

Additionally, developed countries are to 'provide such financial resources, including for the transfer of technology, needed by the developing country Parties to meet the agreed full incremental costs of implementing measures' under the Convention and to generally assist them in adapting to the adverse effects of climate change.[128] The Convention, like the Montreal Protocol, expressly accepts that the implementation of their commitments by developing countries will depend on 'the effective implementation of financial commitments by developed countries'.[129] Special attention is to be accorded to the needs of least-developed countries, in particular those states most vulnerable to the adverse effects of climate change, for instance low-lying states.[130]

The Convention establishes more specific commitments under Article 4(2), although the compromised language has meant that the provision does not, in substance, ascribe significantly stronger obligations than those general commitments outlined in Article 4(1), described above.[131]

Under Article 4(2)(a) of the Convention, developed countries and other Annex I parties are to 'adopt national policies and to take corresponding measures on the mitigation of climate change, by limiting [their] anthropogenic emissions of greenhouse gases and protecting and enhancing [their] greenhouse gas sinks and reservoirs'. Non-Annex I countries (developing countries) are exempted from having to assume responsibilities under Article 4(2). In deciding upon measures to be undertaken under this provision, Annex I countries are able to take account of their individual circumstances, resources and economies in order to achieve the 'equitable and appropriate contributions of each of these Parties to the global effort'.[132] This accords a considerable degree of flexibility to states in transposing commitments.

Article 4(2)(b) refers to the 'aim' of returning emission to 1990 levels 'by the end of the decade' (2000) without specifying a date by which the return is to be achieved. To be clear, the above provisions describe 'soft targets', rather than concrete and binding terms, with the aim of returning emissions to the 1990 levels by the end of the decade.[133] Developed countries and other Annex I parties are merely required to submit within six months of the Convention coming into force, and periodically thereafter, detailed information on national measures implemented with the aim of returning anthropogenic emissions to the 1990 levels.[134] This information is to be reviewed by the Conference of the Parties (COP) on a periodic basis.[135]

---

[127] Birnie and Boyle, *International Law and the Environment*, p. 523.
[128] *UNFCCC*, Article 4(3).
[129] Ibid., Article 4(3) and 4(7).
[130] Ibid., Article 4(8).
[131] Birnie and Boyle, *International Law and the Environment*, p. 525.
[132] *UNFCCC*, Article 4(2)(a).
[133] Sands and Peel, *Principles of International Environmental Law*, p. 280.
[134] *UNFCCC*, Article 4(2)(b).
[135] Ibid., Article 4(4).

International environmental law 167

The Convention establishes reporting requirements for the communication of certain information. Parties are required to communicate information on implementation, national inventories of anthropogenic emission by sources and removal of sinks not controlled by the Montreal Protocol, general information on steps taken to implement the Protocol, as well as any other information relevant to the implementation of the Convention.[136]

Annex I parties are to provide information relating to measures and policies taken to fulfil commitments under Article 4(2)(a) and (b) as well as specific estimates on the effect these policies are likely to have on emissions and removals by 2000.[137]

The COP is established as the supreme body of the Convention and performs various functions, inter alia: periodically examining the obligations of the parties and the institutional arrangements of the Convention; considering and adopting regular reports on implementation; and making recommendations on issues relevant to the effective implementation of the Convention.[138] In addition, the Convention provides for a secretariat, together with a subsidiary body for scientific and technological advice and a subsidiary body for implementation.[139]

It was decided at the first session of the COP, following the Convention's entry into force, that the commitments established under the Framework Convention did not constitute an adequate response to the pressing problem of global climate change. Subsequently, preparations began to draft a further legal instrument, which would strengthen the commitments of Annex I parties.[140] This was the Kyoto Protocol.

Protocol to the Framework Convention on Climate Change (the Kyoto Protocol)

The Kyoto Protocol[141] was adopted in 1997. In an important development, the Kyoto Protocol introduces legally binding commitments for Annex I parties to reduce global greenhouse gas (GHG) emissions by more than 5 per cent below 1990 baseline levels by 2008–2012.

The main obligation under the Protocol is set out in Article 3(1), which provides that Annex I parties 'shall individually, or jointly, ensure that their aggregate anthropogenic carbon dioxide equivalent emissions...do not exceed their assigned amounts'.[142] The six main GHGs covered are listed in

---

[136] Ibid., Articles 4(1)(j) and 12(1).

[137] Ibid., Article 12(2).

[138] Ibid., Article 7.

[139] Ibid., Articles 8–10.

[140] See Decision 1/CP. 3. Report of the Conference of the Parties on its third session, Kyoto 1–11 December 1997, FCCC/CP/1997/7/Add.1.

[141] Protocol to the Framework Convention on Climate Change (Kyoto Protocol) (1998) 37 ILM 22, entry into force 16 January 2005.

[142] Ibid., Article 3(1).

168 *Part II: Evolution in public international law*

Annex A of the Protocol. Reductions in the three most important gases – CO_2, CH_4 and N_2O – will be measured against a base year of 1990.[143]

In accordance with Article 4(2)(a) of the UNFCCC, different limits are set for each party in deference to the particular circumstance pertaining to the individual state. Therefore, Annex I countries are obliged to limit and reduce their greenhouse gas emission levels in accordance with their respective assigned amounts, inscribed in Annex B of the Protocol. The reduction commitments for each Annex B party (Annex I parties under the Framework Convention) range from an 8 per cent reduction to a 10 per cent increase by the first commitment period of 2008–2012, calculated as an average over these five years. The Protocol also allows states to aggregate their emissions, thus enabling European Union members to be treated as a unit.[144] To date, the Kyoto Protocol has been ratified by almost all Annex I states and 192 states in the world, an astonishing number; but as with the Statute of the International Criminal Court, the most notable exception is the United States. However, in this case, most regrettably and egregious to this author, Canada renounced the Convention effective 15 December 2012.[145]

Article 2 of the Protocol contains an indicative list of measures that may be implemented by parties in order to achieve their emissions limitation and reduction commitments, which include: the protection and enhancement of sinks, energy efficiency, increased research on new and renewable forms of energy, measures to reduce emissions from the transport sector and so on. These measures are to be taken in accordance with considerations of the 'national circumstances' of the contracting state.[146]

The structure of the Protocol is the most robust application of the principle of common but differentiated responsibility. Developing countries do not assume any emission reduction commitments and are consequently not included in Annex B; their commitments continue to be limited to those detailed in Article 4(1) UNFCCC. Article 10 of the Protocol explicitly reaffirms the principle, stating that all parties must take into account 'their common but differentiated responsibilities and their specific national and regional development priorities, objectives, and circumstances, without introducing any new commitments for Parties not included in Annex I [i.e., developing countries]'.[147]

One of the Protocol's most innovative features is its inclusion of mechanisms aimed at maximizing the cost-effectiveness of climate change mitigation

---

[143] Ibid., Annex A. This list is further expanded in the 2012 Doha Amendment to the Protocol.

[144] Ibid., Article 4.

[145] I. Doucet, 'Canada: The Surprise "Pariah" of the Kyoto Protocol', *The Guardian*, 26 November 2012, available at www.theguardian.com/world/2012/nov/26/canada-kyoto, accessed 8 August 2015.

[146] Kyoto Protocol, Article 2(1)(a).

[147] Ibid., Article 10.

International environmental law 169

by allowing parties to reduce emissions, or enhance carbon sinks, abroad instead of domestically. However, resort to these 'flexible mechanisms' is to be 'supplemental' to domestic action.[148] In sum, Annex B states can meet their obligations not just 'individually' but also 'jointly'.[149] To be eligible to participate in the mechanisms, Annex I parties must have ratified the Kyoto Protocol and be in compliance with their methodological and reporting commitments under the Protocol.

The mechanisms consist of:

- 'Joint implementation' (JI), which allows Annex I parties to implement projects that reduce emissions, or increase removals by sinks, in the territories of other Annex I parties.[150]
- The clean development mechanism (CDM). CDM, defined in Article 12, allows Annex I parties to implement projects that reduce GHG emissions in non-Annex I parties.[151]
- The final flexible mechanism provided for is Emissions Trading, which permits Annex B parties to participate in emissions trading for the purposes of fulfilling their commitments under Article 3.[152] This enables parties to utilize lower-cost opportunities to reduce emissions levels or increase removals, in order to reduce the overall cost of mitigating climate change.

The Protocol establishes one of the most innovative and complex regimes for supervising compliance known to international environmental law.[153] For one thing, it establishes detailed reporting requirements under Articles 5, 7 and 8 of the Protocol. Article 5(1) of the Kyoto Protocol requires each Annex I party to have a 'national system for the estimation of anthropogenic emissions by sources and removals by sinks of all greenhouse gases not controlled by the Montreal Protocol' by no later than 2007. Article 7 of the Convention builds on existing reporting requirements under the Framework Convention in requiring annual submission of greenhouse gas inventories, more comprehensive but periodic national communications and 'any supplemental information' that may be required to demonstrate fulfilment of Kyoto Commitments.[154]

The reports are to be considered by the subsidiary body on implementation to the Convention[155] and Protocol[156] and the COP. One of

---

[148] Ibid., Articles 6(d) and 17. See also Birnie and Boyle, *International Law and the Environment*, pp. 527–528.
[149] The concept of joint implementation was included in the *UNFCCC*, Articles 3(3) and 4(2)(a).
[150] Kyoto Protocol, Article 6.
[151] Ibid., Article 12(2).
[152] Ibid., Article 17.
[153] Birnie and Boyle, *International Law and the Environment*, p. 529.
[154] Kyoto Protocol, Article 7(2).
[155] Ibid., Article 12.
[156] Ibid., Article 7.

170 Part II: Evolution in public international law

the main innovations of the Protocol is that parties are also required to avail themselves of independent auditing and review by 'expert review teams', who will consider national reports prior to their submittal to the subsidiary bodies and the COP.[157] These reviews are coordinated by the secretariat and are intended to provide 'a thorough and comprehensive technical assessment of all aspects of implementation by any party',[158] thereby providing the expert teams with an opportunity to identify and report factors that may affect a party's ability to fulfil its commitments.[159] The export team drafts a report, which is then circulated to all parties to the Convention and the COP, who consider these reports along with the information transmitted to them under Article 7, upon which they will 'take any decision on any matter required for the implementation of [the] Protocol'.[160]

The COP is entrusted with the task of keeping both the Convention and the Protocol under review.[161] Its functions include the convening of periodic meetings designed to review the implementation and effectiveness of both instruments.[162] The COP may establish and receive advice from a supplementary body for science and technology and a body on implementation.[163]

Under the Protocol's dispute settlement provision, states are free to settle disputes by negotiation or by other peaceful means of their own choice.[164] However, the only compulsory measures envisaged are non-binding conciliation and negotiation, unless both parties submit to International Court of Justice jurisdiction or arbitration. Where a dispute cannot be settled by recourse to conciliation and if the parties have not consented to the jurisdiction of the International Court of Justice or arbitration, either party may request the convening of a conciliation commission, which can make a non-binding recommendation.[165] A compliance system to ensure parties are meeting their commitments is also established.[166]

The Kyoto Protocol established a far-reaching and complex structure, many aspects of which remain unresolved at the intergovernmental level.[167] One pressing concern relates to the financing of the considerable adaptation

---

[157] Ibid., Article 8(1).
[158] Ibid., Article 8(3).
[159] Ibid.
[160] Ibid., Article 8(5)–(6).
[161] Ibid., Article 13(1).
[162] Ibid., Article 13(4).
[163] Ibid., Article 13(4)(h).
[164] Article 14 of the UNFCCC; Article 19 of the Kyoto Protocol.
[165] UNFCCC, Article 14(5)–(6).
[166] For detailed information on compliance see http://unfccc.int/kyoto_protocol/compliance/items/2875.php, accessed 8 August 2015.
[167] Chester Brown, 'The Kyoto Protocol Enters into Force' (2005) 9(8) *ASIL Insights*, available at http://asil.org/insights/volume/9/issue/8/kyoto-protocol-enters-force, accessed 8 August 2015.

International environmental law   171

costs to worsening climate change, particularly with respect to the countries most directly affected by climate change, that is small-island developing states and least-developed countries, who are generally unable to meet the costs of adaptation.[168]

The Kyoto Protocol is undoubtedly one of the most high-profile environmental agreements, both in terms of its complexity and groundbreaking provisions, but also in terms of the deeply contested nature of some of its provisions and politicized international negotiation of the agreement. One of the main challenges is to encourage non-participating states to ratify the treaty. Securing concessions from developing countries in the fight against climate change presents another delicate challenge, when viewed in light of considerations of equity and historic responsibility. The Kyoto Protocol was amended on 8 December 2012 by the 'Doha Amendment'. This set out a second commitment period from 2013 to 2020 when parties committed to reducing their greenhouse gas emission levels by at least 18 per cent below 1990 levels.[169] Many activists argue, however, that climate change is already so advanced that these measures on reduction targets are not stringent enough.[170]

Convention on Biological Diversity

The Biodiversity Convention,[171] also adopted in 1992, reaffirms the bedrock principle of sovereignty, which endows states with the right to exploit their own resources pursuant to their own environmental policies, albeit limited by the responsibility to ensure that activities within their own jurisdiction or control do not cause damage to the environment of other states.[172] The Convention, however, innovates by adding a qualification to the principle of sovereignty. It introduces the notion that the conservation of biological diversity is a 'common concern of humankind', whereby states have a duty to cooperate in the sustainable management of resources found under their jurisdiction.[173] The Biodiversity Convention also provides a general legal framework regulating access to biological resources and the sharing of benefits arising from their use.

---

[168] Ibid.

[169] For detailed information on the Protocol and amendments see http://unfccc.int/kyoto_protocol/items/2830.php, accessed 8 August 2015.

[170] Carbon Trust, 'Doha: It Kept the Show on the Road – But Only Just', 23 January 2013, available at www.carbontrust.com/news/2013/01/doha-it-kept-the-show-on-the-road-but-only-just/, accessed 8 August 2015.

[171] Convention on Biological Diversity (CBD), 5 June 1992, 31 ILM 818, and for detailed discussion see Birnie and Boyle, *International Law and the Environment*, pp. 568–59; Sands and Peel, *Principles of International Environmental Law*, pp. 453–464, 505–523.

[172] CBD, Article 3.

[173] CBD, Preamble. See also Birnie and Boyle, *International Law and the Environment*, p. 571.

172 *Part II: Evolution in public international law*

Central to the Biodiversity Convention is an attempt to achieve an equitable balance between the interests of developing and developed states.[174] Article 1 sets out the Convention's three main objectives: (a) the conservation of biodiversity, (b) the sustainable use of its components and (c) the fair and equitable sharing of the benefits of the utilization of genetic resources. These guiding objectives are translated into substantive obligations in Articles 6–20 of the Convention. Negotiations leading up to conclusion of the Convention were contentious and polarized. As a result, the text of the Convention is formulated in broad language with virtually all provisions framed as 'soft' rather than 'concrete' obligations, which are further qualified by phrases such as 'as appropriate' and 'as far as possible'.[175]

On the other hand, although in the context of the Biodiversity Convention the legal status of 'common concern' is left ambiguous and while obligations created under it are 'soft', the Convention does provide a general basis for international action, which confers to parties and even non-parties a right to observe and comment on global goals and the fulfilment of Convention obligations, both within their own national jurisdiction and beyond it.[176]

The Convention applies to biodiversity from all sources including terrestrial, marine and other aquatic sources. With respect to the components of biodiversity, the Convention applies within the limits of national jurisdiction.[177] For processes and activities carried out under the jurisdiction and control of the party, the Convention applies within the areas of national jurisdiction or beyond the limits of national jurisdiction, regardless of where the effects of such processes and activities occur.[178]

The Biodiversity Convention establishes a number of general obligations for states parties. Pursuant to Article 5, parties are to cooperate for the conservation and sustainable use of biodiversity with respect to areas beyond national jurisdiction and on matters of mutual interest. Parties are to develop national strategies, plans or programmes for the conservation and sustainable use of biological diversity.[179] States parties, where possible and appropriate, are to integrate conservation and sustainable use of biological diversity into relevant sectoral or cross-sectoral plans, programmes and policies.[180] Obligations relating to research and training, public education and awareness, the exchange of information and technical and scientific cooperation are also included in the Convention.[181]

The central objective of the Convention is the conservation of biological diversity and biological resources. As established earlier, parties are to adopt

---

[174] Birnie and Boyle, *International Law and the Environment*, p. 571.
[175] Ibid., p. 572.
[176] Ibid., p. 573.
[177] CBD, Article 4(a).
[178] Ibid., Article 4(b).
[179] Ibid., Article 6.
[180] Ibid.
[181] Ibid., Articles 12, 13, 17 and 18.

International environmental law **173**

national plans and programmes for conservation and sustainable use, which, according to Birnie and Boyle, has the effect of constraining national sovereignty.[182] The Convention lists a wide range of measures to be undertaken by parties in protecting the elements of in situ biodiversity,[183] including inter alia: the designation of protected areas; regulation and management of biological resources both inside outside these areas; the protection of ecosystems and natural habitats; rehabilitation and restoration of areas that have degraded ecologically; regulation and management of activities that threaten biodiversity.[184]

Ex situ conservation outside the natural habitats of the protected biodiversity components is also proposed and is to complement in situ conservation.[185] Ex situ measures are preferably undertaken in the country of origin. These measures include: a duty to maintain facilities for the conservation of and research on plants, animals and micro-organisms; seeking the rehabilitation of threatened species and their reintroduction into their natural habitats; regulation of the collection of biological resources from natural habitats for ex situ conservation so as not to unnecessarily threaten ecosystems and in situ populations of species; to provide financial support for ex situ conservation, especially to developing countries.[186]

These protective measures are somewhat weakened by qualifiers as in Article 8(b) of the Convention, in relation to in situ measures that call upon states to 'develop, where necessary, guidelines'. States are therefore given the choice to create guidelines on 'selection, establishment and management of protected areas'.

Obligations relating to the application of protective measures to areas beyond national jurisdiction are also weak and the Convention merely directs the states parties to 'as far as possible and as appropriate, co-operate with other Contracting Parties'.[187] The Convention reiterates the sovereign right of a state to exploit its own resources, although this is qualified by the dictate prohibiting damage to other states or areas beyond national jurisdiction.[188] The Convention does not specify the kind of activities that would constitute 'damage' for the purposes of the said provision, and therefore the legal implications of the responsibility not to harm areas outside national jurisdiction are unclear.[189]

---

[182] Birnie and Boyle, *International Law and the Environment*, p. 576.
[183] In situ conservation relates to 'the conservation of ecosystems and natural habitats and the maintenance and recovery of viable populations of species in their natural surroundings where they have developed their distinctive properties'. CBD, Article 2.
[184] Ibid., Article 8.
[185] Ibid., Article 2 of the Convention defines ex situ conservation as 'conservation of components of biological diversity outside their natural habitats'.
[186] Ibid.
[187] Ibid., Article 5.
[188] Ibid., Article 3.
[189] Birnie and Boyle, *International Law and the Environment*, p. 575.

174 *Part II: Evolution in public international law*

Article 14 does, however, provide that states parties are to '[introduce appropriate procedures' requiring environmental impact assessment on proposed projects 'that are likely to have significant adverse impacts on biological diversity with a view to avoiding or minimising such effects'.[190] The Convention provides for notification, exchange of information and consultation on activities that are likely to have significant adverse effects on biological diversity of other states or in areas beyond national jurisdiction. An obligation of notification is provided for in cases of grave or imminent danger or damage, and emergency responses are to be promoted for activities or events that pose a grave and imminent danger to biodiversity.[191]

Article 15 of the Convention establishes a regime for access to shared genetic resources. The development of genetic engineering and inventions derived from biological resources opens up new avenues for the acquisition of intellectual property rights.[192] As the majority of biological resources are found in developing countries, the question of access was a particularly important one in the negotiations leading up to the Convention.

The Convention attempts to balance donor countries' sovereign rights over their biological and genetic resources whilst facilitating access to users.[193] Access must therefore be provided on 'mutually agreed terms'[194] and is subject to the 'prior informed consent'[195] of the country of origin. Article 15 reaffirms the sovereignty of parties over their genetic resources, and recognizes the authority of states to determine access to those resources. Under assertions inscribed in Article 15(7), parties are to 'take legislative, administrative or policy measures, as appropriate', 'with the aim of sharing, in a fair and equitable' way, benefits derived from commercial use of biodiversity.[196] Benefit-sharing can also take the form of non-monetary benefits including the sharing of research and development results.[197]

An aspect of the Convention that merits special attention is the number of incentives available under the agreement aimed at encouraging participation in, and facilitating implementation of, the Convention. Article 16 specifically recognizes the need to facilitate the transfer of technologies that are relevant to the conservation and sustainable use of biological diversity or make use of genetic resources that do not cause significant damage to the environment.[198] Access to, and transfer of, technology for developing countries is to

---

[190] CBD, Article 14(a) and also Article 10, Annex I of the Convention, titled 'Identification and Monitoring', requires systematic monitoring by contracting nations of the following components of biological diversity within their borders: ecosystems, habitats, species, communities, genomes and genes.

[191] Ibid., Article 14(1)(c) to (e).

[192] Sands and Peel, *Principles of International Environmental Law*, p. 458.

[193] CBD, Article 15, in particular 15(10) and (3).

[194] Ibid., Article 15(4).

[195] Ibid., Article 15(5).

[196] Sands and Peel, *Principles of International Environmental Law*, p. 454.

[197] Ibid.

[198] CBD, Article 16(1).

International environmental law **175**

be provided under 'fair and most favourable terms, including on concessional and preferential terms where mutually agreed'.[199]

The Convention, adopting language that is similar to that which was used in the context of the Montreal Protocol, argues that the ability of developing countries to effectively implement their commitments under the Convention will depend on the 'effective implementation by developed country Parties of their commitments under this Convention related to financial resources and transfer of technology'.[200] Furthermore, the Convention states that developed countries will provide 'new and additional financial resources' to assist developing countries in meeting additional ('incremental') costs of implementation and fulfilment of their obligations.[201]

The provision of funds under Article 21 is subject to monitoring and evaluation by the COP, who 'shall determine the policy, strategy, programme priorities and eligibility criteria relating to the access to and utilization of such resources'.[202] This somewhat modifies the application of Article 3, which permits contracting states to determine their own environmental policies in connection with their sovereign right over their resources, subject of course to the proviso that activities within their jurisdiction or control do not cause harm to areas beyond their national jurisdiction.[203]

The Biodiversity Convention does not establish a reporting procedure for complaints to be reviewed by treaty bodies, which is common to some other environmental treaties.[204] Nor does it establish a compliance inspection and monitoring system.[205] Parties are instead encouraged to review exiting legislation and policies, as well as to identify and promote incentives for conservation and sustainable use.[206] The emphasis is therefore on self-regulation. Parties are, however, required to report on measures undertaken to implement the objectives of the Convention.[207] Birnie and Boyle consider this institutional dynamic to be appropriate for a 'soft' framework of obligations that call for the adoption of national legislation for the protection of resources found mainly within national jurisdictions.[208]

The Convention's supreme governing body is the Conference of the Parties,[209] whose primary function is to review implementation of the Convention. The Convention establishes the Subsidiary Body in Scientific, Technical and Technological Advice and a Clearing House Mechanism.[210]

---

[199] Ibid., Article 16(2).

[200] Ibid., Article 20(4).

[201] Ibid., Article 20(2).

[202] Ibid., Article 20(2).

[203] Birnie and Boyle, *International Law and the Environment*, p. 584.

[204] Ibid., pp. 586–587.

[205] Ibid.

[206] Ibid., p. 587.

[207] CBD, Article 26.

[208] Birnie and Boyle, *International Law and the Environment*, p. 587.

[209] CBD, Article 23(4).

[210] Ibid., Article 25.

176 *Part II: Evolution in public international law*

A secretariat is also established with reporting duties to Conference of the Parties and which can perform any function assigned to it by any Protocol.[211]

Article 27 provides for dispute resolution concerning 'interpretation and application' of the Convention and its protocols, and Annex II sets out arbitration procedures.[212] However, the only form of compulsory dispute avoidance is negotiation.

Article 19(3) of the Convention of Biodiversity calls upon parties to the Convention to consider the need for and content of a protocol to the Convention to address the safe transfer, handling and use of living modified organisms derived from modern biotechnology 'that may have adverse effects on the conservation and sustainable use of biological diversity'. Subsequently, the Cartagena Protocol was adopted, which regulates the:

> transboundary movement, transit [movement through countries other than the country of initial export and final import], handling and use of living modified organisms that may have adverse effects on the conservation and sustainable use of biological diversity, taking also into account risks to human health.[213]

At the core of the Protocol is the obligation on parties to apply an 'advanced informed agreement' or 'AIA' procedure to the first intentional transboundary movement of a living modified organism (LMO), but LMOs intended for direct use as food or feed are not subject to the AIA procedure. Under the AIA process, a party from which an LMO is exported (party of export) to another party (party of import) for the first time must provide advance notice to the party of import.[214] The party of import then has the right to permit, to permit subject to conditions or to deny permission to import the LMO.[215]

The party of import must ensure that a scientifically sound risk assessment is carried out prior to making its decision as to whether to refuse, permit or permit with conditions imports of LMOs. In an application of the precautionary principle, Articles 10 and 11 explicitly recognize the right of parties of import to make decisions that would avoid or reduce potential adverse effects in the face of scientific uncertainty due to insufficient scientific information and knowledge.[216] Once again, this Convention places prevention at its core.

---

[211] Ibid., Article 24(1)(b).

[212] Ibid., Annex II of the CBD sets forth detailed procedures for arbitration and conciliation of disputes arising under the Convention.

[213] Article 4, Cartagena Protocol on Biosafety to the Convention on Biological Diversity, 19 January 2000, 3 ILM 1027. For detailed discussion see Sands and Peel, *Principles of International Environmental Law*, pp. 466–472.

[214] Cartagena Protocol, Article 8.

[215] Ibid., Article 10.

[216] Ibid., Articles 10(8) and 11(8).

International environmental law 177

This provision also arguably grants parties of import substantial discretion to regulate trade in LMOs, not only for environmental protection purposes, but also to protect domestic social and economic interests. The Protocol imposes time limits for the party of import to respond to the advance notice and to make a final decision, and requires the party of import both to justify its decisions and to make a summary of its risk assessment and its final decision generally available through a 'Biosafety Clearing-House'.[217]

These treaties were followed by a number of environmental conventions and court decisions outlining the scope of legal obligation. The added dimension, lacking from the responsibility to protect or indeed aggravated state responsibility, was the codification of sophisticated monitoring provisions like the ones set out under these two conventions. Environmentalists managed to achieve international supervision in a more systematic way than the ad hoc criminal tribunals or even the International Criminal Court, with many fewer parties to the ICC (now 123) than the Kyoto Protocol (192) or the Convention on Biological Diversity (196).

Environmental degradation, the responsibility to protect and aggravated state responsibility

One difficulty in this analysis of environmental law is that state practice, to date, has only attached *erga omnes* status to norms of human rights law. As a result, aggravated state responsibility might not be triggered by environmental harm. However, it could be argued that there are two situations that might trigger aggravated state responsibility and indeed the responsibility to protect. The first is a violation of the paramount environmental principles resulting in serious harm to another state's or the global environment, thus triggering aggravated state responsibility, and the second is the failure of the state in the grip of an environmental catastrophe to aid its own people, engaging the responsibility to protect. Scholar Rachel Johnstone is examining the issues in the first aspect of environmental damage.[218] She cites an Advisory Opinion of the Seabed Disputes Chamber, which specifically cites Article 48 of ARSIWA. The opinion states:

> 180. No provision of the Convention can be read as explicitly entitling the Authority to make such a claim. It may, however, be argued that such entitlement is implicit in article 137, paragraph 2, of the Convention, which states that the Authority shall act 'on behalf' of mankind. Each State Party may also be entitled to claim compensation in light of the

---

[217] Ibid., Articles 9, 10, 20.

[218] R. Johnstone, *Offshore Oil and Gas Development in the Arctic under International Law: Risk and Responsibility* (Dordrecht: Martinus Nijhoff, 2014), pp. 222–224; R. Johnstone, 'Invoking Responsibility for Environmental Injury in the Arctic Ocean' (2014) 6 *The Yearbook of Polar Law Online* 1.

178   *Part II: Evolution in public international law*

erga omnes character of the obligations relating to preservation of the environment of the high seas and in the Area. In support of this view, reference may be made to article 48 of the ILC Articles on State Responsibility, which provides: Any State other than an injured State is entitled to invoke the responsibility of another State…if: (a) the obligation breached is owed to a group of States including that State, and is established for the protection of a collective interest of the group; or (b) the obligation breached is owed to the international community as a whole.[219]

Although, as Johnstone herself points out, this passage might give support to the notion of aggravated state responsibility on the high seas, it does not give support to the idea in national territory pollution cases that might affect neighbouring states.[220] Nevertheless, it does point out that aggravated state responsibility is emerging in international environmental law, further supporting the emergence of the doctrine generally.

The second element of obligation to rescue people from environmental disaster is perhaps more developed. Given the weakness in environmental protection in the face of human-induced climate change, natural disasters have increased five-fold.[221] In 2009 Rebecca Barber published an article concerning Cyclone Nargis, which struck Myanmar on the 2 and 3 May 2008.[222] In particular it devastated the Irrawaddy Delta, affected 2.4 million people and left an estimated 130,000 dead or missing. The repressive regime in Burma restricted aid to the victims as they were part of minority ethnic groups. Barber argued that although this situation may not reach that level, if a government refused to allow access to survivors and there was immense humanitarian need, an intervention by force may be warranted.[223]

Although the notion of responsibility to the international community is embedded within international environmental law, it is too big a leap to suggest a responsibility to protect within an environmental disaster. The trigger point for the responsibility to protect could be within a natural disaster if, and only if, massive abuses of human rights occur concurrently with the natural disaster. The environmental catastrophes that might already be occurring in

---

[219] Seabed Disputes Chamber of the International Tribunal for the Law of the Sea, *Advisory Opinion on Responsibilities and Obligations of States Sponsoring Persons and Entities with Respect to Activities in the Area*, 1 February 2011, Case No. 17 Advisory Opinion (2011) 50 ILM 458.

[220] Johnstone, *Offshore Oil and Gas Development*, p. 224.

[221] S. Goldenberg, 'Eight Ways Climate Change is Making the World More Dangerous', *The Guardian*, 14 July 2014, available at www.theguardian.com/environment/blog/2014/jul/14/8-charts-climate-change-world-more-dangerous, accessed 8 August 2015.

[222] R. Barber 'The Responsibility to Protect Survivors of Natural Disaster: Cyclone Nargis, a Case Study' (2009) 14 *Journal of Conflict and Security Law* 3.

[223] Ibid.

the context of climate change do not in themselves trigger the responsibility to protect.

Conclusion

Of all of the international legal regimes, international environmental law is probably the furthest along the continuum towards true international responsibility. Yet paradoxically it has achieved little of its promise. Climate change continues unabated and international conferences remain deadlocked over control of harmful emissions. However, it is clear that there are a network of treaty, customary and soft law principles, all of which argue responsibility to the international community. The remaining question is what consequences are there when these responsibilities are breached.

In spite of Barber's plea for the responsibility to protect the victims of natural disasters, it seems that the doctrine of the responsibility to protect from the practice of the United Nations is limited to those international crimes outlined in the original resolution. However, the law of the environment is very instructive in its core principles, which mirror those of the responsibility to protect. Notions of common concerns of mankind echo the sentiments in the original reports recommending the responsibility to protect. This is a developed area of the law replete with obligations to the international community, which could serve as a model for future enforcement of the responsibility to protect and may well illustrate how a principle can quickly evolve into a doctrine of customary law.

Part III

The responsibility to protect in practice

This part of the book consciously fails to follow the format in the UN implementation report, which asserts three pillars in the doctrine. These are:

1. The State carries the primary responsibility for protecting populations from genocide, war crimes, crimes against humanity and ethnic cleansing, and their incitement;
2. The international community has a responsibility to encourage and assist States in fulfilling this responsibility;
3. The international community has a responsibility to use appropriate diplomatic, humanitarian and other means to protect populations from these crimes. If a State is manifestly failing to protect its populations, the international community must be prepared to take collective action to protect populations, in accordance with the Charter of the United Nations.[1]

Even though these pillars discuss levels of responsibility, the operational dimension of the doctrine focuses on what action the international community might take at the third pillar, if the state fails to fulfil its primary responsibility to protect populations, and what might be the international law basis for those actions. Therefore, the next three chapters focus on the three types of activities incorporated in the original report recommending the doctrine: prevention, reaction and rebuilding, all of which would fall into the third pillar of implementation.

The purpose of this review is to discuss the specific international legal obligations that might be contained in each of the three operational elements of prevention, reaction and rebuilding. At this point it is premature and inaccurate to argue that each element is a public international law obligation, but contained within each are existing legal obligations binding on sovereign states, individuals and international organizations. There is also evidence of emerging international practice, particularly within the United Nations system, that might eventually result in binding international law obligations to

---

[1] UN Doc. A/63/677 of 12 January 2009.

182 Part III: The responsibility to protect in practice

prevent conflict, react to conflict and rebuild post-conflict. In each of these chapters we review the specific elements of each responsibility as set out in the reports recommending the responsibility to protect, view these elements in light of current practice and discuss the international law elements of these responsibilities.

7 The responsibility to prevent

Introduction

The responsibility to prevent, as argued in *The Responsibility to Protect* report, is the most important dimension of the responsibility to protect, and yet is the least developed in international practice.[1] In all of UN practice since 1945 there has been only one specific conflict prevention action, the United Nations mission in Macedonia.[2] The classic example of the failure to prevent is the case of Rwanda. As the UN report investigating that genocide states: 'the failure by the United Nations to prevent, and subsequently, to stop the genocide in Rwanda is a failure by the United Nations system as a whole.'[3] In his separate report on the Prevention of Conflict Kofi Annan acknowledges that:

> Estimates by the Force Commander at the time, General Romeo Dallaire, that a deployment of approximately 5,000 troops to Rwanda in April 1994 would have been sufficient to halt the genocide have been borne out in subsequent investigations.[4]

The explanation for a noted lack of prevention activities is that there is a serious legal bar to a more systematic use of prevention. In order for there to be United Nations intervention – without the consent of the sovereign state – the situation must reach the threshold of Article 39 of the United Nations Charter, a determination by the Security Council of a threat to or breach of the peace. In contrast, prevention activities, to be successful, must ordinarily take place prior to such a determination. As the Netherlands

---

[1] International Commission on Intervention and State Sovereignty (ICISS), *The Responsibility to Protect* (Ottawa, 2001), p. 20.

[2] Discussion of this mission is available at www.un.org/en/peacekeeping/missions/past/unpredep.htm, accessed 30 June 2015, and see also UN Doc. S/Res/983, 31 March 1995.

[3] UN Doc. S/1999/1257, Report of the Independent Inquiry of the actions of the United Nations during the 1994 genocide in Rwanda, p. 3.

[4] UN Doc. A/55/985 and S/2001/574, Prevention of Armed Conflict, Report of the Secretary-General, 7 June 2001.

184   *Part III: The responsibility to protect in practice*

Advisory Council's report *Humanitarian Intervention* asserts, the conflict is between respect for territorial sovereignty and the duty to uphold and promote human rights.[5]

The first part of this chapter reviews the various reports on conflict prevention and describes the recommendations supporting a responsibility to prevent. The responsibility to prevent is a doctrine that is little understood and it is only the detailed analysis in the ICISS report that links all of the elements: from the necessity within a failed or failing state of economic, political and social reform to the now entrenched international activity of early warning and political response.

The second part of the chapter analyses the limited UN practice in this area, including the debacle in Rwanda and the hopeful action in Macedonia, and identifies the international legal barrier to prevention activity: the necessity for a finding of threat to international peace and security. The third and final part of the chapter attempts to reconcile international prevention activities with the rules of public international law and argues for an appropriate application by the Security Council of the concept of a threat to international peace and security, which would allow for robust prevention activities.

The reports on the responsibility to prevent

Even though the first step in any potential conflict should be prevention, this has been sadly neglected in the results of UN reforms, and in the practice of collective security since the end of the cold war. Although it was not until 2001 that a responsibility to prevent was asserted, there has been a long-standing process of examining conflict prevention that began in 1992 with the influential report by the then UN Secretary-General Boutros Boutros-Ghali, entitled *An Agenda for Peace*.[6] He devoted a chapter to conflict prevention. His key recommendation in this report was that the UN should 'seek to identify at the earliest possible stage situations that could produce conflict, and to try through diplomacy to remove the sources of danger before violence results'.[7] He defined preventative diplomacy as: 'action to prevent disputes from arising between parties, to prevent existing disputes from escalating into conflicts and to limit the spread of the latter when they occur'.[8] He identified several facets to the prevention of conflict: confidence-building measures such as exchanges of military missions; fact-finding missions; early warning systems; and preventive deployment.

The major contribution of this report was the recommendation that potential conflict situations should be identified by an early warning system.

---

[5] Advisory Council on International Affairs and Advisory Committee on Issues of Public International Law, *Humanitarian Intervention* (The Hague, 2000).
[6] UN Doc. A/47/277-S/24111, Boutros Boutros-Ghali, *An Agenda for Peace*.
[7] Ibid., para. 15.
[8] Ibid., para. 20.

The responsibility to prevent   185

There is an existing model in the UN system for this, as the Economic and Social Council (ECOSOC) has initiated a network of early warning systems for environmental threats, risk of nuclear accident, natural disasters, the mass movement of populations, threat of famine and the spread of disease.[9] What was missing, in Boutros-Ghali's view, were arrangements in order that this information could be joined with political indicators to determine whether a threat to the peace existed and to analyse what action the UN could take by way of preventive action. He suggested that a 'reinvigorated and restructured Economic and Social Council' could provide reports to the Security Council on the 'economic and social developments that may, unless mitigated, threaten international peace and security'.[10]

The second important recommendation in *An Agenda for Peace* is to develop a system called 'preventive deployment', in which armed forces could be strategically deployed in trouble spots prior to the eruption of conflict.[11] There is an important legal caveat to this procedure, which is that the state involved would have to consent to the UN presence in order for it to be lawful. Activities would include military support for humanitarian assistance, creating conditions of safety and security to limit or control the violence in order that negotiations could take place, and finally participation in conciliation efforts.[12] However, Boutros-Ghali argued that, in these situations of internal crisis, the UN would need to respect the sovereignty of the state. He quoted General Assembly Resolution 46/182 of 19 December 1991, which specified guidelines for humanitarian assistance, including that assistance must be provided in accordance with the principles of humanity, neutrality and impartiality, and that the sovereignty, territorial integrity and national unity of states must be fully respected in accordance with the Charter.[13] This model of preventive deployment rested on the pivotal aspect of consent, which, if withheld, would result in emergence of conflict.

In response to this influential report, the General Assembly passed two consensus resolutions adopting some of the recommendations in *An Agenda for Peace*. In one, they adopted provisions on preventive deployment:

1. *Acknowledges* the importance of considering, on a case-by-case basis, the use of preventive deployment and/or the establishment of demilitarized zones as a means to prevent existing or potential disputes from escalating into conflicts and to promote efforts to achieve the peaceful settlement

---

[9] B.G. Ramcharan, *The International Law and Practice of Early Warning and Preventive Diplomacy: The Emerging Global Watch* (Dordrecht: Martinus Nijhoff, 1991), p. 154, and see also ECOSOC Resolution 1989/85 of 26 July 1989.

[10] Ramcharan, *The International Law and Practice of Early Warning*, para. 26.

[11] Ibid., para. 28.

[12] Ibid., para. 29.

[13] Ibid., para. 30, and UN Doc. A/RES/182 (1991). This resolution led to the creation of the Department of Humanitarian Affairs.

186 Part III: The responsibility to protect in practice

of such disputes, the continuance of which is likely to endanger the maintenance of international peace and security;

2. *Reaffirms* that a United Nations preventive deployment and/or the establishment of a demilitarized zone should be undertaken with the consent of and, in principle, on the basis of a request by the Member State or Member States involved, having taken into account the positions of other States concerned and all other relevant factors.[14]

The movement on conflict resolution continued, as Boutros-Ghali repeated these recommendations in his *Supplement to an Agenda for Peace* on the occasion of the fiftieth anniversary of the UN in 1995. His second report highlighted the increase in activity of the Security Council in maintaining peace and security and pointed out the change in the type of armed conflict as a result of the end of the cold war. He characterized these conflicts as internal conflicts, often of a religious or ethnic character, involving unusual violence and cruelty.[15] As part of the suggestion for responding to these conflicts, he stated:

> It is evidently better to prevent conflicts through early warning, quiet diplomacy and, in some cases, preventive deployment than to have to undertake major politico-military efforts to resolve them after they have broken out.[16]

Boutros-Ghali considered how preventative action could be undertaken. In this report he dealt with the difficult issue of lack of consent. He argued that the Secretary-General would have to play an active role in this field, even though 'the United Nations cannot impose its preventive and peacemaking services on Member States who do not want them'.[17] He argued that the solution for this lack of consent would be in 'creating a climate of opinion, or ethos, within the international community in which the norm would be for Member States to accept an offer of United Nations good offices'.[18]

Boutros-Ghali was realistic about the difficulties involved in prevention activities. First, there would be the difficulty in finding senior persons who would have the diplomatic skills and who would be willing to serve as a special representative of the Secretary-General. The second problem would be the establishment and financing of small field missions for preventive diplomacy and peacemaking. There is no clear view amongst member states about whether 'legislative authority' for establishing such missions rested with the Security Council or the General Assembly, nor are there budgetary

---

[14] UN Doc. A/RES/47/120 B, 20 September 1993, original emphasis.
[15] UN Doc. A/50/60-S/1995/1, Boutros Boutros-Ghali, *Supplement to an Agenda for Peace*, 3 January 1995, para. 10.
[16] Ibid., para. 26.
[17] Ibid., para. 28.
[18] Ibid., para. 29.

The responsibility to prevent 187

procedures.[19] Boutros-Ghali's solution was to include this as a regular budget item and also to enlarge the existing provisions for unforeseen and extraordinary activities for preventive and peacemaking activities.[20]

Throughout the 1990s there were systematic efforts to examine conflict prevention, with the most influential study released by the Carnegie Commission on Preventing Deadly Conflict in 1997.[21] Furthermore, two important studies on the conflict in Rwanda and the genocide in Srebrenica were published in 1999 and contained recommendations on conflict prevention.[22]

During his term as Secretary-General, Kofi Annan took up the mantle of reform initiatives on conflict prevention and his important contribution was in expanding the existing analysis of the root causes of conflict within the framework of human security. He commissioned a panel of experts to examine peacekeeping operations. The *Report of the Panel on United Nations Peace Operations*, known as the Brahimi Report (named after Lakhdar Brahimi, the Chair of the Panel), addressed the root causes of conflict including poverty, competition for resources and issues of ethnicity, and how it was vital that the negotiators, the Security Council and the mission planners understood the political–military environment they were entering.[23] The panel endorsed the statement of the Secretary-General in his Millennium Report that 'every step towards reducing poverty and achieving broad-based economic growth is a step toward conflict prevention'.[24] As a result, the report proposed that development entities in the UN system view development work through a 'conflict prevention lens' and that long-term prevention should be a key focus of their work.[25] The key component in conflict prevention in their view was in coordination of activities. Two key recommendations were:

(a) The Panel endorses the recommendations of the Secretary-General with respect to conflict prevention contained in the Millennium Report and in his remarks before the Security Council's second open meeting on conflict prevention in July 2000, in particular his appeal to 'all who are engaged in conflict prevention and development – the United Nations,

---

[19] Ibid., paras 30–31.

[20] Ibid., para. 32.

[21] Preventing Deadly Conflict: Final Report, with Executive Summary, Carnegie Commission on Preventing Deadly Conflict, New York, December 1997, and see also F. Tanner, 'Conflict Prevention and Conflict Resolution: Limits of Multilateralism' (2000) 839 *International Review of the Red Cross* 541.

[22] Report of the Secretary-General pursuant to General Assembly Resolution 53/35: The fall of Srebrenica, General Assembly Doc. A/54/549, 15 November 1999. Report of the independent inquiry into the actions of the United Nations during the 1994 Genocide in Rwanda, United Nations, 15 December 1999.

[23] *Report of the Panel on United Nations Peace Operations* (Brahimi Report), UN Doc. A/55/305, 21 August 2000, paras 24 and 26.

[24] K. Annan, Millennium Report of the Secretary-General, UN Doc. A/54/2000.

[25] Brahimi Report, para. 30.

188 *Part III: The responsibility to protect in practice*

the Bretton Woods institutions, Governments and civil society organizations – [to] address these challenges in a more integrated fashion';

(b) The Panel supports the Secretary-General's more frequent use of fact-finding missions to areas of tension, and stresses Member States' obligations, under Article 2(5) of the Charter, to give 'every assistance' to such activities of the United Nations.[26]

As a result of the Brahimi Report, in 2000 the Security Council adopted the first of many subsequent resolutions recognizing the vital role of all parts of the United Nations system in conflict prevention, and pledging to enhance their effectiveness.[27]

Annan himself prepared a seminal report on the Prevention of Armed Conflict, presented to the General Assembly and Security Council on 7 June 2001. The first sentence of his executive summary revealed the importance of conflict prevention to Annan. He asserted that, since assuming office, he had pledged to move the United Nations 'from a culture of reaction to a culture of prevention'.[28] His report acknowledged his reliance on the pivotal 1997 *Carnegie Commission Report on the Prevention of Deadly Conflict*.[29] The Carnegie Corporation established the private commission in 1994 and one of the co-chairs was Cyrus Vance (Former US Secretary of State), and members included Gro Harlem Brundtland (former prime minister of Norway), Gareth Evans (subsequently chair of International Crisis Group and co-chair of ICISS) and David Owen (former UK Foreign Minister). The Carnegie Commission on Preventing Deadly Conflict provided a typology of prevention by dividing it into two categories: structural prevention, which were measures ensuring that crises did not arise in the first place or, if they did, that there were long-term structural adjustments made in order that they did not recur; and operational prevention, which were the measures necessary in an immediate crisis.[30]

The Secretary-General adopted this typology in his report and adopted many of the recommendations of the Carnegie Commission report. In the area of structural prevention he emphasized sustainable development, as an investment in development assistance could prevent a more expensive armed conflict. In operational prevention the tools that were available to the United Nations included preventive diplomacy, preventive deployment of military and civil

---

[26] Ibid., para. 34.

[27] UN Doc. S/RES/1327 (2000), 13 November 2000; S/RES/1366 (2001), 30 August 2001; S/RES/1625 (2005), 14 September 2005; S/RES/1631 (2005), 17 October 2005; S/RES/1653 (2006), 27 January 2006.

[28] UN Doc. A/55/985 and S/2001/574, Prevention of Armed Conflict, Report of the Secretary-General, 7 June 2001. The General Assembly adopted a resolution on the prevention of armed conflict: A/RES/55/289 (2001), 1 August 2001.

[29] Available at www.dtic.mil/dtic/tr/fulltext/u2/a372860.pdf, accessed 18 November 2015.

[30] Ibid., Chapter 3 (Operational Prevention) and Chapter 4 (Structural Prevention).

The responsibility to prevent   189

police contingents, preventive disarmament and allied measures and effective post-conflict peace-building strategies.[31] His two-pronged approach was set out in detail, including HIV/AIDS prevention strategies, food aid, disarmament and use of the International Court of Justice to deal with state disputes.

The previous work on conflict prevention directly influenced the Commissioners in the International Commission on Intervention and State Sovereignty, as the co-chair Gareth Evans served on the Carnegie Commission. In *The Responsibility to Protect* released later the same year, the Commissioners asserted that prevention was the 'single most important dimension of the responsibility to protect' and that prevention options should 'always be exhausted before intervention is contemplated'.[32] The report defined prevention as addressing 'both the root causes and direct causes of internal conflict and other man-made crises putting populations at risk'.[33] As the most important facet of the responsibility to protect, the report advocated that all prevention options should be exhausted before intervention is contemplated and that more commitment and resources should be devoted to it. It follows that the key theme throughout the report was that the least intrusive and coercive measures should be considered before more coercive and intrusive ones were applied.

The Responsibility to Protect endorsed the idea of risk assessment contained in the Brahimi Report. The body of the report considered the responsibility to prevent in detail and argued that there were three methods to be employed for the effective prevention of conflict. These were:

(1) There has to be knowledge of the fragility of the situation and the risks associated with it – 'early warning';
(2) There has to be an understanding of the policy measures available that are capable of making a difference – the 'preventive toolbox';
(3) There has to be the willingness to apply those measures – the issue of 'political will'.[34]

The commission supported the Brahimi Report recommendations that the UN play a clearing house role and the need for more effective collection and assessment of information at UN Headquarters, which could be accomplished by a special unit reporting directly to the Secretary-General.[35]

With respect to structural prevention issues, the report stressed that national efforts to ensure good governance, protection of human rights, social and economic development and fair distribution of resources would be

---

[31] UN Doc. A/55/985 and S/2001/574, Prevention of Armed Conflict, Report of the Secretary-General, 7 June 2001, paras 8–13.
[32] ICISS, *The Responsibility to Protect*, p. XI.
[33] Ibid.
[34] Ibid., p. 20.
[35] Ibid., p. 20.

190   Part III: The responsibility to protect in practice

the first step.[36] However, prevention is not just a local affair and the report argued that strong support from the international community was needed, often in the form of development assistance and other efforts to address the root causes of conflict, which meant support for local initiatives to advance good governance, human rights and the rule of law.[37]

One of the major features of the analysis in this report was the continuing problem with development assistance. It was pointed out that there has been a marked decline in the overall level of assistance worldwide and debts accumulated during the cold war continued to place a tremendous repayment burden on developing country economies.[38] The trade policies adopted by richer countries tended to unfairly disadvantage or restrict access to markets, thus not assisting the capacity of poorer countries to meet the social and economic development needs of their populations.[39] In this important area the report argued for a broader view of peace and security and that there was 'a growing and widespread recognition that armed conflicts cannot be understood without reference to such "root" causes as poverty, political repression, and uneven distribution of resources'.[40] The report recommended that preventive strategies must therefore work to promote human rights, to protect minority rights and to institute political arrangements in which all groups were represented.[41] Political measures could include democratic institution- and capacity-building; constitutional power-sharing, power-alternating and redistribution arrangements; confidence-building measures between different communities or groups; support for press freedom and the rule of law; the promotion of civil society; and other types of similar initiatives that broadly fit within the human security framework.[42] Economic measures should be development assistance and cooperation to address inequities in the distribution of resources or opportunities; promotion of economic growth and opportunity; better terms of trade and permitting greater access to external markets for developing economies; encouraging necessary economic and structural reform; and technical assistance with strengthening regulatory instruments and institutions.[43]

The report also suggests legal reforms such as: protecting the integrity and independence of the judiciary; promoting honesty and accountability in law enforcement; enhancing protections for vulnerable groups, especially minorities; and providing support to local institutions and organizations working to advance human rights.[44]

---

[36] Ibid., p. 19.
[37] Ibid., p. 20.
[38] Ibid. This cause was subsequently taken up by Bob Geldof and Bono with a successful campaign to write off much of the debt of the poorest countries.
[39] Ibid., p. 20.
[40] Ibid., p. 22.
[41] Ibid., pp. 22–23.
[42] Ibid., p. 24.
[43] Ibid., p. 23.
[44] Ibid.

The responsibility to prevent 191

The final structural prevention effort recommended was that states embark upon needed sectoral reforms to the military and other state security services. This could be: enhanced education and training for military forces; reintegration of ex-combatants; strengthening civilian control mechanisms, including budget control; encouraging efforts to ensure that security services are accountable for their actions and operate within the law; promoting adherence to arms control, disarmament and non-proliferation regimes, including control over the transfer of light weapons and small arms; and the prohibition of landmines.[45]

To use another common analysis, these efforts are directed at states that could be described as failing, as they are not able to meet the needs of their population. Under the ICESCR, as discussed in the chapter on human rights, there is an existing international obligation to ensure basic standards of living for all peoples.[46] One cannot help but agree with the Commissioners for both Carnegie and the ICISS, and with Secretary-General Annan, that when these basic items are not provided, conflict is an inevitable result.

In the second category of operational prevention, the ICISS report was very detailed and argued the need for good office missions and mediation efforts to promote dialogue and reconciliation. But uniquely in this report, in terms of operational prevention, the ICISS recommended that this might involve 'a willingness to apply tough and perhaps even punitive measures'.[47] The report called for the UN system to adopt responses similar to the Organization of African Unity (OAU), which in 1993 established a Mechanism for Conflict Prevention, Management, and Settlement, with support from external donors, and the Organization for Security and Cooperation in Europe (OSCE), which developed a number of innovative internal mechanisms and practices toward preventing conflict in Europe.[48] They also pointed to the increasingly significant role played by NGOs in the context of early warning efforts.[49]

However, in the event of an imminent conflict, there was a need for operational prevention action by the international community. The report argues that early warning about deadly conflict has been ad hoc and unstructured. The range of players involved includes embassies and intelligence agencies, UN peacekeeping forces, relief and development NGOs, national and

---

[45] Ibid. pp. 23–24.
[46] UN General Assembly, International Covenant on Economic, Social and Cultural Rights, 16 December 1966, UNTS 993 3, Article 2(1), and see also I. Carr and S. Breau, 'Towards Achieving a Balance: Humanitarian Aid, Human Rights and Corruption' in M. Odello and S. Cavandoli (eds), *Emerging Areas of Human Rights in the 21st Century: The Role of the Universal Declaration on Human Rights* (London: Routledge, 2010).
[47] ICISS, *The Responsibility to Protect*, p. 19.
[48] Ibid., p. 54.
[49] R. Van Steenberghe, 'Non-State Actors' in G. Zyberi (ed.), *An Institutional Approach to the Responsibility to Protect* (Cambridge: Cambridge University Press, 2013).

192 *Part III: The responsibility to protect in practice*

international human rights groups, the International Committee of the Red Cross (ICRC), faith groups, academics and the media. The coordination amongst these groups was argued to be rudimentary or non-existent.[50] The report maintained that UN Headquarters was the logical place to centralize early warning, but that the organization's capacity had fallen short and the Commission supported the recommendations of the Brahimi Report that the UN play a clearing house role within the UN Secretariat. This would include a special unit that would receive and analyse sensitive information from member states and others and would report directly to the Secretary-General.[51] It must be pointed out that in Brussels such an organization exists and flourishes, and that is the International Crisis Group, established by Gareth Evans. Its reports can be seen as the model for this type of early warning activity. The sad reality is that the reports, although transmitted to the United Nations, seem to the outsider to be rarely acted upon.

The Responsibility to Protect addressed in detail the operational/direct prevention efforts, known colloquially as the 'toolbox'.[52] This toolbox describes activities that rise in levels of interference with state sovereignty. On the first level are political and diplomatic measures, which may include the involvement of the UN Secretary-General, as well as fact-finding missions, friends groups, eminent persons commissions, dialogue and mediation through good offices, international appeals and non-official 'second track' dialogue and problem-solving workshops. At the more robust and negative end of the scale, political and diplomatic direct prevention might encompass the threat or application of political sanctions, diplomatic isolation, suspension of organization membership, travel and asset restrictions on targeted persons, 'naming and shaming' and other such actions.[53]

The second level of seriousness in interference in state sovereignty are economic/social direct prevention measures, which include positive as well as negative inducements. Positive inducements include promises of new funding or investment, or the promise of more favourable trade terms. The report argued that a distinction must be drawn between regular developmental and humanitarian assistance programmes on the one hand, and those implemented as a preventive or peace-building response to problems that could lead to the outbreak or recurrence of violent conflict on the other. Special care was required to ensure that such assistance prevented or alleviated conflict issues, and did not exacerbate them. However, economic direct prevention efforts could also be of a more coercive nature, including threats of trade and financial sanctions, withdrawal of investment, threats to withdraw IMF or World Bank support and the curtailment of aid and other assistance.[54]

---

[50] ICISS, *The Responsibility to Protect*, para. 3.12.

[51] Ibid., paras 3.14–3.16.

[52] For an excellent visual representation of the tool-box, see G. Evans, *The Responsibility to Protect* (Washington DC: Brookings Institution Press, 2008), p. 87.

[53] Ibid., paras 3.25–3.26.

[54] Ibid., para. 3.27.

The responsibility to prevent 193

The third level of interference in sovereignty are direct prevention measures of a legal nature. These measures might include offers of mediation, or arbitration or perhaps adjudication – though in cases of domestic dispute these options may not be readily available or acceptable to all parties. The deployment of monitors to observe compliance with human rights standards, and help reassure communities or groups feeling themselves to be at risk, is another measure that might usefully be considered. The report asserted correctly that the threat to seek or apply international legal sanctions has in recent years become a major new weapon in the international preventive armoury. In the first place, the establishment of specialist tribunals to deal with war crimes committed in specific conflicts – for the former Yugoslavia, Rwanda and most recently Sierra Leone – concentrated the minds of potential perpetrators of crimes against humanity on the risks they ran of international retribution. Second, the establishment of the International Criminal Court meant there was new jurisdiction over a wide range of established crimes against humanity and war crimes, some of which, such as the categories of sexual violence constituting crimes against humanity, are described in greater detail in the Statute than in existing instruments, and some of which, such as the prohibition on the enlistment of child soldiers, are new. The establishment of the International Criminal Court was also to be welcomed as a measure to avoid the accusations of double standards, or 'victor's justice', that are periodically aimed at the specialist tribunals referred to above.

Apart from international courts, the report maintained that the Geneva Conventions and Additional Protocols (as well as the Convention against Torture) establish universal jurisdiction over the crimes listed in them. Universal jurisdiction was in any case held to exist under customary international law for genocide and crimes against humanity, and it was revealed that a number of countries had enacted legislation to give their courts jurisdiction in such cases. The report acknowledged that these provisions have in the past usually been more honoured in their breach, but pointed to the prosecution and conviction in 2001 in a Belgian court of Rwandan nuns charged with complicity in the Rwandan genocide, and the British House of Lords decision in 1998–1999 in the General Pinochet extradition case.[55] As we have seen previously in the chapter on international criminal law, too much reliance is placed on what is still a very controversial concept in international criminal law, especially in light of the International Court of Justice decision in *Democratic Republic of the Congo* v. *Belgium* (2002).[56]

Uniquely this report argued that there is scope for a fourth level of interference in state sovereignty by direct prevention measures of a military nature. These could include stand-off reconnaissance, or a consensual preventive

---

[55] *R* v. *Bow Street Metropolitan Stipendiary Magistrate, Ex Parte Pinochet Ugarte* (*No. 3*) [1998] UKHL 41; [1998] *3* WLR 1456.
[56] *Case Concerning the Arrest Warrant of 11 April 2000 (Democratic Republic of the Congo* v. *Belgium)*, Judgment of 14 February 2002 [2002] ICJ Rep 3.

194　*Part III: The responsibility to protect in practice*

deployment. However, the report proposed controversially that, in extreme cases, direct prevention might involve the threat to use force. It is argued that this move from incentives for prevention to more intrusive and coercive preventive measures, such as threats of economic sanctions or military measures, was significant and should never be undertaken lightly. This type of action would require a relatively high level of political commitment on the part of the external actors. The use of threats and other coercive measures was also much more likely to engender greater political resistance from the targeted state than would prevention based on positive inducements. Nonetheless, tough threatened direct prevention efforts could be important in eliminating the need to actually resort to coercive measures, including the use of force.[57]

The report concludes the section on prevention with a plea for this approach by stating:

> Underlying all the specifics, what is necessary is for the international community to change its basic mindset from a 'culture of reaction' to that of a 'culture of prevention'. To create such a culture will mean, as the Secretary-General reminds us, 'setting standards for accountability of member states and contributing to the establishing of prevention practices at the local, national, regional and global levels'. It is a task long overdue.
>
> Without a genuine commitment to conflict prevention at all levels – without new energy and momentum being devoted to the task – the world will continue to witness the needless slaughter of our fellow human beings, and the reckless waste of precious resources on conflict rather than social and economic development. The time has come for all of us to take practical responsibility to prevent the needless loss of human life, and to be ready to act in the cause of prevention and not just in the aftermath of disaster.[58]

The High-Level Panel on Threats, Challenges and Change, commissioned by the Secretary-General to examine collective security in the wake of the crisis over Iraq, released a report entitled *A More Secure World*, which took up some of the previous recommendations for prevention, but not in nearly as much detail. This is probably due to the fact that this panel was only examining the process when it reached the level of threats to the peace. Its first recommendation was the appointment of skilled, experienced and regionally knowledgeable envoys, mediators and special representatives, who could make as important a contribution to conflict prevention as they did to conflict resolution.[59] The report also recommended that there be a facility established

---

[57]　Ibid., paras 3.32–3.33.

[58]　Ibid., paras 3.42–3.43.

[59]　High-Level Panel on Threats, Challenges and Change, *A More Secure World: Our Shared Responsibility*, para. 100.

The *responsibility to prevent* 195

for training and briefing new or potential special advisors or mediators.[60] The members of the panel proposed that the Department of Political Affairs be given additional resources and should be restructured to provide more consistent and professional mediation support.[61]

The second significant recommendation was in the field of preventive deployment. However, these recommendations did not differ from the previous reports in that they encourage 'national leaders and parties to conflict to make constructive use of preventive deployment'.[62] Once again this was based on the consent of sovereign states. The report regrettably does not take up the call in *The Responsibility to Protect* for more robust and perhaps non-consensual prevention activities.

Finally, just before the sixtieth anniversary General Assembly Summit, Kofi Annan released his report on the state of the United Nations entitled *In Larger Freedom*, in which he again voiced an extensive plea for prevention. The major contribution of this report was to tie in the freedom from fear with the freedom from want, arguing again that poverty was the single biggest source of conflict. Annan asserted that 'we have no choice but to tackle the whole range of threats. We must respond to HIV/AIDS as robustly as we do to terrorism and to poverty as effectively as we do to proliferation'.[63] The long-term tools he recommended were combating poverty and promoting sustainable development, strengthening national capacity to manage conflict, promoting democracy and the rule of law and curbing the flow of small arms and light weapons. Operational prevention included the use of good offices, Security Council missions and preventive deployment.[64] He requested that member states allocate additional resources to the Secretary-General for his good offices function.[65] Interestingly, Annan then suggested the use of sanctions as a vital tool at the disposal of the Security Council for dealing preventively with threats to international peace and security. In some cases sanctions could be combined with military pressure to weaken and isolate rebel groups or states who are in violation of Security Council resolutions.[66] His key recommendation with respect to sanctions was that:

> All Security Council sanctions should be effectively implemented and enforced by strengthening State capacity to implement sanctions, establishing well resourced monitoring mechanisms and mitigating humanitarian consequences.[67]

---

[60] Ibid., para. 101.
[61] Ibid., para. 102.
[62] Ibid., para. 104.
[63] K. Annan, *In Larger Freedom: Towards Development, Security and Human Rights for All*, UN Doc. A/59/2005, 21 March 2005, paras 80–81.
[64] Ibid., para. 106.
[65] Ibid., para. 107.
[66] Ibid., para. 109.
[67] Ibid., para. 110.

196 *Part III: The responsibility to protect in practice*

In spite of all of these reports from the Carnegie Commission, two Secretary-Generals of the United Nations, two independent commissions established by the United Nations and the ICISS, the only reference to preventive activities in the sixtieth Anniversary Summit Outcome Resolution in the General Assembly is in the clause preceding the endorsement of the responsibility to protect:

> 138. ...The international community should, as appropriate, encourage and help States to exercise this responsibility and should support the United Nations to establish an early warning capability.[68]

An explanation for this disappointing result may lie in the international legal context of these proposed actions. These early warning/prevention systems proposed in the various reports are far more sophisticated than the steps proposed in Chapter VI of the Charter and involve the whole of the UN system with a particular role for the Economic and Social Council. They contemplate measures short of armed intervention at a much earlier stage than finding that a situation constitutes a threat to international peace and security. The threshold in intervention in internal affairs of a nation seems to be much lower and involves every facet of society, including economic development, human rights and political stability.[69] This might be why there has been reluctance on the part of sovereign states to support these recommendations explicitly, as it would be a fundamental reframing of the notion of state sovereignty.

Ban Ki-moon also understands that the key element in the responsibility to protect is prevention. His first report, released subsequent to his implementation plan, was entitled *Early Warning, Assessment and the Responsibility to Protect.*[70] This report emphasized the importance of prevention, and proposed ways to improve the UN's ability to use available early warning information effectively. Importantly, it refers to Chapters VI and VIII of the UN Charter, which offer 'a wide range of tools that could be employed to protect populations by peaceful means'.[71] Ban Ki-moon indicated that these measures are likely to be effective if they are untaken at an early stage, and this requires early warning.[72] The report criticizes the lack of coordination of information within the UN system and that early warning mechanism does not look at the information 'through the lens of the responsibility to protect'.[73] The report emphasizes the key roles of the Special Advisors on Genocide and the Responsibility to Protect in

---

[68] UN Doc. A/Res/60/1, 24 October 2005, emphasis added.
[69] The International Crisis Group in Brussels already operates as an early warning NGO and provides reports to every level of the UN system and to other governments.
[70] UN Doc. A/64/864, 9 August 2010.
[71] Ibid., para. 3.
[72] Ibid.
[73] Ibid., para. 10.

The responsibility to prevent 197

coordination and assessment of the information received in order that there be 'early and flexible response tailored to the circumstances of each case'.[74]

Recently there has been a significant breakthrough on conflict prevention. On 21 August 2014 the Security Council passed yet another resolution on conflict prevention.[75] However, on this occasion there was an acknowledgement in the debate that although the Security Council had addressed the issue in several meetings, that body had failed 'to prevent the onset or escalation of conflicts'.[76] Situations such as Syria, South Sudan, Libya, Mali and the Central African Republic were specifically mentioned.[77] The UN Secretary-General presented five key actions including the Rights Up Front Initiative, which 'seeks to ensure that we avoid the systematic failures of the past and recognize that human rights violations are early warning signals of mass atrocities'.[78] During the debate the High Commissioner for Human Rights, Navi Pillay, framed the argument in responsibility to protect language, stating that 'when governments are unwilling or unable to protect their people, it is the responsibility of the international community, and singularly this Council to intervene'.[79] In this Resolution 2171 the Security Council committed to 'consider and use the tools of the UN system to ensure that warning signals about potential conflicts trigger early concrete prevention action'.[80] There were two references to the responsibility to protect, first reaffirming the primary responsibility of each individual state to protect its populations from genocide, war crimes, ethnic cleansing and crimes against humanity, but second, and importantly, recalling the important role of the UN Special Advisers on the Prevention of Genocide and the Responsibility to Protect and their functions to act as an early warning mechanism to prevent situations that could result in these crimes.[81] Five years earlier, Alex Bellamy had also emphasized the important role of the two advisors in the 'building of real capacity' for prevention.[82] Yet the roles seem to be confined to the preparations of reports and statements of warning. In spite of this language and a plethora of other resolutions, there is no real breakthrough concerning the thorny issue of sovereignty and the perceived necessity of consent. The United Nations practice belies the verbiage of Resolution 2171. State consent seems to be an impermeable barrier to prevention as the paucity of practice discussed below reveals.

---

[74] Ibid., para. 19.
[75] UN Doc. S/Res/2171, 21 August 2014.
[76] UN Doc. S/PV.7247 Security Council debate, 21 August 2014.
[77] Ibid.
[78] Ibid.
[79] Ibid.
[80] UN Doc. S/Res/2171, 21 August 2014.
[81] Ibid.
[82] A. Bellamy, *Responsibility to Protect* (Cambridge: Polity Press, 2009), p. 131.

198   *Part III: The responsibility to protect in practice*

United Nations practice in the responsibility to prevent

The classic example of a failure in practice of prevention is the 11 January 1994 cable from Roméo Dallaire, Force Commander of the United Nations Assistance Mission in Rwanda (UNAMIR), to Maurice Baril, Military Advisor to the Secretary-General, sent in the lead-up to the genocide in Rwanda. In the cable headed 'Request for Protection for Informant' Dallaire set out three main points of information from an allegedly top-level trainer with the Interahamwe militia. The first was that there was a strategy to provoke the killing of some of the Belgian peacekeepers to bring about their withdrawal. The second was that the Interahamwe had trained 1,700 men, now scattered in groups of 40 throughout Kigali, that the informant had been ordered to register all Tutsis in Kigali and that these trained men could kill up to 1,000 Tutsis in 20 minutes. The third was that there was a weapons cache of 135 AK47 and G3 rifles and the informant was willing to show the soldiers of UNAMIR its location in return for protection for his family. Dallaire informed Baril that he intended to take action within 36 hours and that he wished to protect the man's family. The responding cable from UN Headquarters suggested that Dallaire and the Secretary-General's representative in Rwanda, Ambassador Booh Booh, meet with President Habyarimana. The cable ended with specific instructions that there needed to be an avoidance of entering into a course of action that might 'lead to a use of force and unanticipated repercussions'.[83] It should be pointed out that in his Draft Rules of Engagement in paragraph 17 Dallaire had previously attempted to allow his troops to use force to respond to crimes against humanity and other abuses, but UN Headquarters never responded to Dallaire's request for approval.[84] Sadly, we all know the results of the lack of approval for an early preventive action in this case; almost a million Tutsis and moderate Hutus were killed. But one must also acknowledge the international legal context – that such an authorization for robust prevention activities had never been given in the past. Security Council Resolution 792 establishing the operation had granted no such mandate, so on a legal basis Director of Peacekeeping, Kofi Annan, was right to point out the limitation in the mandate given by sovereign states.[85] In the Report of the Independent Inquiry the first conclusion was that:

> UNAMIR, the main component of the United Nations presence in Rwanda, was not planned, dimensioned, deployed or instructed in a way which provided for a proactive and assertive role in dealing with a peace process in serious trouble.[86]

[83] UN Doc. S/1999/1257, pp. 10–11.
[84] Ibid., p. 9.
[85] Ibid., p. 14.
[86] Ibid., p. 30.

The responsibility to prevent 199

The key difficulty lay in a mandate that did not anticipate the peace process getting into trouble, nor the possibility of genocide. This is in spite of the history of genocidal activity in Rwanda and Burundi between the Tutsis and the Hutus and the fragile state of the truce. Although, strictly speaking, this might be a situation of post-conflict due to the existence of a peace agreement, prevention activities in these circumstances were essential. In terms of the typology of prevention, this would have been at the more robust end of direct prevention efforts that might have slipped into the responsibility to react, although it would have been more like a police action to seize the cache of arms and arrest persons suspected of complicity in a plan of extermination.

The difficulty not addressed in the independent inquiry report is the difficulty in obtaining a mandate for robust action in the face of a peace process and resistance on the part of states to act. The Security Council clearly failed to respond to the genocide once it began with a peace enforcement action, but there was a sea change required in United Nations collective security mandates to permit action prior to the traditional threat to international security barrier. As the inquiry stated:

> The United Nations and its member states must also be prepared to mobilise political will to act in the face of gross violations of human rights, which have not reached the ultimate level of genocide. Particular emphasis must be placed on the need for preventive action: the will to act needs to be mobilised before a situation escalates to a genocide.[87]

Two key recommendations emerge from this inquiry that as yet do not seem to have been acted upon to any great extent. The first is that the United Nations, and in particular the Security Council, must be prepared to act to prevent genocide and gross violations of human rights, and the second is that the early warning capacity of the United Nations has to be improved through cooperation with NGOs and academics, as well as the Secretariat.[88]

On the tenth anniversary of the Rwandan genocide in 2004, the Secretary General finally introduced his action plan to prevent genocide. He argued that one of the reasons for failure in genocide prevention is in not facing the fact that genocide is a real possibility. He argued that the United Nations must not be held back by 'legalistic arguments' about whether a particular atrocity met the definition of genocide. Civil society would play a vital role, as its reports would draw attention to the impending catastrophe. Annan accepted the recommendation for an early warning system and outlined these specific recommendations for the United Nations:

> The United Nations human rights system, too, has a special responsibility. This Commission, through the work of its Special Rapporteurs,

[87] Ibid., p. 38.
[88] Ibid., p. 53, Recommendations 3 and 4.

200   *Part III: The responsibility to protect in practice*

independent experts and working groups, as well as the treaty bodies and the Office of the High Commissioner, should be well placed to sound the alarm. Indeed, your Special Rapporteur on Extrajudicial Killings described many warning signs in Rwanda the year before the genocide happened. Alas, no one paid attention.

[…]

One decision I have already taken is to create a new post of Special Adviser on the Prevention of Genocide, who will report through me to the Security Council and the General Assembly, as well as to this Commission.

This adviser's mandate will refer not only to genocide but also to mass murder and other large-scale human rights violations, such as ethnic cleansing. His or her functions will be:

First, to work closely with the High Commissioner to collect information on potential or existing situations or threats of genocide, and their links to international peace and security;

Second, to act as an early-warning mechanism to the Security Council and other parts of the UN system;

And third, to make recommendations to the Security Council on actions to be taken to prevent or halt genocide.[89]

It seems that, generally, the situation still exists that the Security Council will not be able to muster the will to respond to early warning with robust direct prevention efforts. Hopefully, there are two organs within the United Nations that will have an *unofficial* prevention mandate. The first as discussed above is the Special Advisor roles in Genocide and Responsibility to Protect, and the second is the Peacebuilding Commission. Although we will discuss this commission in much more detail in the responsibility to rebuild, it actually involves prevention activities, albeit in localities that have already experienced conflict.

In the practice that has emerged since the genocide in Rwanda, there is one example of how this is already put into place, albeit in a region that has already exploded into conflict. *The Responsibility to Protect* gave an example of United Nations practice in preventive deployment. This is the United Nations Preventive Deployment Force (UNPREDEP), which deployed in Macedonia from 1992 to 1999. This is the first mission in UN history to have a preventive mandate. The Security Council authorized the establishment of the United Nations Protection Force (UNPROFOR)'s presence in the Former Yugoslav Republic of Macedonia by its Resolution 795 (1992) of 11 December 1992 as 'UNPROFOR's Macedonia Command'. Its mandate was to: monitor the border areas with Albania and the Federal Republic of Yugoslavia (Serbia and Montenegro); strengthen, by its presence, the

---

[89]   K. Annan, *Action Plan to Prevent Genocide*, UN Doc. Press Release SG/SM/9197 AFR/893, HR/CN/107, 7 April 2004, original emphasis.

The responsibility to prevent   201

country's security and stability; and report on any developments that could threaten the country.[90] Subsequently, on 18 June 1993 the Council welcomed the offer by the United States to provide about 300 troops to reinforce UNPROFOR's presence in the republic and, in its Resolution 842 (1993), authorized the deployment of the additional personnel.[91]

On 31 March 1995 the Security Council decided to replace UNPROFOR with three separate but interlinked peacekeeping operations. Within the Former Yugoslav Republic of Macedonia, the Council decided, by adopting Resolution 983 (1995), that UNPROFOR would be known as the United Nations Preventive Deployment Force (UNPREDEP) with the mandate, responsibilities and composition identical to those in place in UNPROFOR.[92] The original force has been created under a Chapter VII mandate, so it can be argued that preventive deployment fell within the ambit of action under Chapter VII.[93] This mission was very successful in preventing the spillover from the conflict in Yugoslavia to Macedonia. *The Responsibility to Protect* argues that the mere presence of the force had 'a stabilizing influence on the fragile internal system' and deterred any possible hostility from Yugoslavia.[94] To this day, this has been the only mission with a purely preventive mandate.[95]

Notwithstanding the lack of effort within the United Nations, there is an active civil society movement involved in prevention activities. One organization deserves special mention and attention: it is the International Crisis Group based in Brussels. On an almost daily basis alerts are sent to the governments of member states of the United Nations, the various organs of the United Nations, the media and civil society on developing crises around the world.[96] It produces analytical reports containing practical recommendations targeted at key international decision-makers. The alerts are entitled Crisis Watch, which along with the more detailed reports highlight the current potential or actual crises around the globe. This organization joins efforts of other organizations that monitor and report human rights violations, such as Amnesty International (AI), Human Rights Watch (HRW) and the Fédération internationale des ligues des droits de l'homme (FIDH). These organizations, which previously spent much of their time and effort reporting on human rights violations against individuals and groups, since the end of the cold war have shifted their focus, and they have expanded

---

[90] Security Council Resolution 795 (1992) of 11 December 1992.

[91] Security Council Resolution 842 (1993) of 18 June 1993.

[92] Security Council Resolution 983 (1995) of 31 March 1995.

[93] See N.D. White, *Keeping the Peace* (Manchester: Manchester University Press, 1990), pp. 32–47 for discussion of the legal regime of 'threat to the peace' and controversy over Chapter VI or Chapter VII mandates in the threat to the peace.

[94] ICISS, *The Responsibility to Protect*, para. 7.5.

[95] D.J. Ludlow, 'Preventive Peacemaking in Macedonia: An Assessment of U.N. Good Office Diplomacy' (2003) 2 *Brigham Young Law Review* 761, p. 767.

[96] Available at www.crisisgroup.org/home/index.cfm?id=208&l=1, accessed 2 August 2007.

202   *Part III: The responsibility to protect in practice*

their work to include early warning about conflicts that could result in massive violations of human rights or even genocide.[97] Finally, the most recent effort at early warning has been launched by the United States Holocaust Memorial Museum, which has launched The Early Warning Project in order to produce risk assessments of the potential for mass atrocities around the world by using 'state-of-the-art quantitative and qualitative analysis' focused on a global map.[98] The aim of the project is to 'give governments, advocacy groups, and at-risk societies earlier and more reliable warning, and thus more opportunity to take action, before such killings occur'.[99]

Yet the sovereignty barrier in prevention activity remains to this day in spite of many resolutions and the concerted activity in April 2014. The question remains as to whether the UN Charter could provide an international law basis for early prevention activities, which would defeat this sovereignty barrier.

The responsibility to prevent in international law

Kofi Annan, in his report on conflict, reviewed in detail the legal basis for prevention activities. He argued that the cardinal mission set out in the UN Charter was 'to save succeeding generations from the scourge of war' and that member states committed themselves to 'to take effective collective measures for the prevention and removal of threats to the peace', as set out in Article 1, paragraph 1 of the Charter. He also pointed out that Article 55 of the Charter explicitly recognized that solutions to international economic, social, health and related problems, international, cultural and educational cooperation and universal respect for human rights were essential for 'the creation of conditions of stability and well-being which are necessary for peaceful and friendly relations among nations'. He therefore concluded that the 'Charter provides the foundation for a comprehensive and long-term approach to conflict prevention based on an expanded concept of peace and security'.[100]

Annan discussed the specific legal basis for Security Council and General Assembly activity with regard to prevention. In respect of the Security Council he stated:

> The basis for preventive action by the Security Council can be seen in Chapter VI of the Charter of the United Nations, which stresses the necessity to seek a solution to the continuance of a dispute or situation likely to endanger the maintenance of international peace and security.

[97] ICISS, *The Responsibility to Protect*, para. 3.13.
[98] Description of the project available at www.earlywarningproject.com/about, accessed 27 September 2015.
[99] Ibid.
[100] UN Doc. A/55/985 and S/2001/574, Prevention of Armed Conflict, Report of the Secretary-General, 7 June 2001, paras 17–20.

The responsibility to prevent 203

According to Chapter VI, the Security Council may investigate any dispute or any situation, which might lead to international friction or give rise to a dispute.[101]

In respect of the General Assembly he said:

Within the framework of Articles 10 and 11 of the Charter, the General Assembly has a broad authority to consider conflict prevention in all its aspects; develop recommendations, as appropriate; or call the attention of the Security Council to situations, which are likely to endanger international peace and security. According to Article 14, the General Assembly may also recommend measures for the peaceful adjustment of any situation, regardless of origin, which it deems likely to impair the general welfare or friendly relations among nations.[102]

Annan unwittingly disclosed in this analysis a definite flaw in preventive activity, that it is recommendatory not mandatory and any recommendation can only come into operation with the consent of the state involved. Annan suggested in his concluding paragraphs that certain measures under Chapter VII of the Charter, such as sanctions, can have an important deterrent effect.[103]

The Responsibility to Protect also addressed the international law issues. It first referred to the Security Council, stressing the importance of responding to root causes of conflict and the need to pursue long-term effective preventive strategies, and that these were part of the role of that body in maintaining international peace and security. The report also cited Article 55 of the Charter, which explicitly states that solutions to international economic, social and health problems and that universal respect for human rights are all essential for 'the creation of conditions of stability and well-being which are necessary for peaceful and friendly relations among nations'. The ICISS concluded that this article provided the foundation for a comprehensive and long-term approach to conflict prevention based on an expanded concept of peace and security.[104] Yet even this report did not analyse the nature of threats to international peace and security and did not attempt to breach the sovereignty barrier.

All of these recommendations seem to go towards the less robust and earlier prevention activities, which have to involve a comprehensive plan for a failing state. But there are occasions, such as those that emerged in Rwanda, where the earlier peace process is not successful and more direct, immediate and robust prevention efforts are required. These reports and

---

[101] Ibid., para. 33.
[102] Ibid., para. 25.
[103] Ibid., para. 169.
[104] ICISS, *The Responsibility to Protect*, para. 3.18.

204   *Part III: The responsibility to protect in practice*

all of the others cited here seem to neglect the basic analysis that could be conducted with respect to Article 39 of the United Nations Charter. It states:

> The Security Council shall determine the existence of any threat to the peace, breach of the peace, or act of aggression and shall make recommendations, or decide what measures shall be taken in accordance with Articles 41 and 42, to maintain or restore international peace and security.

Surely after 60 years of practice the history of what has constituted a threat to the peace can be considered. From Somalia to the recent mandate in Darfur, it is clear that the consistent recent practice has been to intervene in situations of internal armed conflict. The tangential nature of connection is made by the argument of 'spill-over' effects into other territories by flows of refugees and arms. The word threat implies that a developing situation can constitute a threat to international peace and security. This was acknowledged in the mandate given to the mission in Macedonia. If the situation in Rwanda proves anything, it is that the information relayed to UN Headquarters was absolutely correct. Had an operation been mounted, it might not have prevented all of the slaughter, but that – and stopping the broadcasting from Radio Milles Collines – could well have saved thousands of lives. The genocide spread from the capital, and so preventing the operation in Kigali from commencing would have been hugely significant. Surely a threat to international peace and security can arise at a much earlier point, allowing for the recommended preventive deployment actions.

This type of activity involves a sea change in international activity for sovereign states. It often requires a state to inform the Security Council that another state is at risk of exploding into civil violence. This is something that states have thus far not attempted, save for the Macedonian situation, where the history of the dispute in Yugoslavia and the failure of protection at Srebrenica was well known. One way around this situation is to allow regular briefings from both the International Crisis Group and the Special Advisor on Genocide on where there are real risks to human security, and to invite all interested states to make presentations. Instead of waiting for a state to send the usual letter to the president of the Security Council, there is a constant early warning watch. This could also be accomplished by a recommendation in *The Responsibility to Protect*:

> UN headquarters is often identified as the logical place to centralize early warning. Efforts have been made for over two decades to improve the world organization's information gathering and analytical capacities. One of the principal strengths is the special mandate provided to the Secretary-General under Article 99 of the UN Charter to 'bring to the attention of the Security Council any matter that in his opinion may threaten the maintenance of international peace and security'. The

The *responsibility to prevent* 205

Secretariat possesses, in other words, a formidable capacity to alert the world of impending conflicts, either loudly or discreetly.[105]

Therefore, the UN Charter already provides the Secretary-General with the legal capacity to bring these situations to the Security Council's attention and he could do so in conjunction with the International Crisis Group and the Special Advisor on Genocide.

Second, there should be a rapid reaction force, a measure recommended from the earliest report by Boutros Boutros-Ghali.[106] This type of robust prevention activity cannot successfully take place without a military presence that can move quickly. Once again, this depends on mandates being properly given. If the existence of a threat to international peace and security is declared by the Security Council under Article 39, the sovereignty and consent barrier is thus eliminated, and a preventive deployment/rapid reaction force can be launched.

Even if Article 39 is interpreted more narrowly than this author might suggest, Gill has suggested that the practice of the Security Council can change and adapt. He states that 'the Council has been forced to find other ways to carry out its task of maintaining or restoring international peace and security'.[107] He argues that the development and practice of UN peacekeeping has resulted in its evolution into a 'multifaceted instrument which often includes provisions relating to the protection of civilians from violence'.[108] Surely the evolution in practice towards human rather than state security can result in an earlier conclusion of a threat to international peace and security in the most serious cases and deployment of preventative forces.

Conclusion

It is frankly heartbreaking that in spite of years of efforts in this area, progress is almost non-existent with only one truly preventative UN action successful in Macedonia. In spite of many General Assembly and Security Council resolutions dealing with this issue and hours of debate, it seems unlikely that in the foreseeable future the sovereignty barrier in this area will be broken. In a way this is understandable as this reluctance is being supported by such efforts as the National Security Strategy, which called for armed intervention in pre-emptive self-defence.[109] This seems to give the hegemonic power the right to determine which other country might be a possible threat to its

---

[105] Ibid., pp. 21–22.

[106] UN Doc. A/50/60-S/1995/1, Boutros Boutros-Ghali, *Supplement to an Agenda for Peace*, 3 January 1995, para. 10.

[107] T. Gill, 'The Security Council' in G. Zyberi (ed.), *An Institutional Approach to the Responsibility to Protect* (Cambridge: Cambridge University Press, 2013), p. 91.

[108] Ibid.

[109] The National Security Strategy of the United States 2002, available at http://nssarchive.us/national-security-strategy-2002/, accessed 27 September 2015.

206   *Part III: The responsibility to protect in practice*

interest. This has caused understandable angst amongst nations, as a colonialist agenda might be seen to be operating when one labels a nation as a failed or failing state.[110]

These two issues must be separated. The risks in the situations that give rise to the responsibility to prevent are internal. Although there certainly may be a risk of these conflicts spilling over into other territories, such as in the Great Lakes conflict, the initial impetus is a lack of attention to human security issues within sovereign states. This might be as a result of a lack of capacity, necessitating international assistance. Preventive deployment could have saved almost a million lives in Rwanda. It has to be part of the tool kit of the responsibility to protect and Article 39 can be interpreted to allow just such action to be taken. There are sophisticated mechanisms that have been put in place by the NGO community to provide all the information that is required for the responsibility to prevent to be invoked; it is just left to the states making up the international community to realize that prevention is part and parcel of their protection obligations.

---

[110] See the discussion in Chapter 10 on the situation in Syria.

8 The responsibility to react

Introduction

The responsibility to react in a timely fashion is the part of the doctrine most closely related to humanitarian intervention, and scholarly articles to this day still confuse or conflate the two concepts.[1] As discussed in Chapter 1, the debate on humanitarian intervention focused on the issue of whether countries could intervene on a unilateral basis, without an enabling Security Council resolution. The responsibility to react, on the other hand, is predicated on multilateral intervention, where the international community responds to its responsibility to protect, most preferably with Security Council authorization. Instead of a traditional model of peacekeeping with the consent of parties to a conflict, this doctrine contemplates the use of force to halt international crimes, whether or not a peace process is in place. Therefore, the purpose of this chapter, as indeed is the purpose of the original report, is to consider the role of the United Nations and delegated regional organizations in interventions for human protection purposes. The question addressed here is whether the United Nations architecture and practice has embraced its collective responsibility to protect.

As with the previous chapter, we will consider, first, the recommendations contained in *The Responsibility to Protect* report regarding the responsibility to react and its adoption in subsequent reports, and second, we will consider the change in the practice of the United Nations. Although not all of the extensive discussion in the original reports were incorporated into the subsequent United Nations reports or the resulting General Assembly Resolution, they have been carefully studied by personnel at the United Nations, states and non-governmental organizations, and much of the language has become part of the dialogue of intervention. It thus is important to include it in our review.

---

[1] See for example: G. Cronogue, 'Responsibility to Protect: Syria, the Law, Politics, and Future of Humanitarian Intervention Post-Libya' (2012) 3 *International Humanitarian Legal Studies* 124; L. Jubilut, 'Has the Responsibility to Protect Been a Real Change in Humanitarian Intervention? An Analysis from the Crisis in Libya' (2012) 14 *International Community Law Review* 309.

208   *Part III: The responsibility to protect in practice*

In the second part, the chapter will survey whether or not the responsibility to react is emerging within United Nations practice as an obligation. It can be seen from the examples given here that, together with the responsibility to rebuild, the responsibility to react is becoming an integral part of United Nations practice in peace enforcement. There is also important regional practice, particularly embodied in the African Union and the Great Lakes Peace Process. Finally, the third part of this chapter will discuss what is arguably the first responsibility to react mission outside of peacekeeping missions: the NATO intervention in Libya authorized by a Security Council mandate.

The reports

This second element of the responsibility to protect – the responsibility to react – forces an evolution within the practice of the Security Council. The responsibility to react requires an enforcement action under Chapter VII of the Charter in situations of massive abuses of human rights, if preventive actions fail. This responsibility entails a dramatic transformation from peacekeeping to active intervention and peace enforcement. Murphy argues that the litmus test for determining if an operation is peacekeeping or peace enforcement is the ability and willingness to resort to the use of force.[2] The responsibility to react inevitably involves the use of force and, therefore, mandates peace enforcement operations. It is argued here that, in fact, traditional peacekeeping operations in the twenty-first century have evolved into peace enforcement operations, at least to the extent of protecting the civilian population from human rights abuses.[3]

There were reports prior to the ICISS report that recommended peace enforcement. In his supplement to *An Agenda for Peace*, Boutros Boutros-Ghali discussed a new kind of United Nations operation, with the use of force to protect humanitarian operations. He gave the example of the operations in Bosnia–Herzegovina and Somalia. He discussed the fact that in both cases the use of force was authorized under Chapter VII of the Charter, but that this was not peacekeeping as practised hitherto because the hostilities continued and there was no agreement between the warring parties. He highlighted the 'safe areas' concept in Bosnia–Herzegovina as giving the United Nations forces a humanitarian mandate under which the use of force was authorized, but only for 'limited and local purposes and not to bring the war to an end'.[4] This limited and local purpose was to protect the civilian population.

[2] R. Murphy, 'United Nations Peacekeeping in Lebanon and Somalia, and the Use of Force' (2003) 8 *Journal of Conflict & Security Law* 71, p. 95.

[3] R. Thakur, *The United Nations, Peace and Security* (Cambridge: Cambridge University Press, 2006), pp. 34–47, in which he discusses the transition from traditional peacekeeping operations to peace operations.

[4] UN Doc. A/50/60-S/1995 /1, 3 January 1995, paras 18 and 19.

The Brahimi Report on United Nations Peace Operations also discussed the new type of peacekeeping operations. Since the end of the cold war United Nations peacekeeping had been combined with peace-building in complex peace operations deployed in situations of intra-state conflict. The report described the mandates of these operations as 'complex and risky', including such tasks as: relief escort duties for humanitarian personnel; protection of civilians in the conflict where the potential victims were at the greatest risk; controlling heavy weapons in possession of local parties where these weapons were being used to threaten the mission and the local population; and, in extreme situations, managing law enforcement and administrative authority where local authority did not exist or was unable to function.[5]

Although the Brahimi Report tended to favour a more traditional view of peacekeeping by consent of sovereign states, critically it recommended changes in the rules of engagement for peacekeepers. It suggested that United Nations peacekeepers 'must be capable of defending themselves, other mission components and the mission's mandate', and that rules of engagement should not 'limit contingents to stroke-for-stroke responses', but should allow the troops to use force sufficient to 'silence a source of deadly fire that is directed at United Nations troops or the people they are charged to protect'.[6] Crucially, the report stated:

> In some cases, local parties consist not of moral equals but of obvious aggressors and victims, and peacekeepers may not only be operationally justified in using force but morally compelled to do so. Genocide in Rwanda went as far as it did in part because the international community failed to use or to reinforce the operation then on the ground in that country to oppose obvious evil. The Security Council has since established, in its resolution 1296 (2000), that the targeting of civilians in armed conflict and the denial of humanitarian access to civilian populations afflicted by war may themselves constitute threats to international peace and security and thus be triggers for Security Council action. If a United Nations peace operation is already on the ground, carrying out those actions may become its responsibility, and it should be prepared.[7]

This is indeed a recommendation not only for a more robust kind of peace operation, but also for the troops to be aware of their responsibility for human protection. These reports and some limited practice in

---

[5] *Report of the Panel on United Nations Peace Operations* (Brahimi Report), UN Doc. A/55/305-S/2000/809, 21 August 2000, paras 18 and 19.

[6] Ibid., para. 49.

[7] Ibid., para. 50.

210 *Part III: The responsibility to protect in practice*

peacekeeping operations during the 1990s, particularly in Somalia and Yugoslavia, set the stage for the recommendations in *The Responsibility to Protect*.[8]

This theme was discussed at great length in the ICISS report, as the responsibility to protect implies above all else a responsibility to react in situations of compelling need for human protection. This is to take place when the preventive measures discussed in the previous chapter have failed to resolve the situation. However, even in this reaction phase there would be gradations of reaction and would include coercive measures represented by various types of political, economic and military sanctions.[9] Sanctions would arguably inhibit the capacity of states to interact with the outside world, but they would still permit the state to carry out actions within its borders. The measures still aim to persuade the authorities to desist from their human rights and humanitarian law violations. The report also cautions against blanket sanctions harming the civilian population (based on the experience in Iraq) and sanctions that target leadership groups and security organizations responsible for gross human rights violations. This would mean a standard exemption for food and medical supplies, which is generally recognized by the Security Council and international law.[10]

The report crucially contains specific recommendations on how to target sanctions effectively. First, in the military area there should be arms embargoes, including on the sale of military equipment as well as spare parts, and the end of military cooperation and training programmes. In the economic area measures could include financial sanctions that target the foreign assets of a country, rebel movement or terrorist organization, or the foreign assets of particular leaders, and this should be expanded to include members of the individual's immediate family. It could also include restrictions on income-generating activities such as oil, diamonds, logging and drugs due to the fact that the funds generated from these activities are a means to start and sustain the conflict and can be the principal motivation for the conflict (such as in the conflicts in Sierra Leone, Liberia and the Democratic Republic of Congo, which were funded by diamonds). Placing restrictions on access to petroleum products would be an important way of restricting military operations, together with aviation bans. In the political and diplomatic area, targeting sanctions can include: restrictions in diplomatic representation, including expulsion of staff; restrictions on travel, not least to major international shopping destinations; suspension of membership or expulsion from international or regional bodies, which could mean the loss of technical

---

[8] For discussion of UN peacekeeping operations since 2001 see S. Breau, 'The Impact of the Responsibility to Protect on Peacekeeping' (2006) 11 *Journal of Conflict and Security Law* 429 and 'Peacekeeping Operations' in G. Zyberi (ed.), *An Institutional Approach to Responsibility to Protect* (Cambridge: Cambridge University Press, 2013).

[9] International Commission on Intervention and State Sovereignty (ICISS), *The Responsibility to Protect* (Ottawa, 2001), p. 29.

[10] Ibid.

The responsibility to react 211

cooperation and financial assistance; and, finally, refusal to admit a country to membership of an international or regional body.[11]

It is not surprising that the report proposes intervention by other means before a discussion of the use of force. The United Nations Charter collective security system as set out in Articles 39 to 42 of the Charter contemplated just such a process.[12] The dramatic development here is that the threshold conditions for collective action set out in Article 39, namely any threat to the peace, breach of the peace or act of aggression, is expanded to include compelling need for human protection, which could (but not usually) include situations that may not be armed conflict and certainly situations of internal strife that might not rise to the level of armed conflict. However, the process of reaction after the threshold is met is very similar to the provisions of Articles 40 (provisional measures), 41 (sanctions) and 42 (use of force).[13]

The report acknowledges that in some cases reaction through sanctions will not be sufficient and in extreme cases there will be a need to resort to military action. The definitional problem is what constitutes an extreme case. The starting point in the report is the principle of non-intervention. All members of the United Nations have an interest in 'maintaining an order of sovereign, self-reliant, responsible, yet interdependent states'. The interest of all states is served if there is abstention from interference in the domestic affairs of other states. This not only protects states, but also enables societies to maintain 'the religious, ethnic and civilizational differences they cherish'.[14] This reflects the vision of an international community of states, an international society based on shared humanitarian values. The report argues that the norm of non-intervention is the equivalent of the Hippocratic principle – 'first do no harm'. This rule against intervention encourages states to solve their own internal problems, otherwise the problems spilling over can constitute a threat to international peace and security.[15] Yet crucially there are times when intervention has to be considered. The report states:

> 4.13 Yet there are exceptional circumstances in which the very interest that all states have in maintaining a stable international order requires them to react when all order within a state has broken down or when civil conflict and repression are so violent that civilians are threatened with massacre, genocide or ethnic cleansing on a large scale…the view was that these exceptional circumstances must be cases of violence which so genuinely 'shock the conscience of mankind', or which present such a clear and present danger to international security, that they require coercive military intervention.[16]

[11] Ibid., p. 30.
[12] United Nations, Charter of the United Nations, 24 October 1945, 1 UNTS XVI, Chapter VII.
[13] Ibid., Articles 39–42.
[14] ICISS, *The Responsibility to Protect*, p. 30.
[15] Ibid., p. 31.
[16] Ibid., p. 31.

212   Part III: The responsibility to protect in practice

The task according to the Commission was to define, with as much precision as possible, what would constitute exceptional circumstances so that consensus could be reached in authorizing intervention. This is an important innovation of the responsibility to protect doctrine – the development of principles for military intervention in the responsibility to react phase. There would have to be tough threshold conditions before military intervention would be contemplated. The report states that these conditions must be high, for if military action is to be defensible, the circumstances requiring it must be grave.[17]

The report proposed six criteria for military intervention. The criteria for intervention were summarized under six headings – right authority, just cause, right intention, last resort, proportional means and reasonable prospects. These will be discussed in turn and in detail, as more than any other recommendations they pose a challenge to the traditional *jus ad bellum* regime both in customary international law and in the Charter.

Right authority

It becomes clear that *The Responsibility to Protect* report attempts to resolve the nagging legal issue of unilateral intervention and to introduce a scheme for intervention. Due to the importance of this discussion, the report is cited in full. It states:

A. There is no better or more appropriate body than the United Nations Security Council to authorize military intervention for human protection purposes. The task is not to find alternatives to the Security Council as a source of authority, but to make the Security Council work better than it has.
B. Security Council authorization should in all cases be sought prior to any military intervention action being carried out. Those calling for an intervention should formally request such authorization, or have the Council raise the matter on its own initiative, or have the Secretary-General raise it under Article 99 of the UN Charter.
C. The Security Council should deal promptly with any request for authority to intervene where there are allegations of large scale loss of human life or ethnic cleansing. It should in this context seek adequate verification of facts or conditions on the ground that might support a military intervention.
D. The Permanent Five members of the Security Council should agree not to apply their veto power, in matters where their vital state interests are not involved, to obstruct the passage of resolutions authorizing military intervention for human protection purposes for which there is otherwise majority support.

---

[17] Ibid., p. 29.

The responsibility to react 213

E. If the Security Council rejects a proposal or fails to deal with it in a reasonable time, alternative options are:
  I. Consideration of the matter by the General Assembly in Emergency Special Session under the 'Uniting for Peace' procedure; and
  II. Action within area of jurisdiction by regional or sub-regional organizations under Chapter VIII of the Charter, subject to their seeking subsequent authorization from the Security Council.
F. The Security Council should take into account in all its deliberations that, if it fails to discharge its responsibility to protect in conscience-shocking situations crying out for action, concerned states may not rule out other means to meet the gravity and urgency of that situation – and that the stature and credibility of the United Nations may suffer thereby.[18]

It is evident that the right authority includes the possibility of a unilateral action in the very last resort, but reading this section as a whole, the focus is on the Security Council fulfilling its responsibility with the Permanent Five members not exercising the veto in these situations. Regrettably, as discussed in the final chapter on Syria, the veto is still used and this recommendation was not adopted in any subsequent resolutions.[19]

Just cause

The just cause threshold criteria are set out as military intervention for human protection purposes to halt or avert:

> large scale loss of life, actual or apprehended, with genocidal intent or not, which is the product either of deliberate state action, or state neglect or inability to act, or a failed state situation; or large scale 'ethnic cleansing', actual or apprehended, whether carried out by killing, forced expulsion, acts of terror or rape.[20]

Although these might seem clear, the Commission expanded what these acts would include. In addition to genocide as defined in the 1948 Genocide Convention, and crimes against humanity and war crimes as defined in the Geneva Conventions and Additional Protocols, it included 'situations of state collapse and the resultant exposure of the population to mass starvation and/or civil war', and 'overwhelming natural or environmental catastrophes, where the state concerned is either unwilling or unable to cope, or call for assistance, and significant loss of life is occurring or threatened'.[21]

[18] Ibid., pp. XII–XIII.
[19] I. Black, 'Russia and China veto UN move to refer Syria to international criminal court', *The Guardian*, 22 May 2014, available at www.theguardian.com/world/2014/may/22/russia-china-veto-un-draft-resolution-refer-syria-international-criminal-court, accessed 7 July 2015.
[20] Ibid., p. 33.
[21] Ibid., p. 32.

214 *Part III: The responsibility to protect in practice*

Another innovation in the report is that military action could be contemplated as 'an anticipatory measure' as a result of 'clear evidence of likely large-scale killing'.[22] Within this just cause discussion is a discussion of what evidence might suffice for an intervention to take place. The Commission rightly points out that obtaining 'fair and accurate information' is essential. Research is currently being conducted under the auspices of Every Casualty Worldwide to ensure accurate recording of civilian casualties.[23] *The Responsibility to Protect* report released in 2001 suggested that there were as yet no impartial non-government sources of such information; the International Committee of the Red Cross was unwilling to take on this role as it needed to remain absolutely removed from political decision-making.[24] Every Casualty Worldwide has a network of casualty recorders, but to date there is no central organization taking on this role.[25] The other places for provision of evidence identified in the report were the UN organs and agencies, such as the High Commissioners for Human Rights and Refugees. The other suggestion, which seems to be quite commonly utilized in practice, was an independent special fact finding mission sent by the Security Council or Secretary-General.[26] The Secretary-General has the authority under Article 99 of the Charter to 'bring to the attention of the Security Council any matter which in his opinion may threaten the maintenance of international peace and security'.[27]

Right intention

This threshold condition contains, once again, a change in the perception of humanitarian intervention. The condition states that '[t]he primary purpose of the intervention must be to halt or avert human suffering'.[28] This means it may not be the sole purpose, just the primary one. The report suggests that one way of ensuring the right intention is to have intervention take place on a collective or multilateral basis.[29] The self-interested parts of the intervention could be concerns about budget and cost in human life, and to avoid refugee outflows.

---

[22] Ibid., p. 32.
[23] S. Breau and R. Joyce, 'The Legal Obligation to Record Civilian Casualties of Armed Conflict', Discussion paper for Every Casualty, available at www.everycasualty.org/downloads/ec/pdf/legal-obligation-to-record-casualties.pdf, accessed 7 July 2015, and see S. Breau and R. Joyce, 'The Responsibility to Record Civilian Casualties' (2013) 5 *Global Responsibility to Protect* 28.
[24] ICISS, *The Responsibility to Protect*, p. 35.
[25] For the list of organizations in the International Practitioner Network see www.everycasualty.org/practice/ipn, accessed 7 July 2015.
[26] ICISS, *The Responsibility to Protect*, p. 35
[27] United Nations, Charter of the United Nations, 24 October 1945, 1 UNTS XVI, Article 99.
[28] ICISS, *The Responsibility to Protect*, p. 33.
[29] Ibid., p. XII.

Last resort

This threshold condition is straightforward. Simply put, the responsibility to prevent has to be fully discharged before the responsibility to react is employed. Every diplomatic and non-military avenue including sanctions has to be attempted first.[30] Sadly, in practice since 2001 there has been little evidence, except for Macedonia discussed in the previous chapter, of any real effort in prevention. Too often the situation comes before the Security Council when the last resort has already arrived.

Proportional means

This is a condition that accords with the international law *jus ad bellum* obligations of necessity and proportionality on the use of force in self-defence.[31] The condition states that '[t]he scale, duration and intensity of the planned military intervention should be the minimum necessary to secure the humanitarian objective in question'.[32] The commentary goes on to argue that all of the rules of international humanitarian law should be strictly observed.[33]

Reasonable prospects

The final threshold condition is another innovation, but again very welcome in the context of intervention for human protection purposes. The condition states that '[m]ilitary action can only be justified if it stands a reasonable chance of success, that is, halting or averting the atrocities or suffering that triggered the intervention in the first place'.[34] The discussion goes on to assert that military intervention should not take place if the consequences of the intervention are likely to be worse than if there is no intervention at all.[35] Examples given are if the intervention would trigger a larger conflict. The other example given of the application of this principle would be that action would be precluded against any one of the five permanent members of the Security Council. The report stated that '[i]t is difficult to imagine a major conflict being avoided, or success in the original objective being achieved, if such action were mounted against any of them'.[36] The report extends this proviso to other major powers and acknowledges the question of double standards, but asserts that this is reality as interventions cannot be commenced in every case.[37]

---

[30] Ibid.
[31] J. Green, *The International Court of Justice and Self-Defence in International Law* (Oxford: Hart, 2009), Chapter 2.
[32] Ibid.
[33] Ibid., p. 37.
[34] Ibid., p. XII.
[35] Ibid., p. 37.
[36] Ibid.
[37] Ibid.

216 *Part III: The responsibility to protect in practice*

In addition to these precautionary principles, the report discusses the rules of engagement in responsibility to react operations. In this robust military reaction phase, the contrast with traditional peacekeeping operations is that these military operations have to be able and willing to engage in much more forceful action than is permitted by traditional peacekeeping.[38] This would impact on the rules of engagement as the 'use of only minimal force in self-defence that characterizes traditional peacekeeping would clearly be inappropriate and inadequate for a peace enforcement action'. Rules of engagement would have to be 'clear and robust'.[39] In addition, the means of intervention must be carefully tailored to objectives with key military and political pressure points identified and targeted. The missions will be comprehensive with the roles of non-military components planned for and taken into account.[40] In terms of United Nations military operations key operational principles were also proposed:

A. Clear objectives; clear and unambiguous mandate at all times; and resources to match.
B. Common military approach among involved partners; unity of command; clear and unequivocal communications and chain of command.
C. Acceptance of limitations, incrementalism and gradualism in the application of force, the objective being protection of a population, not defeat of a state.
D. Rules of engagement, which fit the operational concept; are precise; reflect the principle of proportionality; and involve total adherence to international humanitarian law.
E. Acceptance that force protection cannot become the principal objective.
F. Maximum possible coordination with humanitarian organizations.[41]

Although never discussed in such detail again, these recommendations were taken up in the United Nations reports following the Iraq war. The task of the Secretary-General's High-Level Panel was to review the whole issue of collective security and this particularly involved an examination of the legal authority to intervene. In *A More Secure World*, the High-Level Panel specifically addressed the issue of peacekeeping and the confusions between mandates given to peacekeepers. The report argued that there has been confusion between peacekeeping missions – 'Chapter VI operations' – and peace enforcement missions – 'Chapter VII operations'. The distinction was based on the use of deadly force for purposes other than self-defence in peace enforcement missions.[42] The panel argued that these characterizations

[38] Ibid., p. 57.
[39] Ibid., p. 62.
[40] Ibid., p. 63.
[41] Ibid., see synopsis pp. XI–XIII.
[42] *A More Secure World: Our Shared Responsibility. Report of the Secretary-General's High-Level Panel on Threats, Challenges and Change* (New York: United Nations, 2004), UN Doc. A/59/565, 2 December 2004, para. 211.

The responsibility to react   217

were misleading, as there was a necessary distinction between operations in which the robust use of force was integral from the outset and those in which force may not be needed at all. The kind of operation in which robust force was necessary could be an 'explosion of violence'.[43] The panel supported a Chapter VII mandate for any peacekeeping mission, but the real challenge in any deployment of forces was to ensure that they had '(a) an appropriate, clear and well understood mandate, applicable to all the changing circumstances that might reasonably be envisaged, and (b) all the necessary resources to implement that mandate fully'.[44]

Regrettably, Annan did not take up any extensive discussion on peacekeeping and peace enforcement in his report *In Larger Freedom*, but did pose this question:

> As to genocide, ethnic cleansing and other such crimes against humanity, are they not also threats to international peace and security, against which humanity should be able to look to the Security Council for protection?[45]

The 2005 consensus resolution of the General Assembly's sixtieth anniversary Summit is disappointing in this regard, as there is no specific discussion of the issue of mandate for peace enforcement and the need for Chapter VII authority from the outset. The document, in paragraph 83, confirmed the practice of delegation of peacekeeping to regional organizations. As Kantareva argues: 'Comparing the four texts in substantive terms, one can safely conclude that, textually, R2P has been progressively diluted.'[46] Nevertheless, the actual practice of the United Nations in the last five years has undergone a remarkable transformation, which belies claims of dilution. The practice supports the use of the principles suggested in the original report. Chapter VII mandates have become routine in situations of human rights catastrophes, with robust civilian protection mandates being given, and in doing so, the Security Council is embracing a responsibility to react.

United Nations' adoption of the responsibility to protect in peacekeeping

The responsibility to react as a doctrine of customary international law may not have yet crystallized, but the evolving practice of the United Nations will have to be carefully monitored, as it reflects the practice of the member states. Some of the more recent peacekeeping operations, such as in the Democratic

---

[43] Ibid., para. 212.
[44] Ibid., para. 214.
[45] K. Annan, *In Larger Freedom: Towards Development, Security and Human Rights for All*, UN Doc. A/59/2005, 21 March 2005, p. 33.
[46] S. Kantareva, 'The Responsibility to Protect: Issues of Legal Formulation and Practical Application' (2011–2012) 6 *Interdisciplinary Journal of Human Rights Law* 1.

218 *Part III: The responsibility to protect in practice*

Republic of Congo, Burundi, Ivory Coast and Darfur, Sudan, illustrate a transformation reflecting an international legal obligation towards protection of victims of human rights catastrophes. These peacekeeping operations are in reality peace enforcement actions. Although these missions require extensive analysis, for the purpose of this chapter the examination will be limited to the actual mandates given by the UN Security Council. Africa provides us with most of the current examples of peace enforcement actions, as the conflicts in the Middle East result in substantial division in the Security Council, except for the conflict in Libya.

Democratic Republic of Congo

The mission in the Democratic Republic of Congo (DRC, formerly Zaire) dates to the establishment of the United Nations Organization Mission in the Democratic Republic of Congo (MONUC) established by Security Council Resolution 1279 (1999) on 30 November 1999. This mandate did not give any type of force mandate as, at the time, it was an observation mission for the Lusaka ceasefire agreement, which was to begin the process of ending the international armed conflict between various Great Lake countries fighting in the territory.[47] Resolution 1291 of 24 February 2000 was the first resolution that determined that the threat in the DRC constituted 'a threat to international peace and security in the region as a result of the failure to implement the Lusaka Accord'. The resolution expressed 'deep concern at all violations and abuses of human rights and abuses of international humanitarian law'. This resolution expanded MONUC's mandate, including:

> 7(g) to facilitate humanitarian assistance and human rights monitoring, with particular attention to vulnerable groups including women, children and demobilized child soldiers, as MONUC deems within its capabilities and under acceptable security conditions, in close cooperation with other United Nations agencies, related organizations and non-governmental organizations.

However, the significant change was a robust mandate for the use of force, particularly to protect civilians:

> 8. Acting under Chapter VII of the Charter of the United Nations, decides that MONUC may take the necessary action, in the areas of deployment of its infantry battalions and as it deems it within its capabilities, to protect United Nations and co-located JMC personnel, facilities, installations and equipment, ensure the security and freedom of

---

[47] UN Doc. S/Res/1279 (1999), 30 November 1999; the parties to the conflict were Uganda, Rwanda, Angola, Namibia and Zimbabwe. See the next chapter, which discusses the Great Lakes Peace Process.

The responsibility to react 219

movement of its personnel, *and protect civilians under imminent threat of physical violence.*[48]

Even though Joseph Kabila, who replaced his assassinated father, has been more committed to the peace, violence continues with the presence of militia and foreign-armed groups in the eastern part of the DRC. Therefore, there have been several other resolutions concerning the DRC. Amongst them was Resolution 1355 (2001), which again expressed 'deep concern at all violations of human rights and humanitarian law' including 'atrocities against civilian populations, especially in the eastern provinces'. This resolution continued the mandate of civilian protection and added a couple of elements:

> 34. *Requests* the Secretary-General to expand the civilian component of MONUC, in accordance with the recommendations in his report, in order to assign to areas in which MONUC is deployed human rights personnel, so as to establish a human rights monitoring capacity, as well as civilian political affairs and humanitarian affairs personnel;
>
> 35. *Calls on* the Secretary-General to ensure sufficient deployment of child protection advisers to ensure consistent and systematic monitoring and reporting on the conduct of the parties to the conflict as concerns their child protection obligations under humanitarian and human rights law and the commitments they have made to the Special Representative of the Secretary-General for Children and Armed Conflict.[49]

This practice was further enhanced in the reaction to the troubles in the Ituri province and the deaths of hundreds of people in the capital city of Bunia.[50] In Resolution 1484 (2003), after a declaration that the situation constituted a threat to international peace and security, the Security Council authorized the deployment of an interim emergency multinational force in Bunia in close cooperation with MONUC, which was to:

> contribute to the stabilization of the security conditions and the improvement of the humanitarian situation in Bunia, to ensure the protection of the airport, the internally displaced persons in the camps in Bunia and, if the situation requires it, to contribute to the safety of the civilian population, United Nations personnel and the humanitarian presence in the town.[51]

[48] UN Doc. S/Res/1291 (2000), 24 February 2000, emphasis added.
[49] UN Doc. S/Res/1355 (2001), 15 June 2001, original emphasis.
[50] C.J. Le Mon and R.S. Taylor, 'Security Council Action in the Name of Human Rights: From Rhodesia to the Congo' (2004) 10 *U.C. Davis Journal of International Law & Policy* 197, p. 224.
[51] UN Doc. S/Res/1484 (2003), 30 May 2003.

220 Part III: The responsibility to protect in practice

This was further strengthened in Resolution 1493 (2003), paragraph 27, where the Security Council:

> Requests the Secretary-General to deploy in the Ituri district, as soon as possible, the tactical brigade-size force whose concept of operation is set out in paragraphs 48 to 54 of his second special report, including the reinforced MONUC presence in Bunia by mid-August 2003 as requested in resolution 1484 (2003), particularly with a view to helping to stabilize the security conditions and improving the humanitarian situation, ensuring the protection of airfields and displaced persons living in camps and, if the circumstances warrant it, helping to ensure the security of the civilian population and the personnel of the United Nations and the humanitarian organizations in Bunia and its environs and eventually, as the situation permits, in other parts of Ituri.[52]

It should be noted that these two resolutions had a limitation on use of force to protect civilians 'if the situation requires it' or 'if the circumstances warrant it'.

Resolution 1565 (2004) strengthened MONUC's mandate, as the troop strength was increased by 5,900 personnel to a total of 16,700. The comprehensive and robust mandate, without any limitation clauses as above, included the following provisions:

4. (b) to ensure the protection of civilians, including humanitarian personnel, under imminent threat of physical violence,
5. (g) to assist in the promotion and protection of human rights, with particular attention to women, children and vulnerable persons, investigate human rights violations to put an end to impunity, and continue to cooperate with efforts to ensure that those responsible for serious violations of human rights and international humanitarian law are brought to justice, while working closely with the relevant agencies of the United Nations;
6. *Authorizes* MONUC to use all necessary means, within its capacity and in the areas where its armed units are deployed, to carry out the tasks.[53]

This resolution set up a comprehensive and multidimensional peace enforcement mission including both peace enforcement and peace-building, and it continues to this day.[54] It reveals the extent of activity required of peacekeeping forces, including the use of all necessary means to carry out their mandate. The limitation of 'if circumstances permit' is not included in this

---

[52] UN Doc. S/Res/1493 (2003), 28 July 2003.
[53] UN Doc. S/Res/1565, 1 October 2004, original emphasis.
[54] The mission was just extended until 30 September 2006 in Security Council Resolution 1635 (2005) of 28 October 2005.

The responsibility to react 221

later resolution, which also includes provisions for disarmament, demobilization and the protection of human rights. Although the situation in the DRC clearly contained elements of international armed conflict and was a clear threat to international peace and security, the later resolutions clearly focus on internal human rights abuses and do not mention any trans-border aspects to the conflict.[55]

This operation has undergone many different phases.[56] It is now entitled the United Nations Organization Stabilization Mission in the Democratic Republic of the Congo (MONUSCO), which was established by Security Council Resolution 1925.[57] This resolution continued the civilian protection mandate in addition to supporting the Kabila government in its stabilization and peace consolidation efforts.[58] There was a major resurgence of violence in April 2012 in North Kivu, but this was addressed as part of the Great Lakes Peace Process, which had been ongoing for several years.

Burundi

Burundi has the sad distinction of having experienced the first example of African genocide in modern times.[59] In June of 1993 Burundi elected Melchior Ndadaye, a Hutu, as president in its first national election. In October of that same year Ndadaye was assassinated. This sparked ethnic violence, which resulted in the deaths of an estimated 50,000 Hutu and Tutsi civilians.[60] The world response to the violence was largely non-existent. The violence in Burundi set the stage for the 1994 Rwandan genocide in two ways: first, it gave extremist Rwandan Hutus valuable propaganda in their efforts to incite genocide in that country; and second, it signalled to those same extremists that the international community will do nothing in the face of African ethnic violence. However, by 2003 the Security Council finally decided to intervene in the face of continued massacres and the involvement of several nations in the Great Lakes conflict.

The Security Council debate in late 2003 authorizing the establishment of the peacekeeping operation in Burundi included some tentative language with respect to the sense of a responsibility to protect. Sir Emyr Jones Parry of the United Kingdom stated:

---

55 Le Mon and Taylor, 'Security Council Action', p. 225.
56 See www.un.org/en/peacekeeping/missions/monusco/background.shtml, accessed 27 July 2015.
57 UN Doc. S/Res/1925, 1 July 2010.
58 See www.un.org/en/peacekeeping/missions/monusco/background.shtml, accessed 27 July 2015.
59 R. Lemarchand, *Burundi: Ethnocide as Discourse and Practice* (Washington DC: Woodrow Wilson Center Press, 1994), p. xi.
60 D. Scheffer, 'Commentary: Shameful Inaction in Face of Genocide. In 1994, we in the U.S. government failed Rwanda', *Los Angeles Times*, 5 April 2004, part B, at 11.

222 *Part III: The responsibility to protect in practice*

The obligation on the international community is all the greater because the Africans – within Africa as a whole and within the region – are producing their own solutions. The view of the United Kingdom is that, when that happens, they require, and *we are obliged to give*, support to those solutions.

With regard to the United Nations, we believe that a focused intervention is necessary, covering all those areas and involving all the instruments and elements within the family of the United Nations, including – crucially, as we have heard – the role of the Economic and Social Council: in short, an integrated, coordinated approach that tackles the needs of Burundi and avoids a repetition of some of the disasters we have seen previously.

How do we reinforce the efforts being made on the ground, which demand our support? If that means a peacekeeping operation, then the United Kingdom is very open to that.[61]

Mr Cunningham of the United States of America stated:

I wanted to make a point of commending the African Union for its positive role in overseeing the implementation of the Ceasefire Agreement and to commend the African mission in Burundi, which, as the Deputy President said, that could be considered as a shining example and a model of African engagement…The United States strongly encourages and will support that approach…*we must help our African friends when they step up to the challenge as they are doing here*.[62]

Resolution 1545 (2004), adopted unanimously, contained a robust mandate similar to that adopted for the DRC and Ivory Coast.[63] Its operational paragraph under a Chapter VII mandate contained a mix of peace enforcement and peace-building elements:

5. *Authorizes* ONUB to use all necessary means to carry out the following mandate, within its capacity and in the areas where its armed units are deployed, and in coordination with humanitarian and development communities:
  – to ensure the respect of ceasefire agreements, through monitoring their implementation and investigating their violations,
  – to promote the re-establishment of confidence between the Burundian forces present, monitor and provide security at their pre-disarmament assembly sites, collect and secure weapons and military materiel to dispose of it as appropriate, and

---

[61] S/PV.4876 of 4 December 2003, emphasis added.
[62] Ibid., emphasis added.
[63] UN Doc. S/Res/1545, 21 May 2004.

The responsibility to react   223

contribute to the dismantling of militias as called for in the ceasefire agreements,

– to carry out the disarmament and demobilization portions of the national programme of disarmament, demobilization and reintegration of combatants,

– to monitor the quartering of the Armed Forces of Burundi and their heavy weapons, as well as the disarmament and demobilization of the elements that need to be disarmed and demobilized,

– to monitor, to the extent possible, the illegal flow of arms across the national borders, including Lake Tanganyika, in cooperation with the United Nations Organization Mission in the Democratic Republic of the Congo (MONUC) and, as appropriate, with the group of experts referred to in paragraph 10 of resolution 1533,

– to contribute to the creation of the necessary security conditions for the provision of humanitarian assistance, and facilitate the voluntary return of refugees and internally displaced persons,

– to contribute to the successful completion of the electoral process stipulated in the Arusha Agreement, by ensuring a secure environment for free, transparent and peaceful elections to take place,

– *without prejudice to the responsibility of the transitional Government of Burundi, to protect civilians under imminent threat of physical violence,*

– to ensure the protection of United Nations personnel, facilities, installations and equipment, as well as the security and freedom of movement of ONUB's personnel, and to coordinate and conduct, as appropriate, mine action activities in support of its mandate.[64]

The interesting part of the use of force mandate to protect civilians was the use of similar language to that in the Outcome Document of the sixtieth anniversary General Assembly Summit that recognized the primary obligation to protect civilians was with the sovereign state and, in the case of default of that responsibility, the international community would act. This resolution was again a mixture of peace enforcement and peace-building reflecting the peace process, even though it was extremely fragile.

This operation, ONUB, completed its mandate on 31 December 2006 and was succeeded by the United Nations Integrated office in Burundi (BINUB) established by Security Council Resolution 1719,[65] but recently there have

---

[64] Ibid., emphasis added.
[65] See www.un.org/en/peacekeeping/missions/past/onub/, accessed 28 July 2015, and UN Doc. S/Res/1719, 25 October 2006.

224   *Part III: The responsibility to protect in practice*

been reports of escalating violence as a result of the Burundian president deciding to run for a constitutionally illegal third term.[66]

The African Union and the Great Lakes Peace Process

The African Union has enthusiastically embraced *The Responsibility to Protect*. First, the Constitutive Act of the African Union has adopted amongst its principles:

> (h) the right of the Union to intervene in a Member State pursuant to a decision of the Assembly in respect of grave circumstances, namely: war crimes, genocide and crimes against humanity.[67]

Notwithstanding this provision as Dersso points out, the practice has been to avoid the direct citation of the provision, but instead in Darfur a 'protective role in convincing the Sudanese Government to accept African Union mediation' was adopted.[68] Nevertheless, the treaty establishing the African Union is an important example of a number of states that have adopted this second level of collective responsibility.

However, the African Union did act in the Great Lakes conflict, which had erupted with much violence in the DRC and Burundi (see above). The African Union and the UN mediated a peace process for this large regional conflict, taking place mainly in the DRC, but this long-standing war involved several states in the African Great Lakes Region, growing out of the ethnic conflict and genocides in Burundi and Rwanda. The International Conference on the Great Lakes Region (ICGLR) was established in 2004 by the 11 member states of the Great Lakes Region as a forum for resolving armed conflict, maintaining peace, security and stability and laying the foundation for post-conflict reconstruction in the region. The member states are Angola, Burundi, Central African Republic, Republic of Congo, Democratic Republic of Congo, Kenya, Rwanda, Sudan, Tanzania, Uganda and Zambia. These states adopted the Pact on Stability, Security and Development in the Great Lakes Region in December 2006. The Pact contained detailed obligations for member states relating to the main thematic areas of the Conference, namely peace and security, democracy and good governance, development and human security.[69]

---

[66] BBC News, 'Burundi President votes amid tension', 21 July 2015, available at www.bbc. co.uk/news/world-africa-33605531, accessed 28 July 2015.

[67] Constitutive Act of the African Union, adopted 11 July 2000 and entered into force 26 May 2001, 2158 UNTA 3, Article 4(h).

[68] S.A. Dersso, 'The African Union' in G. Zyberi (ed.), *An Institutional Approach to the Responsibility to Protect* (Cambridge: Cambridge University Press, 2013), p. 225, and 'Report of the Pan-African Parliament Fact Finding Mission on Darfur, the Sudan', AU Doc. AU/PAP/PRT/CIRC/CTTEE, 23 February 2005, para. 1.5.

[69] For the background to the Pact, see www.lse.ac.uk/collections/law/projects/greatlakes/ihl-greatlakes-summary.htm, accessed 27 July 2015.

The responsibility to react   225

A key part of that framework relating to the responsibility to protect is the Protocol on Non-Aggression and Mutual Defence in the Great Lakes Region. This Protocol includes this clause:

> Member States agree that the provisions of this Article and Article 5 of this Protocol shall not impair the exercise of their responsibility to protect populations from genocide, war crimes, ethnic cleansing, crimes against humanity, and gross violations committed by, or within, a State. The decision of the Member States to exercise their responsibility to protect populations in this provision shall be taken collectively with due procedural notice to the Peace and Security Council of the African Union and the Security Council of the United Nations.[70]

Sadly, as with African Union practice, the violence continues in this region and the responsibility to protect activity has not taken place outside of the civilian protection mandates in the DRC peacekeeping mission as discussed above.[71] In response to the resurgence of violence the Peace, Security and Cooperation Framework for the Democratic Republic of Congo and the region was signed by representatives of these same 11 countries in the region, the Chairs of the African Union, the International Conference on the Great Lakes Region, the Southern African Development Community and the United Nations Secretary-General on 24 February 2013 in Addis Ababa, Ethiopia.[72] It remains to be seen whether the Great Lakes Peace Process will truly lead to a lasting peace and whether the African Union will act on its treaty provision with respect to the responsibility to protect.

Darfur, Sudan

Activities within Darfur province were the most violent in Sudan's 22-year civil war. The Sudan Liberation Army/Movement (SLA) and Justice and Equality Movement (JEM) rebelled against the government, beginning in February 2003. The rebels are predominantly made up of African tribes, such as Fur, Zaghawa and Massaleit. After a string of rebel victories in spring 2003, the government responded to the rebellion by arming Arab 'Janjaweed' militia to clear civilian population bases of African tribes thought to be supporting the rebellion. The policy led to displacement of between 1.5 and 2 million civilians in Darfur, and the deaths of at least 50,000. A ceasefire agreement signed between the government and the Darfur rebels in April 2004 failed to stop the violence.[73]

---

[70] International Conference of the Great Lakes Region, Protocol on Non-aggression and Mutual Defence in the Great Lakes Region, 30 November 2006.

[71] Ibid., p. 64.

[72] See www.un.org/en/peacekeeping/missions/monusco/background.shtml, accessed 27 July 2015.

[73] For an excellent history of conflict and breaking of peace deals, see www.responsibilityto protect.org/index.php/crises/crisis-in-darfur, accessed 7 July 2015.

226   *Part III: The responsibility to protect in practice*

The Security Council had been staggeringly slow to respond to the established crimes against humanity in Darfur. In Resolution 1590 (2005) the Security Council established a peacekeeping force to monitor the comprehensive peace agreement that supposedly would end the long-standing civil war, but it did not incorporate any comprehensive solution to the Darfur crisis.[74] The resolution determined that the situation in Sudan was a threat to international peace and security. However, unlike in Burundi, the Democratic Republic of Congo and Côte d'Ivoire, there was no robust mandate given to protect civilians. The United Nations Mission in Sudan was mandated to support the implementation of the comprehensive peace agreement and monitor and verify the implementation of the ceasefire agreement, including the disarmament, demobilization and reintegration programme. In terms of civilian protection there was a mandate to ensure a human rights presence, but not the use of force. In 2005 the International Crisis Group assessed the situation as follows:

> More than two years into the crisis, the western Sudanese region of Darfur is acknowledged to be a humanitarian and human rights tragedy of the first order: as many as 5,000 people – overwhelmingly civilians – are dying every month. The humanitarian, security and political situations continue to deteriorate: atrocity crimes are continuing, people are still dying in large numbers of malnutrition and disease, and a new famine is feared. The international community is failing to protect civilians itself or influence the Sudanese government to do so.[75]

Darfur, Sudan was used as the example of the failure of the United Nations system in spite of the referral of the situation to the International Criminal Court.[76] However, in response to mounting pressure, the Security Council acted in accordance with the responsibility to react, but it was certainly late by years, not by any means a 'timely' intervention. UN Security Council Resolution 1706 of 31 August 2006 authorized the deployment of UN peacekeepers to Darfur, and applied the responsibility to protect principle to a particular context for the first time:

> *Recalling* also its previous resolutions…and 1674 (2006) on the protection of civilians in armed conflict, which reaffirms inter alia the provisions of paragraphs 138 and 139 of the 2005 United Nations World Summit outcome document.[77]

[74] UN Doc. S/Res/1590 (2005), 24 March 2005
[75] See www.crisisgroup.org/en/regions/africa/horn-of-africa/sudan/089-darfur-the-failure-to-protect.aspx, accessed 18 November 2015.
[76] UN Doc. S/Res/1593, 31 March 2005.
[77] UN Doc. S/Res/1706, 31 August 2006, original emphasis.

The responsibility to react 227

In addition to dramatically increasing the number of troops within the United Nations Missions in Sudan (UNMIS) by 17,300 military personnel and 3,200 civilian police personnel, the mandate for these troops was changed:

> 12. Acting under Chapter VII of the Charter of the United Nations:
>
> (a) Decides that UNMIS is authorized to use all necessary means, in the areas of deployment of its forces and as it deems within its capabilities: – to protect United Nations personnel, facilities, installations and equipment, to ensure the security and freedom of movement of United Nations personnel, humanitarian workers, assessment and evaluation commission personnel, to prevent disruption of the implementation of the Darfur Peace Agreement by armed groups, without prejudice to the responsibility of the Government of the Sudan, to protect civilians under threat of physical violence.[78]

It has to be noted that, once again, the civilian protection mandate was only within its areas of deployment and capabilities, which again only partially fulfils the responsibility to react mandate.

The mission in Darfur was changed to the African Union/United Nations hybrid Mission in Darfur (UNAMID) and it remains active to this day. Under Security Council Resolution 1769, the civilian protection mandate continues.[79]

Côte d'Ivoire

The civil war in Côte d'Ivoire has not involved the same degree of humanitarian catastrophe as that in the DRC, but in spite of that fact, the mandates for the peacekeeping mission have been robust as well. ECOWAS and the French forces had intervened after a second government coup attempt in September 2002 when members of the military junta were executed. In January 2003 the political parties signed the French-brokered Linas-Marcoussis Accord agreeing to a power-sharing government of national reconciliation. However, in September 2003 the northern rebel forces suspended their participation in the national reconciliation government and the United Nations expanded its involvement from a political mission to a peace enforcement mission acting under Chapter VII, thereby supporting the French and ECOWAS troops.

In a lengthy and detailed Resolution, 1528 (2004), the peacekeeping mission of the United Nations Mission in Côte d'Ivoire (UNOCI) was established under Chapter VII with a mandate reminiscent of a traditional peacekeeping operation, including 'Monitoring of the ceasefire and movement of armed groups' and a typical post-conflict mandate of 'Disarmament,

---

[78] Ibid.
[79] UN Doc. S/Res/1769, 31 July 2007.

228   *Part III: The responsibility to protect in practice*

demobilization, reintegration, repatriation and resettlement'. Yet there was a clear use of force mandate given as well, where the force was to be used to 'protect civilians under imminent threat of physical violence, within its capabilities and its areas of deployment'. This mandate again contained the limitation clause for the use of force. In addition, the mission was 'to facilitate the free flow of people, goods and humanitarian assistance, inter alia, by helping to establish the necessary security conditions'.[80]

The mission established in April 2004 by this resolution authorized a large force of 7,000 UN peacekeepers and personnel to the country, alongside 4,000 French troops (the French troops would act in accordance with the UN commanders). The mandate of both UN peacekeepers and Operation Licorne (the French operation) was continually extended but changed dramatically with the 2010 presidential election crisis.[81] Incumbent Laurent Gbagbo refused to honour the results of the election that had declared his opponent Alassane Ouattara the winner. The results of the election (which had taken place over two rounds) were announced on 3 December 2010 and the violent clashes between the two camps of supporters began soon after. The Special Adviser of the Secretary-General on the Prevention of Genocide, Francis Deng, and Special Adviser to the Secretary-General on the Responsibility to Protect, Edward Luck, issued two joint statements on the political crisis with the second reminding 'all parties of their responsibility to protect all populations in Côte d'Ivoire, irrespective of their ethnicity, nationality, or religion'.[82]

On 30 March 2011 the Security Council passed Resolution 1975 (2011), repeating its calls for Mr Gbagbo to step down and urging an immediate end to the violence against civilians. The Council reaffirmed the mandate of UNOCI to protect civilians, including preventing the use of heavy weaponry against them.[83] There was an important part of this resolution with reference to the responsibility to protect:

> Condemning the serious abuses and violations of international law in Côte d'Ivoire, including humanitarian, human rights and refugee law, reaffirming the primary responsibility of each State to protect civilians and reiterating that parties to armed conflicts bear the primary responsibility to take all feasible steps to ensure the protection of civilians and facilitate the rapid and unimpeded passage of humanitarian assistance and the safety of humanitarian personnel.[84]

---

[80] UN Doc. S/Res/1528, 27 February 2004.
[81] For a history of the UN operation, see www.un.org/en/peacekeeping/missions/unoci/, accessed 7 July 2015.
[82] UN Press release, available at www.un.org/en/preventgenocide/adviser/pdf/Special%20 Advisers%27%20Statement%20on%20Cote%20d%27Ivoire,%2029%20.12.2010.pdf, accessed 7 July 2015.
[83] UN Doc. S/Res/1975, 30 March 2011.
[84] Ibid.

The responsibility to react 229

In spite of this resolution, by April Ban Ki-moon was reporting that over 1,000 civilians had died in clashes and the UN High Commissioner for Refugees said that more than 500,000 people had been forcibly displaced and 94,000 had fled to Liberia.[85] A military operation began on 4 April with a statement by the UN Secretary-General in which he instructed UNOCI to 'take the necessary measures to prevent the use of heavy weapons against the civilian population'.[86] Gbagbo was arrested on 11 April 2011 by Ouattara's forces after days of fighting with the involvement of UNOCI and the French military.[87]

This last intervention in Côte d'Ivoire in 2011 revealed another substantial change in United Nations peacekeeping practice. On this occasion, the Security Council was prepared to authorize reasonably timely intervention that, in the end, probably saved thousands of lives. This intervention was not limited geographically, was aided by French forces and did, at least for the time being, resolve the prevailing human rights crisis. It led to commentators questioning whether the responsibility to protect was indeed emerging as a legal principle requiring robust use of force mandates to protect civilians.[88] This view was further supported by the final case study in this chapter: the NATO intervention in Libya.

Libya

As a consequence of the Arab Spring, protests began in Libya, with protestors demanding an end to Muammar Gaddafi's 41-year rule. These protests spread from Tripoli to Benghazi, a city that became the centre of opposition activity. Unlike the leaders in Tunisia and Egypt, Gaddafi had no intention of going quietly and he sent the army to crush any dissent. The point at which the responsibility to protect became engaged was a speech Gaddafi made on 22 February 2011 when he called on his supporters to attack the protesting 'cockroaches' (reminiscent of the Rwandan genocide) and 'cleanse Libya house by house'.[89] This was particularly concerning as this was the day after Gaddafi's son Saif had warned of 'rivers of blood' in Libya.[90] The evidence was clear that the

---

[85] See www.responsibilitytoprotect.org/index.php/crises/crisis-in-ivory-coast, accessed 7 July 2015.

[86] Ibid.

[87] Ibid.

[88] M. Serrano, 'The Responsibility to Protect: Libya and Côte d'Ivoire' (2011) 3 *Amsterdam Law Forum* 92; A. Bellamy and P. Williams, 'The New Politics of Protection: Côte d'Ivoire, Libya and the Responsibility to Protect' (2011) 87 *International Affairs* 275.

[89] BBC News, 'Defiant Gaddafi Refuses to Quit', 22 February 2011, available at www.bbc. co.uk/news/world-middle-east-12544624, accessed 7 July 2015.

[90] Al Alarabiya, 'Gaddafi's son warns of "rivers of blood" in Libya', 21 February 2011, available at www.alarabiya.net/articles/2011/02/21/138515.html, accessed 7 July 2015.

230   *Part III: The responsibility to protect in practice*

government was indiscriminately targeting civilians with 233 deaths reported by 20 February 2011.[91]

In this case the reaction by the United Nations was swift and decisive. On 22 February 2011 the Special Advisers on the Prevention of Genocide and the Responsibility to Protect issued a statement on the situation in Libya, in which they reminded the Libyan Government of its responsibility to protect its population and called for an immediate end to the violence.[92] Three days later, the Human Rights Council adopted Resolution S15/2 calling for the Libyan Government to uphold its responsibility to protect and cease all human rights violations; for an international commission of inquiry to be established; and for the General Assembly to suspend Libya from the Council.[93] In response, the General Assembly unanimously suspended Libya's membership of the Council on 1 March.[94] Later, on 1 June 2011, the report submitted to the Human Rights Council by the International Commission of Inquiry asserted that the Libyan Government and opposition forces had been committing crimes against humanity and war crimes since the start of the crisis.[95]

The Security Council, responding swiftly and unanimously, adopted Resolution 1970 on 26 February 2011. Resolution 1970 affirmed Libya's 'responsibility to protect' and imposed an arms embargo, a travel ban on the Gaddafi family and key members of government, froze the assets of the Gaddafi family and referred the situation to the International Criminal Court for investigation into reports of crimes against humanity.[96] When the non-military measures imposed here failed to stop the violence, the Council adopted Resolution 1973, less than a month later, on 17 March 2011. It has to be noted that China, Russia, India, Brazil and Germany abstained from the vote. The resolution accepted a no-fly zone to protect Libyan civilians and authorized member states, in cooperation with the Security Council, to take 'all necessary measures to protect civilians and civilian populated areas under threat.'[97] Ban Ki-moon issued a statement immediately after the meeting, pointing out that Resolution 1973 'affirms, clearly and unequivocally, the international community's determination to fulfill its responsibility to protect civilians from violence perpetrated upon them by their own government'.[98]

---

[91] International Coalition for the Responsibility to Protect, 'Crisis in Libya', available at www.responsibilitytoprotect.org/index.php/crises/crisis-in-libya, accessed 7 July 2015.

[92] UN Press Release, available at www.responsibilitytoprotect.org/UN_Secretary-General%27s_Special_Advisers_on_the_Prevention_of_Genocide_and_the_Responsibility_to_Protect_on_the_Situation_in_Libya%5B1%5D.pdf, accessed 7 July 2015.

[93] UN Doc. A/HRC/S-15/1, 2 February 2011.

[94] UN Press Release, available at www.un.org/press/en/2011/ga11050.doc.htm, accessed 7 July 2015.

[95] International Coalition for the Responsibility to Protect, 'Crisis in Libya'.

[96] UN Doc. S/Res/1970, 26 February 2011.

[97] UN Doc. S/Res/1973, 17 March 2011.

[98] International Coalition for the Responsibility to Protect, 'Crisis in Libya'.

The resolution was acted upon by the imposition of a no-fly zone policed by a coalition of states, which included 15 NATO countries, Sweden, Jordan, Qatar and the United Arab Emirates. The coalition also provided support to the rebel National Transitional Council (NTC) forces in Benghazi and Misrata, and then in Libya's capital Tripoli. The NTC forces prevailed and on 24 October 2011 NTC officials declared the end of the eight-month conflict following the death of Gaddafi and his son Mutassim on 20 October.[99] The UN Security Council voted unanimously on 26 October 2011 to end the no-fly zone in Libya and the NATO mission ended on the 31 October.[100]

The NATO mission was very controversial as there were serious concerns that the aerial bombardment had caused civilian casualties, and there were allegations of 'mission creep' that had strayed into regime change rather than civilian protection particularly expressed by a group of states under the acronym BRICS (Brazil, Russia, India, China and South Africa).[101] An Amnesty International report released on 19 March 2012 found that although NATO had made 'significant efforts to minimize civilian damage', the airstrikes had resulted in the death of scores of civilians and injury to many others.[102] These conclusions were supported in the May 2012 Human Rights Watch report.[103] There were also allegations that Libyan rebel forces had 'repeatedly violated international humanitarian law during the law, where particularly foreign migrants were subjected to arbitrary arrest and in some cases torture and execution'.[104] Human Rights Watch reported that the bodies of 53 that were assumed to be Gaddafi supporters were found on 23 October apparently executed by rebel militias.[105] Finally, the public murder of Gaddafi, broadcast on 20 October around the world, caused real concern about the role of the international community in this violent regime change. As Zifcak asserts, the Libyan intervention demonstrated that much work needed to be done in 'determining the nature and limits of military strategy and tactics in the implementation of a Pillar 3 intervention'.[106] This reaction was particularly

---

[99] Ibid.

[100] UN Doc. S/Res/2016, 26 October 2011.

[101] J. Gifkins, 'The UN Security Council Divided: Syria in Crisis' (2012) 4 *Global Responsibility to Protect* 377; S. Zifcak, 'The Responsibility to Protect after Libya and Syria' (2012) 13 *Melbourne Journal of International Law* 59.

[102] Amnesty International, 'Libya: The Forgotten Victims of NATO strikes', London, 2012.

[103] Human Rights Watch, 'Unacknowledged Deaths: Civilian Casualties in NATO's Air Campaign in Libya', New York, 2012.

[104] Human Rights Council, 'Report of the International Commission of Inquiry to Investigate all Alleged Violations of International Human Rights Law in the Libyan Arab Jamahiriya', UN Doc. A/HRC/17/44, 1 June 2011.

[105] Human Rights Watch, 'Libya: Apparent Execution of 53 Gaddafi Supporters', 24 October 2011, available at www.hrw.org/news/2011/10/24/libya-apparent-execution-53-gaddafi-supporters, accessed 7 July 2015.

[106] S. Zifcak, 'Falls the Shadow: The Responsibility to Protect from Theory to Practice' in S. Sampford and R. Thakur (eds), *Responsibility to Protect and Sovereignty* (Farnham, Surrey: Ashgate, 2013), p. 19.

Conclusion

If one reviews the change in mandates of the UN forces in operations such as Burundi, the Democratic Republic of Congo, Côte d'Ivoire and Darfur, Sudan, one can see a remarkable shift in the way in which peacekeeping is conducted. A much better term has to be peacemaking or robust peace enforcement operations. The complexities of these missions include a mix of peace enforcement with post-conflict peace-building, which will be discussed in the following chapter.

From an international law standpoint it may be argued that the United Nations is finally embarking on its original mandate of collective security but in many cases within a sovereign state's boundaries, something that was not contemplated by the original drafters of the Charter. However, it is acknowledged that many of these situations result in real threats to international peace and security, as one can see from the Great Lakes conflict involving several sovereign states. In our interdependent world there can never be a truly domestic situation. Movements of populations and of goods mean that other nations will be affected by civil wars. Nevertheless, these are truly Chapter VII, not Chapter VI, operations, as there are specific mandates to use force to protect not only the peacekeepers but also the civilian population. As these situations become threats due to the way the civilian population is affected, these mandates seek to stop the very source of the conflict: attacks on civilian populations.

The difficulty in this whole reform process, however, is the lack of adoption of the criteria for force and the precautionary principles recommended in *The Responsibility to Protect*. This means that charges of selectivity and political considerations can still be levelled against the Security Council. There are clearly no-go areas that will not see needed assistance, such as any conflicts involving the Permanent Five members. Furthermore, as Libya demonstrates, civilian protection mandates should never be transitioned into regime change. The opposition to what happened in Libya has had a devastating effect on the conflict in Syria, as will be discussed in the final chapter.

9   The responsibility to rebuild

Introduction

Boutros Boutros-Ghali in his *An Agenda for Peace* provides an excellent definition of post-conflict peace-building, which is – 'action to identify and support structures which will tend to strengthen and solidify peace in order to avoid a relapse into conflict'.[1] The Brahimi Report on peacekeeping adds substance to the term peace-building. It is this expanded definition that seems to have informed all subsequent activities in this area:

> 13. Peace-building…defines activities undertaken on the far side of conflict to reassemble the foundations of peace and provide the tools for building on those foundations something that is more than just the absence of war. Thus, peace-building includes but is not limited to reintegrating former combatants into civilian society, strengthening the rule of law (for example, through training and restructuring of local police, and judicial and penal reform); improving respect for human rights through the monitoring, education and investigation of past and existing abuses; providing technical assistance for democratic development (including electoral assistance and support for free media); and promoting conflict resolution and reconciliation techniques.[2]

It is this feature of the responsibility to protect – the responsibility to rebuild – that, if successful, would prevent the recurrence of conflict. Unlike the responsibility to prevent, which remains undeveloped, the international community has embraced the responsibility to assist in peace-building, which includes helping rebuild the institutions and infrastructures of states that have been involved in civil war or in international conflict to 'build bonds of

---

[1] B. Boutros-Ghali *An Agenda for Peace: Preventive Diplomacy, Peacemaking, and Peace-keeping: Report of the Secretary-General Pursuant to the Statement Adopted by the Summit Meeting of the Security Council on 31 January 1992* (New York: United Nations, 1992); UN Doc. A/47/277-S/24111, 17 June 1992, para. 21.

[2] The Panel on United Nations Peace Operations, chaired by Lakhdar *Brahimi*, reported to the UN Secretary-General on 17 August 2000: UN Doc. A/55/305 (Brahimi Report).

234   *Part III: The responsibility to protect in practice*

peaceful mutual benefit among nations formerly at war' and to address the deepest causes of the conflict including 'economic dispair, social injustice and political oppression'.[3] The subject of this chapter is deliberately not directed at the law of occupation, as post-conflict peace-building missions are encompassed in Chapter VII United Nations resolutions authorizing multilateral action, not occupation in international humanitarian law.

In spite of these noble aspirations, rebuilding a nation after armed conflict or widespread infliction of harm by its leaders towards an ethnic or political group is probably one of the most difficult tasks. Accomplishing these goals after the Second World War took a massive financial and logistical effort in the Marshall Plan.[4] Since that time there has not been a Marshall Plan equivalent for post-conflict recovery and states often limp along from crisis to crisis.[5] It was not until 1992, in an *Agenda for Peace*, that peace-building came to the forefront of the international agenda. Boutros-Ghali argued that there was an 'increasingly common moral perception that spans the world's nations and peoples, and which is finding expression in international law'.[6] He argues that there is an 'obvious connection between democratic practices – such as the rule of law and transparency in decision-making – and the achievement of true peace and security'.[7] This theme of the rule of law is taken up in all of the subsequent reports that examine the concept of post-conflict peace-building. The responsibility to rebuild encompasses international legal obligations that, if satisfied, could prevent future conflict.

In this chapter we again examine the various reports on peace-building, view the practice of the United Nations in this area and draw conclusions concerning the international legal aspect of the responsibility to rebuild. Furthermore, it is possible in this chapter to examine the early initiatives of the Peace-building Commission and the Peace-building Support Office, international institutions that resulted from the recommendations from the sixtieth anniversary summit in 2005.

The reports on peace-building

In the first substantial report recommending post-conflict peace-building, *An Agenda for Peace*, Boutros Boutros-Ghali argued that for peacemaking and peacekeeping operations to be truly successful, they had to include efforts to identify and support structures that would consolidate peace and advance a sense of confidence and well-being among people. This included: disarming the previously warring parties and the restoration of order; the custody and

---

[3] Boutros-Ghali *An Agenda for Peace*, para. 15.
[4] Act of 3 April 1948, European Recovery Act (Marshall Plan), Enrolled Acts and Resolutions of Congress, 1789–1996, General Records of the United States Government, Record Group 11, National Archives.
[5] See discussion of the Great Lakes process in Chapter 8, for example.
[6] Boutros-Ghali *An Agenda for Peace*, para. 15.
[7] Ibid., para. 59.

The responsibility to rebuild **235**

possible destruction of weapons; repatriating refugees; advisory and training support for security personnel; monitoring elections; advancing efforts to protect human rights; reforming or strengthening governmental institutions and promoting formal and informal processes of political participation.[8] Christine Gray refers to this phase as the 'exit strategy for peacekeeping operations', which must be directed towards 'defining an overall objective, not an arbitrary, self-imposed, artificial deadline which encourages belligerents to outwait the outside intervention'.[9]

It was Kofi Annan who was the first to relate economic development to the prevention of conflict (see Chapter 7) and to rebuilding after conflict. He first discussed the nature and rationale of post-conflict peace-building in his 1998 report on *The Causes of Conflict and the Promotion of Durable Peace and Sustainable Development in Africa*.[10] Annan argued that post-conflict peace-building meant actions undertaken at the end of a conflict to consolidate peace. This consolidation would require more than diplomatic and military action, but he expanded on the categories proposed by Boutros-Ghali. He argued that there needed to be an integrated peace-building effort to address the various factors that caused the conflict. This would include the creation or strengthening of national institutions, monitoring elections, promoting human rights, providing for reintegration and rehabilitation programmes, as well as creating conditions for resumed development.[11]

The Brahimi Report on United Nations Peace Operations in 1999 agreed with Annan and recommended that there was a need to build United Nations capacity to contribute to peace-building, both preventive and post-conflict, in a 'genuinely integrated manner'.[12] In a unique aspect of the report, Brahimi acknowledged social and economic causes of conflict by indicating that an essential complement to effective peace-building included support for the fight against corruption, the implementation of humanitarian demining programmes, emphasis on human immunodeficiency virus/acquired immunodeficiency syndrome (HIV/AIDS) education and control and action against other infectious diseases.[13]

An innovative aspect of the Brahimi Report was the discussion of the governance aspect of post-conflict peace-building contained in the section entitled 'the Challenges of Transitional Civil Administration'.[14] The background to the difficulty of post-conflict governance was argued to have emerged in 1999, as until then the UN had conducted just a small handful of operations

---

[8] Boutros-Ghali, *An Agenda for Peace*, para. 55.
[9] C. Gray, *International Law and the Use of Force*, 3rd edition (Oxford: Oxford University Press, 2008), p. 275.
[10] K. Annan, *The Causes of Conflict and the Promotion of Peace and Sustainable Development in Africa*, 16 April 1998.
[11] Ibid., para. 63.
[12] Brahimi Report, para. 6.
[13] Ibid., para. 14.
[14] Ibid., Section H, paras 76–83.

236   *Part III: The responsibility to protect in practice*

with elements of civil administration. However, in June 1999 the Secretariat was directed to develop transitional civil administration for Kosovo and three months later for East Timor. The report correctly pointed out the difficulties with the mundane aspects of the task by stating:

> 77. These operations face challenges and responsibilities that are unique among United Nations field operations. No other operations must set and enforce the law, establish customs services and regulations, set and collect business and personal taxes, attract foreign investment, adjudicate property disputes and liabilities for war damage, reconstruct and operate all public utilities, create a banking system, run schools and pay teachers and collect the garbage – in a war-damaged society, using voluntary contributions, because the assessed mission budget, even for such 'transitional administration' missions, does not fund local administration itself. In addition to such tasks, these missions must also try to rebuild civil society and promote respect for human rights, in places where grievance is widespread and grudges run deep.[15]

Critically, the report indicated that if transitional administration was to continue, there had to be expertise developed within the United Nations. The recommendation on this aspect supported the idea of the crucial importance of the imposition of the rule of law:

6. Transitional civil administration:

> The Panel recommends that the Secretary-General invite a panel of international legal experts, including individuals with experience in United Nations operations that have transitional administration mandates, to evaluate the feasibility and utility of developing an interim criminal code, including any regional adaptations potentially required, for use by such operations pending the re-establishment of local rule of law and local law enforcement capacity.[16]

The Responsibility to Protect adopted all of these approaches and included peace-building as a critical phase in any intervention in human rights catastrophes – the responsibility to rebuild. However, the Commissioners went even further and asserted that there has to be a commitment from the international community to build a durable peace with the promotion of good governance and sustainable development.[17] Too often the responsibility to rebuild had been insufficiently recognized and the exit of the intervention poorly managed, with the underlying problems causing the conflict

---

[15] Ibid., para. 77

[16] Ibid., Recommendation 6.

[17] International Commission on Intervention and State Sovereignty (ICISS), *The Responsibility to Protect* (Ottawa, 2001), para. 5.1, p. 39.

The responsibility to rebuild 237

left unresolved.[18] The critical features, as with *An Agenda for Peace* and the Brahimi Report, were disarmament, demobilization and reintegration of the armed groups.[19] Other critical aspects of post-conflict activity were the necessity for justice, reconciliation and economic growth.[20]

These peace-building aspects were endorsed by the High-Level Panel in their report, *A More Secure World*. The panel argued that resources spent on the implementation of peace agreements and peace-building were the best investments for future conflict prevention, as states that experienced civil war faced a high risk of civil war recurring.[21] The report argued that in the period before the outbreak of civil war and in the transition out of war, neither the UN nor the broader international community, including international financial institutions, were well organized to assist countries attempting to build peace. The report argued that what was needed was a single intergovernmental organ empowered to 'monitor and pay close attention to countries at risk' and 'ensure concerted action by donors, agencies, programmes and financial institutions, and mobilize financial resources for sustainable peace'.[22] This would require coordination between governments, bilateral donors, the international financial institutions and the UN.[23] None of this would be effective unless resources were given for reintegration and rehabilitation. As well as capacity-building of effective public institutions, this included the police, the judiciary and human rights institutions.[24]

Although mentioned briefly in the Brahimi Report, *A More Secure World* expanded on the proposal to establish a Peacebuidling Commission, which would be an intergovernmental organization not contemplated by the drafters of the Charter. The panel acknowledged that there was 'no place in the United Nations system explicitly designed to avoid State collapse and the slide to war or to assist countries in their transition from war to peace'.[25] The panel stated that it was no surprise that this was not included in the Charter as the work in largely internal conflicts by the UN was a fairly recent event. However, there was a clear international obligation to assist states in developing their capacity to perform their sovereign functions effectively and responsibly.[26] This is an astonishing statement considering the emphasis in the Charter on sovereign equality of states. From this point on, states would be identified as fragile, requiring rebuilding in order to avoid further conflict.

---

18 Ibid., para. 5.7, p. 40.
19 Ibid., para. 5.9, p. 41.
20 Ibid., para. 5.19, p. 42.
21 UN General Assembly, Note (transmitting report of the High-Level Panel on Threats, Challenges and Change, entitled 'A more secure world: our shared responsibility'), 2 December 2004, A/59/565, para. 221, p. 71.
22 Ibid., para. 225, p. 71.
23 Ibid., para. 226, p. 71.
24 Ibid., para. 229, p. 72.
25 Ibid., para. 261, p. 83.
26 Ibid.

238 *Part III: The responsibility to protect in practice*

The legal mandate for establishment of the Peace-building Commission would come from Article 29 of the Charter, which permitted the Security Council to establish 'such subsidiary organs as it deems necessary for the performance of its functions'. The panel argued that the UN needed to be able to act in a 'coherent and effective way' on a continuum that ran from early warning, through preventive action to post-conflict peace-building.[27] The functions of the commission would be to identify countries at risk, to organize proactive assistance and to assist in the transition between conflict and post-conflict peace-building for whatever period might be necessary.[28]

Annan's *In Larger Freedom* also supported, in the same phrases, the Peace-building Commission and its Peace-building Support Office. Annan called the lack of such an institution 'a gaping hole in the United Nations institutional machinery'.[29] However, in a very disappointed retreat from his earlier positions, Annan did not support a pivotal part of the Commission's role, stating:

> I do not believe that such a body should have an early warning or monitoring function, but it would be valuable if Member States could at any stage make use of the Peace-building Commission's advice and could request assistance from a standing fund for peace-building to build their domestic institutions for reducing conflict, including through strengthening the rule-of-law institutions.[30]

Sadly, the Outcome Document of the sixtieth anniversary Summit supported the Annan vision of the Peace-building Commission without the early warning/preventive aspect. The document stated:

> 97. Emphasizing the need for a coordinated, coherent and integrated approach to post-conflict peace-building and reconciliation, with a view to achieving sustainable peace; and recognizing the need for a dedicated institutional mechanism to address the special needs of countries emerging from conflict towards recovery, reintegration and reconstruction and to assist them in laying the foundation for sustainable development; and recognizing the vital role of the United Nations in that regard, we decide to establish a Peace-building Commission as an intergovernmental advisory body.
>
> 98. The main purpose of the Peace-building Commission is to bring together all relevant actors to marshal resources and to advise on and propose integrated strategies for post-conflict peace-building and recovery.

---

[27] Ibid., para. 263, p. 83 and Article 29 of the Charter of the United Nations.
[28] Ibid., para. 264, pp. 83–84.
[29] Kofi Annan, *In Larger Freedom: Towards Development, Security and Human Rights for All*, UN Doc. A/59/2005/Add.3, 26 May 2005, para. 114, p. 29.
[30] Ibid., para. 115, p. 29.

The responsibility to rebuild 239

The Peace-building Commission should focus attention on the reconstruction and institution-building efforts necessary for recovery from conflict and support the development of integrated strategies in order to lay the foundation for sustainable development. In addition, it should provide recommendations and information to improve the coordination of all relevant actors within and outside the United Nations, develop best practices, help to ensure predictable financing for early recovery activities and extend the period of attention by the international community to post-conflict recovery. The Peace-building Commission should act in all matters on the basis of consensus of its members.

The Summit also accepted the idea of a Peace-building Support office, but in a much more truncated version:

104. We also request the Secretary-General to establish, within the Secretariat and from within existing resources, a small peace-building support office staffed by qualified experts to assist and support the Peace-building Commission. The office should draw on the best expertise available.

This outcome is disappointing as it does not represent the vision of peace-building contained in *A More Secure World*, as this body would only have a mandate to deal with post-conflict societies and not engage in early warning. Although this might prevent the further emergence of conflict in societies that have already gone through a civil war, and perhaps an armed international intervention, it fails to deal with emerging situations. The Peace-building Commission was established by General Assembly Resolution in 2005.[31] Notwithstanding the fact that peace-building is not joined up institutionally with prevention, the vision for the international body was the comprehensive one proposed by Annan that deals with root causes of conflict including lack of economic development. As Evans points out, '[p]ost-conflict peacebuilding is not the end of the process of conflict resolution; it has to be the beginning of a new process of conflict prevention.'[32]

It is evident that the recommendation for the responsibility to rebuild included in the 2001 report was strongly supported by UN reform efforts within the 2005 sixtieth anniversary Summit. Peace-building has now been institutionalized. It remains to be seen whether this institutionalization has been supported by the practice within the past 10 years. The next section reveals that the practice of rebuilding seems to have become embedded within UN peacekeeping operations and it is often difficult to determine where peacekeeping ends and peace-building begins. These were the type

---

[31] General Assembly Resolution A/Res/60/180, 30 December 2005.
[32] G. Evans, *The Responsibility to Protect* (Washington DC: Brookings Institution Press, 2008), p. 148.

240 *Part III: The responsibility to protect in practice*

of complex operations envisioned in the Brahimi Report.[33] The mandates for Darfur, the Democratic Republic of Congo and Burundi, for example, contain a mixture of peace enforcement and peace-building.[34] There are also operations that are instituted in the post-conflict phase even though there was not a traditional peacekeeping force. Examples of these types of operations are in Kosovo, Afghanistan, East Timor, Haiti and Iraq. Some of these operations follow unilateral armed intervention (Afghanistan, Iraq) or peace agreements (Haiti, East Timor) that did not include peacekeeping forces.

United Nations practice

Prior to *The Responsibility to Protect* and the subsequent reports, there were historical examples of post-conflict peace-building operations. It is outside the scope of this book to examine the recovery efforts in post-war Germany and Japan, but it could be argued that the efforts in these two nations are the model for disarmament, recovery and reconstruction. It is a shame the international community did not learn from its own history. It was not until the 1990s that the international community again engaged in systematic post-conflict recovery.

Cambodia

The first major peace-building operation in this new era was in Cambodia. The international community did little to assist the people of Cambodia during their genocide, but in the 1980s the Secretary-General of the UN assisted in general peace negotiations. As a result of intensive negotiations, a ceasefire was agreed between all parties and a peace treaty signed in Paris in April 1991. Cambodia had two separate UN missions commencing in October 1991 with the authorization of the United Nations Advance Mission in Cambodia by Resolution 717 of 16 October 1991. Its mandate was to assist the four Cambodian parties to maintain their ceasefire and to initiate mine-awareness training of the civilian population.[35] This mandate was enlarged on 8 January 1992 to include a major training programme for Cambodians in mine-detection and mine-clearance.[36] This mission had few personnel and constituted only limited UN involvement. But this changed dramatically a month later.

In February 1992 the Security Council authorized the establishment of the United Nations Transitional Authority in Cambodia (UNTAC). The mandate given to this group was robust and gave the UN an unprecedented

---

[33] Report of the Panel on United Nations Peace Operations, UN Doc. **A**/55/305 – S/2000/809, para. 198, p. 34.

[34] DRC, UN Doc. S/Res/1565, 1 October 2004, Burundi; UN Doc. S/Res/1545, 21 May 2004, Darfur; UN Doc. S/Res/1706, 31 August 2006.

[35] UN Doc. S/Res/717, 16 October 1991.

[36] UN Doc. S/Res/728, 8 January 1992.

role.[37] The role of UNTAC was to supervise the ceasefire, the end of foreign military assistance and the withdrawal of foreign forces; regroup, canton and disarm all armed forces of the Cambodian parties and ensure a 70 per cent level of demobilization; control and supervise the activities of the administrative structures, including the police; ensure and respect human rights; and organize and conduct free and fair elections.[38] The mission assumed control of the key portions of the government including foreign affairs, defence, security, finance and communications. For the first time since the establishment of the UN, a peacekeeping mission was governing a nation. The mandate of UNTAC ended in September 1993 with the formation of a new government of Cambodia following elections when nearly 90 per cent of the voters cast their ballot for a Constituent Assembly.[39]

This mission was only a partial success. The Paris Accords were not fully implemented and civil war continued for some time with the Khmer Rouge. However, the election did bring in a coalition government, which diminished the strength of the Khmer Rouge.[40] Eventually the Cambodians agreed to a hybrid court, the Extraordinary Chambers in the Courts of Cambodia (ECCC), to try a few of the perpetrators of the Cambodian genocide.[41] The reviews of the success of this court are mixed, but notwithstanding the mixed success, there has not been a return to extreme violence in Cambodia.[42]

Kosovo

The administration in Kosovo, following the NATO intervention, is another example of a comprehensive peace-building mission. However, Kosovo and the next example, East Timor, represented the 'cross-over into comprehensive governance of territory'.[43] The mission was established in Security Council Resolution 1244. The critical operative paragraphs stated:

> 10. Authorizes the Secretary-General, with the assistance of relevant international organizations, to establish an international civil presence in Kosovo in order to provide an interim administration for Kosovo under

[37] See www.un.org/en/peacekeeping/missions/past/untac.htm, accessed 11 July 2015.

[38] UN Doc. S/Res/745, 28 February 1992.

[39] See www.un.org/en/peacekeeping/missions/past/untac.htm, accessed 11 July 2015.

[40] S.J. Stedman, 'UN Intervention in Civil Wars: Imperatives of Choice and Strategy' in D. Daniel and B. Hayes, *Beyond Traditional Peacekeeping* (Basingstoke: MacMillan Press, 1995), pp. 43–44.

[41] Extraordinary Chambers Responsible for the Prosecution of Crimes Committed by the Khmer Rouge in Cambodia, UN Doc. A/Res/57 228B, 22 May 2003.

[42] M. Salber, 'The Khmer Rouge Tribunal: successes and failures of an innovative form of justice', Political Science 2013, available at https://hal.archives-ouvertes.fr/dumas-00951111/document, accessed 27 July 2015.

[43] S. Mohamed, 'From Keeping the Peace to Building Peace: A Proposal for a Revitalized United Nations Trusteeship Council' (2005) 105 *Columbia Law Review* 809, p. 819.

242 *Part III: The responsibility to protect in practice*

which the people of Kosovo can enjoy substantial autonomy within the Federal Republic of Yugoslavia, and which will provide transitional administration while establishing and overseeing the development of provisional democratic self-governing institutions to ensure conditions for a peaceful and normal life for all inhabitants of Kosovo;

11. Decides that the main responsibilities of the international civil presence will include:

(a) Promoting the establishment, pending a final settlement, of substantial autonomy and self-government in Kosovo, taking full account of annex 2 and of the Rambouillet accords (S/1999/648);

(b) Performing basic civilian administrative functions where and as long as required;

(c) Organizing and overseeing the development of provisional institutions for democratic and autonomous self-government pending a political settlement, including the holding of elections;

(d) Transferring, as these institutions are established, its administrative responsibilities while overseeing and supporting the consolidation of Kosovo's local provisional institutions and other peace-building activities;

(e) Facilitating a political process designed to determine Kosovo's future status, taking into account the Rambouillet accords (S/1999/648);

(f) In a final stage, overseeing the transfer of authority from Kosovo's provisional institutions to institutions established under a political settlement;

(g) Supporting the reconstruction of key infrastructure and other economic reconstruction;

(h) Supporting, in coordination with international humanitarian organizations, humanitarian and disaster relief aid;

(i) Maintaining civil law and order, including establishing local police forces and meanwhile through the deployment of international police personnel to serve in Kosovo;

(j) Protecting and promoting human rights;

(k) Assuring the safe and unimpeded return of all refugees and displaced persons to their homes in Kosovo.[44]

This resolution encompassed almost every aspect of civilian administration. This operation has not been entirely successful as there is no conclusion about the ultimate status of Kosovo and ethnic conflict has continued, with many of the remaining Serbian population fleeing back to Serbia and Montenegro. The key problem as set out by Alexandros Yannis, the

[44] UN Doc. S/Res/1244, 10 June 1999.

The responsibility to rebuild 243

political advisor to Bernard Kouchner, the Special Representative of the Secretary-General, was:

> In the absence of a consensus over the future status of Kosovo, that status must be frozen: Kosovo should enter a deep winter in which Resolution 1244, with all its ambiguities, will be the only guiding light for both Kosovo Albanians and Serbs as well as for the international administration.[45]

However, since that opinion, there has been an astonishing effort made by various segments of the international community, including the European Union, the OSCE and the UN, in establishing a viable domestic political, legal and social system. It is evidence of just how difficult and longterm the effort to build the peace has to be. Kosovo has recently declared its independence, but that independence is not recognized by powers such as Russia, which has a long-standing connection with Serbia. The matter has been litigated by Advisory Opinion in the International Court of Justice, which recognized the status of the unilateral declaration of independence but did not declare on issues of self-determination.[46] Kosovo is basically self-governing, although its political status remains unresolved.

East Timor

East Timor was the second of these comprehensive missions and again the success could be said to be mixed. Although the political status in this situation is resolved, there are still periodic outbreaks of violence.[47] The resolution establishing this transitional administration was made following a period of conflict where many civilians were murdered in their claim for independence from Indonesia. Resolution 1272 (1999), establishing a peace-building mission in East Timor, was also a Chapter VII resolution and the relevant operative paragraphs were:

> 1. <u>Decides</u> to establish, in accordance with the report of the Secretary-General, a United Nations Transitional Administration in

---

[45] A. Yannis, 'Kosovo under International Administration' (2001) 43 *Survival* 31, p. 44. See also R. Wolfrum, 'International Administration in Post-Conflict Situations by the United Nations and Other International Actors' (2005) 9 *Max Planck UN Yearbook* 649 and R. Wilde, 'From Danzig to East Timor and Beyond: The Role of International Territorial Administration' (2001) 95 *American Journal of International Law* 583.

[46] Advisory Opinion on the Accordance with International Law of Unilateral Declaration of Independence in Respect of Kosovo, 2010 ICJ Rep 141, 22 July 2010, and see E. Cirkovic, 'An Analysis of the ICJ Advisory Opinion on Kosovo's Unilateral Declaration of Independence' (2010) 11 *German Law Journal* 895.

[47] BBC News, East Timor profile: Timeline available at www.bbc.co.uk/news/world-asia-pacific-14952883, accessed 11 July 2015.

244 *Part III: The responsibility to protect in practice*

East Timor (UNTAET), which will be endowed with overall responsibility for the administration of East Timor and will be empowered to exercise all legislative and executive authority, including the administration of justice;

2. <u>Decides also</u> that the mandate of UNTAET shall consist of the following elements:
   (a) To provide security and maintain law and order throughout the territory of East Timor;
   (b) To establish an effective administration;
   (c) To assist in the development of civil and social services;
   (d) To ensure the coordination and delivery of humanitarian assistance, rehabilitation and development assistance;
   (e) To support capacity-building for self-government;
   (f) To assist in the establishment of conditions for sustainable development;

3. <u>Decides further</u> that UNTAET will have objectives and a structure along the lines set out in part IV of the report of the Secretary-General, and in particular that its main components will be:
   (a) A governance and public administration component, including an international police element with a strength of up to 1,640 officers;
   (b) A humanitarian assistance and emergency rehabilitation component;
   (c) A military component, with a strength of up to 8,950 troops and up to 200 military observers;

4. <u>Authorizes</u> UNTAET to take all necessary measures to fulfil its mandate.[48]

A further UN mission, the United Nations Mission of Support in East Timor (UNMISET), was established by Security Council Resolution 1410 (2002) of 17 May 2002 to support the new government with the following mandate:

- To provide assistance to core administrative structures critical to the viability and political stability of East Timor;
- To provide interim law enforcement and public security and to assist in the development of a new law enforcement agency in East Timor, the East Timor Police Service (ETPS); and
- To contribute to the maintenance of the external and internal security of East Timor.

The Security Council also requested UNMISET to give full effect to the following three Programmes of the Mandate Implementation Plan as set out in section III A 3 of the report of the Secretary-General:

---

[48] UN Doc. S/Res/1272, 25 October 1999.

The responsibility to rebuild   245

- Stability, Democracy and Justice;
- Public Security and Law Enforcement; and
- External Security and Border Control.[49]

On 14 May 2004 the Security Council, in Resolution 1543, again extended the mandate of UNMISET for a period of six months. It also decided to reduce the size of the mission and revise its tasks, in accordance with the recommendations of the Secretary-General, to include the following elements:

(i)   support for the public administration and justice system of Timor-Leste and for justice in the area of serious crimes:
(ii) support to the development of law enforcement in Timor-Leste;
(iii) support for the security and stability of Timor-Leste.[50]

On 20 May 2005 UNMISET successfully concluded its mandate in Timor-Leste, the newly independent country. It was succeeded by a small political mission, the United Nations Office in Timor-Leste (UNOTIL), which was established by the Security Council to ensure that the underpinnings of a viable state are firmly in place in that country.[51] However, in May 2006 clashes erupted involving former soldiers who were fired and this evolved into factional violence with 25 dead and 150,000 internally displaced.[52] This resulted in the resignation of the prime minister and yet another UN Mission, the UN Integration Mission in East Timor (UNMIT).[53] UNMIT's mandate was to support the Timor-Leste Government in 'consolidating stability, enhancing a culture of democratic governance, and facilitating political dialogue among Timorese stakeholders, in their efforts to bring about a process of national reconciliation and to foster social cohesion'.[54] Although there were sporadic outbreaks of violence over next few years, the mission was considered a success and its mandate concluded on 31 December 2012.[55]

It has to be noted that, in contrast with Kosovo, Timor-Leste has been recognized as an independent state and is now a member of the United Nations.[56]

---

[49] UN Doc. S/2002/432, 17 April 2002.
[50] UN Doc. S/Res/1543, 14 May 2004.
[51] History of the mission is available at www.un.org/en/peacekeeping/missions/past/unmiset/, accessed 11 July 2015.
[52] BBC News, East Timor profile: Timeline available at www.bbc.co.uk/news/world-asia-pacific-14952883, accessed 11 July 2015.
[53] UN Doc. S/Res/1704, 25 August 2006. For a history of the operation see www.un.org/en/peacekeeping/missions/past/unmit/, accessed 27 July 2015.
[54] Ibid.
[55] Ibid.
[56] BBC News, East Timor profile: Timeline available at www.bbc.co.uk/news/world-asia-pacific-14952883, accessed 11 July 2015.

246   *Part III: The responsibility to protect in practice*

Afghanistan

The United Nations Assistance Mission for Afghanistan (UNAMA) was established on 28 March 2002 after the unilateral intervention in Afghanistan by a coalition of forces led by the United States.[57] UNAMA's mandate includes promoting national reconciliation, fulfilling the tasks and responsibilities entrusted to the UN in the Bonn Agreement, including those related to human rights, the rule of law and gender issues, and managing all UN humanitarian, relief, recovery and reconstruction activities in Afghanistan in coordination with the Afghan Administration.[58]

There are a number of guidelines that characterize the work of UNAMA. The activities of the UN system, which includes 19 UN agencies, were coordinated. The goal was to ensure that as many Afghans as possible were trained in governance and security. This has turned out to be an extremely difficult task given the fragile security situation with many areas of the country remaining ungoverned. There is also friction between the civilian and military missions.[59] The smuggling and opium-based economy do not assist this mission.[60]

In spite of an ongoing civil war in the country and the withdrawal of all foreign forces, which had occurred by the end of 2014, the Afghanistan mission is still ongoing. There is a continuing difficulty with consolidating the security situation and a lack of resources to accomplish the massive peace-building task. One of the major difficulties is the persistent violence requiring peacekeeping forces in large numbers.[61] Financial and personnel resources that might have been available for this important task have been diverted into the ongoing conflict in Iraq. However, at their annual conference on Afghanistan in Tokyo in 2014 donors pledged US$16 billion for the country's economic and development needs.[62]

It is difficult to assess the success or failure of this mission as large parts of Afghanistan are not within the control of the central government. As a result of the resurgence of violence after the Iraq War, significant investment has been poured into the country. It does, however, challenge Annan's view that economic development can lead to peace; the conflict, if anything, seems more intractable than ever. This may well have been a situation where an intervention would not have a reasonable prospect of success due to the nature of the conflict. This was not originally a responsibility to react mission

---

[57] UN Doc. S/Res/1401, 28 March 2002.

[58] Ibid.

[59] W.B. Wood, 'Post-Conflict Intervention Revisited: Relief, Reconstruction, Rehabilitation, and Reform' (2005) 29 *Fletcher Forum of World Affairs* 119, p. 130.

[60] Ibid., p. 125.

[61] Ibid., p. 124.

[62] See http://unama.unmissions.org/Default.aspx?tabid=12255&language=en-US, accessed 23 January 2015.

The responsibility to rebuild   247

but rather an exercise in self-defence against terrorism.[63] It was not a successful armed conflict, the enemy combatants have not surrendered, and that may well be why reconstruction is impossible.

Haiti

On 30 April 2004 the UN once again dealt with the continuing problem of state collapse in Haiti. On this occasion the Security Council established a governance mission with all aspects of civilian administration supporting Haiti's transitional government. Resolution 1542 (2004) established the United Nations Stabilization Mission in Haiti (MINUSTAH).

Again acting under Chapter VII of the Charter, the Security Council established three separate mandates: to ensure a secure and stable environment; to support the constitutional and political process under way; and to support the transitional government and the Haitian human rights institutions and groups in their efforts to promote and protect human rights.

The first part of the mandate is security and stability, which is to be accomplished by a combination military and police mission. It also includes disarmament, demobilization and reintegration (DDR) programmes for all armed groups, together with a mandate to:

   (f)   to protect civilians under imminent threat of physical violence, within its capabilities and areas of deployment, without prejudice to the responsibilities of the Transitional Government and of police authorities.[64]

The second part of the mandate was governance. This included facilitating free and fair elections and supporting all levels of government including the municipal level. A Special Representative of the Secretary-General, currently Juan Gabriel Valdés of Chile, is responsible for heading this mission.

The third mandate, protecting human rights, includes monitoring and reporting on the human rights situation, in cooperation with the Office of the United Nations High Commissioner for Human Rights, and including the situation of returned refugees and displaced persons. This is an acknowledgement of the critical role the promotion and protection of human rights plays in proper peace-building.

This comprehensive resolution attempts to deal with all the facets of reconstruction of a failed state. The mission began on 1 June 2004 and will probably take a considerable period of time. Haiti has been in an ongoing situation

---

[63] For examples see B. Smith and A. Thorp, 'The Legal Basis for the Invasion of Afghanistan', International Affairs and Defence Section, Foreign Office United Kingdom, House of Commons Library Document Number SN/IA/5340 and Gray, *International Law and the Use of Force*, chapter on self-defence and terrorism.

[64] Security Council Resolution 1542 of 30 April 2004.

248   *Part III: The responsibility to protect in practice*

of state collapse[65] with numerous human rights violations and a terrible natural disaster, the earthquake, that made the UN effort even more difficult.

Iraq

Although the current situation of an internationalized armed conflict in Iraq will be discussed in the next chapter, there has been long-standing involvement of the United Nations in Iraq even prior to the invasion in 2003. After the unilateral invasion of Iraq by a coalition again led by the United States, the United Nations Assistance Mission for Iraq (UNAMI), a political mission, was established by Security Council Resolution 1500.[66] Sadly, this first mission was marred by the attack on the UN Headquarters in Baghdad and the deaths of 22 people including the UN Special Representative to Iraq, Sergio Vieira de Mello.[67] The mission had been established only five days before. There was a second bombing a month later that resulted in the withdrawal of 600 UN staff.[68] Interestingly, this mission is not administered by the Department of Peacekeeping, but by the Department of Political Affairs. In spite of these deaths and withdrawal of personnel, the mission has been continuously operational since that time, with its role greatly expanded in 2007 with the passage of Resolution 1770.[69] The mandate is a clear peace-building mandate to advance 'inclusive, political dialogue and national reconciliation', assist 'in the electoral process and in the planning for a national census', facilitate 'regional dialogue between Iraq and its neighbours' and promote the protection of human rights and judicial and legal reform.[70] It has now been extended on an annual basis.[71]

The UN Mission in Iraq had been a complete failure and, if anything, the political instability is even higher than at its worst level during the Iraq War. Evans explains that a fundamental lesson from Iraq is that '*imposing* a peace settlement and democratic institutions of governance on a state and people ravaged by war and atrocity crimes in highly unlikely to work'.[72] Once again, as with Afghanistan, the 'war in Iraq' has never been successfully concluded in spite of the withdrawal of foreign troops. It supports the position that a rebuilding mission can only be successful when there is a

---

[65] Mohamed, 'From Keeping the Peace to Building Peace', p. 813, quoting Helman and Ratner who defined state collapse as 'a nation-state utterly incapable of sustaining itself as a member of the international community'.

[66] UN Doc. S/Res/1500, 14 August 2003.

[67] See www.un.org/en/memorial/baghdad2003.asp, accessed 11 July 2014.

[68] BBC News, Iraq Profile: Timeline, available at www.bbc.co.uk/news/world-middle-east-14546763, accessed 11 July 2015.

[69] UN Doc. S/Res/1770, 10 August 2007. For all information regarding UN role in Iraq, see www.uniraq.org/index.php?lang=en, accessed 11 July 2015.

[70] Ibid., para. 2.

[71] UN Doc. S/Res/2169? (cf. fn 69 above), 30 July 2014.

[72] Evans, *The Responsibility to Protect*, p. 150, original emphasis.

The responsibility to rebuild   249

cessation of hostilities and a true peace agreement with buy-in from the various parties in society. Achieving security is a pre-condition of the activities of peace-builders.[73]

The Peace-building Commission and the rule of law

The above missions were 'ad hoc' established missions after, or even in the midst of, conflict. However, the institutional mechanisms of the UN would like to deal with countries emerging from conflict in a more systematic way as recommended in the various reports discussed above. The Peace-building Commission is described on its website as 'an intergovernmental advisory body'. Its mandate is to 'marshal resources at the disposal of the international community to advise and propose integrated strategies for post-conflict recovery, focusing attention on reconstruction, institution-building and sustainable development, in countries emerging from conflict'. In order to accomplish this task, the Commission is to use the UN's capacities and experience in conflict prevention, mediation, peacekeeping, respect for human rights, the rule of law, humanitarian assistance, reconstruction and long-term development. In summary, the Commission's challenging ambitions are to:

- Propose integrated strategies for post-conflict peace-building and recovery;
- Help to ensure predictable financing for early recovery activities and sustained financial investment over the medium to longer term;
- Extend the period of attention by the international community to post-conflict recovery;
- Develop best practices on issues that require extensive collaboration among political, military, humanitarian and development actors.[74]

Presumably the ongoing missions in Kosovo, Haiti, Afghanistan and Iraq should be absorbed into the Peace-building Commission coordination machinery, but by and large they have not. The Security Council resolutions that established these missions illustrate the three parts of state-building that must be coordinated: safety and security; stable governance; and the promotion and protection of human rights. However, thus far only the African nations of Burundi, Sierra Leone, Côte d'Ivoire, the Central African Republic, Guinea–Bissau and Liberia are on the agenda of the Peace-building Commission.[75]

The Peace-building Commission released its report for its first session June 2006–June 2007 and discussed efforts in coordination for peace-building

---

[73] Ibid., pp. 153–154.
[74] Mandate as described on the website of the Peace-building Commission at www.un.org/en/peacebuilding/, accessed 22 December 2007.
[75] See ibid. for current list of countries.

250   *Part III: The responsibility to protect in practice*

for its first two selected countries, Sierra Leone and Burundi. The reason for their selection was that the governments of those two countries sent letters to the presidents of the Security Council and General Assembly requesting to be placed on the agenda of the Peace-building Commission. On that basis they were referred to the Commission by the Security Council.[76] Therefore, these first two countries have consented to limit their sovereignty in the over-lapping areas of conflict recovery. In Burundi the four main priorities for peace-building have been identified as:

1. Promoting good governance
2. Strengthening the rule of law
3. Reform of the security sector
4. Ensuring community recovery.[77]

In Sierra Leone the four main areas identified as needing both national and international assistance are:

1. Youth unemployment and disempowerment
2. Justice and security sector reform
3. Democracy consolidation and good governance
4. Capacity-building.[78]

In 2008 Guinea–Bissau was added to the agenda.[79] In Guinea–Bissau the priority areas requiring attention are:

1. Reform of public administration
2. Consolidating the rule of law and security sector reform
3. Eliminating drug trafficking
4. Promotion of professional training and youth employment
5. Rehabilitation of the energy sector
6. Addressing the needs of vulnerable groups.[80]

In June of the same year the Central African Republic was added to the agenda. The main areas needing the assistance of the peace-building commission are:

1. Reform of the security sector and the disarmament, demobilization and reintegration process

---

[76] UN Docs A/62/137 and S/2007/458, 25 July 2007, p. 4.

[77] Ibid., pp. 7–8.

[78] Ibid., pp. 9–10.

[79] UN Doc. A/62/686–S/2008/87, 7 January 2008, Letter dated 28 December 2007 from the Chairperson of the Peace-building Commission to the President of the Security Council accepting Guinea–Bissau on the agenda of the Peace-building Commission.

[80] UN Doc. PBC/2/GNB/5, 2 April 2008, pp. 9–12.

The responsibility to rebuild 251

2. Good governance and the rule of law
3. Economic Development.[81]

In 2010 Liberia requested to be the fifth country on the Peace-building Commission's agenda. The main areas needing both national and international effort are:

1. Strengthening the rule of law
2. Supporting security sector reform
3. Promoting national reconciliation.[82]

In 2011 Guinea became the sixth country added to the agenda, and there has not been an addition since. The priority areas in Guinea are:

1. Promotion of national reconciliation and unity
2. Security and defence sector reform
3. Youth and women's employment policy.[83]

It would need an additional volume to analyse the success thus far in these various activities, which involve large elements of nation-building and economic development. The impressive part of these activities is the significant level of engagement between the UN and the various countries that have voluntarily placed themselves on the agenda. However, it remains to be seen whether these activities will truly ensure sustained peace in these nations. There are difficulties in attracting voluntary contributions to the peace-building fund and the monies are nominal compared to the amount really required to rebuild fractured societies. Nevertheless, the Commission has included a wide variety of stakeholders in its deliberations, including civil society, other United Nations agencies and regional organizations, and surely an integrated approach has a better chance of success.[84]

One example of an important initiative in Sierra Leone was the award of a seed grant of US$1.5 million to support the creation of a National Human Rights Commission mandated by the Lome Peace Treaty of 1999. This Commission is mandated by the Sierra Leonean Parliament to receive and act on complains of human rights violations, to monitor, investigate, document and report on human rights situations and to raise public awareness on human rights, and importantly to oversee the government's compliance with its international treaty obligations. The Commission was mandated to compile an annual report for Parliament on the state of affairs in human rights.[85] This is an important example of a legal institution established to ensure peace.

---

[81] UN Doc. PBC/3/CAF/7, 3 June 2009, p. 12.
[82] UN Doc. PBC/4/LRB/2, 16 November 2010, pp. 2–6.
[83] UN Doc. PBC/5/GUI/2, 23 September 2011, pp. 3–8.
[84] See www.un.org/en/peacebuilding/.
[85] UN Doc. Bulletin No. 3, United Nations Peace-building Fund, 18 March 2008.

252   *Part III: The responsibility to protect in practice*

In 2010 there was a five-year review of the activities of the Peace-building Commission entitled 'Review of the United Nations Peace-building Architecture'.[86] It examined the Commission, the Peace-building Support Office and the Peace-building Fund. Disappointingly the report indicated that the hopes expressed on the establishment of these institutions had yet to be realized.[87] Interestingly, the report called for a 'new dynamic' between the Security Council and the Commission, which would contemplate more involvement by the Commission in the Security Council's consideration of peacekeeping mandates.[88] At that time there were four countries to assess and the report indicated that the two countries that had been on its agenda the longest had had the most success, and that Guinea–Bissau still had a way to go to achieve political stability.[89] The recommendations unsurprisingly called for greater coordination, further financial contributions and greater involvement by regional bodies. A 10-year review of the activities of the Commission was conducted in 2015, but the report had not been released as of July 2015, the time of the writing of this chapter.[90]

The responsibility to rebuild in international law

The question remains as to whether the responsibility to rebuild could become a doctrine of public international law. As we can see from the practice, there is a large element of legal obligations contained within the various mission mandates. Particularly critical in the process of rebuilding is the concept of the rule of law recommended in each of the reports on peace-building, with examples of specific mandates for the Peace-building Commission's activities in Burundi and the involvement in justice and security sector reform in Sierra Leone. This aspect of the rule of law includes elements that were discussed previously in this book – the importance of human rights and international criminal justice. Gareth Evans in his Rebuilding Toolbox includes constitutional/legal measures as a critical component; these include rebuilding criminal justice, managing transitional justice and supporting traditional justice.[91] Therefore, if a decision to intervene is taken by the Security Council, it must include the aspect of rebuilding, and practice of the United Nations in the various operations discussed within this chapter point to a developing international practice. It cannot yet be said to be legally mandatory, but the international practice is certainly developing in that direction with numerous legally binding Security Council mandates to rebuild.

---

[86] UN Docs A/64/868 and S/2010/393, 21 July 2010.
[87] Ibid., Executive Summary.
[88] Ibid., p. 4.
[89] Ibid., p. 12.
[90] See www.un.org/en/peacebuilding/review2015.shtml, accessed 28 July 2015.
[91] Evans, *The Responsibility to Protect*, p. 150.

The responsibility to rebuild   253

It must be noted that each of the six country mandates involve both domestic and international obligations. But the missions are wholly predicated on national consent; there is no element of international coercion. Even if there were a responsibility to react mission that contains Chapter VII authorization, the rebuilding element is based on national consent. This is how it should be. The responsibility to rebuild is based on both domestic and international responsibility. The international responsibility to rebuild has to be based not only on consent, but also on a dialogue with a nation emerging from conflict as to what institutions are required. However, careful analysis of the mandates above would determine that they emerge from an international consensus of the importance of the introduction of national institutions such as criminal justice systems and human rights bodies, which will ensure that a framework exists to prevent future conflict. Even though the nations consent, there is a considerable degree of imposition of a model by those from the Peace-building Commission who liaise with these six nations.

Clearly the view of administrations that emerge from conflict is that they must put in place systems to ensure human rights and criminal justice guarantees. In addition, there are elements of imposition of democratic ideals such as free and fair elections with universal suffrage. The debate on whether there is an emerging right of democratic governance is a vigorous one in international law, sparked by the influential article of Thomas Franck.[92] However, democracy is not yet a customary international law right and certainly not a requirement of membership in international society, in spite of the conditions of rule of law, democracy and human rights imposed in such documents as the EC Guidelines on the Recognition of New States in Eastern Europe and in the Soviet Union or the EC Declaration of Yugoslavia.[93] Nevertheless, the institutional structures being put in place in these nations are predicated on democratic institutions. A theoretical question for future debate is whether there is in fact an emerging international constitutional template being suggested for countries that emerge from conflict.

With a public international law analysis, once again as with the responsibility to react, the mandate for the Security Council in securing international peace and security has changed beyond all recognition from its inception in 1945. The five-year review suggested even further involvement by the Security Council and the ten-year review will no doubt point out that the Security Council now has extensive involvement in peace-building, not only

---

[92] T. Franck, 'The Emerging Right to Democratic Governance' (1992) 86 *American Journal of International Law* 46.

[93] EC Guidelines on the Recognition of New States in Eastern Europe and in the Soviet Union, 16 December 1999, UKMIL 1991, (1991) 62 BYI. 559 and EC Declaration on Yugoslavia. 16 December 1991, UKMIL 1991, (1991) 62 BYIL 559.

254   Part III: The responsibility to protect in practice

with these six nations but also continuing in Iraq, Afghanistan, Kosovo, Haiti and the DRC.

Conclusion

The Responsibility to Protect report argues that if military intervention action is taken – because of a breakdown or abdication of a state's own capacity and authority in discharging its 'responsibility to protect' – there should be a genuine commitment to helping to build a durable peace, and promoting good governance and sustainable development. Conditions of public safety and order have to be reconstituted by international agents acting in partnership with local authorities, with the goal of progressively transferring to them the authority and responsibility to rebuild.[94] If the ongoing tragedies of Iraq and Afghanistan have taught the international community anything, it is that if there is an armed intervention, there must also be a systematic plan of reconstruction. Otherwise there is a continuous cycle of responsibility for the international legal community to intervene in situations of threats to international peace and security.

The last 22 years since the original *An Agenda for Peace* report has seen a consolidation of views on what it takes to secure lasting peace. A major contribution of Kofi Annan will always remain his vision for sustainable development alongside the emergence of democratic and rule of law governance. Peace-building means that these nations remain on the agenda of the international community that cannot then ignore its responsibility to protect those nations that are vulnerable to a renewal of conflict.

However, there is one situation that has emerged in the twenty-first century that poses a fundamental threat to international peace and security and that remains outside of the purview of the responsibility to protect. This is the ongoing conflict in Syria and its spillover into the territory of neighbouring countries, particularly Iraq.

[94] ICISS, *The Responsibility to Protect*, para. 5.1.

10 Responsibilities ignored?
Syria and Iraq

Introduction

In spite of the extensive practice outlined in the previous three chapters, there is one situation that, in conjunction with the negative reaction by a number of states over the intervention in Libya, could arguably sound the death knell for the responsibility to protect. This is the crisis concerning Syria, which is now in its fifth year and has catastrophically spilled over into Iraq. In fact, it might be premature for a comprehensive analysis of this conflict as this situation is ongoing, and certainly in flux, with several states embarking on air support for Kurdish and Iraqi army fighters, and conducting air strikes against targets in Syria.[1] However, it is useful to discuss the earlier part of the crisis in Syria and the decision by most of the states within the international community not to intervene at that point. Sadly, it is the argument here that the decision not to intervene in the civil war in Syria was the correct decision. The decision, or to be more precise the lack of international intervention, was in direct accord with Principle 4 of the Precautionary Principles as set out originally in *The Responsibility to Protect*. That is:

> **Reasonable prospects:** There must be a reasonable chance of success in halting or averting the suffering, which has justified the intervention, with the consequences of action not likely to be worse than the consequences of inaction.[2]

It is the contention that at no time since the beginning of the civil war in Syria, up until the involvement of Islamic State (IS or Daesh) forces, was there a moment when intervention would have halted or averted the suffering. Although there is certainly academic opinion that the Russian and Chinese opposition to any sort of armed intervention in Syria was as a result

---

[1] Government of the United Kingdom, 'Update Airstrikes in Iraq', 9 July 2015, available at www.gov.uk/government/news/update-air-strikes-in-iraq, accessed 20 July 2015.

[2] International Commission on Intervention and State Sovereignty (ICISS), *The Responsibility to Protect* (Ottawa, 2001), p. XII.

256 *Part III: The responsibility to protect in practice*

of the 'mission creep' towards regime change in Libya, the actual facts of the situation in Syria itself require interpretation.[3] One major piece of evidence supporting the opinion for non-intervention during that time is the debate and parliamentary vote in the United Kingdom not to support intervention, primarily on the basis that any such intervention would not be successful.[4]

This chapter will be divided into the two historical phases of this latest global conflict. The first part of the discussion will focus on the civil war that emerged in Syria as a result of the 'Arab Spring'. The facts of that situation reveal extensive international response, short of an actual intervention, but with a stalemate in the Security Council. It also reveals a chaotic situation on the ground militating against a successful use of force to halt the human rights abuses that clearly took place.

However, if one moves into the context of 2014–2015, in the second half of this chapter, there is a forceful intervention by an international coalition by means of air strikes and drone attacks. When IS becomes a main actor in this conflict, a strong argument can be made that the current international intervention is necessary and, if anything, should be expanded. That is due to the fact that there is clear evidence of genocide being committed by the IS fighters in the parts of both Syria and Iraq that the Islamic caliphate controls. The second part of this chapter will assert that if the international community does not embrace its responsibility to react in this conflict, the responsibility to protect is indeed in jeopardy as an operating principle in international relations and certainly will not be an evolving international law doctrine.

Syrian uprising and the lack of international response from 2011–2013

The current uprising in Syria began in March of 2011. The context of the uprising was once again the much-vaunted 'Arab Spring', which had begun in Tunisia in December 2010.[5] In response to the demonstrations demanding

---

[3] Hansard Debate on Syria, 29 August 2013, available at www.publications.parliament.uk/pa/cm201314/cmhansrd/cm130829/debtext/130829-0001.htm#1308298000001, accessed 21 July 2015. It should be noted that there was a subsequent debate for air strikes on IS targets in Syria which will be discussed later in the chapter.

[4] See for example: M.-J. Domestici-Met, 'Protecting Libya on Behalf of the International Community' (2011) 3 *Goettingen Journal of International Law* 861; V.P. Nanda, 'The Future under International Law of the Responsibility to Protect after Libya and Syria' (2013) 21 *Michigan State International Law Review* 1; G. Cronogue, 'Responsibility to Protect: Syria, the Law, Politics, and Future of Humanitarian Intervention Post-Libya' (2012) 3 *International Humanitarian Legal Studies* 124; J. Gifkins, 'The UN Security Council Divided: Syria in Crisis' (2012) 4 *Global Responsibility to Protect* 377; S. Zifcak, 'The Responsibility to Protect after Libya and Syria' (2012) 13 *Melbourne Journal of International Law* 59.

[5] BBC News, 'Arab Uprising Country by Country: Tunisia', available at www.bbc.co.uk/news/world-12482315 (last updated 16 December 2013), accessed 18 November 2015.

democratic regimes, the Assad regime in Syria fought back.[6] This has resulted in a major civil war in Syria with various groups of rebel forces trying to overthrow the Assad regime.[7] This first part of this non-international armed conflict began in March 2011 and lasted until the involvement of Islamic State in Syria and Iraq in April 2013, which transformed this conflict into an international armed conflict.

The history of the first two years of the uprising is characterized by Assad's forces being ruthless in supressing dissent, including by the use of chemical weapons.[8] However, the focus here has to be on the international response – or lack of it – and why that might have occurred. The Global Centre for the Responsibility to Protect has monitored the international response to the crisis and has prepared an excellent chronological report.[9] The first killings in the uprising were in Deraa on 23 March 2011, when Syrian forces killed six people in an attack on protesters and then later opened fire on hundreds of people. The situation escalated when on 25 April, the Syrian army began deadly military attacks on other towns, using tanks, infantry carriers and artillery, which led to hundreds of civilian deaths.[10] On 29 April President Obama signed an executive order under which the US Treasury Department blocked the property of the Syrian Intelligence Directorate, the Islamic Revolutionary Guard Corps and three Syrian officials considered to be 'responsible' for human rights abuses. On the same day the Human Rights Council adopted a resolution establishing a Fact-Finding Mission to investigate alleged violations of international human rights law in Syria and to establish the facts and circumstances of such violations.[11] On 10 May the European Union imposed sanctions including an arms embargo on the Syrian regime. The first mention of the responsibility to protect in the context of Syria occurred on 2 June when the Special Advisors on the Prevention of Genocide and the Responsibility to Protect, Francis Deng and Edward Luck, issued a press release expressing their grave concern at the loss of life in Syria as a result of violent suppression of protest, and reminded the Syrian Government of its

---

6   BBC News, 'Arab Uprising Country by Country: Syria', available at www.bbc.co.uk/news/world-12482309 (last updated 16 December 2013), accessed 20 July 2015.

7   L. Charbonneau, 'Syria conflict now a Civil War: U.N. Peacekeeping Chief says', Reuters, 12 June 2012, available at www.reuters.com/article/2012/06/12/us-syria-crisis-un-idUSBRE85B1BI20120612, accessed 20 July 2015.

8   Timeline of Syrian Chemical Weapons Activity available at www.armscontrol.org/factsheets/Timeline-of-Syrian-Chemical-Weapons-Activity, accessed 21 July 2015.

9   Global Centre for the Responsibility to Protect, 'Timeline of the International Response to the Situation in Syria', available at www.globalr2p.org/publications/135, accessed 20 July 2015.

10 Anthony Shadid, 'Syria Escalates Crackdown as Tanks Go to Restive City', *New York Times*, 25 April 2011.

11 UN Doc. Resolution A/HRC/RES/S-16/1, 29 April 2011 and Global Centre for the Responsibility to Protect, 'Timeline of the International Response to the Situation in Syria', p. 2.

258 *Part III: The responsibility to protect in practice*

responsibility to protect its population. They issued another stronger release with similar warnings on 21 July.[12]

From the start of the crisis there were many opposition groups calling for the removal of the Assad regime and there was a large ethnic conflict component from the outset.[13] President al-Assad and his family are members of the Alawite minority group, which is a Shi'a Islamic sect. The majority of the security forces are also Alawite, as is the Shabiha militia group, a well-armed and immune faction who support the regime. However, the majority of Syrians are Sunni Muslim.[14] The largest group (up until the rise of Islamic State) was the Syrian National Council (SNC), an umbrella group with a Sunni majority formed in October 2011.[15] However, the Carnegie Endowment reported that the SNC contained a large Islamist component including the Syrian Muslim Brotherhood and the Group of 74 composed of former brotherhood members.[16]

Another major group, formed early in the conflict, was the Free Syrian Army (FSA), which was made up of defectors from the Syrian Army and civilians who took up arms against the Assad regime. They received arms and funding from Saudi Arabia and Qatar and once more were a Sunni group.[17] Another strong opposition force, existing since before the Arab Spring, are Kurdish opposition parties who seek a federal state in Syria. They also consist of armed militia groups.[18] Although many regime opponents were interested in democratic transition, the presence of Islamic groups gave Assad an opportunity to allege terrorism supported by Iran and Hezbollah from Lebanon.[19]

In spite of allegations of attacks on civilian demonstrators with lethal force, the members of the UN Security Council have not been able to find consensus on what action to take since April of 2011, when the members failed to agree on a presidential statement.[20] A draft Security Council resolution was circulated by the United Kingdom, France, Portugal and Germany in late May 2011. It condemned abuses of human rights and reminded the Syrian Government of its responsibility to protect its citizens.[21] The draft was never voted on as China and Russia said they would

---

[12] Global Centre for the Responsibility to Protect, 'Timeline of the International Response to the Situation in Syria', pp. 2–3 for all the facts contained in this paragraph.

[13] Jonathan Masters, 'Syria's Crisis and the Global Response', Council on Foreign Relations, available at www.cfr.org/syria/syrias-crisis-global-response/p2840, accessed 22 July 2015.

[14] Gifkins, 'The UN Security Council Divided', p. 379.

[15] Carnegie Endowment, 'The Syrian National Council', available at http://carnegieendowment.org/syriaincrisis/?fa=48334, accessed 22 July 2015.

[16] Ibid.

[17] Masters, 'Syria's Crisis and the Global Response', p. 3.

[18] Carnegie Endowment, 'The Syrian National Council'. These groups are aligned to the general Kurdish movement in the Middle East.

[19] Gifkins, 'The UN Security Council Divided', pp. 380–381.

[20] Ibid., p. 381.

[21] Ibid., p. 382.

veto the draft, and Brazil, India, Lebanon and South Africa also opposed the resolution.[22]

The first consensual activity of the United Nations Security Council took place on 3 August when a presidential statement was issued expressing 'grave concern', calling for the Syrian authorities to comply with their obligations under international law and to cease the use of force.[23] The Human Rights Council held a special seventeenth session on 22 and 23 August to address the situation and concluded with a resolution that called for creation of fact-finding missions by the Office of the High Commissioner for Human Rights (OHCHR).[24] By 31 August, Amnesty International's report *Deadly Detentions* had detailed a high number of suspicious deaths in Syrian custody and accused the Syrian Government of 'crimes against humanity'.[25] By 12 September High Commissioner for Human Rights, Navi Pillay, asserted that the death toll in Syria was 2,600.[26] Three days later the European Parliament (EP) demanded an immediate halt to the crackdowns and for Assad and his regime to relinquish power. The EP President stated: '[w]e Europeans must assume our responsibility to protect civilians.'[27] In his speech to the General Assembly in the same month, President Obama stated that there was 'no excuse for inaction' in Syria and called upon the Security Council to issue sanctions.[28]

In spite of the adoption of sanctions against the Assad regime by the United States, Switzerland, Norway, Canada, Turkey and the European Union in late 2011, and the escalation of violence, the Security Council failed to act. There was a draft Security Council Resolution 1831, which condemned Syria's use of force against civilians in Syria, called for member states to impose sanctions and for the International Criminal Court to ensure the investigation and punishment of all crimes. Russia and China

---

[22] Ibid.

[23] S/PRST/2on/i6, 3 August 2011.

[24] 'Human Rights Council decides to dispatch a commission of inquiry to investigate human rights violations in the Syrian Arab Republic', available at www.ohchr.org/EN/NewsEvents/Pages/DisplayNews.aspx?NewsID=11326&LangID=E, accessed 20 July 2015.

[25] Amnesty International, 'Deadly Detentions', London, 31 August 2011.

[26] Opening Statement by Ms Navi Pillay, United Nations High Commissioner for Human Rights at the 18th session of the Human Rights Council, 12 September 2011, available at www.ohchr.org/EN/NewsEvents/Pages/DisplayNews.aspx?NewsID=11326&LangID=E, accessed 20 July 2015.

[27] European Parliament News, 'Syria's Assad must go, and Libya's resources must benefit all Libyans, say MEPs', Plenary Session Press release – External relations – 15-09-2011 – 13:04, available at www.europarl.europa.eu/news/en/news-room/content/20110915IPR26710/html/Syria%27s-Assad-must-go-and-Libya%27s-resources-must-benefit-all-Libyans-say-MEPs, accessed 20 July 2015.

[28] The White House Office of the Press Secretary, 'Remarks by President Obama in Address to United Nations General Assembly', available at www.whitehouse.gov/the-press-office/2011/09/21/remarks-president-obama-address-united-nations-general-assembly, accessed 20 July 2015.

260   *Part III: The responsibility to protect in practice*

vetoed the resolution.[29] By 14 October the OHCHR was urging immediate international action as the official UN death toll in Syria rose to over 3,000, including 187 children, with Pillay using the language of the responsibility to protect.[30] On 9 November 2011, during an open debate in the Security Council on civilian protection, the US, Japan and France suggested that the Security Council had failed to protect civilians in Syria in not adopting a resolution condemning the violence.[31] On 28 November the Human Rights Committee released the report of its Committee of Investigation, which detailed the regime's excessive use of force against the civilian population including summary executions, enforced disappearances, arbitrary arrests and sexual violence.[32] On the same day Amnesty International urged states to act on the report confirming Syria's perpetration of crimes against humanity.[33] Throughout 2011, in spite of numerous reports, draft resolutions and debates, the Security Council failed to act, and by 12 December the OHCHR estimated that the death toll in Syria exceeded 5,000.[34]

The situation of stalemate in the Security Council continued throughout 2012. On 25 January, France, Britain and Germany began to work on another draft resolution, but Russia announced that it would not support any action that included sanctions or military intervention in Syria.[35] This promise was realized when on 4 February, for the second time, Russia and China vetoed the draft resolution that would have condemned the violence.[36] In contrast, the United Nations General Assembly in a vote – 137 in favour, 12 against and 17 abstentions – adopted a resolution that strongly condemned the continued 'widespread and systematic' human rights violations by the Syrian authorities and demanded an immediate cessation of

---

[29] UN Press Release, 'Security Council Fails to Adopt Draft Resolution Condemning Syria's Crackdown on Anti-Government Protestors, Owing to Veto by Russian Federation, China', available at www.un.org/press/en/2011/sc10403.doc.htm, accessed 20 July 2015.

[30] Office of the High Commissioner for Human Rights, 'Pillay urges international action to Protect Syrians', 14 October 2011, available at www.ohchr.org/EN/NewsEvents/Pages/DisplayNews.aspx?NewsID=11493&LangID=E, accessed 20 July 2015.

[31] UN Doc. S/PV.6650, 9 November 2011.

[32] For all the documentation on the Commission see www.ohchr.org/EN/HRBodies/HRC/IICISyria/Pages/IndependentInternationalCommission.aspx, accessed 20 July 2015.

[33] Amnesty International, 'States must act resolutely on UN report on Syria', Press release, 28 November 2011.

[34] OHCHR Press Release, 'As Syrian death toll tops 5,000, UN human rights chief warns about key city', available at www.un.org/apps/news/story.asp?NewsID=40708&Cr=syria&Cr1=#.VazN7UUQSf4, accessed 20 July 2015.

[35] Global Centre for the Responsibility to Protect, 'Timeline of the International Response to the Situation in Syria', p. 14.

[36] UN Press Release, 'Security Council Fails to Adopt Draft Resolution on Syria as Russian Federation, China Veto Text Supporting Arab League's Proposed Peace Plan', 4 February 2012, available at www.un.org/press/en/2012/sc10536.doc.htm, accessed 20 July 2015.

violence.[37] This language is interesting as it contains the threshold condition of widespread and systematic violations required for a finding of crimes against humanity.[38] This clearly is a condition of a responsibility to protect mandate.

In February 2012 Kofi Annan was appointed by Ban Ki-moon as the UN–Arab League Special Envoy on Syria, and was charged with attempting to find a diplomatic end to the violence.[39] By the end of the month, and again at the end of March, the Human Rights Council adopted yet more resolutions condemning the 'widespread and systematic violation of human rights by the Syrian authorities'.[40] The UN High Commissioner for Human Rights, Navi Pillay, had been using the responsibility to protect as the guiding principle throughout the violence and on 5 March, in an interview with Al-Jazeera, she cautioned against arming the Syrian opposition for fear of escalating the violence as the primary concern of her office was the protection of Syrian civilians, given the international community's responsibility to protect.[41] Three days later the UN Special Rapporteur on Torture indicated that the Security Council had a 'responsibility to protect the Syrian people from these very serious crimes' (referring to torture in detention).[42] In spite of these calls, and calls of other groups to intervene in the situation, the Security Council could only agree to adopt a presidential statement expressing its gravest concern at the deteriorating situation in Syria and lending support to the mission of Kofi Annan.[43]

It was on 14 April 2012 that the United Nations Security Council finally acted when it unanimously adopted Resolution 2024, which authorized a team of 30 unarmed observers to report on the implementation of Kofi Annan's brokered ceasefire.[44] This mandate was expanded in Resolution 2043 of 21 April, when the United Nations Supervision Mission in Syria was given a 90-day deployment of 300 unarmed observers to monitor the ceasefire and full implementation of the Annan peace plan.[45] However, as Gifkins asserts,

---

[37] Global Centre for the Responsibility to Protect, 'Timeline of the International Response to the Situation in Syria', p. 16, and UN Doc. A/RES/66/253, 21 February 2012.

[38] Ibid.

[39] UN Press Release, 'Kofi Annan Appointed Joint Special Envoy of United Nations, League of Arab States on Syrian Crisis', 23 February 2012, available at www.un.org/press/en/2012/sgsm14124.doc.htm, accessed 20 July 2015.

[40] UN Doc. A/HRC/19/L.1/Rev.1, 29 February 2012 and A/HRC/19/L.38/Rev.1, 23 March 2012.

[41] Navi Pillay Interview with Al Jazeera, available at www.aljazeera.com/programmes/talktojazeera/2012/03/201232144352254346.html, accessed 20 July 2015.

[42] Global Centre for the Responsibility to Protect, 'Timeline of the International Response to the Situation in Syria', p. 18.

[43] UN Doc. S/PRST/2012/6 SC/10583, 21 March 2012.

[44] UN Doc. S/RES//2024, 14 April 2012.

[45] UN Doc. S/RES/2043, 21 April 2012.

262 *Part III: The responsibility to protect in practice*

'this lowest-common denominator response' was quickly suspended due to the high levels of violence directed against the UN observers.[46]

On 8 May Annan briefed the Security Council on the serious violations of the ceasefire and the 'unacceptable' levels of violence and abuses.[47] It was evident that even the experienced negotiator Annan could not effectively put into operation a plan that would curb the violence in Syria. By mid-May, Ban Ki-moon estimated the death toll in the civil war at 10,000.[48]

The level of human rights abuses in the conflict was supported by the Annual Amnesty International Report 2012, which stated that Syrian Government forces 'used lethal and other excessive force against peaceful protesters' and that the 'patterns and scale of state abuses may have constituted crimes against humanity'.[49] A serious massacre occurred in May in Houla near Homs, where 108 people were killed.[50] The UN Committee on the Rights of the Child issued a statement on 31 May deploring the Houla Massacre in which 49 of the over 100 victims were children killed by Syrian state authorities. The statement reminded Syria of its primary responsibility to protect.[51] In a statement to the Human Rights Council nineteenth Special Session on the situation of human rights in Syria the following day, Navi Pillay called for an investigation into the massacre and also reminded Syria of its responsibility to protect.[52] Once again, the international reaction was limited to a Human Rights Council resolution condemning the government's use of force and calling for an investigation into the killings in Houla.[53]

By June of 2012 the chorus for intervention was joined by Kofi Annan, who addressed the General Assembly, stating that his peace plan was not being implemented and it was the collective responsibility of the international community to act quickly before the situation became more radicalized and polarized.[54] However, it is evident that this radicalization and polarization

---

[46] Gifkins, 'The UN Security Council Divided', p. 377.

[47] Global Centre for the Responsibility to Protect, 'Timeline of the International Response to the Situation in Syria', p. 24.

[48] Ibid., p. 25.

[49] Amnesty International, *Annual Report 2012*, available at www.amnesty.org/en/documents/pol10/001/2012/en/, accessed 21 July 2015.

[50] UN News Centre, 'UN Human Rights Council Calls for Special Investigation into Houla Massacre in Syria', 1 June 2012, available at www.un.org/apps/news/story.asp?NewslD=42140, accessed 22 July 2015.

[51] 'UN Child Rights Committee appalled at deliberate targeting of children in Syria', 31 May 2012, available at www.ohchr.org/en/NewsEvents/Pages/DisplayNews.aspx?NewsID=12205&LangID=E#sthash.qxENtong.dpuf, accessed 21 July 2015.

[52] Statement by Navi Pillay, High Commissioner for Human Rights to the Human Rights Council, 19th Special Session on 'The deteriorating human rights situation in the Syrian Arab Republic and the killings in El-Houleh', Geneva, 1 June 2012, available at www.ohchr.org/EN/NewsEvents/Pages/DisplayNews.aspx?NewsID=12210&LangID=E#sthash.8yI1x0qv.dpuf, accessed 21 July 2015.

[53] UN Doc. A/HRC/RES/S\-19/1, 4 June 2012.

[54] Global Centre for the Responsibility to Protect, 'Timeline of the International Response to the Situation in Syria', p. 27.

Responsibilities ignored? Syria and Iraq 263

had existed throughout the conflict.[55] Amnesty International released a report on 13 June entitled *Deadly Reprisals*, which detailed the evidence of crimes against humanity and war crimes committed by the Syrian army in towns and villages around Idlib and Aleppo from late February through late May. This report with compelling evidence was further indication that the threshold conditions existed for a responsibility to react response from the Security Council.[56] The Special Advisers on the Prevention of Genocide and the Responsibility to Protect expressed alarm at the escalation of targeted attacks against civilians, which underscored 'the Syrian Government's manifest failure to protect its population'.[57]

The commander of the United Nations Supervision Mission in Syria (UNSMIS), General Mood, announced on 16 June that the monitoring activities in Syria were suspended due to escalating violence, and due to the 'lack of willingness by the parties to seek a peaceful transition'.[58] This statement was a clear indication that all parties, including the opposition, were unwilling to pursue a peaceful resolution. In spite of this suspension, the UN Security Council adopted Resolution 2059, renewing the mandate of UNSMIS for a final period of 30 days and stating that any renewal would require a significant reduction in violence.[59] By this time half of the 300 observers had been sent home.[60] This trend continued with the resignation of Annan on 2 August, citing the increasing militarization on the ground and lack of unity in the Security Council.[61] By 13 August General Babacar Gaye, the new interim Head of UNSMIS, stated that none of the parties had prioritized the needs of civilians.[62] The mandate for UNSMIS expired on 21 August as the peace initiative had been a failure, even though Lakhdar

---

[55] A.J. Tabler, 'Syria's Collapse and How Washington Can Stop It' (2013) 92 *Foreign Affairs* 90, pp. 90 and 92.

[56] Amnesty International, *Deadly Reprisals*, 14 June 2012, available at www.amnestyusa. org/research/reports/deadly-reprisals-deliberate-killings-and-other-abuses-by-syria-s-armed-forces, accessed 21 June 2015.

[57] Statement of the Special Advisers of the Secretary-General on the Prevention of Genocide and on the Responsibility to Protect on the situation in Syria, 14 June 2012, available at www.un.org/en/preventgenocide/adviser/pdf/14%20June%20Statement%20-%20English. pdf, accessed 21 July 2015.

[58] Global Centre for the Responsibility to Protect, 'Timeline of the International Response to the Situation in Syria', p. 28.

[59] UN Doc. S/RES/2059, 20 July 2012.

[60] Under Secretary-General of Peacekeeping Operations, Herve Ladsous, Press Conference 26 July 2013, available at www.un.org/en/peacekeeping/missions/unsmis/documents/ Ladsous press conference_26 July 2012.pdf?nid=6201, accessed 21 July 2015.

[61] Annan Statement, 2 August 2012, available at www.un.org/apps/news/infocus/Syria/ press.asp?NewsID=1245&sID=41, accessed 21 July 2015.

[62] Transcript of the press conference by Lieutenant General Babacar Gaye, Head of UN Supervision Mission in Syria ad interim, 13 August 2012, available at www.un.org/ en/peacekeeping/missions/unsmis/documents/Transcript%20of%20the%20press%20 conference_13%20Aug2012.pdf, accessed 21 July 2015.

264   *Part III: The responsibility to protect in practice*

Brahimi was appointed the new Special Envoy for Syria. On 30 August the Security Council held a special session to discuss Syria but remained deadlocked.[63]

On 5 September the General Assembly held an interactive dialogue entitled 'Responsibility to Protect: Timely and Decisive Response'. Within this debate 18 member states raised concern over Syria and Ban Ki-moon states that the Security Council's inaction on the issue had had a high cost for civilians. This was repeated at the opening of the sixty-seventh session of the General Assembly when 118 states mentioned the crisis in Syria during their speeches in the General Assembly.[64] Yet again the only international activity was the 28 September Human Rights Council resolution condemning the violence and calling on Syrian authorities to meet their responsibility to protect.[65] By 2 October the UN High Commissioner for Refugees (UNHCR) reported that there were over 300,000 Syrian refuges in neighbouring countries.[66] Navi Pillay in her annual report urged the Security Council to adopt urgent measures to protect the Syrian people.[67] By the beginning of November the UN Office for Humanitarian Affairs estimated that four million Syrians inside Syria would need humanitarian aid.[68] By November 2012 the National Coalition for Syrian Revolutionary and Opposition forces formed in Qatar but excluded Islamist militias. In December the United States, Britain, France, Turkey and the Gulf States recognized this coalition as the 'legitimate representative' of the Syrian people.[69]

The civil war entered a very serious phase when on 23 December 2012 the first allegation of chemical weapons use was reported. This represented a major turning point in the conflict. Seven people were allegedly killed in Homs by a 'poisonous gas' used by the Assad regime. The coverage included the report of side effects such as nausea, relaxed muscles, blurred vision and breathing difficulties.[70] Previously, in August, President Obama had indicated that there would be a 'red line' regarding the use of chemical weapons in Syria, which would change his view on a military response.[71] The use of

---

[63] Global Centre for the Responsibility to Protect, 'Timeline of the International Response to the Situation in Syria', p. 33.

[64] Ibid., p. 34.

[65] Ibid., p. 36.

[66] UN News Centre, 'Number of Syrian refugees has tripled in three months', available at www.un.org/apps/news/story.asp?NewsID=43187&Cr=Syria&Cr1#.Va3rdEUQSf5, accessed 21 July 2015.

[67] United Nations General Assembly 67th Session, Statement by Ms Navi Pillay United Nations High Commissioner for Human Rights, New York, 24 October 2012, available at www .ohchr.org/en/NewsEvents/Pages/DisplayNews.aspx?NewsID=12690&LangID=E# sthash.UjhQUfqA.dpuf, accessed 21 July 2015.

[68] Global Centre for the Responsibility to Protect, 'Timeline of the International Response to the Situation in Syria', p. 38.

[69] Ibid., and see the coalition website at www.lccsyria.org/10488, accessed 21 July 2015.

[70] Timeline of Syrian Chemical Weapons Activity.

[71] Ibid., reporting statement of Obama on 20 August 2012.

chemical weapons triggered a much more robust international response. On 21 March 2013 Ban Ki-moon launched the United Nations investigation on the possible use of chemical weapons in Syria, together with the World Health Organization (WHO) and the Organisation for the Prohibition of Chemical Weapons (OPCW).[72]

The crisis concerning the use of chemical weapons reached its apex in August 2013. On 21 August 2013 opposition activists claimed that a large-scale chemical attack occurred in the Ghoula region and there were allegations that there were as many as 1,000 victims.[73] The UN Security Council held an emergency meeting regarding the attack. This seemed to be the international community's 'red line' as well. On 23 August it was announced by Ban Ki-moon that the UN would conduct a 'thorough, impartial and prompt investigation' into the attack.[74] In a Machiavellian move, the Assad regime did not wait long to announce cooperation with the UN inspection team.[75] Nevertheless, there was a chorus calling for intervention and on 28 August a second Security Council meeting was held as the United States, Britain and France were convinced chemical weapons had been used in spite of Syrian denials.[76]

A key event occurred at the end of August that put an end to discussion of intervention, until the victories of Islamic State a year later. On 29 August the UK Parliament debated military action in Syria. The Joint Intelligence Committee had released a report that stated that chemical weapons were used on 21 August. In spite of this information David Cameron faced a defeat in the Commons on intervention in Syria.[77] The reasons given by various parliamentarians referred directly to the responsibility to protect, and this will be discussed in detail in the final section of this chapter.[78] Following from this defeat, on 31 August President Obama announced that he would seek authorization for a limited action for air strikes only to deter the further use of chemical weapons.[79] This vote was postponed on 10 September as the Russians had brokered a deal the previous day, where the Syrian Government would agree to place its chemical weapons under international control and

---

[72] Ibid.
[73] Ibid.
[74] Ibid.
[75] Ibid.
[76] BBC News, 'Syria Crisis: UK puts forward UN Proposal', 28 August 2013, available at www.bbc.co.uk/news/world-middle-east-23864124, accessed 21 July 2015.
[77] UK Legal Position, available at www.gov.uk/government/uploads/system/uploads/attachment_data/file/235098/Chemical-weapon-use-by-Syrian-regime-UK-government-legal-position.pdf, and BBC News, 'Syria crisis: Cameron loses Commons vote on Syria action', 30 August 2013, available at www.bbc.co.uk/news/uk-politics-23892783, accessed 21 July 2013.
[78] Hansard Debate on Syria, 29 August 2013, available at www.publications.parliament.uk/pa/cm201314/cmhansrd/cm130829/debtext/130829-0001.htm#1308298000001, accessed 21 July 2015.
[79] Timeline of Syrian Chemical Weapons Activity.

266   *Part III: The responsibility to protect in practice*

dismantle them.[80] On 27 September the Security Council unanimously passed a resolution on Syria that condemned the use of chemical weapons and stated:

> 21. *Decides*, in the event of non-compliance with this resolution, including unauthorized transfer of chemical weapons, or any use of chemical weapons by anyone in the Syrian Arab Republic, to impose measures under Chapter VII of the United Nations Charter.[81]

By 1 October a joint team of OPCW and UN officials arrived in Syria to begin destruction of the chemical weapons and facilities.[82] By June 2014 the UN announced the complete removal of Syria's chemical weapons.

These first years were characterized by many diplomatic and sanction efforts in spite of lack of unanimity in the Security Council. All of these efforts were to no avail as the civil war had intensified, resulting in hundreds of thousands of refugees and thousands of deaths. Nevertheless, it is the contention here that there was never a time in the conflict when a responsibility to react action would have been successful. As Nanda argues:

> Although there is a stronger case for the use of the third pillar of R2P in Syria than there was in Libya, and there is a moral imperative to react when such egregious violations of human rights occur, the situation in Syria is complex. The army is strong and well trained, extremists have reportedly joined the ranks of the rebels, and the opposition lacks unity. Minorities are apprehensive about possible persecution under a new regime, and there is a likelihood that in light of the inflammatory regional setting, a military intervention might trigger regional instability. Furthermore, a nuanced approach under R2P is called for, because R2P may not be invoked unless there are reasonable prospects of success in protecting the lives and well-being of people, so that the situation is made better for them rather than worse.[83]

One has to agree with Nanda, as in spite of the formation of the Syrian Revolutionary and Opposition Forces, there were a number of opposition groups that sadly in the next two years revealed a fundamental division in the opposition between proponents of a transition to a democracy and those who favoured an Iranian-style Islamic state.

Islamic State and the international response 2013–2015

The civil war had escalated during 2013 with chemical weapons use, and thus it was hardly reported that Abu Bakr al-Baghdadi had declared the formation

---

[80] Ibid.
[81] UN Doc. S/Res 2118, 27 September 2013, original emphasis.
[82] Timeline of Syrian Chemical Weapons Activity.
[83] Nanda, 'The Future under International Law of the Responsibility to Protect after Libya and Syria', p. 31.

Responsibilities ignored? Syria and Iraq 267

of an Islamic State of Iraq in the Levant (ISIL) in April 2013, expanding the Islamic State of Iraq (ISI) to include Syria.[84] It was not until late 2013 that the real and substantial threat from ISIL attracted global attention. On 11 December 2013 the US and Britain suspended 'non-lethal' support for rebels in Northern Syria after reports that Islamist rebels had seized some bases of the Western-backed Free Syrian Army.[85] It was reported that during December 2013 nearly 700 people had been killed amid 'infighting' between Syrian rebel groups, and that ISIL increasingly dominated the opposition and looked to spread its influence into Northern Iraq.[86] The next and most lethal phase of this conflict had begun.

On 3 January 2014 ISIL seized control of the Iraqi cities of Fallujah and Ramadi,[87] and then on 10 June they seized control of Mosul, Iraq's second biggest city. There were reports of massacres of minority groups.[88] The next day ISIL overran more of Nineveh province in Iraq and then captured Tikrit and much of the Sunni heartland, nearly to the outskirts of Baghdad. On 29 June ISIL declared the establishment of a 'caliphate' in the territory from Aleppo in Syria to the eastern Iraqi province of Diyala.[89] Baghdadi was declared the caliph and the militants renamed themselves The Islamic State (IS). Territories under its control in Iraq and Syria were united as the sand berms marking the border were knocked down between the two countries.[90]

At this juncture international response, even without an enabling Security Council resolution, was immediate. On 19 June President Obama sent 300 American military advisers into Iraq to plan possible airstrikes to support the Iraqi army. On 24 August 2014 a major Syrian airbase, Tabqa near the northern city of Raqqa, fell to Islamic State, which then controlled the entire Raqqa province.[91] On 7 August President Obama, by executive order, authorized air strikes in areas including the oil-rich Kurdish region and areas where minority groups faced almost certain death, including stranded Yazidi (also spelled Yizidi and Yezidi) people on Mount Sinjar. It had become clear that Islamic State was targeting ethnic groups for extermination.[92] On 8 August the US began airstrikes in Iraq, citing the humanitarian plight of Iraq's minorities, particularly the Yazidis.[93] On 3 September Obama sent

---

[84] CNN News, 'ISIS Fast Facts', available at http://edition.cnn.com/2014/08/08/worldzes-fast-facts/, accessed 21 July 2013.

[85] Global Centre for the Responsibility to Protect, 'Timeline of the International Response to the Situation in Syria', p. 63.

[86] Global News Canada, 'Timeline rise of Isis in Syria, Iraq', available at http://globalnews.ca/news/1597203/timeline-rise-of-isis-in-syria-iraq/, accessed 21 July 2013.

[87] Ibid.

[88] Ibid.

[89] Ibid.

[90] Ibid.

[91] Sam Dagher, 'Islamic State Captures Major Air Base in Syria from Government', *Wall Street Journal*, 24 August 2014.

[92] Statement by President Obama, 7 August 2014, available at www.whitehouse.gov/the-press-office/2014/08/07/statement-president, accessed 21 July 2015.

[93] Ibid.

268   Part III: The responsibility to protect in practice

350 more military personnel to protect American facilities and workers in Iraq.[94] On 23 September 2014 the United States and five Arab countries began air strikes against Islamic State targets around Aleppo and Raqqa in Syria.[95] Because of concerns raised by Iraq regarding human rights abuses perpetrated by IS, the Human Rights Council convened the Special Session on 1 September 2014, and adopted Resolution A/HRC/RES/S-22/1 by consensus. The Council mandated that the OHCHR dispatch a mission to Iraq to investigate the alleged violations and abuses of international human rights law committed by IS and related terrorist groups, and to 'establish the facts and circumstances of such abuses and violations'.[96] On 26 September the British House of Commons voted in favour of joining the air campaign in Iraq (not in Syria) and on 29 September British planes conducted their first air strikes.[97]

Although there were few 'boots on the ground', the Syrian civil war had now become internationalized with fighting in two states – Iraq and Syria – with air support being provided by several states now joined by Turkey, which shares a long border with Syria.[98] Initially the air support seemed successful, with Kurdish Peshmerga fighters regaining control of Eski Mosul and several neighbouring towns and the Syrian border town of Kobane.[99] On 1 April 2015 Iraqi forces, backed by US-led coalition air-strikes, retook Tikrit.[100] However, since mid-May 2015 the tide has clearly turned against the Iraqi army. First, on 17 May Ramadi fell to IS as Iraqi forces abandoned their weapons and armoured vehicles.[101] On 20 May IS captured the ancient desert city of Palmyra in central Syria as Assad's forces also collapsed and withdrew.[102] The only hopeful development was that the Kurdish Peshmerga fighters continued their success by capturing the Syrian town of Tal Abyad on the Turkish border, which had provided a strategic supply route for IS.[103]

The original Syrian civil war also continued into a dangerous new phase. On 10 September 2014 the OPCW confirmed that chlorine gas was being used in Syria but did not assign blame. On 6 March 2015 the UN Security Council adopted a resolution condemning the use of chlorine gas as a weapon in Syria's civil war and again threatening Chapter VII action if chemical weapons were used again (UN Security Council Resolution 2209). It is

---

[94] Global News Canada, 'Timeline rise of Isis in Syria, Iraq'.
[95] BBC News, 'Syria: US begins air strikes on Islamic State targets', 23 September 2014, http://www.bbc.co.uk/news/world-middle-east-29321136, accessed 21 June 2015.
[96] Ibid.
[97] Global News Canada, 'Timeline rise of Isis in Syria, Iraq'.
[98] BBC News, 'Turkey Bombs Islamic State Targets in Syria', 24 July 2015, available at www.bbc.co.uk/news/world-europe-33646314, accessed 25 July 2015.
[99] Global News Canada, 'Timeline rise of Isis in Syria, Iraq'.
[100] Ibid.
[101] Ibid.
[102] Ibid.
[103] Ibid.

estimated that over 200 people were killed in the attacks. Another Islamic rebel alliance, Jaish al-Fatah (Army of Conquest), backed by Turkey, Saudi Arabia and Qatar, captured the provincial capital of Idlib in March 2015.[104] In spite of allegations of continued use of chemical weapons, it is evident that the civil war is now very much out of the public eye, as the focus of international attention is on the threat of IS, particularly as many nations are concerned that their citizens are being recruited as fighters in the IS army.[105] Notwithstanding the rhetoric of concern, even in the wider IS conflict, the international reaction is limited to supply of materiel, training and funding support to those groups, and to air strikes supporting the Iraqi army, Kurdish Peshmerga fighters, and against IS targets in Syria.

Although, it is clear that in the civil war phase there were serious abuses of human rights and use of chemical weapons, the conduct of IS reaches a whole new level of savagery. This was established in the report that had been ordered by the Human Rights Council in September 2014. One allegation established through eye-witness testimony is that members of the Yazidi ethnic group are being forced to convert to Islam or face death and that the policy of IS is 'to destroy the Yezidi as a group'.[106] This rises to the level of the definition in the Genocide Convention.[107] Other findings are of crimes against humanity and serious war crimes including murder, enslavement, deportation or forcible transfer of population, imprisonment and other severe deprivation of physical liberty, torture, rape, sexual slavery, sexual violence and persecution. The report states that 'information strongly suggests that ISIL has perpetrated some of these crimes against Christian, Shi'a and Yezidi communities'.[108]

Although the findings are limited to allegations in Iraq, there was no reason to suppose that these same abuses do not take place in the territory in Syria that IS controls.[109] The Global Centre for the Responsibility to Protect has reported that IS 'poses a direct threat to civilians as its fighters have carried out mass executions and sexual enslavement in areas under their control'. However, they limited their conclusions to crimes against humanity rather than genocide.[110] They report that the total number of civilians killed in Syria is 1,362 with 400 children recruited as child soldiers.[111]

---

[104] Ibid.

[105] Ibid.

[106] UN Press Release, 'ISIL may have committed genocide, war crimes in Iraq, says UN human rights report', 19 March 2015, available at www.un.org/apps/news/story.asp?NewsID= 50369#.VbNyAUUQSf4, accessed 25 July 2015, and UN Doc. A/HRC/28/18, 13 March 2015.

[107] UN General Assembly, Convention on the Prevention and Punishment of the Crime of Genocide, 9 December 1948, 78 UNTS. 277, Articles 2 and 3.

[108] Ibid.

[109] Ibid.

[110] Global Centre for the Responsibility to Protect, 'Populations at Risk, Syria', available at www.globalr2p.org/regions/syria, accessed 25 July 2015.

[111] Ibid.

270 *Part III: The responsibility to protect in practice*

It has to be noted that the allegations against the Syrian regime in the civil war had also been categorized as genocide by various NGOs including Genocide Watch, but the UN human rights system had not confirmed genocide until the IS activities in Iraq in Syria, with the release of the report discussed above. Regrettably, it cannot be argued that the more robust international reaction is due to these new allegations of genocide; rather the states making up the coalition conducting air strikes, including the United States, the United Kingdom, Jordan, Canada and Turkey, emphasize the threat of terrorism and the control of territory in Iraq and Syria. David Cameron again approached the UK Parliament for permission to extend the Royal Air Force role beyond air strikes in Iraq to air strikes in Syria.[112] On this occasion, in the wake of IS attacks in Paris and Istanbul he successfully received a mandate to extend air strikes into Syria.

Consequences for the responsibility to protect

It is evident from the previous two sections that there was concerted and escalating international activity with respect to Syria and Iraq. Notwithstanding this activity, at the time of writing, the killing continues unabated. There is unilateral activity by selected airstrikes against Islamic State forces, but there has never been a United Nations peace enforcement action pursuant to the responsibility to react or Pillar III with respect to the civil war that is ongoing in Syria.

It has to be asserted that in this situation international intervention would not be effective, as can be evidenced by the disastrous results of intervention in previous conflicts in Afghanistan (2002–2013) and Iraq (2003–2012), which also resulted in continuous civil wars. There are so many disparate groups in the conflict that backing one group, for example the moderate Free Syrian Army, will not guarantee that the human rights abuses will cease. Part of the explanation has to be the long-standing ethnic conflicts that occupy the whole Middle East that were exacerbated by the invasions of Afghanistan and Iraq by Western forces. The Sunni–Shi'a conflict has existed throughout the history of Islam and is thus far intractable. Furthermore, there is another centuries-old conflict between the Kurdish peoples in Iraq and Syria who desire their own state. In Syria particularly, an Arab minority group, the Alawites, dominate the government even though they only make up 16 per cent of the population. It is a Sunni Arab sect but divided from the Sunni majority. Outside intervention would fail to resolve these conflicts; only those in the Middle East can resolve these issues.

It is the precautionary principle of reasonable prospects that merits close consideration. The principle states: 'There must be a reasonable

---

[112] P. Wintour, F. Perraudin and N. Watt, 'David Cameron Believes there is a case to do more in Syria', *The Guardian*, 2 July 2015, available at www.theguardian.com/world/2015/jul/02/defence-secretary-michael-fallon-mps-reconsider-air-strikes-isis-in-syria, accessed 25 July 2015.

Responsibilities ignored? Syria and Iraq 271

chance of success in halting or averting the suffering which justified the intervention with the consequence of action not likely to be worse than the consequence of inaction.' In the explanation for this principle the original ICISS report states that 'military intervention is not justified if actual protection cannot be achieved, or if the consequences of embarking upon the intervention are likely to be worse than if there is no action at all'.[113] Although there is no way of being absolutely certain in determining whether intervention would have been worse, this conflict degenerated very quickly into conflict between ethnic groups. There was no way to determine how leadership might emerge. The Western powers backed the Free Syrian Army, but that group did not have the support of the majority of the population and has now splintered into groups that support the Islamic State. The report goes on to state that '[i]n particular, a military action for limited human protection purposes cannot be justified if in the process it triggers a larger conflict'.[114] Sadly, even without intervention, a larger regional conflict has emerged. But it can be argued that in fact this larger regional conflict already existed and intervention would have triggered this conflict as well. The next comment in the report illustrates the stark reality of the situation. 'It will be the case that some human beings simply cannot be rescued except at an unacceptable cost – perhaps of a larger regional conflagration, involving major military powers. In such cases, however painful the reality, coercive military action is no longer justified.' Sadly this larger regional conflagration exists, but may well have been unavoidable.

A useful example of state practice supporting the above opinion on the necessity for 'reasonable prospects' of success in an intervention was the parliamentary debate that took place in the United Kingdom Parliament in August 2013.[115] Parliamentarians reflected on the difficulties of intervention in this region. David Cameron had proposed a motion to Parliament, not authorizing immediate intervention but instead UK support for 'military action that is legal, proportionate and focused on saving lives by preventing and deterring further use of Syria's chemical weapons' after attempts to obtain an enabling Security Council resolution. Cameron acknowledged the difficulty in obtaining approval for this action by stating 'the well of public opinion was well and truly poisoned by the Iraq episode and we need to understand the public scepticism'.[116] In spite of Cameron's eloquence the motion was unsuccessful and the comments of the Members of Parliament are relevant to the precautionary principle.

---

[113] ICISS, *The Responsibility to Protect*, pp. 37–38.
[114] Ibid., p. 38.
[115] Hansard Debate on Syria, 29 August 2013, and see subsequent debate on IS on 26 September 2014, available at www.publications.parliament.uk/pa/cm201415/cmhansrd/cm140926/debtext/140926-0001.htm#1409266000001, accessed 25 July 2015.
[116] Hansard Debate on Syria, 29 August 2013, Column 1428.

272 *Part III: The responsibility to protect in practice*

The parliamentarians made reference to a brief summary of the UK government legal opinion.[117] The opinion stated:

1. If action in the Security Council is blocked, the UK would still be permitted under international law to take exceptional measures in order to alleviate the scale of the overwhelming humanitarian catastrophe in Syria by deterring and disrupting the further use of chemical weapons by the Syrian regime. Such a legal basis is available, under the doctrine of humanitarian intervention, provided three conditions are met:
(i)   there is convincing evidence, generally accepted by the international community as a whole, of extreme humanitarian distress on a large scale, requiring immediate and urgent relief;
(ii) it must be objectively clear that there is no practicable alternative to the use of force if lives are to be saved; and
(iii) the proposed use of force must be necessary and proportionate to the aim of relief of humanitarian need and must be strictly limited in time and scope to this aim (i.e. the minimum necessary to achieve that end and for no other purpose).[118]

It is annoying that the opinion once more referred to humanitarian intervention, rather than endorsing a responsibility to protect. But several speakers had no such restriction. First, Sir Tony Baldry a fellow Conservative stated:

> On the matter of international law, did not the world leaders and the UN sign up unanimously in 2005 to the doctrine of the responsibility to protect, which means that if countries default on their responsibility to defend their own citizens, the international community as a whole has a responsibility to do so? Syria has defaulted on its responsibility to protect its own citizens, so surely now the international community and we have a responsibility to undertake what we agreed to do as recently as 2005.[119]

Significantly, in response, Cameron acknowledged that the motion was about this doctrine, in addition to the Chemical Weapons Convention.[120] It was Glenda Jackson who first introduced the issue of reasonable prospects to the debate. She posed the question:

> What has convinced him – where is the evidence? – that an action by the international community would cease the use of chemical weapons

---

[117] Available at www.gov.uk/government/publications/chemical-weapon-use-by-syrian-regime-uk-government-legal-position/chemical-weapon-use-by-syrian-regime-uk-government-legal-position-html-version#contents, accessed 25 July 2015.

[118] Ibid.

[119] Hansard Debate on Syria, 29 August 2013, Column 1430.

[120] Ibid and *Convention on the Prohibition of the Development, Production, Stockpiling and Use of Chemical Weapons and on their Destruction*, 3 September 1992 (entered into force 29 April 1997) 1974 UNTS 75.

Responsibilities ignored? Syria and Iraq 273

within Syria, the continuing action that is totally destroying that country? Where is the evidence that convinces the Prime Minister that the external world can prevent this?[121]

She was joined by her fellow Labour MP Hugh Bayley, who asked '[c]an he [referring to the Prime Minister] convince the House that military action by our country would shorten the civil war and help herald a post-war Government who could create stability?'[122] These comments were supported by members of the Conservative Party. John Baron stated that the reason many in Parliament opposed arming the rebels was that atrocities had been committed on both sides and 'that there is a real risk of escalating the violence and therefore the suffering...either within the country or beyond Syria's borders.'[123] It was the Labour leader of the opposition Edward Milliband, in proposing amendments to the motion that would delay armed intervention, who specifically referred to the responsibility to protect. He stated that 'the responsibility to protect also demands a reasonable prospect of success in improving the plight of the Syrian people, and that responsibility is an essential part of making this case'.[124] Milliband proposed a subsequent vote with further information, including 'the prospect of successful action'.[125] Dame Tessa Jowell, another Labour MP, supported Milliband, posing the question again: 'How can we be effective, and at what cost?'[126]

Sir Menzies Campbell, Liberal Democrat, reminded the House that the debate concerning humanitarian intervention, a term used by several speakers, should now be about the responsibility to protect. He said: '[w]e must look beyond what might be achieved in the short term, to the medium term and the long term.'[127] Stephen Doughty, a Labour/Co-op Member, reminded Sir Menzies that one of the criteria of the responsibility to protect was the prospects of success. Sir Menzies responded that '[w]e cannot arrive at a conclusion on the prospect of success until we have more information than is currently available'.[128] In spite of this Sir Menzies voted for the Conservative motion, but his words and those of others must have influenced the majority who voted against the motion. Another speaker emphasizing the difficulties with military action was Angus Roberston of the SNP, who spoke eloquently on the issue. He argued that 'surely the aims, objectives and consequences of any intervention must be made clear and must not run the risk of escalating the conflict, causing further deaths and worsening the humanitarian situation'.[129] Therefore, within this debate it became clear that

---

[121] Ibid., Column 1432.
[122] Ibid., Columns 1433, 1434.
[123] Ibid., Column 1437.
[124] Ibid., Column 1444.
[125] Ibid., Column 1447.
[126] Ibid., Column 1454.
[127] Ibid., Column 1455.
[128] Ibid., Column 1456.
[129] Ibid., Column 1458.

274 Part III: The responsibility to protect in practice

speaker after speaker was concerned about the lack of a coherent long-term plan. A significant factor in the defeat of this motion is that in response to the queries about reasonable prospects for success, the Prime Minister acknowledged that he could make no such assurances. What had been lacking in any of the debate was a plan for intervention that might succeed, and in this case it may well be because any such plan was impossible.

This debate indicates that, in one state at least, an intelligent debate was conducted with respect to the responsibility to protect in all of its elements. In spite of these precautionary principles not being part of any General Assembly resolution, the reasonable prospects of success has influenced decision-making on intervention. It may well be that this is due to the catastrophic failures in Afghanistan, Iraq and Libya, but clearly the element missing from these interventions was real attention to rebuilding shattered societies. Please see attached word doc to be inserted as a paragraph below this one and before the conclusion. After the attacks in Paris and Istanbul, the UK parliament once again debated intervention in Syria.[130] However, the action taken was to constitute bombing of IS targets in Syria and not an intervention in the Syrian civil war, which was the subject of the previous debate. This bombing campaign was never contemplated to be a responsibility to react mission and was justified on the basis of self-defence against terrorism. The House did support with a large majority and air attacks began with the purpose to degrade IS.[131] The situation with respect to international intervention on the basis of the responsibility to protect in Syria remains unchanged.[132]

Conclusion

The precautionary principle, as previously discussed, exists particularly in international environmental law as a customary international law rule, but one can assert that an element of the international legal responsibility of states is to avoid large-scale civilian casualties in armed conflict. The proportionality principle in international humanitarian law indicates that a balance must be struck between the military advantage and civilian casualties and targets containing large numbers of civilians should be avoided. This section of *The Responsibility To Protect* arguably extends this legal principle to the decision to initiate an armed conflict for human protection purposes. This must surely be welcomed. There is scant evidence that the nations of the Security Council considered this fact at the time and, if anything, it was

---

[130] BBC News, 'Syria Airstrikes: What you need to know', 3 December 2015, accessed 11 January 201

[131] Ibid

[132] Space does not permit here a detailed consideration of the unilateral action by the UK and the conclusions to this chapter about the pressing need for an international intervention authorised by the UN remain the same.

the risk to the military forces of the possible participating states that governed the decision. Nevertheless, one cannot argue that the lack of intervention in these situations marks the end of the responsibility to protect. These are two in a large number of cases that have resulted in intervention. Sadly, however, the casualty total for both conflicts is now in the hundreds of thousands with millions of refugees, many of whom are now seeking asylum in Europe.

It cannot seriously be argued that there has been complete 'inaction', but the calls for military intervention have not been answered. One reason given by Gill is that 'the scope for collective intervention in Libya has reinforced the position of some States within and outside the Council which are reluctant to implement collective enforcement measures in response to human rights violations'.[133] The 'mission creep' in Libya to regime change did have a detrimental effect on the responsibility to protect and there is a reluctance on the part of the Russians and Chinese particularly to countenance regime change in Syria.[134] However, at this point action against Islamic State would not in any way result in the downfall of the Assad regime; in fact, expelling Islamic State might strengthen Assad. Now is the time for the Security Council and member states to embrace their responsibility to protect in Syria and Iraq. But in doing so they must develop long-term, coherent plans for reconstruction, recovery and rebuilding.

[133] T. Gill, 'The Security Council' in G. Zyberi (ed.), *An Institutional Approach to the Responsibility to Protect* (Cambridge: Cambridge University Press, 2013), p. 105.

[134] Nanda, 'The Future under International Law of the Responsibility to Protect after Libya and Syria', p. 39.

Conclusion

> R2P gives expression to a growing, global conviction that it is immoral and unacceptable for States to commit or allow serious international crimes against their people. It holds the international community responsible for preventing and addressing these crimes.
>
> Ban Ki-moon, remarks to the American
> Society of International Law, 2012[1]

To respond to the new norm in global discourse that it is not acceptable for massive human rights abuses to occur within any territory, two new doctrines are emerging within international law and international relations discourse – the responsibility to protect and aggravated state responsibility. Both have a long historical pedigree as they emerge from the continuing theoretical debate about the nature and scope of the international system. It seems clear from an extensive review of the literature and the international treaties and customs of various areas in international law that there is an international community with established norms, one of which is that states owe a responsibility to this international community of states to abide by the rules of international law. When one state violates those norms that are paramount, norms of *jus cogens*, it is the obligation of other states to react in some fashion to enforce community norms to fulfil obligations *erga omnes*. The question remains, even at the end of this comprehensive study, as to what form that reaction should take and whether the duty to respond is or will be legally obligatory.

It has been the thesis of this book that these two doctrines are interrelated due to emergence of international responsibility within various areas of international law, including international human rights law, international criminal law and international environmental law. If the rules of international

---

[1] Remarks by the Secretary-General to a lunch hosted by the American Society of International Law, 7 May 2012, available at www.responsibilitytoprotect.org/index.php/component/content/article/35-r2pcs-topics/4148-remarks-by-un-secretary-general-ban-ki-moon-at-a-lunch-hosted-by-the-american-society-of-international-law-, accessed 29 September 2015.

Conclusion 277

environmental law are any example, it is evident that principles of international responsibility such as precaution can emerge as doctrines of customary international law. Although it remains the case that we are still in the period of emergence, there is a momentum within international law towards crystallization of a responsibility to protect.

It is evident from the third part of this book that the responsibility to protect as a principle, rather than as a legal obligation, has become embedded in international affairs. Practice is critical in the emergence of international law doctrine and there is extensive practice in all three areas of responsibility: prevention, reaction and rebuilding. However, as of yet this practice is not consistent or uniform, particularly in the areas of prevention and reaction.

In spite of the potential of this doctrine to save millions of persons at risk of genocide, crimes against humanity, ethnic cleansing and war crimes, there are evident problems with implementation. The intervention in Libya with its 'mission creep' towards regime change resulted in a backlash against the concept that has had tragic consequences for the people of Syria.[2] Misuse of the doctrine also occurred in Iraq with public statements by politicians that the war in this nation was partly for the purposes of protection.[3] In the annual report of Human Rights Watch, entitled *World Report 2004: Human Rights and Armed Conflict*, Executive Director Kenneth Roth embarked on extensive analysis of the relationship between the responsibility to protect and regime change in a chapter entitled: 'War in Iraq: Not a Humanitarian Intervention'.[4] Roth stated that as time went on, the Bush administration's 'dominant remaining justification for the war is that Saddam Hussein was a tyrant who deserved to be overthrown', which was an argument of humanitarian intervention.[5] Roth described 'the effort to justify it even in part in humanitarian terms risks giving humanitarian intervention a bad name'.[6]

Roth described the Human Rights Watch position as supporting rare occasions of humanitarian intervention, but there were certain conditions that had to be met. He relied on threshold conditions set out in *The Responsibility*

---

[2] M.-J. Domestici-Met, 'Protecting Libya on Behalf of the International Community' (2011) 3 *Goettingen Journal of International Law* 861; V.P. Nanda, 'The Future under International Law of the Responsibility to Protect after Libya and Syria' (2013) 21 *Michigan State International Law Review* 1; G. Cronogue, Responsibility to Protect: Syria the Law, Politics, and Future of Humanitarian Intervention Post-Libya' (2012) 3 *International Humanitarian Legal Studies* 124; J. Gifkins, 'The UN Security Council Divided: Syria in Crisis' (2012) 4 *Global Responsibility to Protect* 377; S. Zifcak, 'The Responsibility to Protect after Libya and Syria' (2012) 13 *Melbourne Journal of International Law* 59.

[3] See, for example, Jack Straw, 'Military action was the only way', *The Observer*, 18 November 2001, and Tony Blair, 'Statement to Parliament on Iraq', *The Guardian*, 24 September 2002.

[4] Human Rights Watch, *World Report 2004: Human Rights and Armed Conflict* (New York: Human Rights Watch, 2004).

[5] Ibid., pp. 15–16.

[6] Ibid., p. 14.

278   *Conclusion*

to Protect and as a result was speaking to the possibility of abuse of the emerging doctrine. The first minimum threshold would have to be ongoing or imminent genocide or mass slaughter or loss of life.[7] In the case of Iraq, Roth argued that Hussein's killings had ebbed. The time when intervention was justified was when killing was intense, such as the 1988 Anfal genocide and the suppression of the uprisings in 1991. But by the eve of the conflict no one contended that the killing was near that level and 'better late than never' was not a justification.[8]

The second condition was that the intervention by force had to be the last reasonable option to stop mass killings. In this case Roth argued that the possibility of criminal prosecution should have been tried, as the experiences of Milosevic and Taylor pointed out that an international indictment 'profoundly discredits even a ruthless, dictatorial leader'. Roth argued that the international community should have availed itself of this option years before 2003.[9]

The third condition was a humanitarian purpose for the intervention. Roth accepted that there was no necessity for 'purity of motive', but the humanitarian motive should be 'dominant'. In the case of Iraq he argued that humanitarianism was at best only a subsidiary motive. US officials had spoken of a democratic Iraq transforming the Middle East. His chapter examines the aftermath of the intervention in the failure to provide security for the people, and the mechanism used to try Hussein, which resulted in his public execution.[10] As with the later intervention in Libya, Roth's main objection was converting an intervention into an exercise of regime change. This seems to be the main objection that has emerged in state practice with vehement opposition from a group of nations known as BRICS (Brazil, Russia, India, China and South Africa).[11] One cannot minimize the risk to the doctrine when it is used to disguise another more important political goal, which is to replace rogue regimes. However, there may be occasions when negotiation with an existing regime to preserve human life may well be futile. Hitler, for example, would never have been deterred from his destruction of the Jews. No one seriously argues that the Nazis could have remained in power. The current regime that seems to be a close relative of this type of madness is IS in Syria and Iraq. A regime intent on destroying an ethnic, cultural or religious group manifestly fails in its responsibility to protect.

The risk of the responsibility to protect being used to accomplish regime change is only one of the problems with implementation of the doctrine. These problems emerge from the examination of international and state

---

[7] Ibid., p. 17.
[8] Ibid., pp. 21–22.
[9] Ibid., p. 24.
[10] Ibid., pp. 26–29.
[11] B.S. Chimni, 'R2P in Syria, Imperialism with a human face', Open Democracy, available at www.opendemocracy.net/openglobalrights/bschimni/r2p-and-syria-imperialism-with-human-face, accessed 28 July 2015.

Conclusion 279

practice in the last part of this book. The first is the lack of true prevention activities. The international community is unwilling to act beyond negotiation and sanctions. The innovative and successful prevention mission in Macedonia has never been repeated. The sovereignty barrier with respect to prevention has yet to be crossed. Unless the members of the United Nations embrace this responsibility in its full sense of targeted prevention deployment to disarm potential combatants, they will be faced again and again with having to decide whether to exercise their responsibility to react after many have already died. This is why regime change occurs, as the international community has been unwilling to act at an earlier stage.

The second issue that emerges from the civil war in Syria is revealed in the quite eloquent parliamentary debate in the United Kingdom. Even though the responsibility to rebuild is entrenched in the United Nations system, that knowledge is not translated into proper resourced reaction missions that remain into the rebuilding phase. As several of the parliamentarians pointed out with respect to Syria, the reasonable prospects for success aspect was missing. Reasonable prospects for success means lasting peace. What mechanisms are in place for ensuring that lasting peace? There are many precedents in Kosovo, East Timor and back even further in history in Germany and Japan following the Second World War. It takes investment of funds and people to ensure proper governance. Sadly, as the debacles in Iraq, Afghanistan and Libya reveal, a 'cut and run' regime change operation fails spectacularly. It takes years and substantial financial backing to properly reconstruct nations, with innovations along the lines of a 'Marshall Plan'.[12] If that is not done, nations descend again into conflict very quickly.

International law can assist in those reconstruction efforts. Within the original responsibility to protect report international law is embedded into the responsibility to rebuild. Nations that have emerged from conflict require legal regimes that address the root causes of conflict and the criminality that results. International human rights law and international criminal law provide mechanisms for ensuring not only accountability but also a regime of respect for dignity of those who reside within the former conflict zone.

It can be argued that the responsibility to protect might have wider use than combating international criminality. Its use has been proposed in situations of natural rather than man-made disasters.[13] There is not the space within this monograph to properly analyse this view, but it is evident from our discussion of various international law fields, particularly the law of state responsibility and international environmental law, that the underpinning idea of responsibility to the international community as a whole for grievous

---

[12] Act of 3 April 1948, European Recovery Act (*Marshall Plan*), Enrolled Acts and Resolutions of Congress, 1789–1996, General Records of the United States Government, Record Group 11, National Archives.

[13] R. Barber, 'The Responsibility to Protect Survivors of Natural Disaster: Cyclone Nargis, a Case Study' (2009) 14 *Journal of Conflict and Security Law* 3.

280   *Conclusion*

violations of international law can extend beyond the categories of genocide, crimes against humanity, war crimes and ethnic cleansing. When a state manifestly fails to protect its population or causes hazards to other states, then the international community has an obligation to respond.

Finally, it is difficult to crystal ball-gaze and predict the future of this controversial concept. Will it evolve into an international law obligation? This may well not matter as it already incorporates a number of international law obligations within its underlying roots and within its practice. Even its use on an ad hoc and occasional basis is better than global history thus far, with the numerous failures to protect. It is astonishing that within less than two decades it has become a constant feature of the global conversation. Although not all of its aspects have become embedded in the practice of the United Nations, the offices of the Special Advisors on Genocide and the Responsibility to Protect and the United Nations High Commissioner for Human Rights constantly remind nations of their responsibility to protect their own citizens, and the members of the United Nations of their responsibility to act if this first level of responsibility fails. It seems that there is an unstoppable momentum towards the preservation of life and human dignity. From the Universal Declaration of Human Rights, originally a General Assembly resolution, it seems evident that core principles of our existence eventually evolve into binding customary international law obligations. It also seems evident that aggravated state responsibility will at some future point, emerge as a doctrine of customary law due to the general acceptance of the rules of state responsibility. For the sake of coming generations, we can only hope that the responsibility to protect, in all three of its components of prevention, reaction and rebuilding, also becomes a binding legal obligation on all states making up the international community.

Bibliography

Abella I. and Troper H., *None Is Too Many: Canada and the Jews of Europe 1933–1948* (Toronto: L&O Dennys, 1986)

Abiew F.K., *The Evolution of the Doctrine and Practice of Humanitarian Intervention* (Dordrecht: Kluwer Law International, 1999)

Advisory Council on International Affairs and Advisory Committee on Issues of Public International Law, *Humanitarian Intervention* (The Hague, 2000)

Akehurst M., 'Humanitarian Intervention' in Hedley Bull (ed.), *Intervention in World Politics* (Oxford: Oxford University Press, 1984)

Allott P., *Eunomia* (Oxford University Press, 1990)

Alston P. and Goodman R., *International Human Rights* (Oxford: Oxford University Press, 2012)

Aquinas St Thomas, *Summa Theologica, Part II Question 40* (Cincinnati: Benziger Bros. edition, 1947)

Archibugi D. and Held D., 'Introduction' in D. Archibugi and D. Held (eds), *Cosmopolitan Democracy* (Cambridge: Polity Press, 1995)

Augustine of Hippo St, *City of God*, Book 19

Barber R., 'The Responsibility to Protect Survivors of Natural Disaster: Cyclone Nargis, a Case Study' (2009) 14 *Journal of Conflict and Security Law* 3

Barry B., 'International Society from a Cosmopolitan Perspective' in D. Mapel and T. Nardin (eds), *International Society* (Princeton: Princeton University Press, 1998)

Bellamy A., 'A Chronic Protection Problem: The DPRK and the Responsibility to Protect' (2015) 91 *International Affairs* 225

Bellamy A., *Responsibility to Protect* (Cambridge: Polity Press, 2009)

Bellamy A. and Williams P., 'The New Politics of Protection: Côte D'Ivoire, Libya and the Responsibility to Protect' (2011) 87 *International Affairs* 275

Birnie P. and Boyle A., *International Law and the Environment*, 2nd edition (Oxford: Oxford University Press, 2002)

Bogdandy A. Von, 'Constitutionalism in International Law: Comment on a Proposal from Germany' (2006) 47 *Harvard International Law Journal* 223

Blockmans S., 'Moving into Unchartered Waters: An Emerging Right of Unilateral Humanitarian Intervention?' (1999) 12 *Leiden Journal of International Law* 759

Boutros-Ghali B., *An Agenda for Peace: Preventive Diplomacy, Peacemaking, and Peace-keeping: Report of the Secretary-General Pursuant to the Statement Adopted by the Summit Meeting of the Security Council on 31 January 1992* (New York: United Nations, 1992)

282   Bibliography

Breau S., 'Peacekeeping Operations' in G. Zyberi (ed.), *An Institutional Approach to the Responsibility to Protect* (Cambridge: Cambridge University Press, 2013)

Breau S., 'The Impact of the Responsibility to Protect on Peacekeeping' (2006) 11 *Journal of Conflict and Security Law* 429

Breau S., *Humanitarian Intervention: The United Nations and Collective Responsibility* (London: Cameron May, 2005)

Breau S. and Joyce R., 'The Responsibility to Record Civilian Casualties' (2013) 5 *Global Responsibility to Protect* 28

Brenfors M. and Petersen M., 'The Legality of Humanitarian Intervention – A Defence' (2000) 69 *Nordic Journal of International Law* (2000) 449

Brierly J.L., *The Law of Nations*, 6th edition (Oxford: Oxford University Press, 1963)

Brownlie I., *Principles of Public International Law*, 5th edition (Oxford: Oxford University Press, 1998), 7th edition 2008, 8th edition 2012

Brownlie I., *The Rule of Law in International Affairs: International Law at the Fiftieth Anniversary of the United Nations* (The Hague: Kluwer Law, 1998)

Brownlie I., *System of the Law of Nations: State Responsibility (Part 1)* (Oxford: Clarendon Press, 1983)

Brownlie I., *International Law and the Use of Force by States* (Oxford: Clarendon Press, 1963)

Brownlie I. and Apperley C.J., 'Kosovo Crisis Inquiry: Memorandum on the International Law Aspects' (2000) 49 *The International and Comparative Law Quarterly* 878

Buzan B., *From International to World Society? English School Theory and the Social Structure of Globalization* (Cambridge: Cambridge University Press, 2004)

Bull H., *The Anarchical Society* (Basingstoke: Palgrave, 1977)

Bull H., 'The Grotian Conception of International Society' in H. Butterfield and M. Wight (eds), *Diplomatic Investigations* (London: Allen & Unwin, 1966)

Bull H., Kingsbury B. and Roberts A. (eds), *Hugo Grotius and International Relations* (Oxford: Clarendon Press, 1990)

Buzan B., *From International to World Society? English School Theory and the Social Structure of Globalization* (Cambridge: Cambridge University Press, 2004)

Carr I. and Breau S., 'Towards Achieving a Balance: Humanitarian Aid, Human Rights and Corruption' in M. Odello and S. Cavandoli (eds), *Emerging Areas of Human Rights in the 21st Century: The Role of the Universal Declaration on Human Rights* (London: Routledge, 2010)

Cassese A., *International Criminal Law*, 2nd edition (Oxford: Oxford University Press, 2008)

Cassese A., *International Law*, 2nd edition (Oxford: Oxford University Press, 2005)

Cassese A., 'International Criminal Law' in M. Evans (ed.), *International Law* (Oxford: Oxford University Press, 2003)

Cassese A., 'Ex Injuria ius Oritur: Are We Moving towards Legitimation of Forcible Humanitarian Countermeasures in the World Community?' (1999) 10 *European Journal of International Law* 23

Cassese A., Gaeta P. and Jones J.R.W.D. (eds), *The Rome Statute of the International Criminal Court: A Commentary* (Oxford: Oxford University Press, 2002)

Chesterman S., *Just War or Just Peace? Humanitarian Intervention in International Law* (Oxford: Oxford University Press, 2001)

Cicero Marcus Tullius, *De Officiis*, translated by W. Miller (Cambridge, MA: Harvard University Press, 1913)

Bibliography   283

Cirkovic E., 'An Analysis of the ICJ Advisory Opinion on Kosovo's Unilateral Declaration of Independence' (2010) 11 *German Law Journal* 895

Claude I., *The Changing United Nations* (New York: Random House, 1967)

Colás A., *International Civil Society* (Cambridge: Polity Books, 2002)

Crawford J., *State Responsibility: The General Part* (Cambridge: Cambridge University Press, 2013)

Crawford J., *The International Law Commission's Articles on State Responsibility: Introduction, Text and Commentaries* (Cambridge: Cambridge University Press, 2002)

Crawford J., 'The Earl A. Snyder Lecture in International Law: Responsibility to the International Community as a Whole' (2001) 8 *Indiana Journal of Global Legal Studies* 303

Cronogue G., 'Responsibility to Protect: Syria, the Law, Politics, and Future of Humanitarian Intervention Post-Libya' (2012) 3 *International Humanitarian Legal Studies* 124.

Cullet P., 'Differential Treatment in International Law: Towards a New Paradigm of Inter-state Relations' 10 *European Journal of International Law* 542

Danish Institute of International Affairs, *Humanitarian Intervention: Legal and Political Aspects* (Copenhagen: Danish Institute of International Affairs, 1999)

Deng, F.M. *et al.*, *Sovereignty as Responsibility: Conflict Management in Africa* (Washington DC: The Brookings Institute, 1996)

Dennis M.J. and Stewart D.P., 'Justiciability of Economic, Social and Cultural Rights: Should There Be an International Complaints Mechanism to Adjudicate the Rights to Food, Water, Housing and Health?' (2004) 98 *American Journal of International Law* 462

Dersso S.A., 'The African Union' in G. Zyberi (ed.), *An Institutional Approach to the Responsibility to Protect* (Cambridge: Cambridge University Press, 2013)

Domestici-Met M.-J., 'Protecting Libya on Behalf of the International Community' (2011) 3 *Goettingen Journal of International Law* 861

Dunoff J.L., 'From Green to Global: Towards the Transformation of International Environmental Law' (1995) 19 *Harvard Environmental Law Review* 241

Dupuy P.-M., 'The Constitutional Dimension of the Charter of the United Nations Revisited' (1997) 1 *Max Plank Yearbook of International Law* 1

Dupuy P.-M., 'Soft Law and the International Law of the Environment' (1991) 12 *Michigan Journal of International Law* 420

Dupuy P.-M. and Vinales J.E., *International Environmental Law* (Cambridge: Cambridge University Press, 2015)

Eide A., 'Economic, Social and Cultural Rights as Human Rights' in A. Eide, C. Krause and A. Rosas (eds), *Economic, Social and Cultural Rights: A Textbook* (Dordrecht: M. Nijhoff, 1995)

Evans G., *The Responsibility to Protect* (Washington DC: Brookings Institution Press, 2008)

Farer T., 'Problems of an International Law of Intervention' (1962) 3 *Stanford Journal of International Studies* 20

Fassbender B., 'The United Nations Charter as Constitution of the International Community' (1998) 36 *Columbia Journal of Transnational Law* 529

Fassbender B., *UN Security Council Reform and the Right of Veto* (The Hague: Kluwer Law, 1998)

284 Bibliography

Fawn R. and Larkins J., 'International Society after the Cold War: Theoretical Interpretations and Practical Implications' in R. Fawn and J. Larkins (eds), *International Society after the Cold War* (Basingstoke and London: MacMillan Press, 1996)

Focarelli C., 'The Responsibility to Protect and Humanitarian Intervention: Too Many Ambiguities for a Working Doctrine' (2008) 13 *Journal of Conflict and Security Law* 191

Fox H., 'The Objections to Transfer of Criminal Jurisdiction to the UN Tribunal' (1997) 46 *International and Comparative Legal Quarterly* 434

Franck T., 'The Emerging Right to Democratic Governance' (1992) 86 *American Journal of International Law* 46

Fuller L.L., 'Positivism and Fidelity to Law – A Reply to Professor Hart' (1958) 71 *Harvard Law Review* 630

Gallant K.S., 'Securing the Presence of Defendants before the International Tribunal for the Former Yugoslavia: Breaking with Extradition' in R.S. Clark and S. Sann (eds), *The Prosecution of International Crimes* (New Brunswick, NJ: Transaction Publishers 1996)

Gifkins J., 'The UN Security Council Divided: Syria in Crisis' (2012) 4 *Global Responsibility to Protect* 377

Gill T., 'The Security Council' in G. Zyberi (ed.), *An Institutional Approach to the Responsibility to Protect* (Cambridge: Cambridge University Press, 2013)

Goodwin-Gill G.S., *The Refugee in International Law* (Oxford: Clarendon Press, 1996)

Goodwin-Gill G.S., 'The Limits of the Power of Expulsion in Public International Law' (1976) 47 *British Yearbook of International Law* 56

Grahl-Madsen A., *The Status of Refugees in International Law*, Vol. 2 (Leiden: A.W. Sijthoff, 1972)

Gray, Christine, 'The Legality of NATO's Military Action in Kosovo' in Sienho Yee and Tieya Wang (eds), *International Law in the Post-Cold War World: Essays in Memory of Li Haopei* (London: Routledge, 2001)

Gray Christine, *International Law and the Use of Force*, 3rd edition (Oxford: Oxford University Press, 2008)

Green J., *The International Court of Justice and Self-Defence in International Law* (Oxford: Hart, 2009)

Greenwood C., 'Humanitarian Intervention: The Case of Kosovo' (2002) 10 *Finnish Yearbook of International Law* 141

Greenwood C., 'International Law and the NATO Intervention in Kosovo' (2000) 49 *International and Comparative Law Quarterly* 926

Greig D.W., *International Law* (London: Butterworths, 1976)

Grotii H., *De Jure Belli ac Pacis, libri tres, In quibus ius naturae & Gentium: item iuris publici preciptae expilicantur* (Paris: Apud Nicalaum Buom, 1625, cum privilegio regis via Gallica (the French National Library))

Habermas J., *The Divided West* (Cambridge: Polity Press, 2006)

Handl G., 'Environmental Security and Global Change: The Challenge to International Law' (1991) 1 *Yearbook of International Environmental Law* 3

Harris K.J. and Kushen R., 'Surrender of Fugitives to the War Crimes Tribunals for Yugoslavia and Rwanda: Squaring International Legal Obligations with the U.S. Constitution' (1997) 7 *Criminal Law Forum* 561

Hart H.L.A., *The Concept of Law* (Oxford: Clarendon Press, 1961)

Bibliography 285

Heffter A., *Le Droit International Public de l'Europe* (Berlin: H.W. Muller, 1857)

Held D., 'Law of States, Law of Peoples: Three Models of Sovereignty' (2002) 8 *Legal Theory* 1

Held D., 'Democracy and the International Order' in D. Mapel and T. Nardin (eds), *International Society* (Princeton: Princeton University Press, 1998)

Held D. and McGrew A., *Globalization/Anti-Globalization* (Cambridge: Polity Press 2003)

Henckaerts J.-M. and Doswald Beck L., *Customary International Humanitarian Law, Volume I: Rules* (Cambridge: Cambridge University Press, 2005)

Higgins R., *Problems and Process* (Oxford: Oxford University Press, 1994)

Holzgrefe J.L. and Keohane R. *Humanitarian Intervention: Ethical, Legal, and Political Dilemmas* (Cambridge: Cambridge University Press, 2003)

Human Rights Watch, *World Report 2004: Human Rights and Armed Conflict* (New York: Human Rights Watch, 2004)

Independent International Commission on Kosovo (Chair Richard Goldstone), *The Kosovo Report: Conflict, International Response, Lessons Learned* (Oxford: Oxford University Press, 2000)

International Commission on Intervention and State Sovereignty, *The Responsibility to Protect* (Ottawa, 2001)

Iwama T., 'Emerging Principles and Rules for the Prevention and Mitigation of Environmental Harm' in E. Weiss (ed.), *Environmental Change and International Law* (New York: United Nations University Press, 1992)

Jackson R., 'The Political Theory of International Society' in K. Booth and S. Smith (eds), *International Relations Theory Today* (Cambridge: Polity Press, 1995)

Jackson R., *Quasi-states: Sovereignty, International Relations and the Third World* (Cambridge: Cambridge University Press, 1990)

Johnston D.M., 'World Constitutionalism in the Theory of International Law' in R. St John Macdonald and D.M. Johnston, *Towards World Constitutionalism: Issues in the Legal Ordering of the World Community* (Leiden: Martinus Nijhoff, 2005)

Johnstone, R., 'Invoking Responsibility for Environmental Injury in the Arctic Ocean' (2014) 6 *The Yearbook of Polar Law Online* 1

Johnstone R., *Offshore Oil and Gas Development in the Arctic under International Law: Risk and Responsibility* (Dordrecht: Martinus Nijhoff, 2014)

Jubilut L., 'Has the Responsibility to Protect Been a Real Change in Humanitarian Intervention? An Analysis from the Crisis in Libya' (2012) 14 *International Community Law Review* 309

Kant I., *Perpetual Peace: A Philosophical Essay* (London: G. Allen & Unwin Limited, 1903)

Kantareva S., 'The Responsibility to Protect: Issues of Legal Formulation and Practical Application' (2011–2012) 6 *Interdisciplinary Journal of Human Rights Law* 1

Kapur A., 'Humanity as the A and Ω of Sovereignty: Four Replies to Anne Peters' (2009) 20 *European Journal of International Law* 560

Keohane R.O., 'International Institutions: Two Approaches' in R.J. Beck, A.C. Arend and R. Vander Lugt (eds), *International Rules: Approaches from International Law and International Relations* (Oxford: Oxford University Press, 1996)

Keohane R.O., *After Hegemony: Cooperation and Discord in the World Political Economy* (Princeton: Princeton University Press, 1984)

Keohoane R.O., 'The Demand for International Regimes' in S.D. Krasner (ed.), *International Regimes* (London: Cornell University Press, 1983)

286   Bibliography

Keohane R.O. and Nye J.S., *Power and Interdependence* (Boston, MA: Little, Brown & Co., 1977)

Kiss A., 'The Implications of Global Change' in E. Weiss (ed.), *Environmental Change and International Law* (New York: United Nations University Press, 1992)

Kittichaisaree K., *International Criminal Law* (Oxford: Oxford University Press, 2001)

Krasner S.D., *Sovereignty: Organised Hypocrisy* (Princeton: Princeton University Press, 1999)

Krasner S.D., 'Structural Causes and Regime Consequences: Regimes as Intervening Variables' in S.D. Krasner, *International Regimes* (London: Cornell University Press, 1983)

Krisch N., 'Unilateral Enforcement of the Collective Will: Kosovo, Iraq and the Security Council' (1999) 3 *Max Planck United Nations Yearbook* 59

Kritsiotis D., 'The Kosovo Crisis and NATO's Application of Armed Force against the Federal Republic of Yugoslavia' (2000) 49 *International and Comparative Law Quarterly* 330

Kwakwa E., 'Regulating the International Economy: What Role for the State' in M. Byers (ed.), *The Role of Law in International Politics* (Oxford: Oxford University Press, 2000)

Lauterpacht H., *International Law and Human Rights* (New York: Frederick Praeger, 1950)

Lemarchand R., *Burundi: Ethnocide as Discourse and Practice* (Washington DC: Woodrow Wilson Center Press, 1994)

LeMon C.J. and Taylor R.S., 'Security Council Action in the Name of Human Rights: From Rhodesia to the Congo' (2004) 10 *U.C. Davis Journal of International Law & Policy* 197

Lowe V., 'International Legal Issue Arising in the Kosovo Crisis' (2000) 49 *International and Comparative Law Quarterly* 934

Ludlow D.J., 'Preventive Peacemaking in Macedonia: An Assessment of U.N. Good Office Diplomacy' (2003) 2 *Brigham Young Law Review* 761

Macdonald R. St John and Johnston D.M., *Towards World Constitutionalism: Issues in the Legal Ordering of the World Community* (Leiden: Martinus Nijhoff, 2005)

McDougal M., 'The Impact of International Law upon National Law: A Policy Oriented Perspective' in M. McDougal and Associates, *Studies in World Public Order* (New Haven: Yale University Press, 1960)

McDougal M.S. and Associates, *Studies in World Public Order* (New Haven: Yale University Press, 1960)

McDougal M.S. and Reisman W.M., 'International Law in Policy-Oriented Perspective' in R. St John Macdonald and D.M. Johnston, *Towards World Constitutionalism: Issues in the Legal Ordering of the World Community* (Leiden: Martinus Nijhoff, 2005)

McDougal M.S. and Feliciano F.P., *Law and Minimum World Public Order: The Legal Regulation of International Coercion* (New Haven: Yale University Press, 1961)

Mbazira C., 'A Path to Realizing Economic, Social and Cultural Rights in Africa? A Critique of the New Partnership for Africa's Development' (2004) 4 *African Human Rights Law Journal* 34

Meron T., 'On a Hierarchy of International Human Rights' (1986) 80 *American Journal of International Law* 1

Bibliography 287

Meyer M. and McCoubrey H., *Reflections on the Law of Armed Conflict: The Selected Works of Colonel Draper* (The Hague: Kluwer, 1998)

Mohamed S., 'From Keeping the Peace to Building Peace: A Proposal for a Revitalized United Nations Trusteeship Council' (2005) 105 *Columbia Law Review* 809

Molier G., 'Humanitarian Intervention and the Responsibility to Protect after 9/11' (2006) 53 *Netherlands International Law Review* 37

Mosler H., *The International Society as a Legal Community* (Alphen aan den Rijn, The Netherlands: Sijthoff & Noordhoff, 1980)

Mosler H., 'The International Society as a Legal Community' (1974) 140 *Recueil Des Cours* 1

Mowbray A.R., *The Development of Positive Obligations under the European Convention on Human Rights by the European Court of Human Rights* (Oxford: Hart Publishing, 2004)

Murphy R., 'United Nations Peacekeeping in Lebanon and Somalia, and the Use of Force' (2003) 8 *Journal of Conflict & Security Law* 71

Murphy S.D., *Humanitarian Intervention: The United Nations in an Evolving World Order* (Philadelphia: University of Pennsylvania Press, 1996)

Nanda V.P., 'The Future under International Law of the Responsibility to Protect after Libya and Syria' (2013) 21 *Michigan State International Law Review* 1

Neff S., 'Rescue across State Boundaries: International Legal Aspects of Rescue' in M. Menlove and A. McCall Smith (eds), *The Duty to Rescue: The Jurisprudence of Aid* (Aldershot: Dartmouth Publishing Company, 1993)

Noortmann M., *Enforcing International Law* (Aldershot: Ashgate, 2005)

Orford, A., *International Authority and the Responsibility to Protect* (Cambridge: Cambridge University Press, 2011)

O'Shea S., 'Interaction between International Criminal Tribunals and National Legal Systems' (1996) 28 *New York University Journal of International Law & Policy* 367

Petersmann E.-U., 'Time for a United Nations "Global Compact" for Integrating Human Rights into the Law of Worldwide Organizations: Lessons from European Integration' (2002) 13 *European Journal of International Law* 621

Portela C., *Humanitarian Intervention, NATO and International Law* (Berlin: BITS, 2000)

Pronto A.N., 'The International Law Commission' in G. Zyberi (ed.), *An Institutional Approach to the Responsibility to Protect* (Cambridge: Cambridge University Press, 2013)

Ramcharan B.G., *The International Law and Practice of Early Warning and Preventive Diplomacy: The Emerging Global Watch* (Dordrecht: Martinus Nijhoff, 1991)

Rawls J., *The Law of Peoples* (Cambridge, MA: Harvard University Press, 1999)

Rieff D., 'Charity on the Rampage: The Business of Foreign Aid' (1997) 76 *Foreign Affairs* 132

Roberts A., 'NATO's "Humanitarian War" over Kosovo' (1999) 41 *Survival* 102

Robertson G., *Crimes against Humanity. The Struggle for Global Justice* (London: Penguin, 2002)

Ronzitti N., 'Lessons of International Law from NATO's Armed Intervention against the Federal Republic of Yugoslavia' (1999) 34 *The International Spectator* 45

Sand P., 'International Environmental Law after Rio' (1993) 4 *European Journal of International Law* 377

Sands P. and Peel J., *Principles of International Environmental Law*, 3rd edition (Cambridge: Cambridge University Press, 2012)

288   *Bibliography*

Schabas W., *Introduction to the International Criminal Court*, 2nd edition (Cambridge: Cambridge University Press, 2004)

Schachter O., 'The Relationship between Permanent Sovereignty and the Obligation Not to Cause Transboundary Environmental Damage' (1996) 26 *Environmental Law* 1187

Scharf M., 'The Letter of the Law: The Scope of the International Legal Obligations to Prosecute Human Rights Crimes' (1996) 59 *Law & Contemporary Problems* 41

Serrano M., 'The Responsibility to Protect: Libya and Côte D'Ivoire' (2011) 3 *Amsterdam Law Forum* 92

Shaw M., *International Law*, 7th edition (Cambridge: Cambridge University Press, 2014)

Shaw M., *International Law*, 5th edition (Cambridge: Cambridge University Press, 2003)

Shaw M., 'Global Society and Global Responsibility' in R. Fawn and J. Larkins (eds), *International Society after the Cold War* (Basingstoke and London: MacMillan Press, 1996)

Simma B., 'NATO, the UN and the Use of Force: Legal Aspects' (1999) 10 *European Journal of International Law* 1

Simma B., 'From Bilateralism to Community Interest in International Law' (1994) 250 *Recueil Des Cours* 217

Simms B. and Trim J.D.B., *Humanitarian Intervention: A History* (Cambridge: Cambridge University Press, 2011)

Simpson G., *Great Powers and Outlaw States* (Cambridge: Cambridge University Press, 2004)

Slaughter A.M., *A New World Order* (Princeton: Princeton University Press, 2005)

Slaughter A.M., 'A Global Community of Courts' (2003) 44 *Harvard International Law Journal* 191

Slaughter A.M., 'Global-Government Networks, Global Information Agencies and Disaggregated Democracy' (2002–2003) 24 *Michigan Journal of International Law* 1041

Slaughter A.M., 'International Law in a World of Liberal States' (1995) 6 *European Journal of International Law* 503

Slaughter A.M. and Burke-White W., 'An International Constitutional Moment' (2003) 43 *Harvard International Law Journal* 1

Sloan B., 'General Assembly Resolutions Revisited (Forty Years Later)' (1987) *British Yearbook of International Law* 37

Sofaer A.D., 'International Law and Kosovo' (2000) 36 *Stanford Journal of International Law* 1

Sohn L.V., 'The Stockholm Declaration of the Human Environment' (1973) 14 *Harvard International Law Journal* 423

Spinedi M., 'International Crimes of State: The Legislative History' in J.H.H. Weiler, A. Cassese and M. Spinedi (eds), *International Crimes of State: A Critical Analysis of the ILC's Draft Article 19 on State Responsibility* (Berlin/New York: De Gruyter, 1989)

Stedman S.J., 'UN Intervention in Civil Wars: Imperatives of Choice and Strategy' in D. Daniel and B. Hayes, *Beyond Traditional Peacekeeping* (Basingstoke: MacMillan Press, 1995)

Steiner H.J. and Alston P., *International Human Rights in Context*, 2nd edition (Oxford: Oxford University Press, 2000)

Bibliography   289

Susskind L.J., 'A New World Order in Environmental Policy Making? A Review of the State and Social Power in Global Environmental Politics' (1995) 25 *Environmental Law* 239

Tabler A.J., 'Syria's Collapse and How Washington Can Stop It' (2013) 92 *Foreign Affairs* 90

Tanner F., 'Conflict Prevention and Conflict Resolution: Limits of Multilateralism' (2000) 839 *International Review of the Red Cross* 541

Tesón F.R., *Humanitarian Intervention: An Inquiry into Law and Morality* (Dobbs Ferry, NY: Transnational Publishers Inc., 1988)

Tesón F.R., 'Kantian International Liberalism' in David R. Mapel and Terry Nardin (eds), *International Society* (Princeton: Princeton University Press, 1998)

Tesón F.R., *A Philosophy of International Law* (Boulder, CO: Westview, 1998)

Thakur R., *The United Nations and Peace and Security* (Cambridge: Cambridge University Press, 2006)

de Than C. and Shorts E., *International Criminal Law and Human Rights* (London: Sweet & Maxwell, 2003)

Timoshenko A.S., 'Ecological Security: Responses to Global Challenges' in E. Weiss (ed.), *Environmental Change and International Law* (New York: United Nations University Press, 1992)

Tomuschat C., 'Multilateralism in the Age of US Hegemony' in R. St John Macdonald and D.M. Johnston (eds), *Towards World Constitutionalism: Issues in the Legal Ordering of the World Community* (Leiden: Martinus Nijhoff, 2005)

Tomuschat C., 'International Law: Ensuring the Survival of Mankind on the Eve of a New Century' (1999) 288 *Recueil Des Cours* 1

Tomuschat C., 'Obligations Arising for States without or against their Will' (1993) 241 *Recueil Des Cours* 195

Trachtman, J.P., *The Future of International Law: Global Government* (Cambridge: Cambridge University Press, 2013)

Triffterer O. *et al.*, *Commentary on the Rome Statute of the International Criminal Court*, 2nd edition (Oxford: Hart, 2008)

Tuck R., *The Rights of War and Peace: Political Thought and the International Order from Grotius to Kant* (Oxford: Oxford University Press, 1999)

United Nations Department of Public Information, *The United Nations and Rwanda, 1993–1996* (New York: UN, 1996)

Van Steenberghe R., 'Non-State Actors' in G. Zyberi (ed.), *An Institutional Approach to the Responsibility to Protect* (Cambridge: Cambridge University Press, 2013)

Verdirame G., *The UN and Human Rights: Who Guards the Guardians?* (Cambridge: Cambridge University Press, 2011)

Verdross A. and Simma B., *Universelles Völkerrecht: Theorie und Praxis*, 3rd edition (Berlin: Duncker & Humblot, 1984)

Vevrey W.D., 'Legality of Humanitarian Intervention after the Cold War' in E. Ferris (ed.), *The Challenge to Intervention: A New Role for the United Nations* (Uppsala: Life and Peace Institute, 1992)

Vevrey W.D., 'Humanitarian Intervention under International Law' (1985) 32 *Netherlands International Law Review* 357

Vicunna F.O., 'State Responsibility, Liability and Remedial Measures under International Law: New Criteria for Environmental Protection' in E. Weiss (ed.), *Environmental Change and International Law* (New York: United Nations University Press, 1992)

290   Bibliography

Vincent R.J., *Human Rights and International Relations* (Cambridge: Cambridge University Press, 1986)

Vincent R.J., *Nonintervention and International Order* (Princeton: Princeton University Press, 1974)

Wallach E.J., 'Extradition to the Rwandan War Crimes Tribunal: Is Another Treaty Required?' (1998) 3 *UCLA Journal of International Law & Foreign Affairs* 59

Waltz K., *Theory of International Politics* (Reading, MA: Addison-Wesley Publishing Company, 1979)

Warbrick C. and McGoldrick D., 'Co-operation with the International Criminal Tribunal for Yugoslavia' (1996) 45 *International and Comparative Legal Quarterly* 947

Watts R.L., *Comparing Federal Systems*, 2nd edition (Montreal and Kingston: McGill-Queen's University Press, 1999)

Weis P., 'The Draft United Nations Convention on Territorial Asylum' (1979) 50 *British Yearbook of International Law* 151

Weller M. (ed.), *The Oxford Handbook of the Use of Force in International Law* (Oxford: Oxford University Press, 2015)

Welsh J., 'Implementing the Responsibility to Protect', Policy Brief No. 1 2009, Oxford: Oxford Institute for Ethics, Law and Armed Conflict

Wheatley S., 'The NATO Action against the Federal Republic of Yugoslavia: Humanitarian Intervention in the Post-Cold War Era' (2000) 50 *Northern Ireland Legal Quarterly* 47

Wheeler N., *Saving Strangers* (Oxford: Oxford University Press, 2000)

Wheeler N., 'Pluralist or Solidarist Conceptions of International Society: Bull and Vincent on Humanitarian Intervention' (1992) 21 *Millennium: Journal of International Studies* 464

White N.D., *Keeping the Peace* (Manchester: Manchester University Press, 1990)

Wilde R., 'From Danzig to East Timor and Beyond: The Role of International Territorial Administration' (2001) 95 *American Journal of International Law* 583

Wolfrum R., 'International Administration in Post-Conflict Situations by the United Nations and Other International Actors' (2005) 9 *Max Planck UN Yearbook* 649

Wood W.B., 'Post-Conflict Intervention Revisited: Relief, Reconstruction, Rehabilitation, and Reform' (2005) 29 *Fletcher Forum of World Affairs* 119

Xenos D., *The Positive Obligations of the State under the European Convention of Human Rights* (Routledge Research in Human Rights Law) (Abingdon: Routledge, 2013)

Yannis A., 'Kosovo under International Administration' (2001) 43 *Survival* 31

Zifcak S., 'Falls the Shadow: The Responsibility to Protect from Theory to Practice' in S. Sampford and R. Thakur (eds), *Responsibility to Protect and Sovereignty* (Farnham, Surrey: Ashgate, 2013)

Zifcak S., 'The Responsibility to Protect after Libya and Syria' (2012) 13 *Melbourne Journal of International Law* 59

Zyberi G. (ed.), *An Institutional Approach to the Responsibility to Protect* (Cambridge: Cambridge University Press, 2013)

Index

abuses, 92–3, 99, 102, 104, 218, 228, 233, 268–9; massive, 1, 30, 32, 73, 137, 178, 208
accountability, 55, 83, 91, 135, 143, 190, 194, 279; international, 94, 103
action plan to prevent genocide, 23, 150–1, 199
administration, 66–7, 74, 241, 244, 253; international, 63, 243; transitional, 235–6, 242–3
Afghanistan, 21, 240, 246–9, 253–4, 270, 274, 279
Africa, 218, 222, 235
African Charter, 106–7, 112
African Commission, 106
African Union, 208, 222, 224–5
Agenda 21, 151, 165
Agenda for Peace, 184–6, 208, 234, 237
aggravated state responsibility, 3, 6, 61–2, 79–93, 115–16, 123–4, 145–6, 177–8
aid, 15, 83, 86, 88–9, 99, 117–18, 177, 192
air strikes, 231, 256, 265, 267–70
air support, 255, 268
Albania, 72, 200
Aleppo, 263, 267–8
aliens, 63, 66–8, 73, 79
allegations, 66, 212, 231, 258, 264–5, 269–70
Alston, P., 104
Amnesty International, 201, 260, 263
Annan, Kofi, 188, 191, 195, 199, 202–3, 235, 238–9, 261–3
anthropogenic emissions, 165–7, 169
apartheid, 85, 129–30

arbitration, 70, 170, 193; commissions, 62–3, 67–8
Archibugi, D., 56
Argentina, 103, 134
armed conflict, 12, 14, 23, 26, 124–5, 138, 211, 274; international, 128, 218, 221, 257; non-international, 257
armed forces, 64, 73, 90, 125, 185, 241
armed groups, 74, 227, 237, 247, 258
armed intervention, 16, 19, 196, 205, 254–5, 273; unilateral, 21, 240
arrest, 65, 138–9, 231, 260
ARSIWA (Articles on the Responsibility of States for Internationally Wrongful Acts), 3, 61–2, 68–79, 83, 86, 89, 91, 146
Articles on the Responsibility of States for Internationally Wrongful Acts, see ARSIWA
Assad regime, 257–9, 264–5, 268, 275
Assembly of States Parties, 140–1, 143
assessment, 28, 151, 155, 157, 174, 189, 196–7, 227
assistance, 83, 86, 89, 119–20, 138–9, 141–2, 190, 192; development, 188, 190, 244; humanitarian, 118–19, 185, 218, 223, 228, 244, 249; international, 27, 29, 99, 117, 120, 206, 250; judicial, 138–9; technical, 161–2, 190, 233
asylum, 108–9, 111–13, 121, 274; law, 93, 108, 114; seekers, 92–3
Australia, 29, 112
Austria, 82, 114, 124–5
authorities, 72, 110, 127, 133–4, 144, 177, 212, 254; governmental, 72–4
authorization, 15, 73, 198, 212–13, 240, 265

292 *Index*

balance of consequences, 23
Ban Ki-moon, 13, 196, 261–2,
    264–5, 276
Barcelona Traction, 80, 85, 116
Baril, M., 198
Belgium, 88, 114, 135, 145, 193
Benghazi, 229, 231
binding obligations, 115, 137
biodiversity, 157–8, 162, 171–4, 176–7
Biodiversity Convention, 171–7
biological resources, 171–4
Birnie, P., 153–4, 162–4, 169, 173, 175
Bosnia–Herzegovina, 14, 16, 85–6, 208
Boutros-Ghali, Boutros, 185–7, 205,
    208, 233–5
Boyle, A., 153–4, 162–4, 169, 173, 175
Brahimi Report, 187–9, 192, 209, 235,
    237, 240
Brazil, 230–1, 259, 278
Brownlie, I., 14, 64, 67, 71–2,
    75, 81, 89
Bull, H., 50–1
Bunia, 219–20
Burundi, 199, 218, 221–4, 226, 232,
    240, 249–50, 252

Cambodia, 15, 139, 240–1
Cameron, David, 270–2
Canada, 17, 19, 21, 168, 259, 270
capabilities, 157, 218, 227–8, 247
capacity, 25, 39–40, 206, 210, 220,
    222, 249, 254
capacity-building, 27–8, 190, 237, 250
Carnegie Commission, 187–9, 196
Cartagena Protocol, 176
Cassese, A., 64–5, 69–70, 75–6, 84–5,
    88, 91, 131–2, 141
CDM (clean development
    mechanism), 169
ceasefires, 222–3, 225–7, 240–1,
    261–2
Central African Republic, 15, 197,
    224, 249–50
CESCR (Committee on Economic,
    Social and Cultural Rights),
    106, 117–20
change, 22–3, 194, 205, 207, 214, 218,
    229, 232
chemical weapons, 257, 264–6,
    269, 271–2
children, 97, 218–20, 260, 262, 269
China, 25, 230–1, 259–60, 278
circumstances precluding
    wrongfulness, 70, 76

citizens, 47–9, 51–2, 54–6, 92, 104–5,
    107, 114–15, 272
civil administration, transitional, 235–6
civilian casualties, 214, 231, 274
civilian populations, 24, 126, 208–10,
    219–20, 229, 232, 240, 260
civilians, 209, 211, 218–20, 223,
    225–31, 258–60, 263–4, 269;
    protection, 4, 23, 205, 209,
    219–21, 225–8, 231–2, 260
civil society, 19, 34, 41, 117, 190, 199,
    201, 236; global, 51; international,
    95; organizations, 101, 188
civil war, 15, 137–8, 225–7, 232–3,
    237, 255–6, 266, 268–70
clean development mechanism
    (CDM), 169
climate change, 148, 157, 161, 163–7,
    171, 179
coalitions, 21, 231, 246, 248, 264
coercive measures, 20, 28, 189,
    194, 210
Cold War, 35–7, 95–6, 128, 133, 184,
    186, 190, 201
collective humanitarian intervention, 5,
    51, 146
collective interests, 86, 178
collective responsibility, 4, 23, 29, 57,
    120, 207, 224, 262
collective security system, 56, 211
Commission, Peacebuilding, 6, 200
commitments, 40, 52, 55, 161, 165–70,
    175, 189, 194
Committee on Economic, Social and
    Cultural Rights, *see* CESCR
common but differentiated
    responsibility, 160–1, 165, 168
common concern, 161–4, 172
common humanity, 19, 93
common property, 163–4
commons, global, 163–4
communitarian norms, 80–1, 90
community interest, 39–40, 163
community of states, 1, 7, 42, 57, 63,
    92, 119, 122
community of values, 3, 85
compensation, 64, 79, 103, 123,
    133, 142–3
compliance, 15–16, 76, 81–2, 90,
    99–101, 138–40, 148, 169–70
comprehensive peace agreement, 226
conduct, 35–6, 63–4, 67, 70, 72–4,
    121, 123–4, 127; obligations of,
    105, 117

Index 293

Conference of the Parties, *see* COP
confiscation, 67
conflict, 184–7, 189–91, 193–5,
    200–203, 209–10, 231–9, 253–8,
    269–71; ethnic, 224, 242; internal,
    20, 186, 189, 237; prevention,
    184, 187–9, 191, 194, 197, 202–3,
    237, 239; resolution, 186, 194,
    233, 239
Congo, 136, 210, 218, 221, 223–6,
    232, 240
consensus: international, 162, 253;
    resolutions, 13, 25, 27, 30–1,
    185, 217
consent, 86, 88, 183, 185–6, 195, 197,
    207, 209; national, 253
consequences, balance of, 23
conservation and sustainable use, 172–6
constitution, 33, 37–9, 47–8, 115–16
constitutionalism, 41
constitutionalization, 47
contacts, 45, 53, 102, 123
contracting states, 108, 110, 114,
    168, 175
control, 72, 74–5, 152, 154–5, 171–2,
    241, 267, 269–70
Convention on the Rights of the Child,
    see CRC
conventions, multilateral, 68,
    94, 115–16
cooperation, 83, 86, 115, 117, 119,
    125, 138–42, 155; international,
    54, 96–9, 117–19, 155, 164
coordination, 196–7, 237, 239, 242,
    244, 246, 249, 252
COP (Conference of the Parties),
    166–7, 169–70, 175–6
cosmopolitan democracy, 54–5
cosmopolitanism, 33, 41–3, 54–7
Côte d'Ivoire, 226–9, 232, 249
countermeasures, peaceful, 70, 86
courts, 65–6, 103, 125–7, 134–5,
    138–40, 241; domestic, 68, 103,
    108, 145; international, 26, 89,
    126, 139, 145, 193
Crawford, J., 3, 62–3, 69–73, 75–7,
    81–3, 86, 88, 90
CRC (Convention on the Rights of the
    Child), 97–8, 100
crimes, 1–2, 24–5, 85–6, 122–4,
    126–38, 143–7, 193, 260–1;
    against humanity, 2, 6, 24–5, 92,
    144–6, 193, 197, 213; atrocity,
    226, 248; international, 80–2, 92,

122–5, 131–3, 136–7, 139, 144,
    146; war, 1–2, 6, 24–5, 124–8,
    143–6, 193, 224–5, 230
criminal justice, 92, 122, 139, 144, 253;
    international, 122–4, 126, 133,
    137, 143–4, 146, 252
criminal law, international, 6, 121–3,
    125, 127, 135, 137, 143–7, 193
criminal responsibility, 80–1, 135;
    individual, 89, 128–30
cultural rights, 96, 99–100, 105–8,
    116–18, 121
customary human rights law, 93, 116
customary international law, 2, 6–7, 61,
    63–4, 66–9, 75–6, 115–16, 145–6
customary law, 38, 68, 116, 150, 152,
    155, 158, 179
customs, 64, 68–9, 125–6, 129, 276

Dallaire, Roméo, 183, 198
damage, 64, 69, 133, 142, 154,
    156, 173–4
danger, 36, 108, 110, 174, 184
Darfur, 22, 75, 204, 218, 224–7,
    232, 240
deaths, 219, 221, 230–1, 248, 259–60,
    262, 266–7, 269
decent regimes, 44
defences, 67, 69, 76, 79, 241
demilitarized zones, 185–6
demobilization, 221, 223, 226, 228,
    237, 241, 247, 250
democracy, 43, 47, 55, 195, 224, 245,
    253, 266; cosmopolitan, 54–5
democratic governance, 45–6, 245, 253
Democratic Republic of the Congo
    (DRC), 88, 193, 210, 218–27,
    232, 253
denial, 44, 64, 66, 209
Dennis, M.J., 118–19
deployment, 183, 193–4, 201, 205,
    217–19, 226–8, 242, 247;
    preventive, 184–6, 188, 195,
    200–201, 204, 206
deportation, 114, 126, 269
destruction, 67, 235, 266, 278
detention, 66, 101–2, 114, 138–9, 261
developing countries, 97–8, 119–20,
    148–9, 160–2, 165–6, 168,
    171, 173–5
development, 5–6, 61–2, 95–6, 116–17,
    123, 137–9, 158–9, 244–6;
    assistance, 188, 190, 244; social,
    120, 185; sustainable, 150–1,

294   *Index*

157–60, 165, 235–6, 238–9, 244, 249, 254
diamonds, 210
dignity, 23, 41–3, 93, 96, 106, 115, 150, 279–80
direct international wrongs, 65
direct prevention, 192, 194, 199–200
direct prevention measures, 192–3
disappearances, enforced, 98, 260
disarmament, 189, 191, 221, 223, 226–7, 237, 240, 247
discrimination, 67, 79, 97, 100, 130; racial, 97
displaced persons, 119, 219–20, 223, 242, 247
disputes, 47, 170, 184, 186, 202–4
Draft Articles on Responsibility of States for Internationally Wrongful Acts, 68, 75, 77–8, 80, 83, 85, 90
drafters, 20–1, 83, 86, 95, 237
DRC, *see* Democratic Republic of the Congo
Dupuy, P.-M., 33
durable peace, 236, 254
duties, 50–2, 90, 104, 107–12, 117–18, 127–9, 132–4, 154–5; international, 18, 127; positive, 83, 104, 107, 121

early warning, 26, 184–6, 191–2, 196–7, 199–200, 202, 204, 238–9
East Timor, 236, 240–1, 243–5, 279
ECHR (European Convention on Human Rights), 94, 104, 113
Economic and Social Council (ECOSOC), 185, 196, 222
economic development, 150, 189–90, 194, 196, 235, 239, 246, 251
ECOSOC (Economic and Social Council), 185, 196, 222
ecosystems, 164, 173
ECOWAS (Economic Community of West African States), 15, 227
ECtHR, *see* European Court of Human Rights
effective implementation, 166–7, 175
egregious violations, 62, 79, 116, 266
elections, 228, 241–2
emergency: powers, 99–100; states of, 99
emissions, 148, 166–9; trading, 169
enforcement, 20, 35, 81, 94, 99, 103, 125, 137; action, 24, 208, 270;

international criminal justice, 133–43; mechanisms, 6, 93, 103, 128; peace, 199, 208, 216–18, 220, 222–3, 227, 232, 240
English school, 33, 49–53
enjoyment of rights, 105, 108, 119, 133
environment, 105, 107, 149–50, 152–5, 157–8, 169, 174–5, 178–9; global, 154, 161, 177; human, 149–50
environmental agreements, multilateral, 154, 157, 161
environmental catastrophes, 177–8, 213
environmental damage, 153–4, 177
environmental degradation, 107, 148, 157, 177
environmental harm, 149, 153–4, 156, 177
environmental law, 91, 149, 161, 163, 177, 277; international, 6, 147–53, 155, 157, 159, 161–3, 169, 177–9; principles, 149–61
environmental legislation, 151
environmental policies, 152, 160, 165, 171, 175
environmental principles, 163, 177
environmental protection, 6, 150, 153–4, 157, 161, 178
environmental treaties, 148–9, 175
EP (European Parliament), 56, 259
equality, 97, 106; sovereign, 38–9, 47, 237
equity, 160–1, 171
escalating violence, 224, 263
ethnic cleansing, 1–2, 22–5, 197, 200, 211–13, 217, 277, 280
ethnic groups, 84, 178, 267, 269, 271
European Convention on Human Rights (ECHR), 94, 104, 113
European Court of Human Rights (ECtHR), 103–4, 107, 113–14, 121
Evans, G., 19, 22, 188–9, 192, 252
evidence, 138–9, 142, 144, 149, 157–8, 214–15, 263, 272–3
exceptional circumstances, 142, 211–12
existence of international society, 33, 35
expulsion, 66–7, 110–12, 114, 210
extermination, 126, 199, 267
extradition, 111, 131, 139

fact-finding missions, 102, 184, 188, 192, 259
fair trial, 95–6, 116

Index 295

families, 15, 98, 118, 198, 210, 222, 258
Fassbender, B., 39–40, 56–7
fault, 70–1
fear, well-founded, 110–11, 114
Federal Republic of Yugoslavia, 85, 200, 242
financial institutions, international, 237
financial resources, 149, 161, 166, 175, 237
Fitzmaurice, G., 76, 87
food, 105–9, 117–18, 120, 176, 210
force, use of, 11–18, 21–2, 77–8, 207–9, 211, 217–18, 228–9, 259–60
forcible humanitarian intervention, 77
foreigners, 65, 69, 113
foreign forces, 241, 246
Former Yugoslavia, 138
Former Yugoslav Republic of Macedonia, 200–201
Fortress Europe, 112
Framework Convention on Climate Change, 161, 164, 167–9
France, 14–15, 81–2, 125–6, 258, 260, 264–5
freedom, 79, 81, 85, 95–7, 102, 106–7, 110, 195; fundamental, 79, 94–5, 115
Free Syrian Army (FSA), 258, 271
frontiers, 108, 110–12, 120
FSA (Free Syrian Army), 258, 271
Fuller, L., 20
fundamental human rights, 14, 19, 45, 92, 94–6, 115

Gabčikovo-Nagymaros Project case, 76, 154
Gaddafi family and supporters, 230–1
Gbagbo, Laurent, 228–9
General Assembly, 2–3, 23–5, 28, 68–9, 112, 185–6, 203, 264; resolutions, 98, 116, 146, 164, 207, 239, 274, 280; Summits, 19, 195, 223
general comments, 99–100, 103–4, 117–19, 121, 132
general international law, 64, 70, 76, 82–4, 160
genetic resources, 172, 174
Geneva Conventions, 87, 89, 109, 111, 128–9, 131, 138, 141
genocide, 22–7, 84–6, 128, 131–2, 144–6, 196–200, 204–5, 269–70;

action plan to prevent, 23, 199; Rwandan, 23, 26, 145, 193, 199, 221, 229
Genocide Convention, 71, 87, 129, 131, 144, 213, 269
German school, 34–41, 57
Germany, 19, 72, 78, 81, 125, 230, 258, 260
Global Centre, 29, 257, 269
global civil society, 51
global commons, 163–4
globalization, 35, 41, 55, 148, 164; of international environmental law, 161–77
global responsibilities, 51, 162–3
good faith, 38, 67, 140, 154, 156
good neighbourliness, 155
governance, 38, 49, 55, 244, 246–8, 279; democratic, 45–6, 245, 253; good, 189–90, 224, 236, 250–1, 254
governmental authority, 72–4
governments, 73, 102, 107–8, 125–6, 132, 201–2, 225, 230; national, 55; new, 74–5, 241, 244; transitional, 223, 247
grave and imminent peril, 77
Great Lakes Peace Process, 208, 221, 224–5
greenhouse gases, 157, 164–6, 168–9, 171
gross violations, 199, 225
Grotius, 11–12, 33, 50–1
groups: armed, 74, 227, 237, 247, 258; ethnic, 84, 178, 267, 269, 271; opposition, 258, 266; religious, 71, 129, 278; vulnerable, 143, 190, 218, 250
Guantánamo Bay, 46
Guinea–Bissau, 249–50, 252

Habermas, J., 34, 46–8, 57
Hague Academy, 34, 37–9
Haiti, 85, 240, 247–9, 253
harm, 1, 20, 72, 105, 151, 153–7, 177, 234
health, 106–7, 119, 122, 124, 153, 155, 157, 202–3; mental, 118–19
Held, D., 55–6, 148
High Commissioner, 29, 200
High Commissioner for Human Rights, 29, 197, 214, 259, 261
High Commissioner for Refugees, 214, 229, 264

296 *Index*

High-Level Panels, 21–3, 194, 216, 237
high seas, 64, 109, 153, 178
horizontal obligations, 104, 107–8
Houla Massacre, 262
housing, 106, 108, 117–18
HRC, *see* Human Rights Committee
HRW, *see* Human Rights Watch
human dignity, 41–3, 106, 280
humanitarian action, 77–8
humanitarian assistance, 118–19, 185,
    218, 223, 228, 244, 249
humanitarian intervention, 4–6, 11–19,
    25, 29–31, 51–2, 76–8, 83–5, 277;
    collective, 5, 51, 146; doctrine, 77,
    272; legality, 19; reports, 17–21;
    reports, international reaction,
    21–6; and responsibility to protect,
    11–31; unilateral, 4–6, 12, 30
humanitarian law, international, 23, 26,
    89–90, 128–9, 138–9, 215–16,
    218, 220
humanitarian personnel, 209, 220, 228
humanity, 1–2, 24–5, 126–7, 137–8,
    143–6, 193, 224–6, 260–3; offices
    of, 108–9
human life, 66, 121, 194, 212,
    214, 278
human protection, 7, 21, 209–11;
    purposes, 17, 20–1, 144, 207,
    212–13, 215, 274
human rights, 40–4, 83–5, 90–7,
    100–104, 106–7, 113–16, 246–9,
    251–3; abuses, 14, 105, 144,
    208, 256–7, 262, 268, 270;
    catastrophes, 4, 51, 138, 217–18,
    236; conventions, 68, 87, 99, 101,
    103–5, 115–16, 132; experts, 99,
    119; fundamental, 14, 19, 45,
    92, 94–6, 115; international, 94,
    144; international protection of, 3,
    6, 92; law, 26, 45, 93, 104, 177,
    219; law, customary, 93, 116; law,
    international, 92–3, 95, 97, 99,
    101, 103, 113–17, 121; obligations,
    79, 99, 103, 105; protection, 92–3,
    103, 247; system, 6, 199, 270;
    treaties, 6, 68, 89, 93, 99, 101, 104,
    146; violations, 197, 200–201, 210,
    220, 230, 248, 251, 260
Human Rights Commission, 25,
    95, 101–3
Human Rights Committee (HRC),
    99–101, 103, 105, 113, 121,
    132, 260

Human Rights Council, 26, 29, 103,
    230, 257, 259, 261–2, 268
Human Rights Watch (HRW), 201,
    231, 277
human security, 51, 187, 190, 204, 224
Hutus, 198–9, 221
hybrid courts, 139, 241

ICC, *see* International Criminal Court
ICCPR (International Covenant on
    Civil and Political Rights), 96–7,
    100–101, 104
ICESCR (International Covenant on
    Economic and Social and Cultural
    Rights), 96–7, 117, 119, 191
ICGLR (International Conference on
    the Great Lakes Region), 224–5
ICISS (International Commission
    on Intervention and State
    Sovereignty), 19–20, 22–3, 143–4,
    184, 188–9, 191, 208, 210
ICJ, *see* International Court of Justice
ICRC (International Committee of the
    Red Cross), 116, 192, 214
ICTR (International Criminal Tribunal
    for Rwanda), 138–40, 142
ICTY (International Criminal Tribunal
    for Yugoslavia), 73–4, 89, 138,
    140, 142
ILC (International Law Commission),
    3, 61–2, 68–9, 74, 76, 87,
    127, 129
implementation, 27–9, 166–7, 169–70,
    174–5, 222, 226–7, 261, 277–8;
    effective, 166–7, 175; reports, 13,
    28, 30, 181
incentives, 174–5, 194
independence, 19, 116, 143, 190,
    243
India, 15, 25, 82, 108, 114, 230–1,
    259, 278
indirect international wrongs, 65
indirect responsibility, 65
individual criminal responsibility/
    liability, 89, 128–30
individual responsibility, 119, 129,
    139, 146
information, 26–7, 100–101, 166–7,
    170, 172, 174, 196–8, 273
injured states, 70, 85–8, 178
injury, 65, 78–9, 142, 231
innovations, 48, 212, 214–15, 279
institutions, 33–4, 36, 45, 50,
    139–40, 233–5, 242, 252–3

Index 297

instructions, 72–5, 198
intention, 11, 28, 71–2, 229
Inter-American Court of Human Rights, 103, 107
interest, 43, 45, 77, 81–2, 87–8, 120, 122, 211; collective, 86, 178; international, 134–5
interference, 192–3, 211
internal conflict, 20, 186, 189, 237
international accountability, 94, 103
international action, 150, 172, 260
international administration, 63, 243
international armed conflicts, 128, 218, 221, 257
international assistance, 27, 29, 99, 117, 120, 206, 250
International Bill of Rights, 93–103, 106
international civil society, 95
International Commission on Intervention and State Sovereignty, *see* ICISS
International Committee of the Red Cross (ICRC), 116, 192, 214
international community, 1–3, 5–7, 20–5, 30–3, 37–40, 84–9, 115–22, 278–80; in international legal theory, 33–49; responsibility/ obligations of states towards, 115–16; responsibility of, 116–21
International Conference on the Great Lakes Region (ICGLR), 224–5
international constitution, 37–8, 40, 46, 49, 56
international cooperation, 54, 96–9, 117–19, 155, 164
International Court of Justice (ICJ), 5–6, 62, 71, 73–4, 76, 78, 153–4, 170
International Covenant on Civil and Political Rights, *see* ICCPR
International Covenant on Economic and Social and Cultural Rights, *see* ICESCR
international crimes, 80–2, 92, 122–5, 131–3, 136–7, 139, 144, 146
international criminal code, 128–9
International Criminal Court (ICC), 122–3, 133, 135, 139–45, 147, 177, 193, 226
international criminal justice: enforcement, 133–43; responsibility within system, 122–47

international criminal law, 3, 6, 85, 90, 121–47, 193, 276, 279; as international responsibility, 143–6
International Criminal Tribunal for Rwanda, *see* ICTR
International Criminal Tribunal for Yugoslavia, *see* ICTY
International Crisis Group, 192, 201, 204–5, 226
international environmental law, 3, 6, 147–79, 274, 276, 279
international financial institutions, 237
international humanitarian law, 23, 26, 89–90, 128–9, 138–9, 215–16, 218, 220
international human rights law, 92–121, 257, 268, 276, 279
international interests, 134–5
international intervention, 255–6, 270
internationalism, liberal, 43, 45, 54
international law, 1–5, 33–41, 43–52, 61–3, 65–77, 87–91, 125–30, 134–7; classical, 45, 47; customary, 2, 6–7, 61, 63–4, 66–9, 75–6, 115–16, 145–6; modern, 40–1, 77, 108; obligations on states in, 61–91; peremptory norms, 6, 76–7, 82–4, 86, 136; primary rules of, 63, 69
International Law Commission, *see* ILC
international legal community, 34–7, 39–40, 46, 48–9, 84, 91, 122, 145
international legal obligations, 7, 49, 181, 218, 234
international legal order, 5, 35, 38, 122, 136
international legal sanctions, 143, 193
international liberalism, 43, 94
International Military Tribunal, 125, 129
international morality, 125
international obligations, 69–71, 75–6, 80, 84, 89–90, 117–19, 121, 140
international order, 45, 50–1, 162
international organizations, 4, 36, 42, 47, 81, 86, 111, 117
international peace, 38, 40, 184–6, 195–6, 200, 202–5, 217–19, 254
international reaction, 21, 112, 144, 262, 269–70
international relations, 1–2, 5, 31–3, 35, 47, 49–51, 53–4, 57; theory, 5, 33, 41, 44, 49–56

298 *Index*

international response, 29, 116, 256–7, 266–7
international responsibility, 5–7, 25, 29–31, 93, 120–1, 123–4, 146–7, 276–7; evolution, 114–21; international criminal law as, 143–6; and positive obligations, 103–14
international society, 5–7, 32–3, 35–7, 39–43, 45, 47, 49–55, 57; in international relations theory, 49–56
international standards, 63, 124, 166
international system, 5, 32–6, 38–9, 41–6, 49, 52–3, 99–100, 103
international treaties, 61, 114, 126, 131, 276
international tribunals, 94, 103, 123, 125, 128, 130–1, 137–9, 142
international wrongs, 65, 75
intervention, 12–15, 17–21, 211–12, 214–16, 255–6, 270–1, 273–4, 277–8; collective, 14, 274; humanitarian, *see* humanitarian intervention; international, 255–6, 270; military, 20–2, 144, 212–13, 215, 260, 266, 271, 274; unilateral, 4, 14, 17, 212, 246
invasions, 47, 65, 248, 270
Iran, 28, 73, 102, 258
Iraq, 30, 240, 246, 248–9, 253–7, 267–70, 274–5, 277–9; army, 267–9; invasion, 47; Northern, 6–7, 267
ISI (Islamic State of Iraq), 267
ISIL (Islamic State of Iraq in the Levant), 267, 269
Islamic State, 255, 257–8, 265–75; consequences of response for responsibility to protect, 270–4; of Iraq (ISI), 267; of Iraq in the Levant (ISIL), 267, 269
issue of universal jurisdiction, 136
Italy, 81, 125

Japan, 81–2, 125, 240, 260, 279
Johnston, D.M., 40–1
judicial assistance, 138–9
jurisdiction, 111, 126, 130–8, 140–1, 143, 145, 152–4, 170–2; national, 152–3, 162, 172–5; universal, *see* universal jurisdiction
jus ad bellum, 4, 32

jus cogens, 3, 37, 76–7, 80, 84, 92–3, 121, 136; and obligations *erga omnes*, 37, 115
just cause, 21, 212–14

Kant, I., 11, 43, 47, 54, 94
key principles, 43, 115, 135, 149
Khmer Rouge, 241
killings, 132, 198, 202, 213, 257, 262, 270, 278; large-scale, 22–3, 214
knowledge, 71–2, 125, 156, 176, 189, 279
Kosovo, 12–13, 16–17, 32, 236, 240–3, 245, 249, 253
Krasner, 54
Kyoto Protocol, 161, 167–71, 177

language, 30, 94–5, 98, 172, 197, 221, 223, 260–1; mandatory, 25, 100–101
Larger Freedom, 23, 96, 115, 195, 217, 238
last resort, 19–23, 28, 212–13, 215
Lauterpacht, H., 94
League of Nations, 69, 125
Lebanon, 139, 258–9
legal basis, 62, 131, 150, 202, 272
legal community, 34–6, 47
legality, 4, 17, 19, 21, 47, 90, 99, 153
legal obligations, 2, 18, 61, 91, 100, 177, 277, 280; international, 7, 49, 181, 218, 234
legal order, 36, 46, 70, 100; international, 5, 35, 38, 122, 136
legal status, 41, 159, 163, 172
legitimacy, 7, 12, 52
liberal democracies, 44–5, 56
liberal internationalism, 43, 45, 54
liberalism, 43–6; international, 43, 94
Liberia, 15, 85, 210, 229, 249, 251
Libya, 85, 208, 218, 229–32, 255–6, 266, 274–5, 277–9
life, 20–1, 93, 95–6, 110, 115–16, 132–3, 150, 213; human, 66, 121, 194, 212, 214, 278; normal, 242
limited universal jurisdiction, 134
LMOs (living modified organisms), 176–7
local parties, 209
London Charter, 126–7
Luck, E., 27

Macedonia, 14, 183–4, 200–201, 204–5, 215, 279

Index 299

McGrew, A., 55, 148
mandatory language, 25, 100–101
mankind, 1, 38, 94, 129, 131, 134,
  163–4, 177; common concern
  of, 161–4
Marshall Plan, 234, 279
massacres, 211, 221, 262, 267
massive violations, 5, 48, 92, 123,
  132, 202
MEAs (multilateral environmental
  agreements), 154, 157, 161
mediation, 192–3, 249
mediators, 194–5
mental health, 118–19
Mexico, 66
migrant workers, 97–8
military action, 26, 78, 88, 211–12,
  214, 235, 271, 273
military intervention, 20–2, 144,
  212–13, 215, 260, 266, 271, 274
Millennium Report, 187
minimum standards, 44, 66–8
mission creep, 231, 255, 274, 277
missions: fact-finding, 102, 184, 188,
  192, 259; peace-building, 234,
  241, 243; peacekeeping, 208,
  216–17, 227, 241; political, 227,
  245, 248
mixture of peace enforcement and
  peace-building, 223, 240
monitoring, 99, 101–2, 193, 200–201,
  222–3, 226, 251, 261
Montreal Protocol, 148, 157, 164–7,
  169, 175
MONUC (United Nations
  Organization Mission in the
  Democratic Republic of Congo),
  218–20, 223
morality, international, 125
Morocco, 131
Mosler, H., 34, 36–7, 39
multilateral conventions, 68,
  94, 115–16
multilateral environmental agreements
  (MEAs), 154, 157, 161
multilateralism, 46
multilateral treaties, 84–5, 88, 130

Nanda, V.P., 266, 275
national consent, 253
national governments, 55
nationality, 14, 110, 134–6, 228
national jurisdiction, 152–3, 162, 172–5

national law, 126, 141
national reconciliation, 227, 245–6,
  248, 251
nationals, 65, 67, 73, 79, 84, 130
national security, 110
National Security Strategy, 47, 205
National Transitional Council
  (NTC), 231
NATO (Northern Atlantic Treaty
  Organization), 12, 16–17, 88, 208,
  229, 231, 241
natural disasters, 148–9, 178–9, 185
natural law theories, 42–4, 46, 50,
  93–4, 115
natural resources, 152–3, 158–9
necessity, 63, 66, 76–8, 184, 197, 202,
  271, 278
Neff, S., 108–9
negotiations, 70, 155–7, 170, 172, 174,
  176, 185, 278–9
Netherlands, 5, 17–18, 21, 82, 107,
  125, 183
neutral countries, 108–9
neutrality, 109, 185
New Haven school, 39, 41–3, 53, 57
NGOs, *see* non-governmental
  organizations
Nicaragua, 28, 73–5, 88, 116
Nigeria, 29, 106–7
non-compliance, 141, 266
non-discrimination, 67, 106, 115–16
non-governmental organizations
  (NGOs), 2, 29, 102, 206–7, 218
non-international armed conflicts, 257
non-intervention, 15, 20, 51–2,
  211, 256
non-military options, 21, 23
non-refoulement, 108, 110–14
non-repetition, 78–9, 87
non-states parties, 140–1
Noortmann, M., 53–4
Northern Atlantic Treaty Organization,
  see NATO
Northern Iraq, 6–7, 267
Nottebohm, 67
NTC (National Transitional
  Council), 231
Nuremberg, 123–7; legacy, 124–33

OAU (Organization of African Unity),
  112, 191
obligations, 1–3, 6–7, 75–89, 103–8,
  121–3, 133–6, 153–7, 172–6;

300 Index

binding, 115, 137; of conduct, 105, 117; *erga omnes*, 3, 80–1, 85–6, 89, 91, 93, 115–16, 121; general, 140, 153, 165, 172; horizontal, 104, 107–8; international, 69–71, 75–6, 80, 84, 89–90, 117–19, 121, 140; legal, 2, 18, 61, 91, 100, 177, 277, 280; legal, international, 7, 49, 181, 218, 234; positive, 83, 103–5, 107–8, 113, 117, 121; primary, 62, 66, 76, 223; of result, 105, 117; on states in international law, 61–91; substantive, 69, 172; treaty, 64–6, 76, 93, 99, 101, 132, 134, 139
observations, 101, 120–1
observers, 244, 261–3
OECD (Organisation for Economic Co-operation and Development), 160
offences, 123, 125, 127, 129–31, 136
offenders, 66, 130, 136–7, 145
Office of the High Commissioner for Human Rights, *see* OHCHR
offices of humanity, 108–9
OHCHR (Office of the High Commissioner for Human Rights), 259–60, 268
omissions, 69–70, 72
OPCW (Organisation for the Prohibition of Chemical Weapons), 265–6, 268
operational prevention, 188, 191, 195
operations, 203–4, 208–9, 217, 220–1, 223, 232, 235–6, 240
opposition: forces, 230, 258, 264, 266; groups, 258, 266
ordinary state responsibility, 62, 86
Orford, A., 7
Organisation for Economic Co-operation and Development (OECD), 160
Organisation for the Prohibition of Chemical Weapons (OPCW), 265–6, 268
Organization for Security and Cooperation in Europe (OSCE), 191, 243
Organization of African Unity, *see* OAU
OSCE (Organization for Security and Cooperation in Europe), 191, 243

PCIJ, *see* Permanent Court of International Justice

peace, 47–8, 125–9, 183–6, 202–4, 211, 224–5, 233–4, 237; agreements, 199, 237, 240, 249; agreements, comprehensive, 226; durable, 236, 254; enforcement, 199, 208, 216–18, 220, 222–3, 227, 232, 240; international, 38, 40, 184–6, 195–6, 200, 202–5, 217–19, 254; sustainable, 237–8; Uniting for Peace procedure, 18, 21, 213
peace-building, 209, 220, 223, 233–5, 237–40, 247, 249–54; fund, 251–2; missions, 234, 241, 243; post-conflict, 232–5, 238, 249; reports, 234–40; *see also* responsibility, to rebuild
Peacebuilding Commission, 6, 200, 234, 238–9, 249–50, 252–3
Peace-building Support Office, 234, 238–9, 252
peaceful countermeasures, 70, 86
peacekeepers, 26, 138, 209, 216, 226, 228, 232
peacekeeping, 4, 205, 207–9, 216–17, 232–3, 239, 248–9, 252; forces, 191, 220, 226, 240, 246; missions, 208, 216–17, 227, 241; operations, 187, 201, 209–10, 217–18, 221–2, 234–5, 239; operations, traditional, 208, 216, 227; traditional, 216
peacemaking, 186, 232, 234
peace process, 198–9, 203, 207, 223–4
Peel, J., 158–9
peremptory norms, 3, 6, 76–8, 82–4, 86, 89, 116, 121
Permanent Court of International Justice (PCIJ), 63, 65, 72, 125
Permanent Five members, 21, 212–13, 232
perpetrators, 123, 128, 134–5, 138–9, 144, 147, 241
persecution, 67, 108–12, 114, 126, 266, 269
personal petitions, 100, 106, 131
personnel, 201, 207, 219–20, 228, 240, 248
petitions, personal/individual, 100, 106, 131
physical violence, 219–20, 223, 227–8, 247
Pillay, Navi, 29, 197, 259–62, 264
Pinochet extradition case, 145, 193
piracy, 135–7

political missions, 227, 245, 248
political rights, 44, 100, 104, 107
polluter-pays principle, 160
positive obligations, 6, 83, 86, 93,
    103–8, 113–14, 117–18, 121;
    in refugee and asylum law,
    108–14; under human rights
    conventions, 103–8
post-conflict peace-building, 232–5,
    238, 249
post-conflict reconstruction, 6, 224
post-conflict recovery, 234, 239, 249
poverty, 44, 96, 187, 190, 195
powers, 33–4, 36, 42, 52–3, 55–6,
    99–100, 140–1, 143; emergency,
    99–100; veto, 55, 212
precautionary approach, 151, 157, 163
precautionary principles, 13, 21, 156–8,
    160, 165, 176, 270–1, 274
prevention, 26–9, 85–6, 154, 181,
    183–4, 188–90, 194–200, 202;
    activities, 183–4, 186, 195,
    198–203, 205, 279; direct, 192,
    194, 199–200; operational, 188,
    191, 195; structural, 188
preventive action, 156, 185, 196,
    198–9, 202–3, 208, 238
preventive deployment, 184–6, 188,
    195, 200–201, 204, 206
Preventive Diplomacy, 186
primary obligations, 62, 66, 76, 223
primary responsibility, 61, 122, 181,
    197, 228, 262
primary rules, 62–4, 66, 68–9, 79,
    83–4
private individuals/persons, 75, 102,
    104–5, 107–8, 122, 128–9
proper purpose, 23
property, 63–9, 72, 104, 153, 257;
    common, 163–4
proportionality, 215–16, 274
proportional means, 21, 23, 212,
    215
prosecution, 48, 123, 126, 128, 136,
    138–41, 145, 193
protection, 91–4, 98, 110–11, 121–3,
    155, 163, 216–21, 247–9;
    international, 3, 6, 92–3, 98,
    112–13; responsibilities, 12,
    25, 29–30
protective measures, 173
provisional institutions, 242
punishment, 85–6, 97, 102, 111, 124,
    126, 128–9, 133

race, 95, 97, 104, 110
Rawls, J., 43–4
reaction, 26, 28–9, 84–5, 144, 181,
    210–11, 230–1, 276–7; culture of,
    188, 194; international, 21, 112,
    144, 262, 269–70
reasonable prospects of success, 21,
    212, 215–17, 246, 255, 266,
    270–4, 279
rebuilding, 4, 6–7, 143–4, 233–7, 239,
    251–4, 274–5, 279–80
recommendations, 100, 184–8,
    194–6, 199–201, 203–4, 209–10,
    212–13, 239
reconciliation, 20, 191, 233, 237–8;
    national, 227, 245–6, 248, 251
reconstruction, 6, 238–40, 242, 246–7,
    249, 254, 275, 279
recovery, 20, 238–40, 246, 249, 275
reforms, 26, 55–6, 103, 184, 190–1,
    233, 248, 250–1
refoulement, see non-refoulement
refugees, 108–14, 119, 214, 223, 229,
    264, 266, 274; law, 108, 111, 114,
    121, 228
regime change, 231–2, 256, 274, 277–9
regime theory, 44, 53–4
regional conflict, larger, 271
rehabilitation, 142, 173, 237, 244, 250
reintegration, 191, 223, 226, 228, 235,
    237–8, 247, 250
relations, international law and
    international, 2, 5, 12, 31–3, 35
relief, 64, 191, 246, 272
religious groups, 71, 129, 278
removals, 111, 165, 167, 169, 202, 258
reparations, 63, 70, 78–9, 81, 87–8,
    123, 142, 154
research, 172–4, 214
resources, 106–7, 171, 173–5, 187,
    189–90, 195, 237, 239; biological,
    171–4; financial, 149, 161, 166,
    175, 237
responsibility, 1–7, 11–14, 22–32,
    75–81, 83–93, 143–9, 177–9,
    181–280; aggravated, see
    aggravated state responsibility;
    collective, 4, 23, 29, 57, 120,
    207, 224, 262; common but
    differentiated, 160–1, 165, 168;
    global, 30, 51, 162–3; indirect,
    65; individual, 119, 129, 139,
    146; international, 5–7, 25,
    29–31, 93, 120–1, 123–4, 146–7,

302 *Index*

276–7; international, evolution, 114–21; international, and positive obligations, 103–14; invocation of, 86–7; levels of, 4–5, 20, 144, 181, 280; to prevent, 4–6, 13, 20, 27, 99, 123, 183–206, 215; to prevent, in international law, 202–5; to prevent, reports, 184–97; to prevent, United Nations practice, 198–202; primary, 61, 122, 181, 197, 228, 262; to protect, *see Introductory Note*;

to react, 4, 6, 143–4, 207–32, 253, 263, 266, 270; to react, reports, 208–17; to react, United Nations adoption of responsibility to protect in peacekeeping, 217–29; to react, United Nations practice - Libya, 229–32; to rebuild, 4, 6, 13, 20, 143–4, 200, 233–54, 279; to rebuild, in international law, 252–3; to rebuild, peace-building reports, 234–40; to rebuild, United Nations practice, 240–9; to save the planet, 148–79; shared, 120; within international criminal justice system, 122–47

restrictions, 210, 272
return, 110–12, 114, 166, 198, 241; *see also* non-refoulement
review, 6, 13, 30–1, 99–100, 149, 170, 181–2, 252–3
right authority, 13, 21, 212–13
right intention, 21, 212, 214–15
rights, 44, 50–2, 86, 92–9, 101–2, 104–9, 116–18, 132–3; abuse of, 64, 72; of individuals, 18, 91, 104; political, 44, 100, 104, 107
Rio Declaration, 149–52, 155–6, 158, 160, 162
Rio treaties, 162
risk, 156–7, 189, 193, 204, 206, 237–8, 273–4, 277–8; assessments, 177, 189, 202
Rome Statute, 123, 140–1
Roth, K., 277–8
rule of law, 55–6, 143, 147, 190, 233–4, 236, 246, 249–54
Russia, 14, 148, 230–1, 243, 259–60, 278
Rwanda, 25–6, 139, 183–4, 187, 198–200, 203–4, 206, 224; genocide, 23, 26, 145, 193, 199, 221, 229; nuns, 135, 145, 193

sanctions, 29, 36, 47–8, 195, 210–11, 215, 257, 259
Sands, P., 154, 158–9
secondary rules of state responsibility, 61, 68–9, 77, 83, 85
Second World War, 68–9, 123, 125, 127–8, 139, 234, 279
security, 129–30, 184–6, 195–6, 202–5, 217–27, 244–7, 249, 253–4; collective, 32, 184, 194, 199, 216, 232; conditions, 218–20, 223, 228; human, 51, 187, 190, 204, 224; national, 110; public, 244–5
Security Council, 21–4, 26–7, 140–1, 183–8, 199–205, 212–15, 217–21, 258–66; authorization, 18, 21, 207, 212; Permanent Five members, 21, 212–13, 232; resolutions, 137–8, 195, 198, 205, 207, 226–7, 248–9, 258–9
security forces, 132, 258
security sector reform, 250–2
self-defence, 14–15, 17, 21, 215–16, 247
self-determination, 42, 84–5, 89, 243
Serbia, 16–17, 200, 242–3
sexual violence, 145, 193, 260, 269
shared responsibility, 120
Shaw, M., 51
Sierra Leone, 15, 82, 139, 143, 193, 210, 249–52
Simma, B., 39–40
sinks, 165, 167–9
Slaughter, A.-M., 34, 43–5
SNC (Syrian National Council), 258
Social and Economic Rights Action Center for Economic and Social Rights, 106
social developments, 120, 185
social justice, 48, 55
soft law principles, 159–61, 179
solidarist position, 51–2
Somalia, 204, 208, 210
South Africa, 19, 85, 145, 231, 259, 278
sovereign equality, 38–9, 47, 237
sovereignty, 19–20, 36, 46, 146–7, 152–5, 164, 171, 185; barrier, 202–3, 205, 279; state, 4–5, 18–20, 25, 149, 152, 189, 192–3, 196; territorial, 69, 184
Special Advisers, 13, 19, 26–9, 196–7, 200, 204–5, 228, 230

specialist tribunals, 143, 145, 193
Special Rapporteurs, 69, 80–1, 87–8, 101–2, 199
Special Representatives, 27, 194, 219, 243, 247–8
Special Session, 262, 264, 268
Srebrenica, 19, 25–6, 187, 204
stability, 201–3, 224, 245, 247, 273
state failure, 1, 20
state responsibility, 2–3, 6, 57, 61–91, 115–16, 123, 141, 144–6; aggravated, 3, 6, 61–2, 79–93, 115–16, 123–4, 145–6, 177–8; in international law, 63, 65, 67, 69, 71, 73, 75, 77; law of, 3, 6, 61–3, 65, 69, 71, 73, 75–6; ordinary, 62, 86; primary rules, 79, 84; secondary rules, 61, 68–9, 77, 83, 85; traditional rules, 63–8
states of emergency, 99
state sovereignty, 4–5, 18–20, 25, 149, 152, 189, 192–3, 196
status, legal, 41, 159, 163, 172
Steiner, H. J., 104
Stewart, D.P., 118–19
Stockholm Declaration, 149–50, 152, 155, 162
structural prevention, 188
St Thomas Aquinas, 11
subsidiary body, 167, 169–70, 175
success, 125, 215, 241, 243, 245–6, 251–2, 268, 271; reasonable prospects of, 21, 212, 215, 246, 255, 266, 270–4, 279
Sudan, 22, 28, 75, 142, 147, 218, 224–7, 232
Sudan Liberation Army/Movement (SLA), 225
support, 117, 158, 178, 190–1, 222–3, 238–9, 244–5, 247
Surinam, 132
surrender, 67, 125, 137–40, 142
sustainable development, 150–1, 157–60, 165, 235–6, 238–9, 244, 249, 254
sustainable peace, 237–8
sustainable use, 158–9, 172–6
Syria, 2, 6–7, 14, 29–30, 232, 254–73, 275, 277–9; government, 257–9, 263, 265
Syrian National Council (SNC), 258
Syrian people, 261, 264, 273
systems theory, 52–3

Tadić case, 73, 75
technical assistance, 161–2, 190, 233
territorial asylum, 112
territorial sovereignty, 69, 184
territory, 72–4, 108–10, 112–13, 130–1, 136–8, 152–3, 267, 269–70
terrorism, 129, 132, 195, 247, 258, 270
Tesón, 17, 43–4
threats, 22–3, 183–5, 192–6, 202–5, 211, 217–20, 226–8, 269–70
threshold conditions, 2, 211–12, 214–15, 261, 263
Timor-Leste, 245
Tomuschat, C., 34, 37–40, 46, 57
torture, 85, 88–9, 95–7, 111, 113, 115–16, 130–5, 261
Trail Smelter case, 152–5
transition, 34, 162, 165, 237–8, 258, 263, 266
transitional administration, 235–6, 242–3
treaties, 6, 68, 75–6, 93–4, 98–9, 130–2, 136, 148–9; extradition, 131; human rights, 6, 68, 89, 93, 99, 101, 104, 146; international, 61, 114, 126, 131, 276; multilateral, 84–5, 88, 130
treatment, 63, 65, 67, 69, 109, 114, 128, 133; degrading, 97, 111, 113–14, 133; of foreigners/aliens, 64–5, 69, 79
treaty-monitoring bodies, 99, 101
treaty obligations, 64–6, 76, 93, 99, 101, 132, 134, 139
tribunals, 56, 68, 89, 107, 123, 125–7, 130, 138; International Military, 125, 129; specialist, 143, 145, 193
troops, 183, 198, 201, 209, 227, 244
Tunisia, 229, 256
Turkey, 114, 259, 264, 268–70
Tutsis, 198–9

UDHR (Universal Declaration of Human Rights), 95–7, 109, 115–16, 144, 280
UNAMA (United Nations Assistance Mission for Afghanistan), 246
UNAMI (United Nations Assistance Mission for Iraq), 248
UNAMID (Union/United Nations hybrid Mission in Darfur), 227
UNAMIR (United Nations Assistance Mission in Rwanda), 198

304 *Index*

UNCED (United Nations Conference on Environment and Development), 148, 160–1
UNEP (United Nations Environment Programme), 150
UNFCCC (United Nations Framework Convention on Climate Change), 157, 161, 164–70
UNHCR (United Nations High Commissioner for Refugees), 112–13, 264
unilateral intervention, 4, 14, 17, 212, 246; armed, 21, 240; humanitarian, 4–6, 12, 30
United Kingdom, 21, 38, 80–2, 221–2, 256, 258, 270, 279
United Nations, 4, 20–2, 24–30, 46–9, 54–7, 186–8, 198–202, 216–20; Assistance Mission for Afghanistan (UNAMA), 246; Assistance Mission for Iraq (UNAMI), 248; Assistance Mission in Rwanda (UNAMIR), 198; Charter, 5, 12, 14, 17, 22, 37, 39, 204; Conference on Environment and Development (UNCED), 148, 160–1; Environment Programme (UNEP), 150; Framework Convention on Climate Change, *see* UNFCCC; General Assembly, *see* General Assembly; Human Rights Committee (HRC), 99–101, 103, 105, 113, 121, 132, 260; Human Rights Council, 26, 29, 103, 230, 257, 259, 261–2, 268; Mission of Support in East Timor (UNMISET), 244–5; Missions in Sudan (UNMIS), 227; Office in Timor-Leste (UNOTIL), 245; Preventive Deployment Force (UNPREDEP), 200–201; Protection Force, *see* UNPROFOR; Security Council, *see* Security Council; Special Advisers, 13, 19, 26–9, 196–7, 200, 204–5, 228, 230; Supervision Mission in Syria, *see* UNSMIS; system, 4, 25–7, 29, 35, 181, 183, 188, 226; system, action within, 26–30; Transitional Administration in East Timor (UNTAET), 243–4; Transitional Authority in Cambodia (UNTAC), 240–1

United States, 46–7, 66, 78, 80, 82, 125–7, 222, 264–5; National Security Strategy, 47, 205
Uniting for Peace procedure, 18, 21, 213
Universal Declaration of Human Rights, *see* UDHR
universality, 93, 96–9, 114–15, 131
universal jurisdiction, 88–9, 123, 128, 130, 133–7, 145, 193; limited, 134
universal order, 40–3
UNMIS (United Nations Missions in Sudan), 227
UNMISET (United Nations Mission of Support in East Timor), 244–5
UNOTIL (United Nations Office in Timor-Leste), 245
UNPREDEP (United Nations, Preventive Deployment Force), 200–201
UNPROFOR (United Nations Protection Force), 200–201
UNSMIS (United Nations Supervision Mission in Syria), 261, 263
UNTAC (United Nations Transitional Authority in Cambodia), 240–1
UNTAET (United Nations Transitional Administration in East Timor (UNTAET)), 243–4
Uruguay, 29, 132
use of chemical weapons, 257, 264–6, 269, 272
use of force, 11–18, 21–2, 77–8, 207–9, 211, 217–18, 228–9, 259–60
Uzbekistan, 113

values, 39–40, 42, 48, 51, 55, 57, 85, 134
veto, 21, 55–6, 212–13, 259
Vevrey, W.D., 14
victims, 84, 88, 103–4, 108–9, 123, 134–6, 142–3, 178–9
victor's justice, 145, 193
Vienna Convention, 38, 76, 86, 156, 164
Vincent, R.J., 51
violations, 62–4, 90–1, 113–15, 125–7, 129, 132–3, 138–9, 218–20; egregious, 62, 79, 116, 266; gross, 199, 225; massive, 5, 48, 92, 123, 132, 202; of peremptory norms of international law, 77, 83; systematic, 19, 261; systemic, 101

Index   305

violence, 185–6, 219, 221, 224–5, 228, 230, 241, 259–64; escalating, 224, 263; physical, 219–20, 223, 227–8, 247; resurgence of, 225, 246; sexual, 145, 193, 260, 269
von Bogdandy, A., 35
vulnerable groups, 143, 190, 218, 250

war crimes, 1–2, 6, 24–5, 124–8, 143–6, 193, 224–5, 230
war theory, 11–12, 17, 32
weakness, 48–9, 178
well-founded fear, 110–11, 114
Wheeler, N., 51–2
WHO (World Health Organization), 119, 265
Wight, M., 50–1
withdrawal, 192, 198, 241, 246, 248
women, 96–7, 100, 115, 218, 220
workers, migrant, 97–8
world citizenship, 34

World Commission on Environment and Development, 158
world community, 41, 51, 85, 91
World Health Organization (WHO), 119, 265
world politics, 50–1, 54
World Trade Organization (WTO), 47, 54
wrongful acts, 64–5, 67–8, 70, 75–6, 78–80, 87, 89
wrongfulness, 69, 76–7; circumstances precluding, 70, 76
WTO (World Trade Organization), 47, 54

Yazidis, 267, 269
Yugoslavia, 15, 85–6, 138, 143, 193, 200–201, 204, 210; Former, 138

Zaire, 132, 218
Zifcak, 231